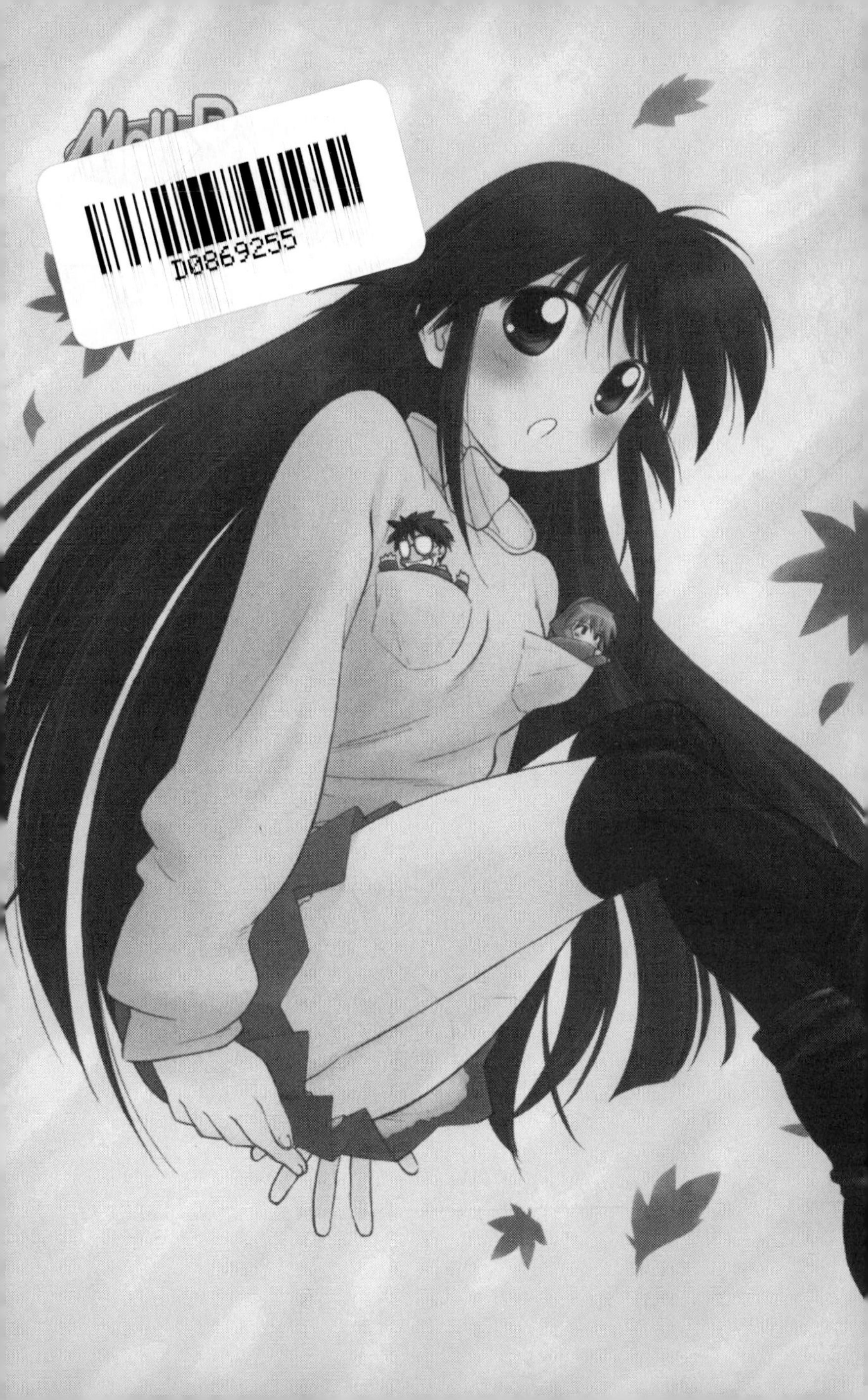

Table of Contents

☆ Story thus far ☆☆☆☆☆☆☆☆☆☆☆☆☆☆☆

MAHORO, the most powerful **COMBAT ANDROID** ever invented by the anti-war organization **VESPER**, after completing a successful tour of duty, has come to spend the rest of her operating days taking care of the orphan **SUGURU MISATO**, a junior high school student and the apple of every girl's eye. Everyone loves Suguru and Mahoro—including **SOARI SHIKIJO** (Suguru's homeroom teacher)—which means that the Misato residence is very popular with everyone, thereby making every day quite interesting. And now they have a new addition to the group: the cyborg **MINAWA ANDOU**, a spy from the evil anti-alien organization **THE KEEPERS.** Mahoro thinks she is keeping Minawa safe by allowing her to masquerade as her little sister, but in reality Minawa is taking orders from the evil **PROFESSOR METHRIS!** Poor Minawa is torn by her love and admiration for Mahoro and the orders she feels she must follow. Upon learning from the Keeper's "Android #184" that Mahoro can only operate at 30% of her active duty capabilities, Professor Methris plans to capture her! But the disarmed Mahoro only has a short time yet to live—her systems are going to stop functioning in a mere 126 days...

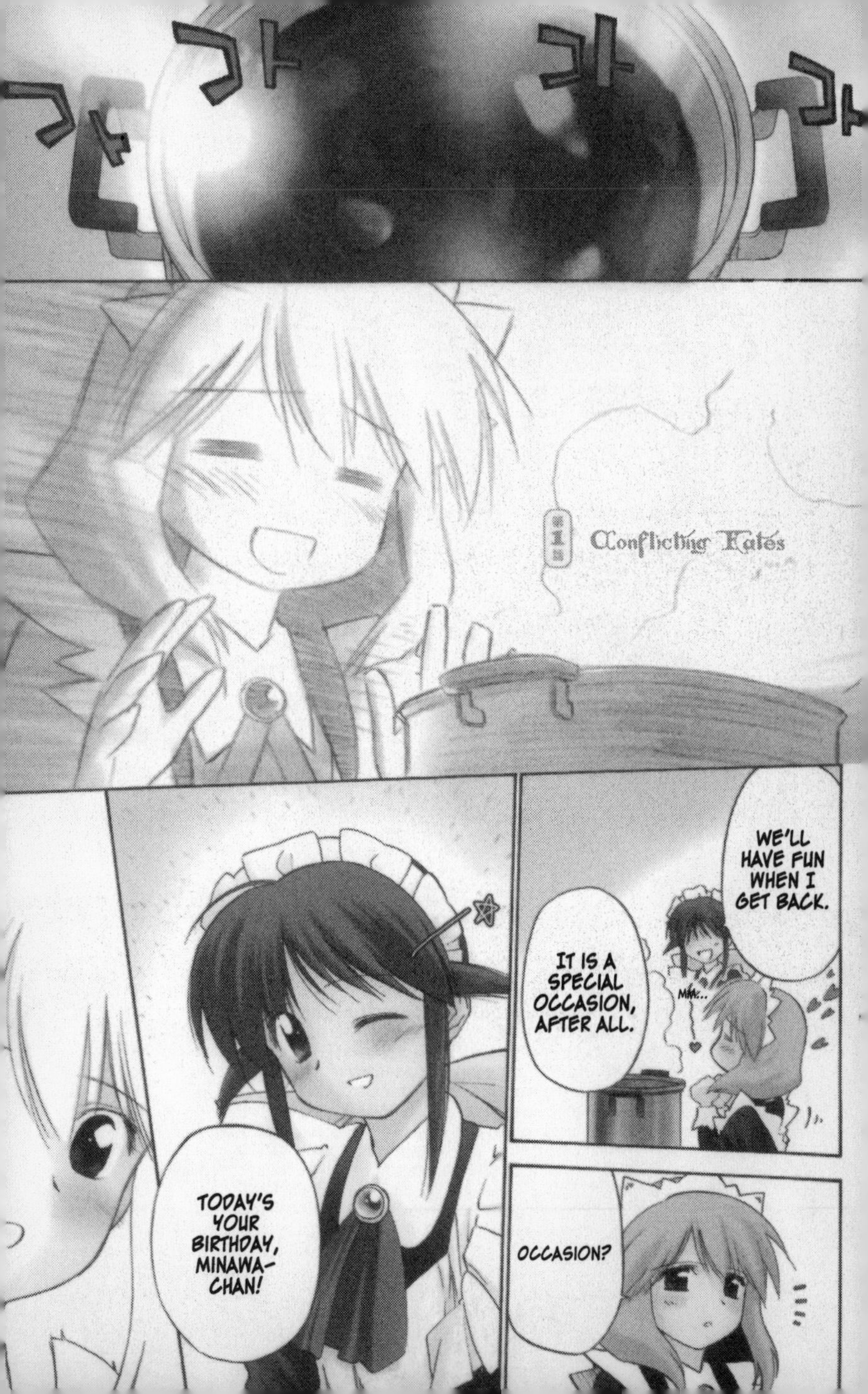
コトコト
コトコト
Conflicting Fates
WE'LL HAVE FUN WHEN I GET BACK.
IT IS A SPECIAL OCCASION, AFTER ALL.
MIA...
OCCASION?
TODAY'S YOUR BIRTHDAY, MINAWA-CHAN!

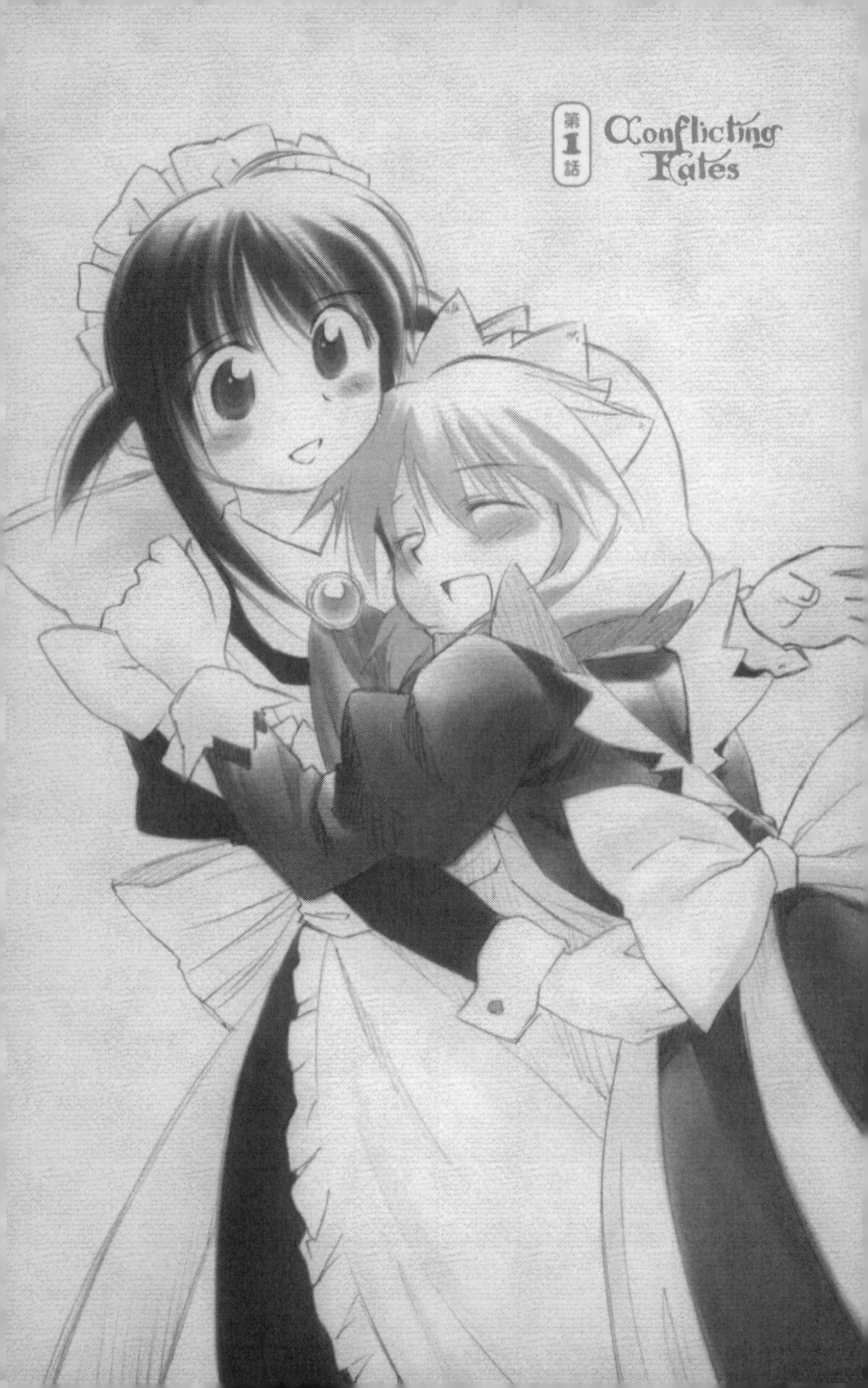
第1話
Conflicting Fates

MAHOROMATIC™
AUTOMATIC MAIDEN

Vol. 7

The Maid Moved by Tears

Art by Bow Ditama
Story by Bunjuro Nakayama

TOKYOPOP®

HAMBURG // LONDON // LOS ANGELES // TOKYO

Mahoromatic: Automatic Maiden Vol. 7
Art by Bow Ditama
Story by Bunjuro Nakayama

Translation - Jeremiah Bourque
English Adaptation - Anna Wenger
Retouch and Lettering - Lucas Rivera
Production Artists - Gloria Wu and Jose Macasocol, Jr.
Cover Design - Al-Insan Lashley

Editor - Luis Reyes
Digital Imaging Manager - Chris Buford
Production Managers - Jennifer Miller and Mutsumi Miyazaki
Managing Editor - Jill Freshney
VP of Production - Ron Klamert
Publisher and E.I.C. - Mike Kiley
President and C.O.O. - John Parker
C.E.O. - Stuart Levy

A  Manga

TOKYOPOP Inc.
5900 Wilshire Blvd. Suite 2000
Los Angeles, CA 90036

E-mail: info@TOKYOPOP.com
Come visit us online at www.TOKYOPOP.com

ISBN: 1-59532-625-1

First TOKYOPOP printing: October 2005
10 9 8 7 6 5 4 3 2 1
Printed in Canada

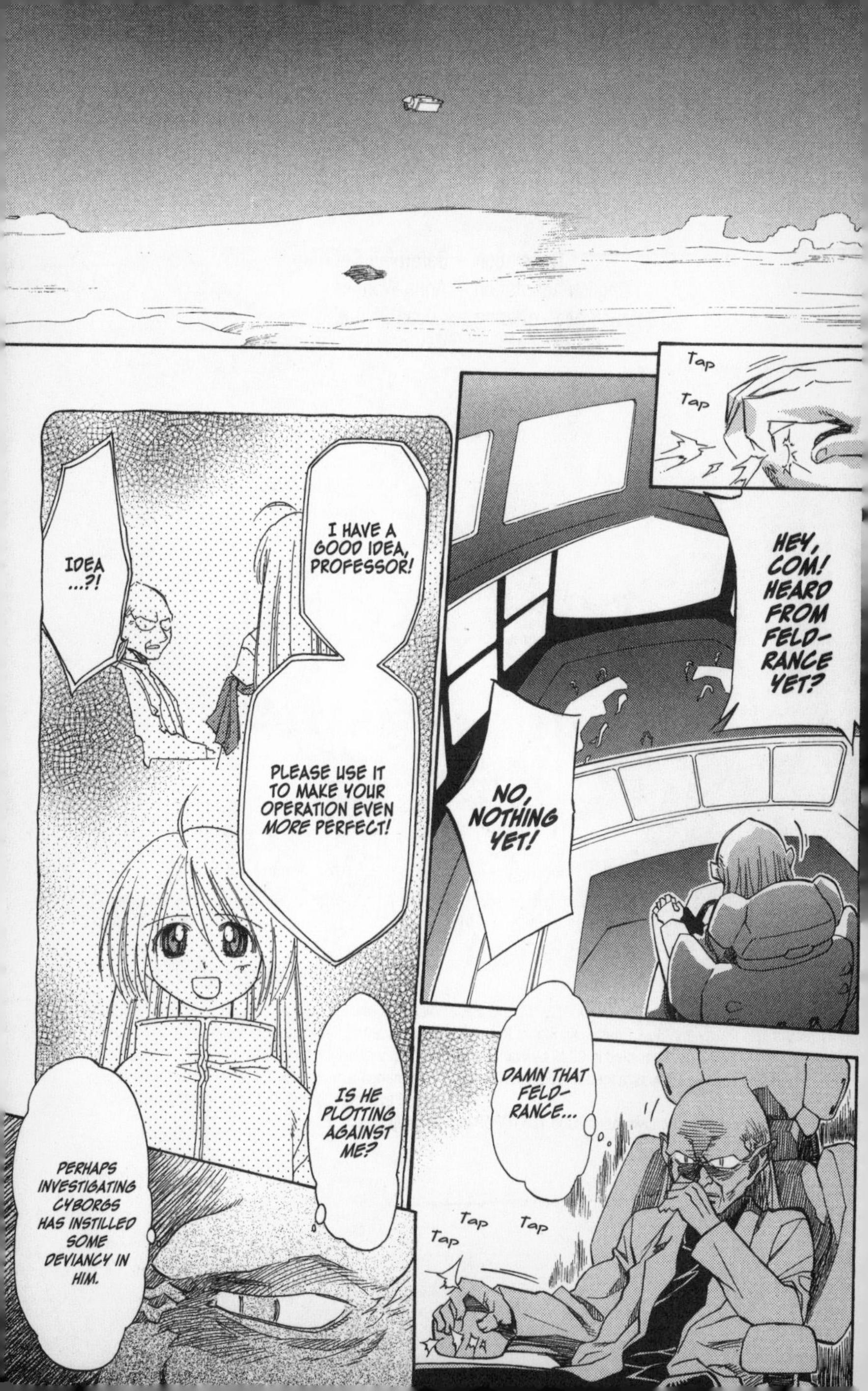
Tap
Tap
HEY, COM! HEARD FROM FELD-RANCE YET?
NO, NOTHING YET!
DAMN THAT FELD-RANCE...
Tap
Tap
Tap
I HAVE A GOOD IDEA, PROFESSOR!
IDEA ...?!
PLEASE USE IT TO MAKE YOUR OPERATION EVEN MORE PERFECT!
IS HE PLOTTING AGAINST ME?
PERHAPS INVESTIGATING CYBORGS HAS INSTILLED SOME DEVIANCY IN HIM.

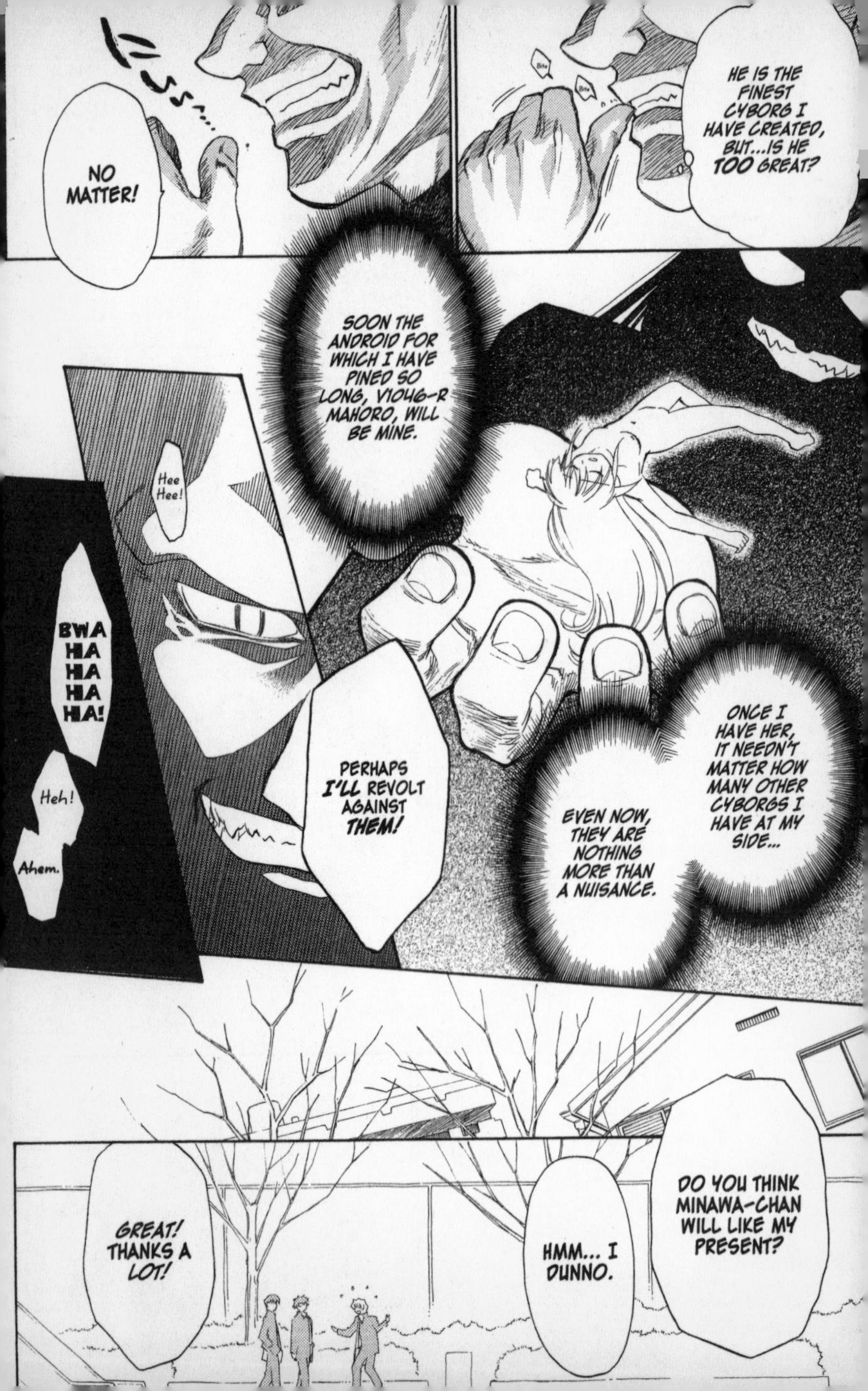
HE IS THE FINEST CYBORG I HAVE CREATED, BUT...IS HE TOO GREAT?
NO MATTER!
SOON THE ANDROID FOR WHICH I HAVE PINED SO LONG, V1046-R MAHORO, WILL BE MINE.
ONCE I HAVE HER, IT NEEDN'T MATTER HOW MANY OTHER CYBORGS I HAVE AT MY SIDE...
EVEN NOW, THEY ARE NOTHING MORE THAN A NUISANCE.
PERHAPS I'LL REVOLT AGAINST THEM!
Hee Hee!
BWA HA HA HA HA!
Heh!
Ahem.
DO YOU THINK MINAWA-CHAN WILL LIKE MY PRESENT?
HMM... I DUNNO.
GREAT! THANKS A LOT!

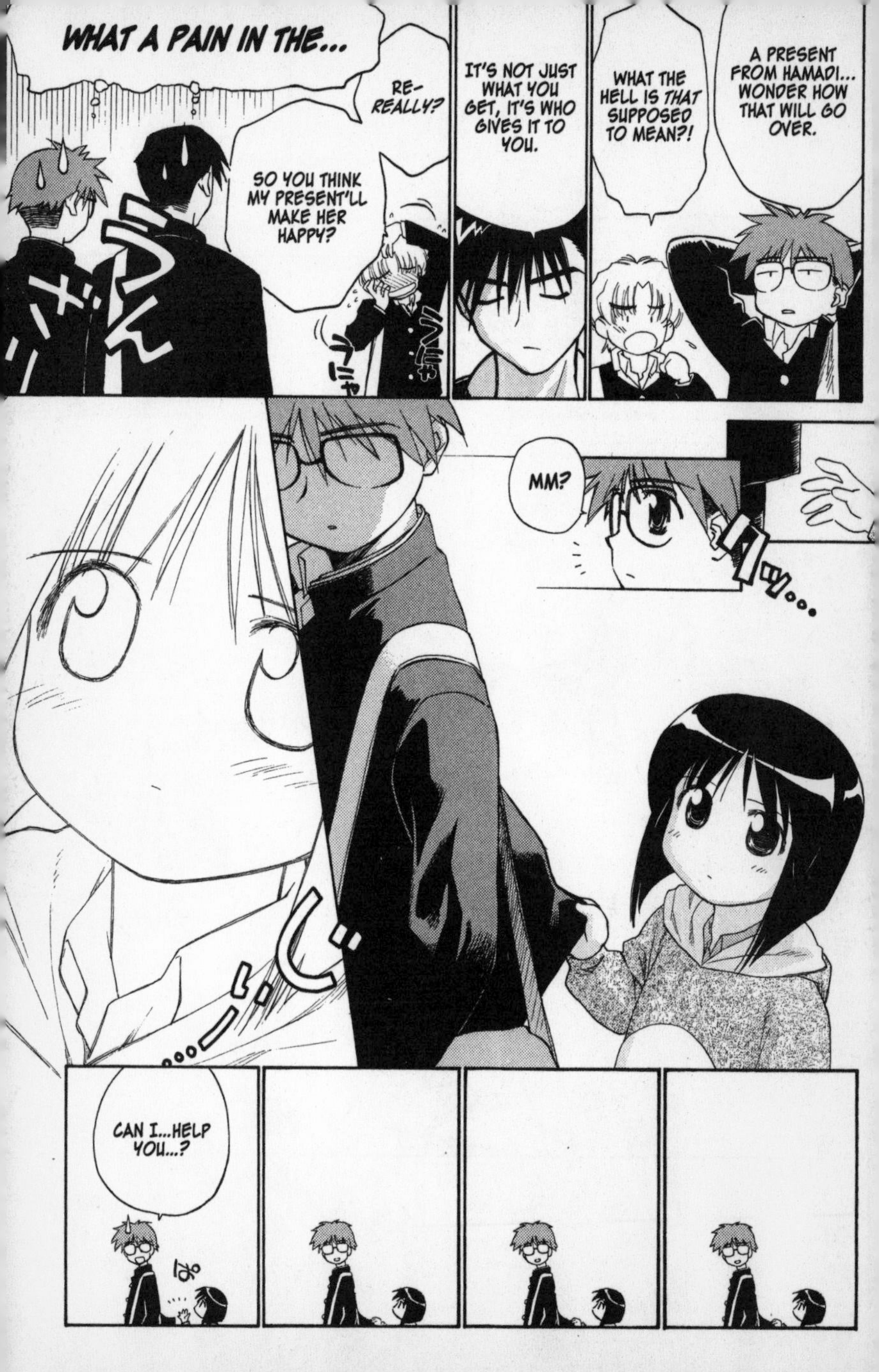

A PRESENT FROM HAMADI... WONDER HOW THAT WILL GO OVER.
WHAT THE HELL IS THAT SUPPOSED TO MEAN?!
IT'S NOT JUST WHAT YOU GET, IT'S WHO GIVES IT TO YOU.
RE-REALLY?
SO YOU THINK MY PRESENT'LL MAKE HER HAPPY?
WHAT A PAIN IN THE...
MM?
CAN I...HELP YOU...?

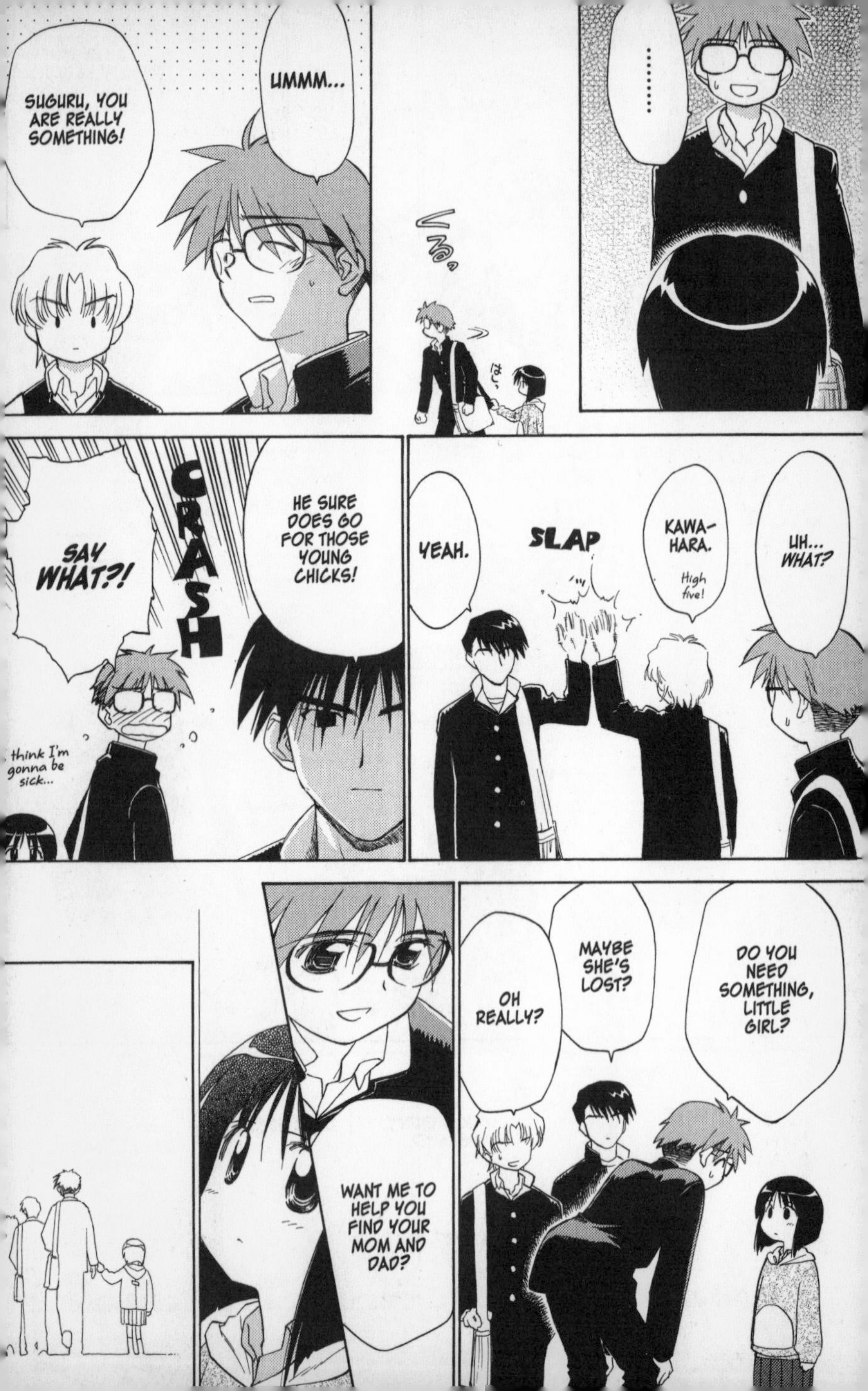
......
くるっ
はっ
UMMM...
SUGURU, YOU ARE REALLY SOMETHING!
UH... WHAT?
KAWA-HARA.
High five!
SLAP
YEAH.
HE SURE DOES GO FOR THOSE YOUNG CHICKS!
CRASH
SAY WHAT?!
think I'm gonna be sick...
DO YOU NEED SOMETHING, LITTLE GIRL?
MAYBE SHE'S LOST?
OH REALLY?
WANT ME TO HELP YOU FIND YOUR MOM AND DAD?

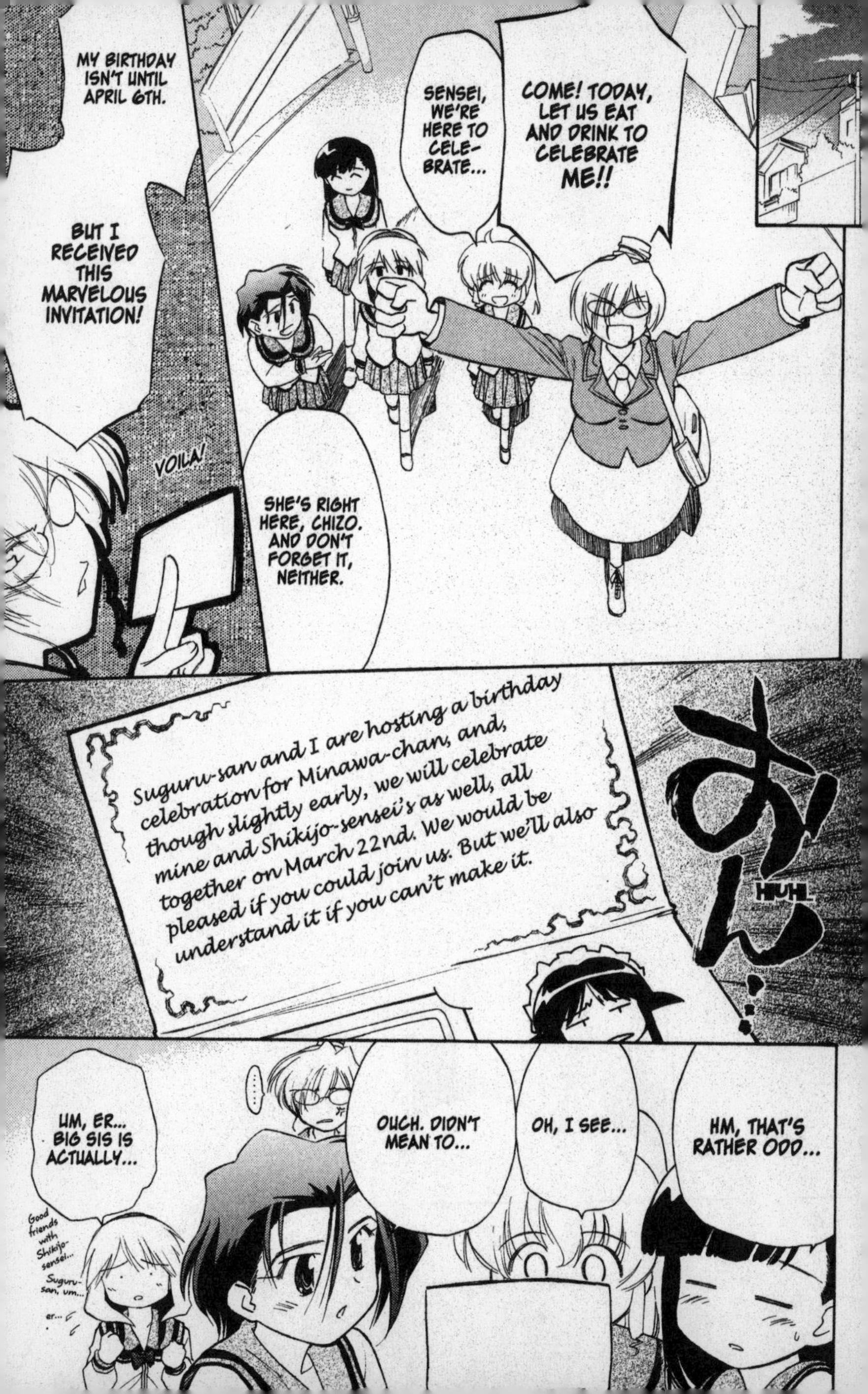

COME! TODAY, LET US EAT AND DRINK TO CELEBRATE ME!!
SENSEI, WE'RE HERE TO CELE-BRATE...
SHE'S RIGHT HERE, CHIZO. AND DON'T FORGET IT, NEITHER.
MY BIRTHDAY ISN'T UNTIL APRIL 6TH.
BUT I RECEIVED THIS MARVELOUS INVITATION!
VOILA!
おん!
HUH
Suguru-san and I are hosting a birthday celebration for Minawa-chan, and, though slightly early, we will celebrate mine and Shikijo-sensei's as well, all together on March 22nd. We would be pleased if you could join us. But we'll also understand it if you can't make it.
HM, THAT'S RATHER ODD...
OH, I SEE...
OUCH. DIDN'T MEAN TO...
......
UM, ER... BIG SIS IS ACTUALLY...
Good friends with Shikijo-sensei...
Suguru-san, um...
er...

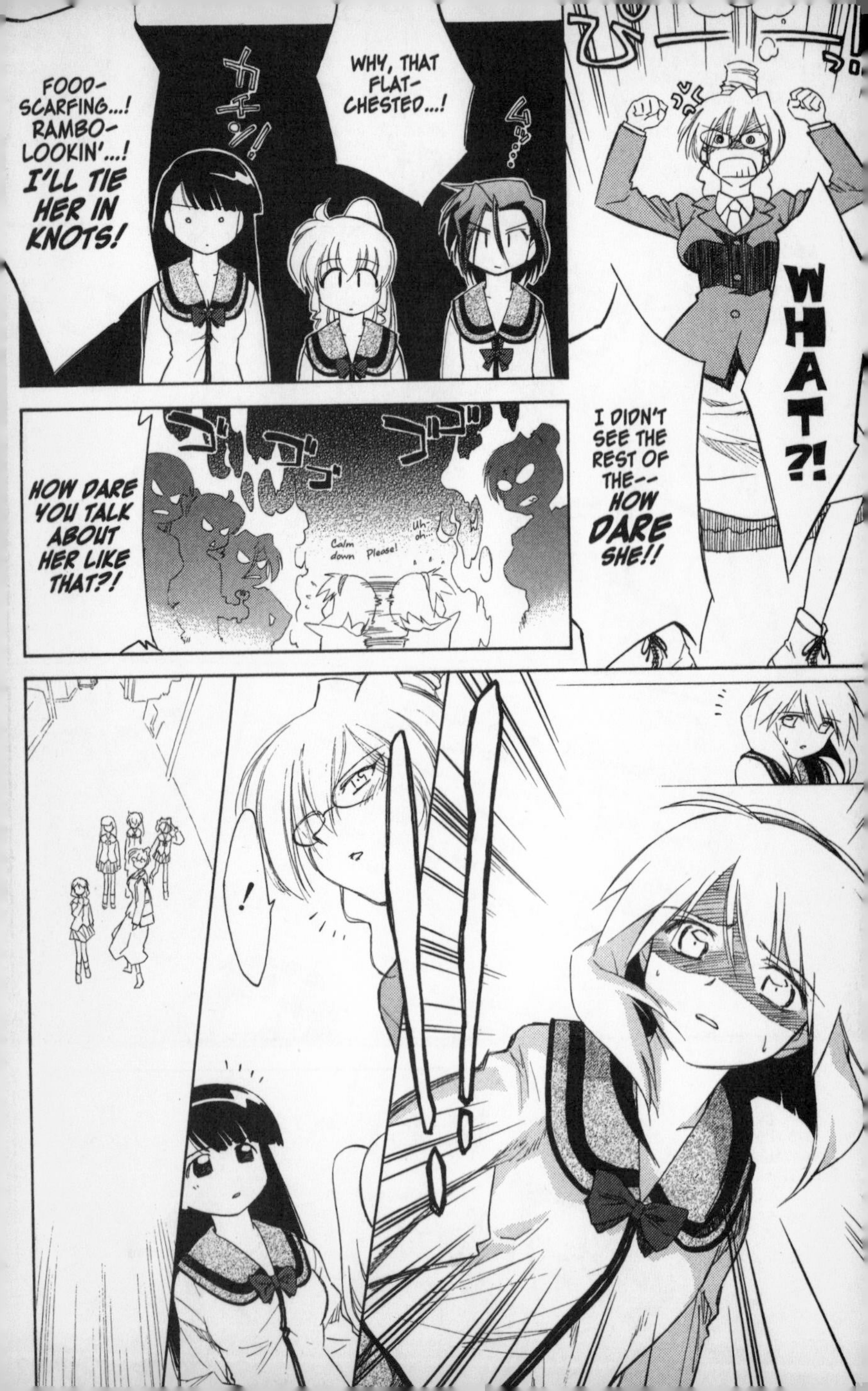
WHAT?!
I DIDN'T SEE THE REST OF THE-- HOW DARE SHE!!
WHY, THAT FLAT-CHESTED...!
FOOD-SCARFING...! RAMBO-LOOKIN'...! I'LL TIE HER IN KNOTS!
HOW DARE YOU TALK ABOUT HER LIKE THAT?!
Uh oh...
Please!
Calm down
!

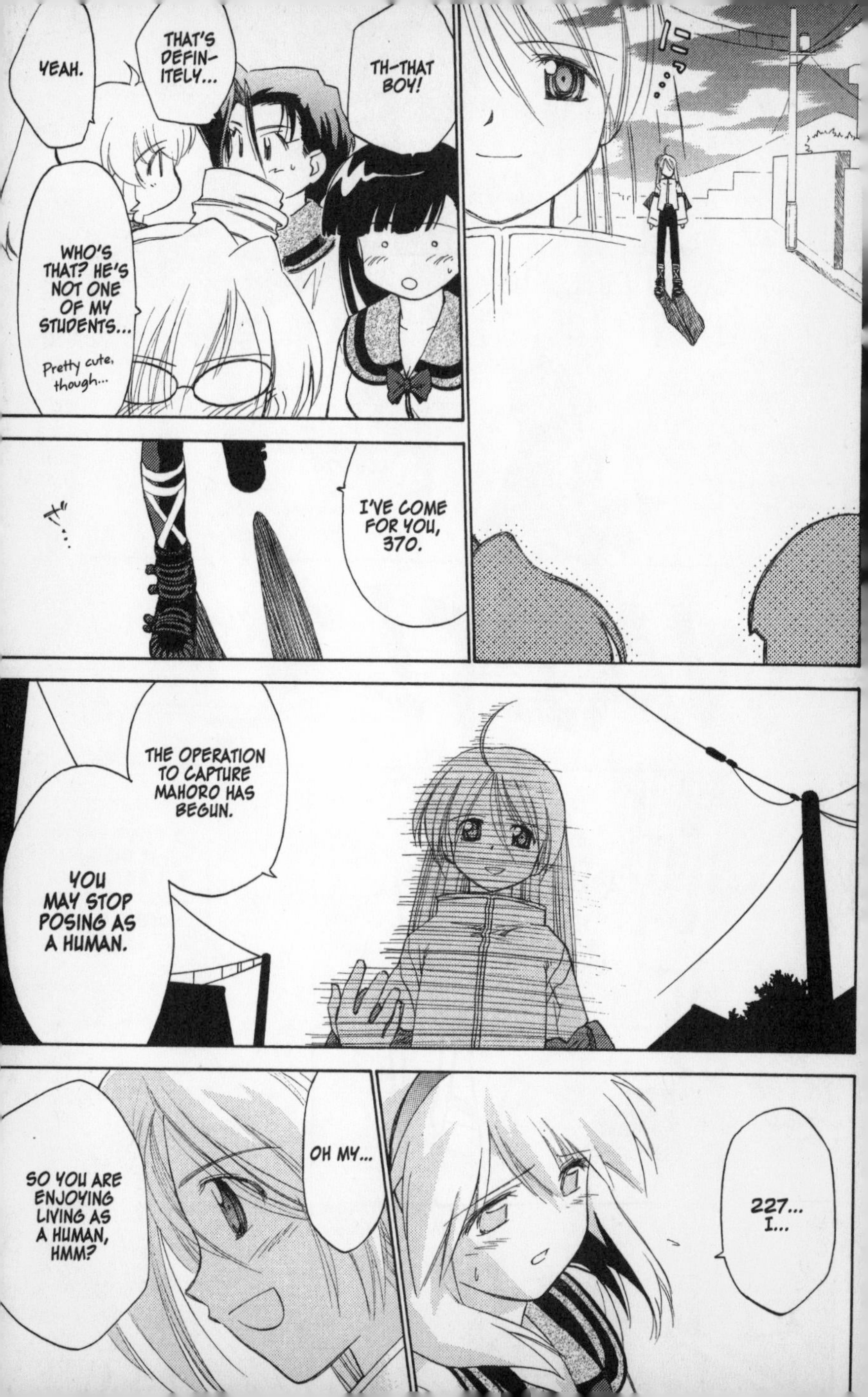
TH-THAT BOY!
THAT'S DEFIN-ITELY...
YEAH.
WHO'S THAT? HE'S NOT ONE OF MY STUDENTS...
Pretty cute, though...
I'VE COME FOR YOU, 370.
THE OPERATION TO CAPTURE MAHORO HAS BEGUN.
YOU MAY STOP POSING AS A HUMAN.
227... I...
OH MY...
SO YOU ARE ENJOYING LIVING AS A HUMAN, HMM?

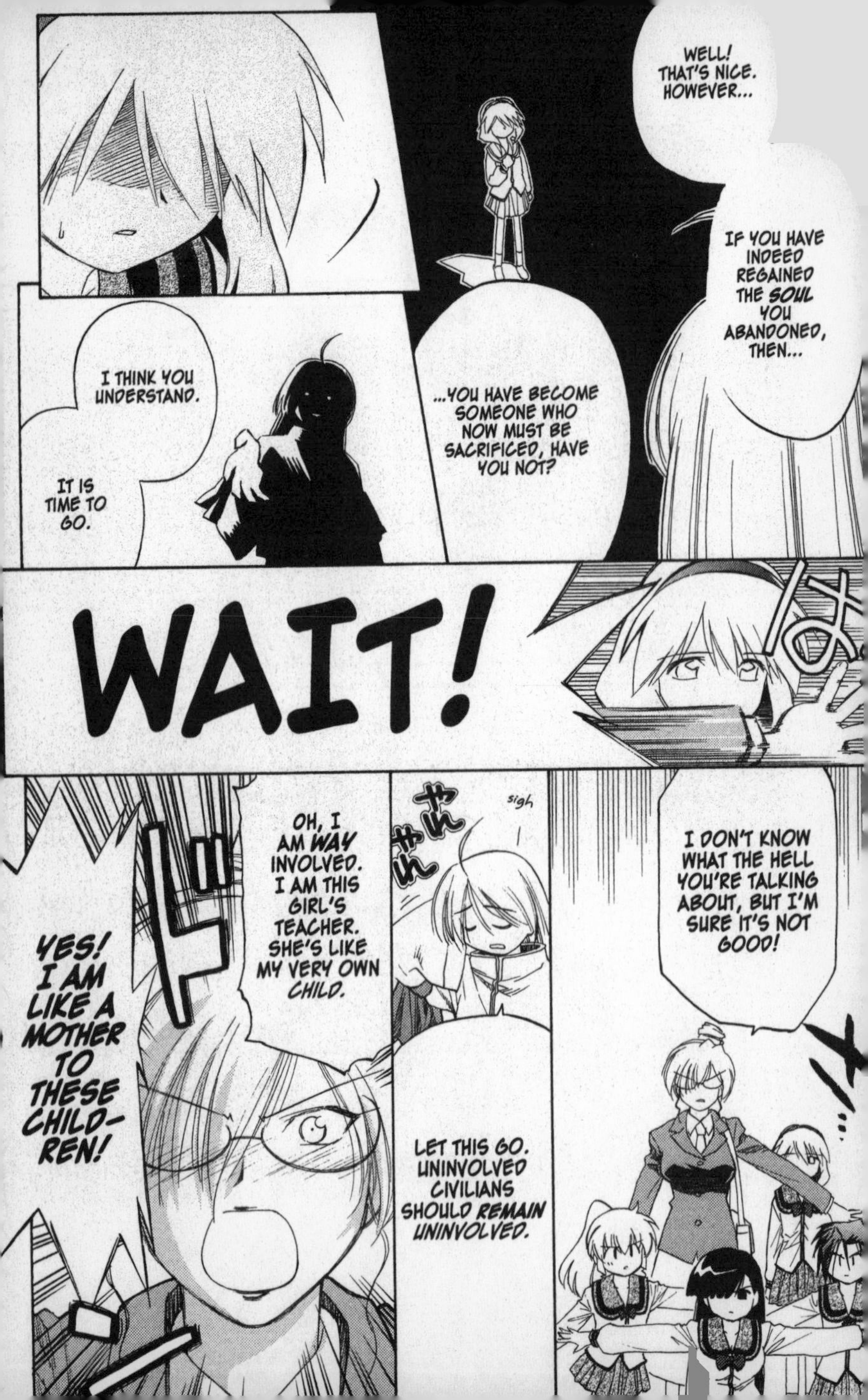
WELL! THAT'S NICE. HOWEVER...
IF YOU HAVE INDEED REGAINED THE *SOUL* YOU ABANDONED, THEN...
...YOU HAVE BECOME SOMEONE WHO NOW MUST BE SACRIFICED, HAVE YOU NOT?
I THINK YOU UNDERSTAND.
IT IS TIME TO GO.
WAIT!
I DON'T KNOW WHAT THE HELL YOU'RE TALKING ABOUT, BUT I'M SURE IT'S NOT GOOD!
sigh
LET THIS GO. UNINVOLVED CIVILIANS SHOULD *REMAIN UNINVOLVED.*
OH, I AM *WAY* INVOLVED. I AM THIS GIRL'S TEACHER. SHE'S LIKE MY VERY OWN *CHILD.*
YES! I AM LIKE A MOTHER TO THESE CHILDREN!

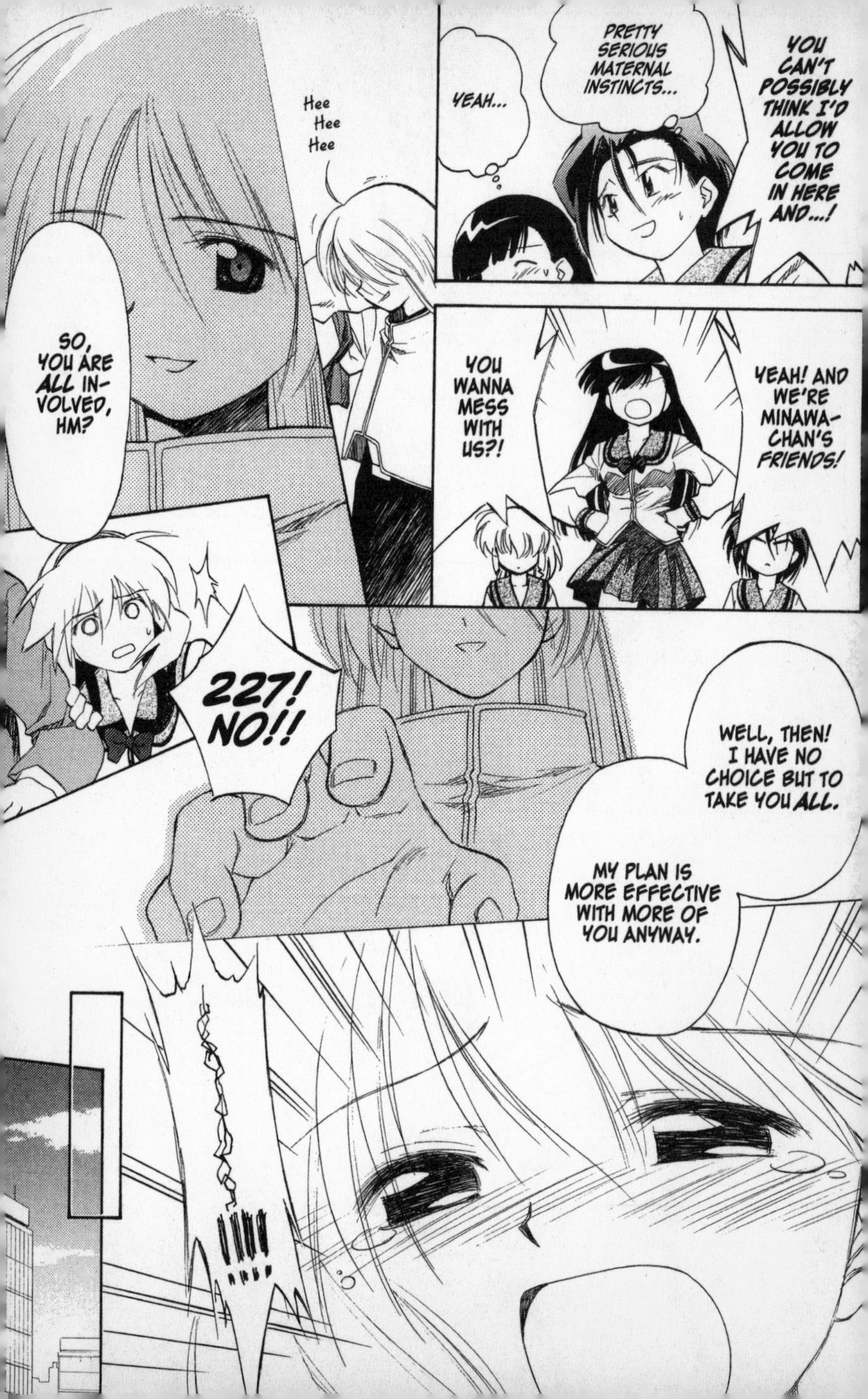
YOU CAN'T POSSIBLY THINK I'D ALLOW YOU TO COME IN HERE AND...!
PRETTY SERIOUS MATERNAL INSTINCTS...
YEAH...
YEAH! AND WE'RE MINAWA-CHAN'S FRIENDS!
YOU WANNA MESS WITH US?!
Hee Hee Hee
SO, YOU ARE ALL IN-VOLVED, HM?
WELL, THEN! I HAVE NO CHOICE BUT TO TAKE YOU ALL.
MY PLAN IS MORE EFFECTIVE WITH MORE OF YOU ANYWAY.
227! NO!!

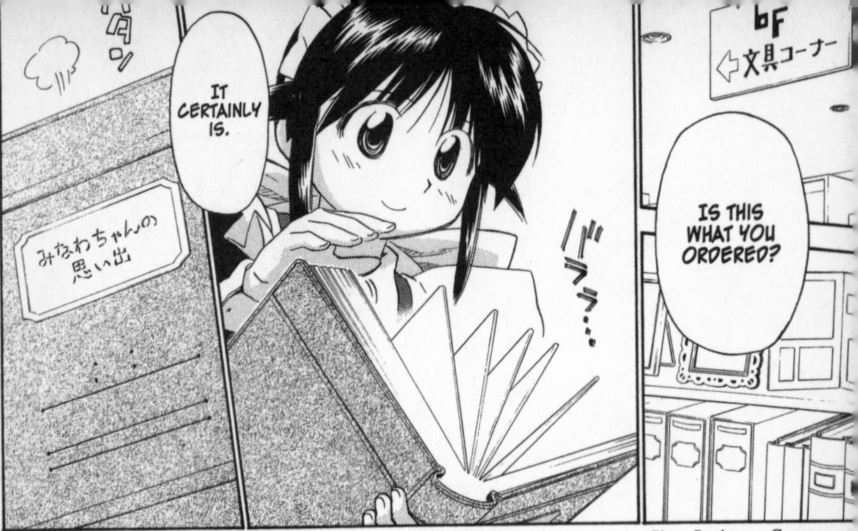
6F
⇦文具コーナー
IS THIS WHAT YOU ORDERED?
IT CERTAINLY IS.
バラ...
みなわちゃんの思い出

Sign: Stationary Corner

Book: Minawa-chan's Memories

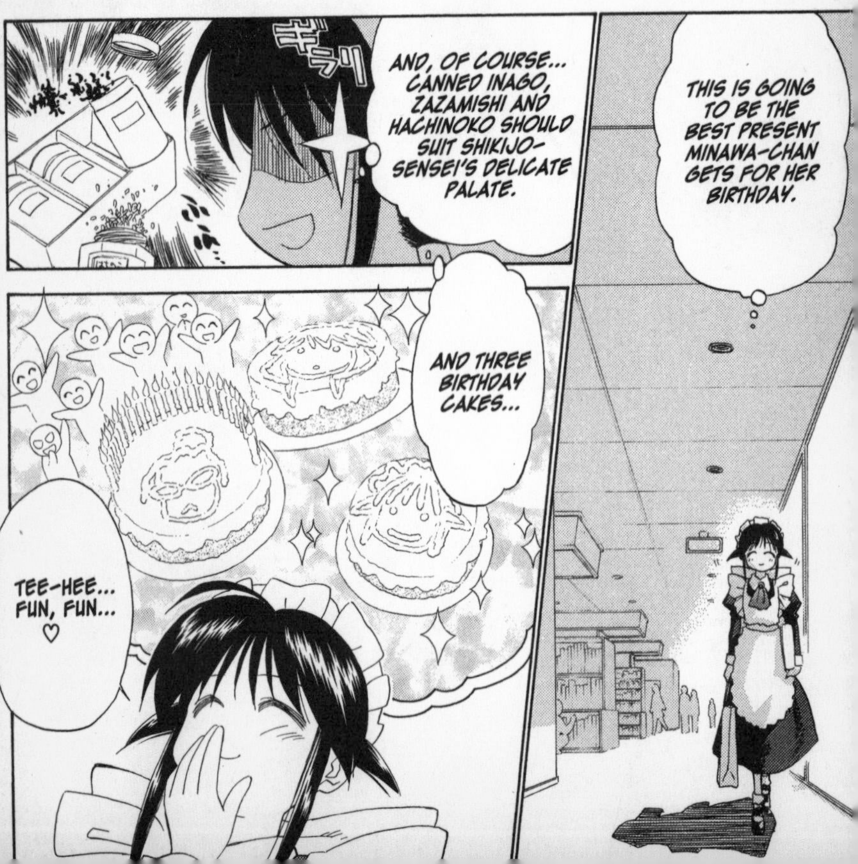
THIS IS GOING TO BE THE BEST PRESENT MINAWA-CHAN GETS FOR HER BIRTHDAY.
ギラリ
AND, OF COURSE... CANNED INAGO, ZAZAMISHI AND HACHINOKO SHOULD SUIT SHIKIJO-SENSEI'S DELICATE PALATE.
AND THREE BIRTHDAY CAKES...
TEE-HEE... FUN, FUN... ♡

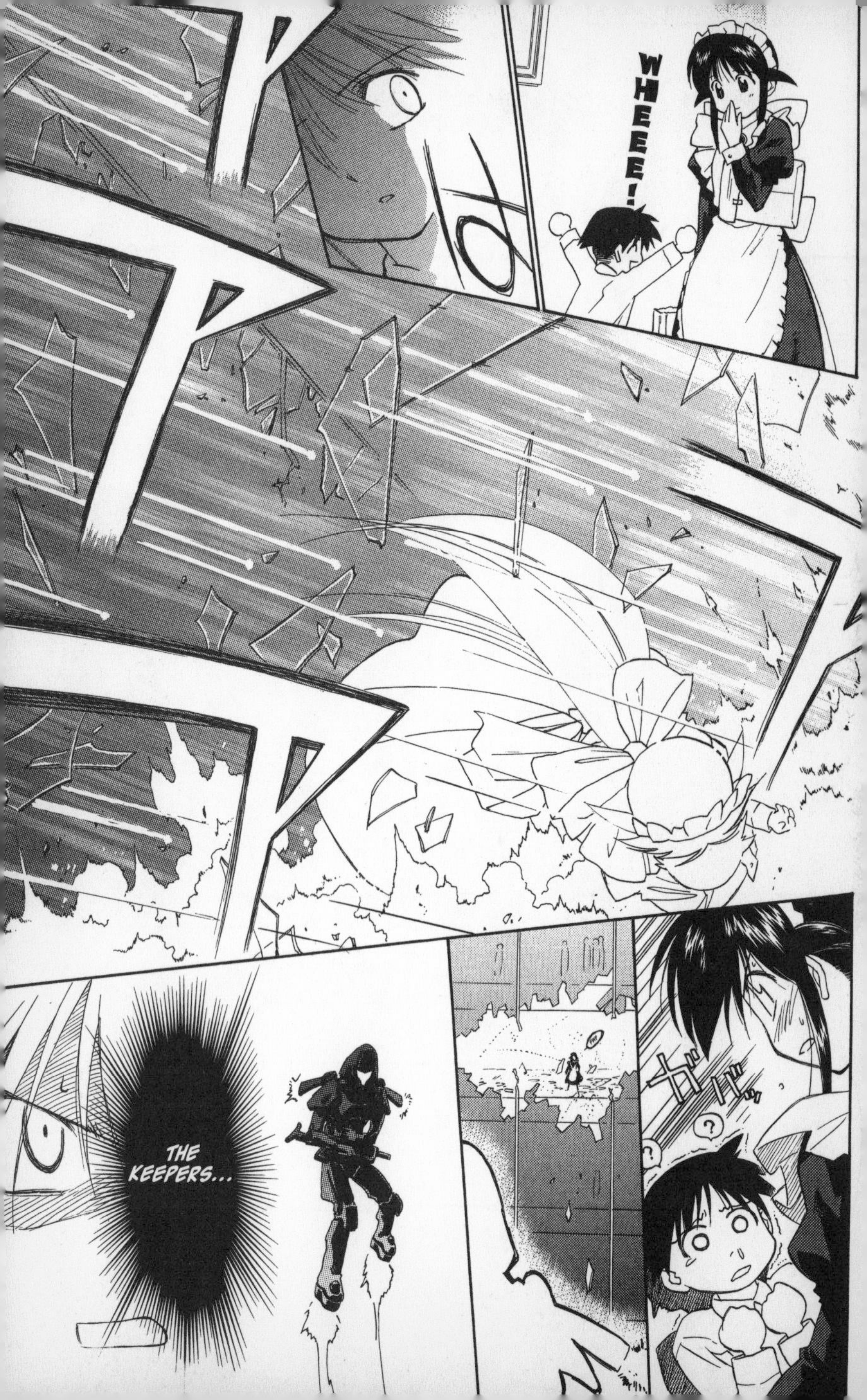
WHEEEE!!
ガバッ
?
THE KEEPERS...

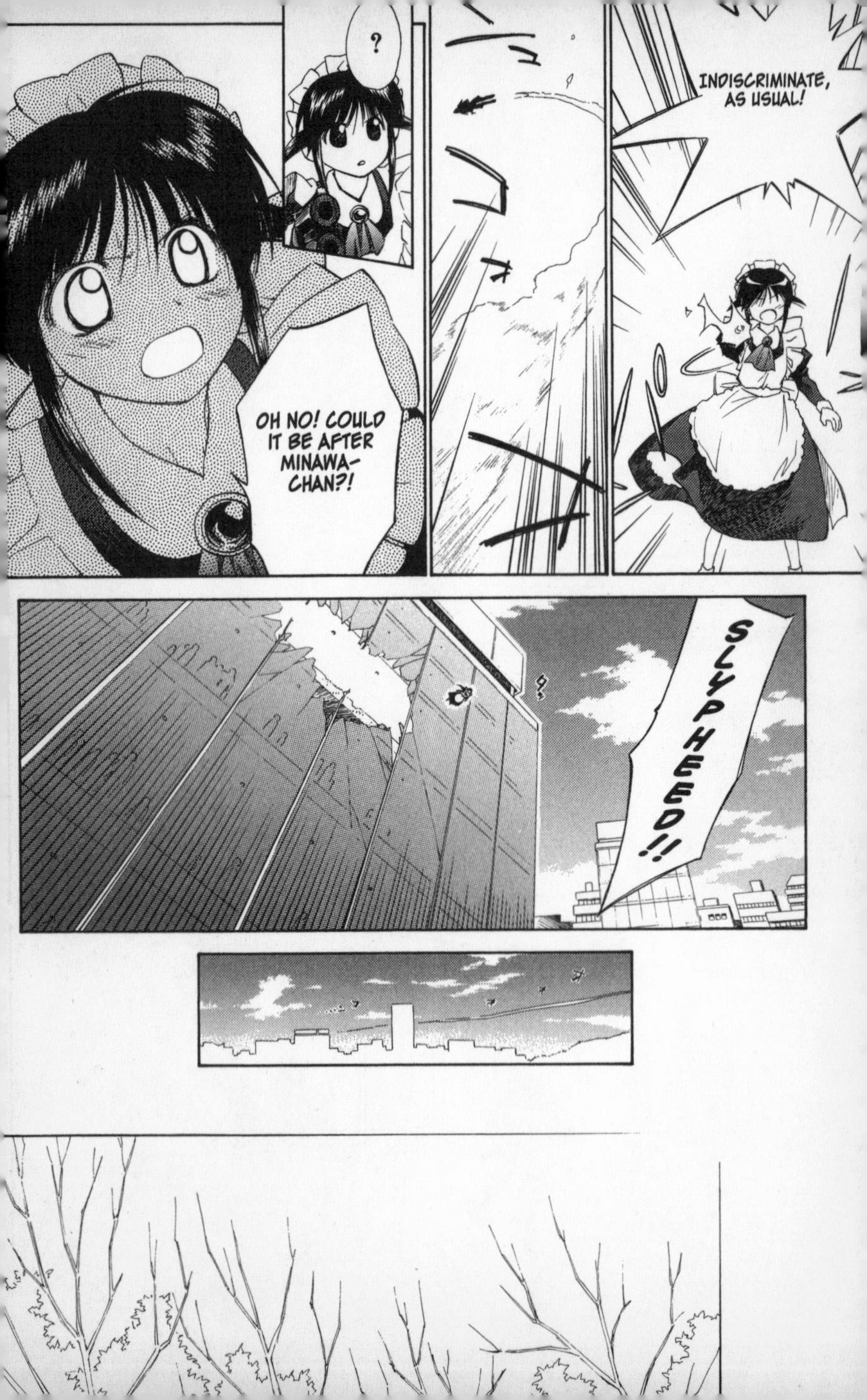
INDISCRIMINATE, AS USUAL!
?
OH NO! COULD IT BE AFTER MINAWA-CHAN?!
SLYPHEEED!!

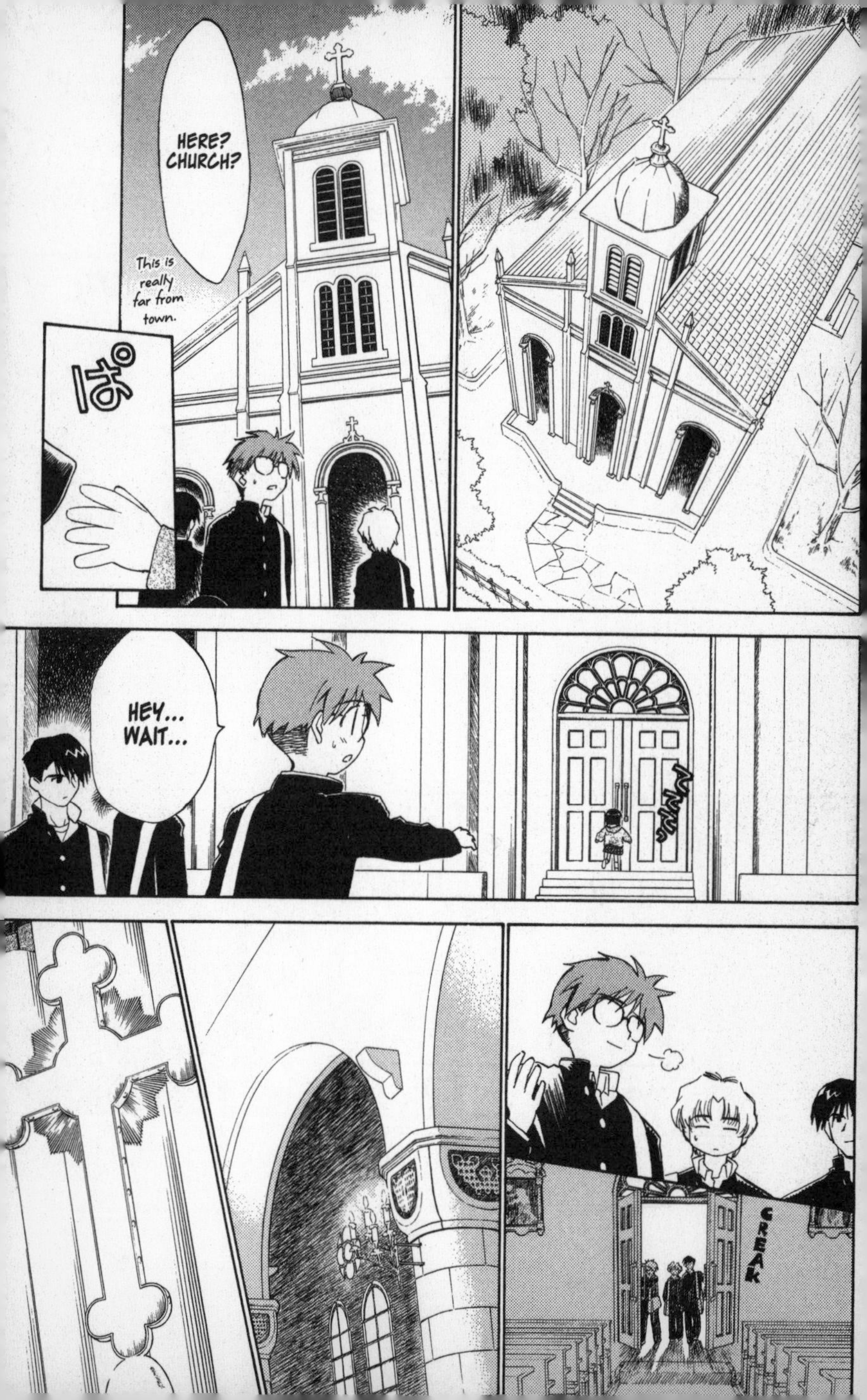
HERE? CHURCH?
This is really far from town.
HEY... WAIT...
CREAK

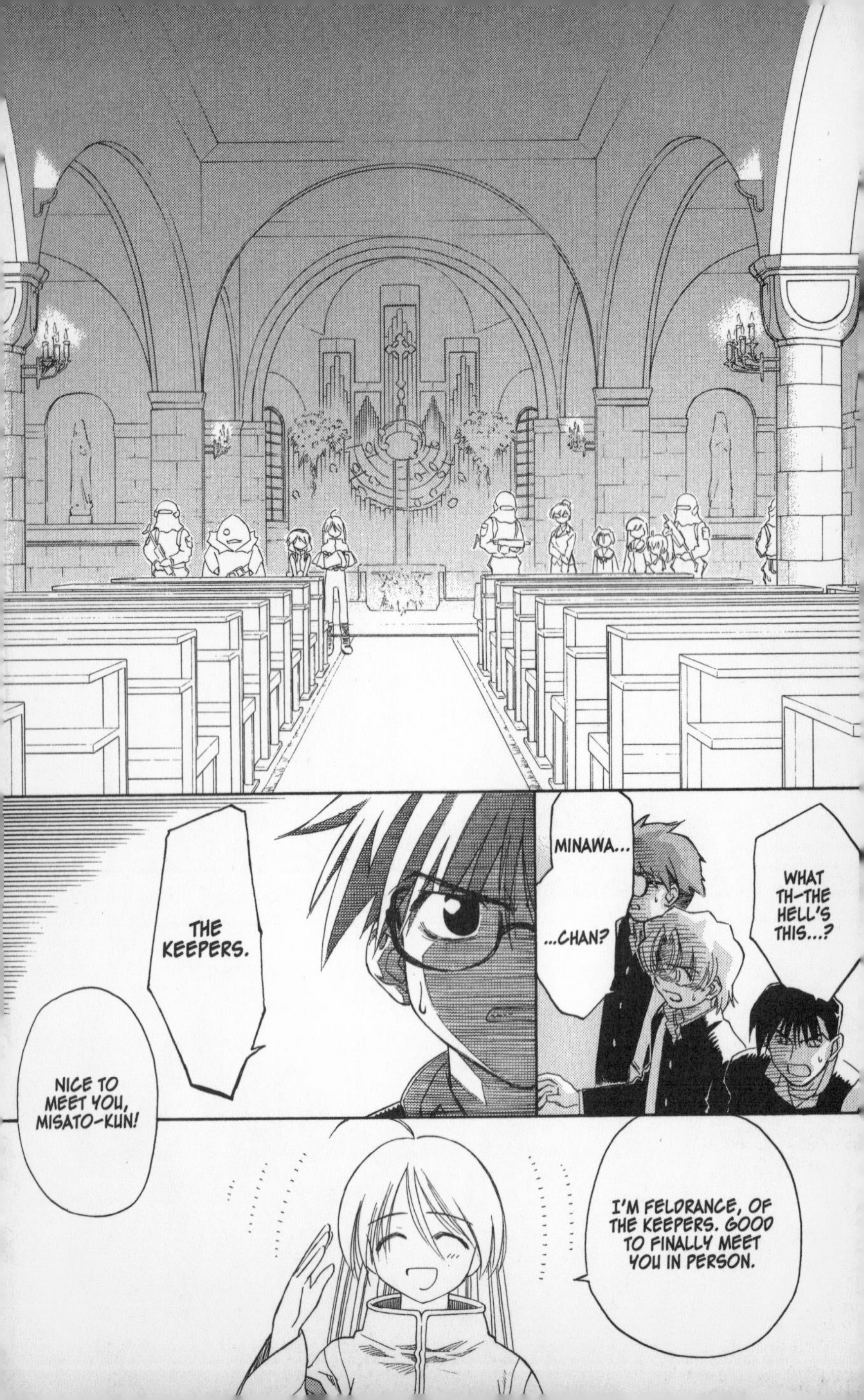
WHAT TH-THE HELL'S THIS...?
MINAWA...
...CHAN?
THE KEEPERS.
NICE TO MEET YOU, MISATO-KUN!
I'M FELDRANCE, OF THE KEEPERS. GOOD TO FINALLY MEET YOU IN PERSON.

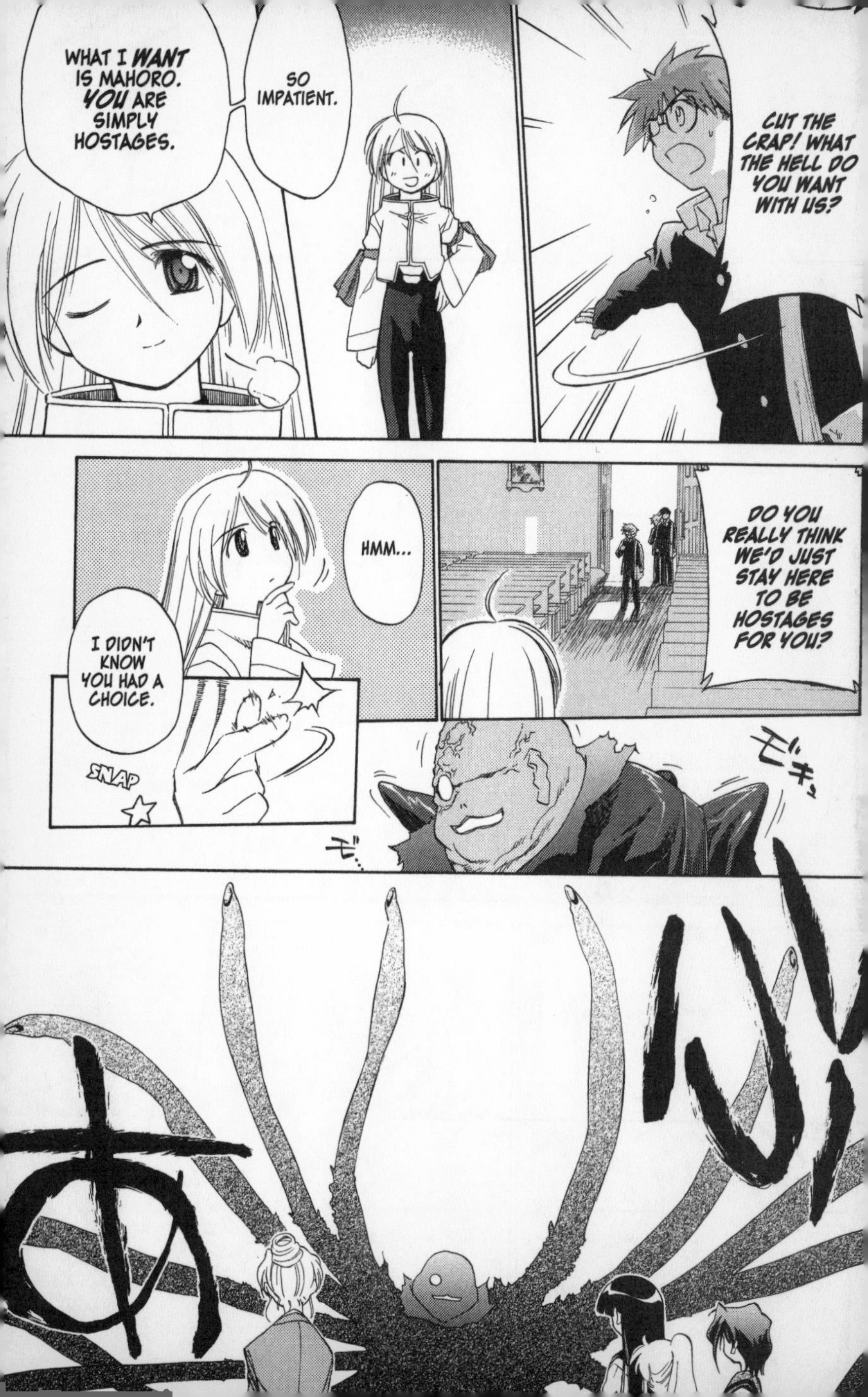
CUT THE CRAP! WHAT THE HELL DO YOU WANT WITH US?
SO IMPATIENT.
WHAT I WANT IS MAHORO. YOU ARE SIMPLY HOSTAGES.
DO YOU REALLY THINK WE'D JUST STAY HERE TO BE HOSTAGES FOR YOU?
HMM...
I DIDN'T KNOW YOU HAD A CHOICE.
SNAP

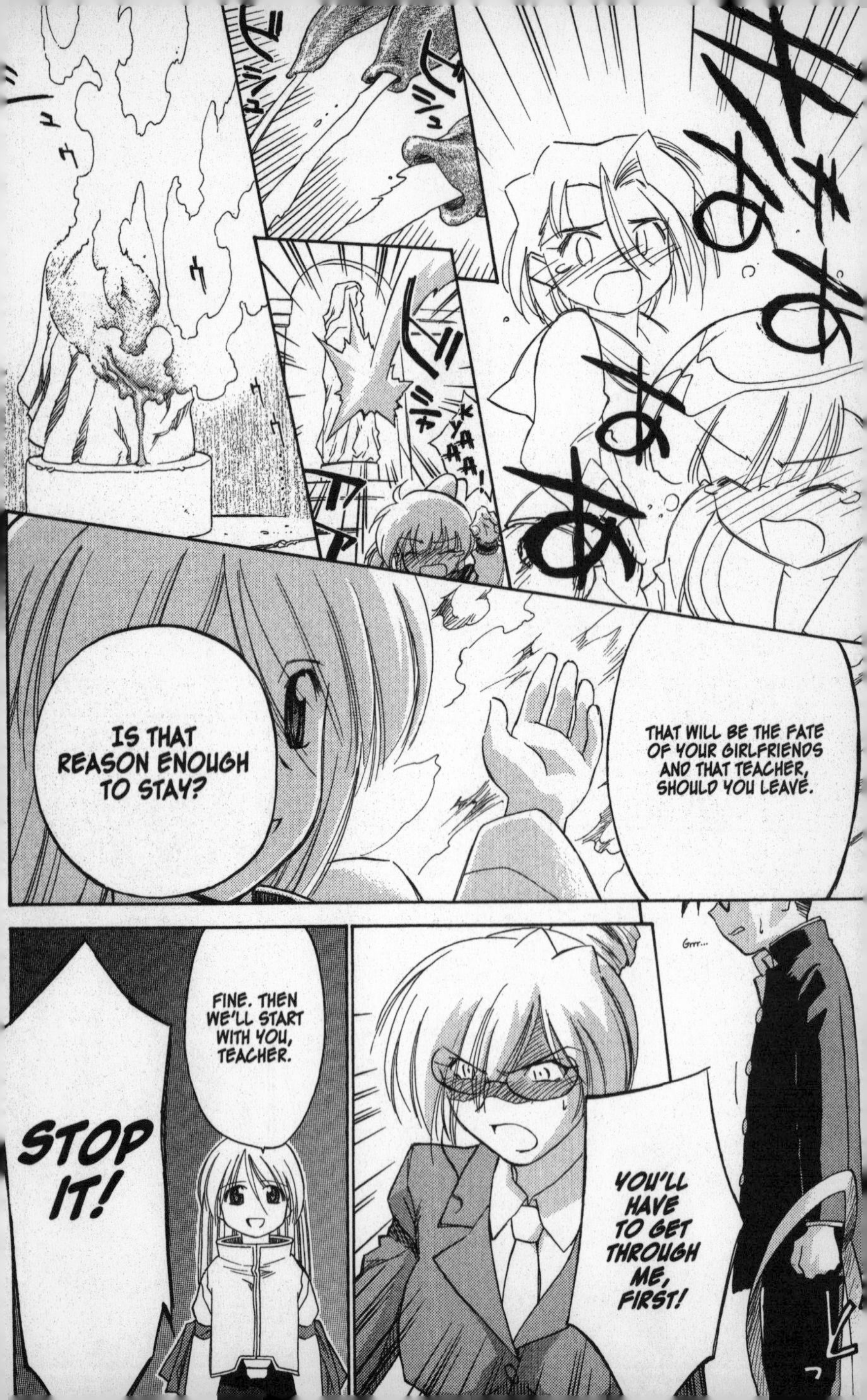
KYAAAA!
THAT WILL BE THE FATE OF YOUR GIRLFRIENDS AND THAT TEACHER, SHOULD YOU LEAVE.
IS THAT REASON ENOUGH TO STAY?
Grrr...
YOU'LL HAVE TO GET THROUGH ME, FIRST!
FINE. THEN WE'LL START WITH YOU, TEACHER.
STOP IT!

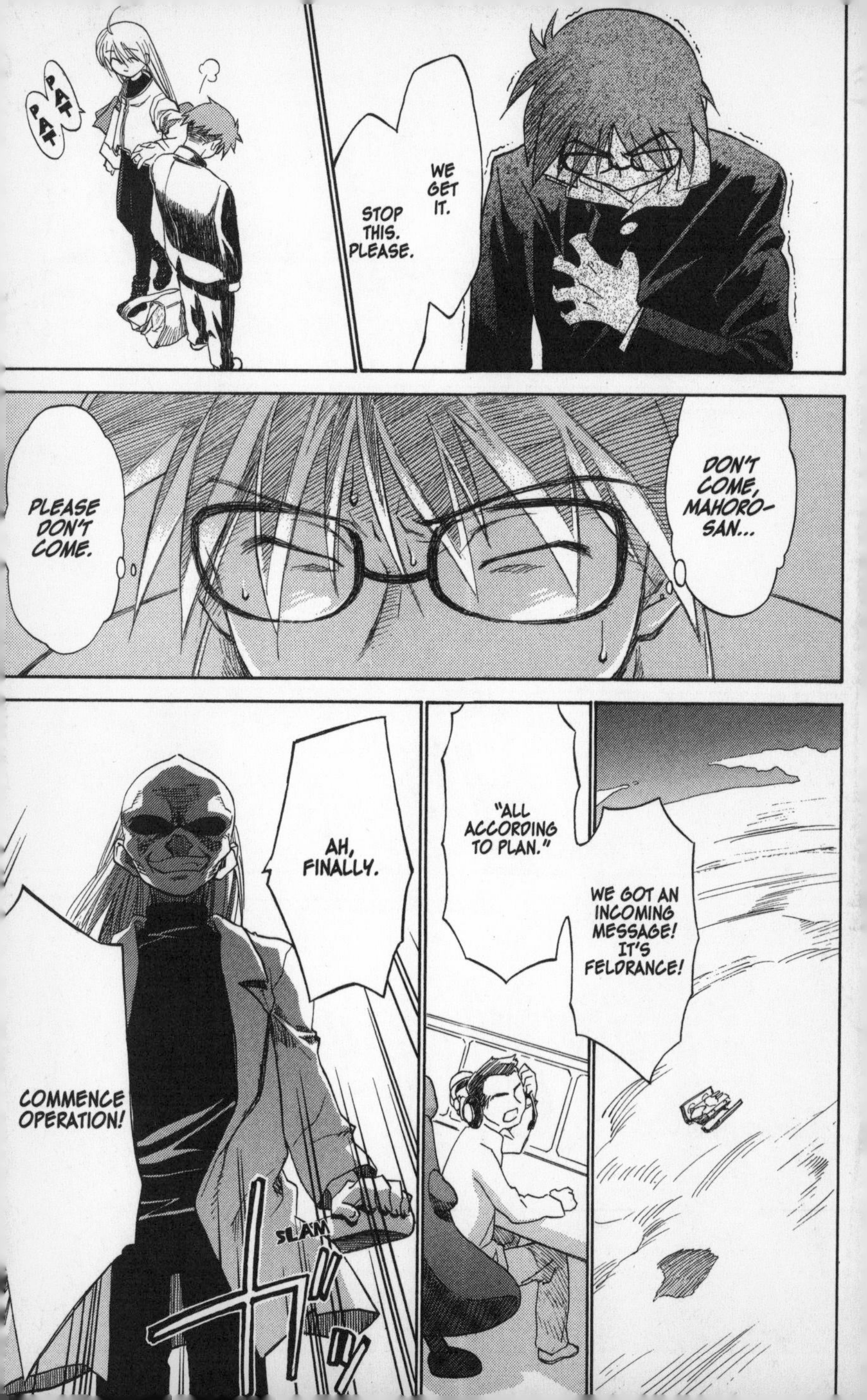
WE GET IT.
STOP THIS. PLEASE.
PAT PAT
DON'T COME, MAHORO-SAN...
PLEASE DON'T COME.
WE GOT AN INCOMING MESSAGE! IT'S FELDRANCE!
"ALL ACCORDING TO PLAN."
AH, FINALLY.
COMMENCE OPERATION!
SLAM

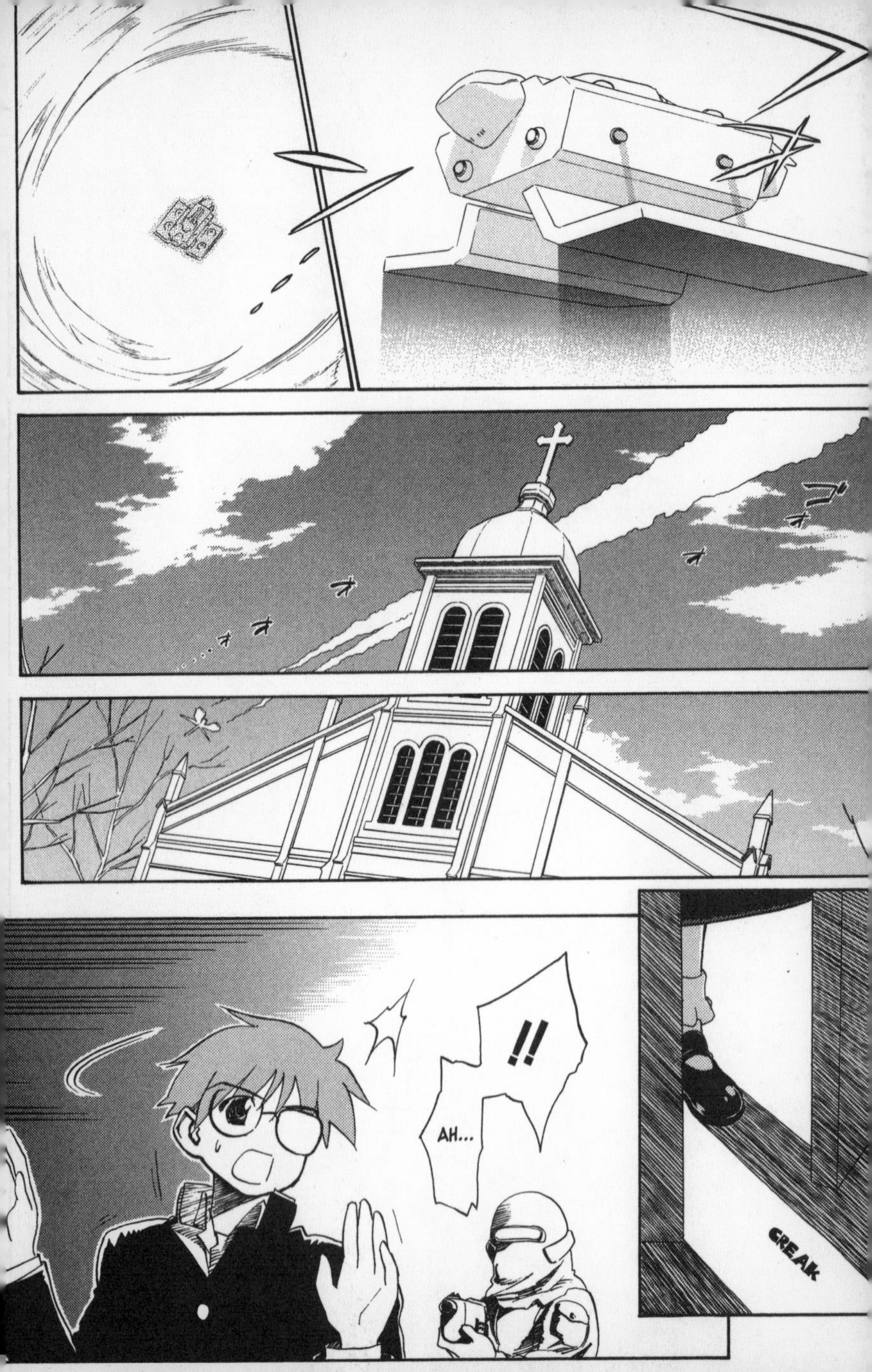
ゴォォォォォ…
CREAK
!!
AH...

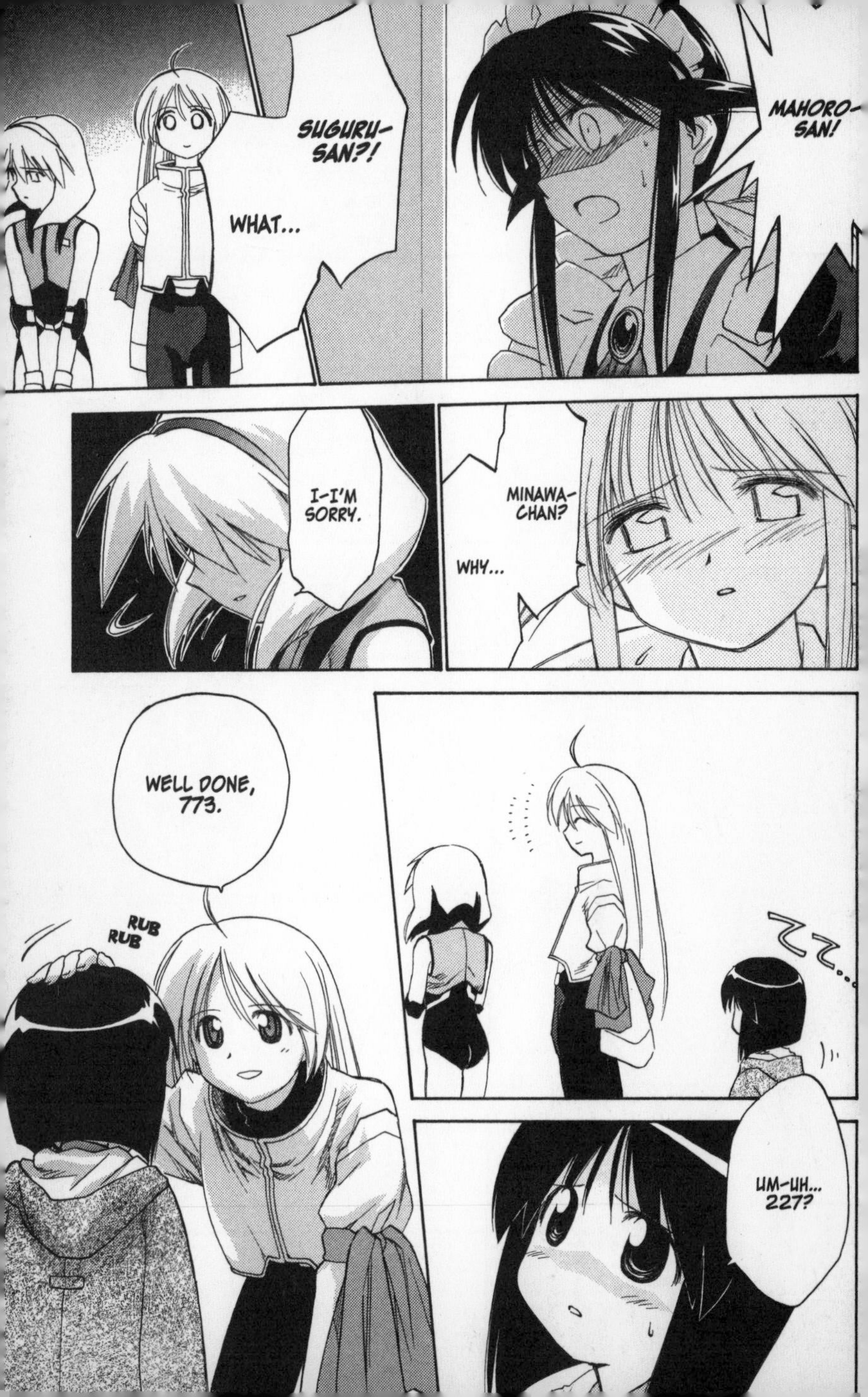
MAHORO-SAN!
SUGURU-SAN?!
WHAT...
MINAWA-CHAN?
WHY...
I-I'M SORRY.
ZZ...
UM-UH... 227?
WELL DONE, 773.
RUB RUB

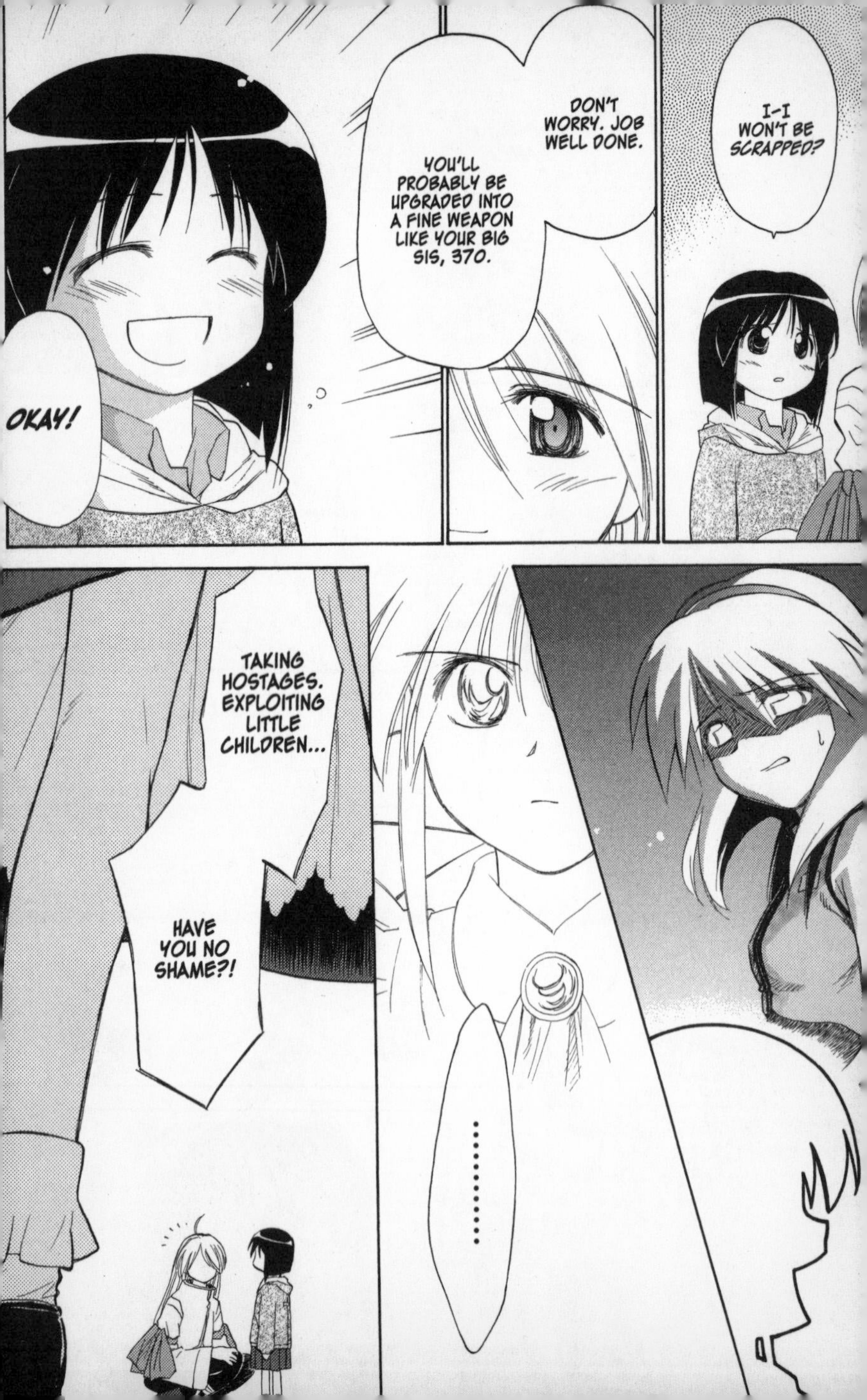
I-I WON'T BE SCRAPPED?
DON'T WORRY. JOB WELL DONE.
YOU'LL PROBABLY BE UPGRADED INTO A FINE WEAPON LIKE YOUR BIG SIS, 370.
OKAY!
....
TAKING HOSTAGES. EXPLOITING LITTLE CHILDREN...
HAVE YOU NO SHAME?!

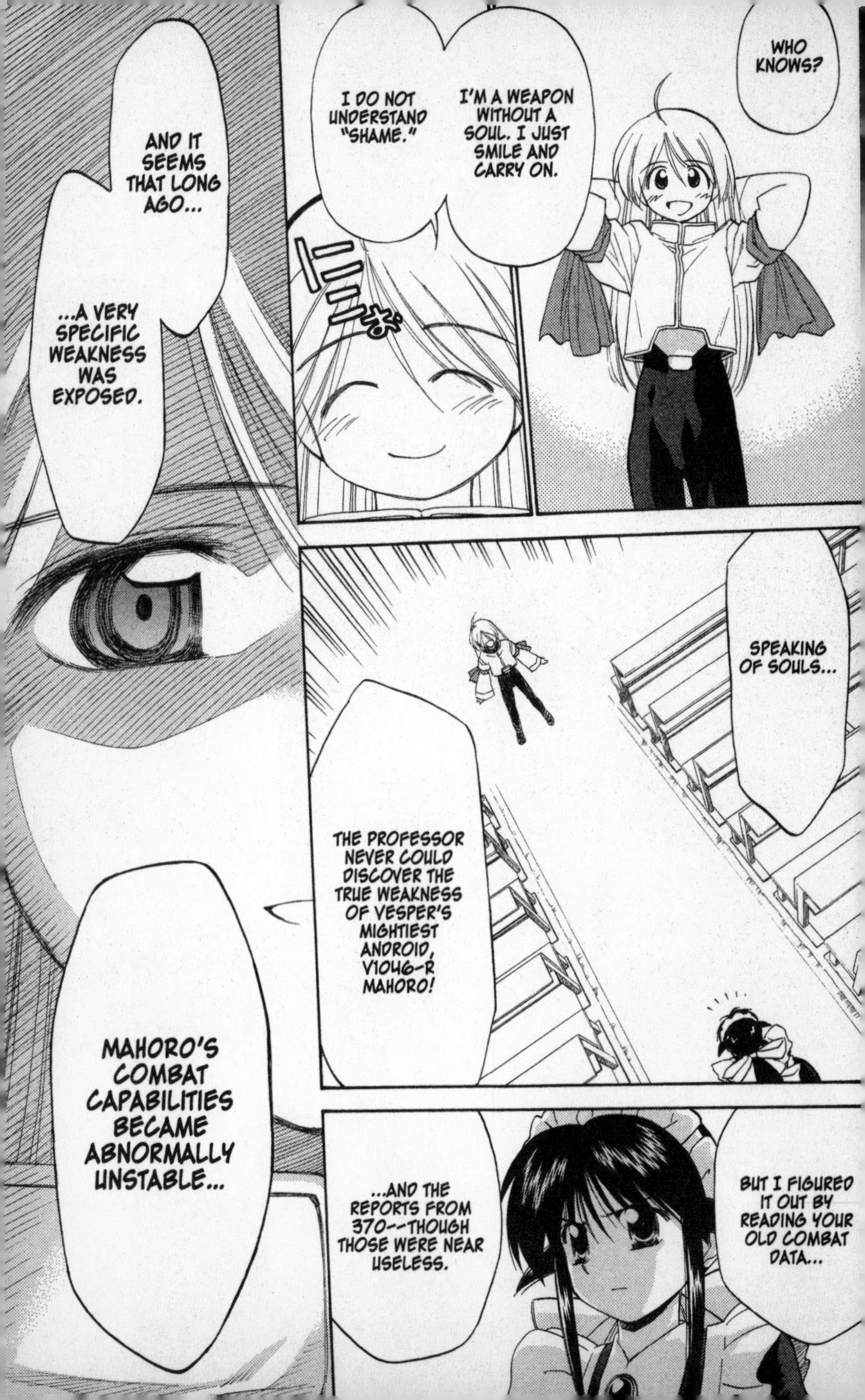
WHO KNOWS?
I'M A WEAPON WITHOUT A SOUL. I JUST SMILE AND CARRY ON.
I DO NOT UNDERSTAND "SHAME."
SPEAKING OF SOULS...
THE PROFESSOR NEVER COULD DISCOVER THE TRUE WEAKNESS OF VESPER'S MIGHTIEST ANDROID, V1046-R MAHORO!
BUT I FIGURED IT OUT BY READING YOUR OLD COMBAT DATA...
...AND THE REPORTS FROM 370--THOUGH THOSE WERE NEAR USELESS.
AND IT SEEMS THAT LONG AGO...
...A VERY SPECIFIC WEAKNESS WAS EXPOSED.
MAHORO'S COMBAT CAPABILITIES BECAME ABNORMALLY UNSTABLE...

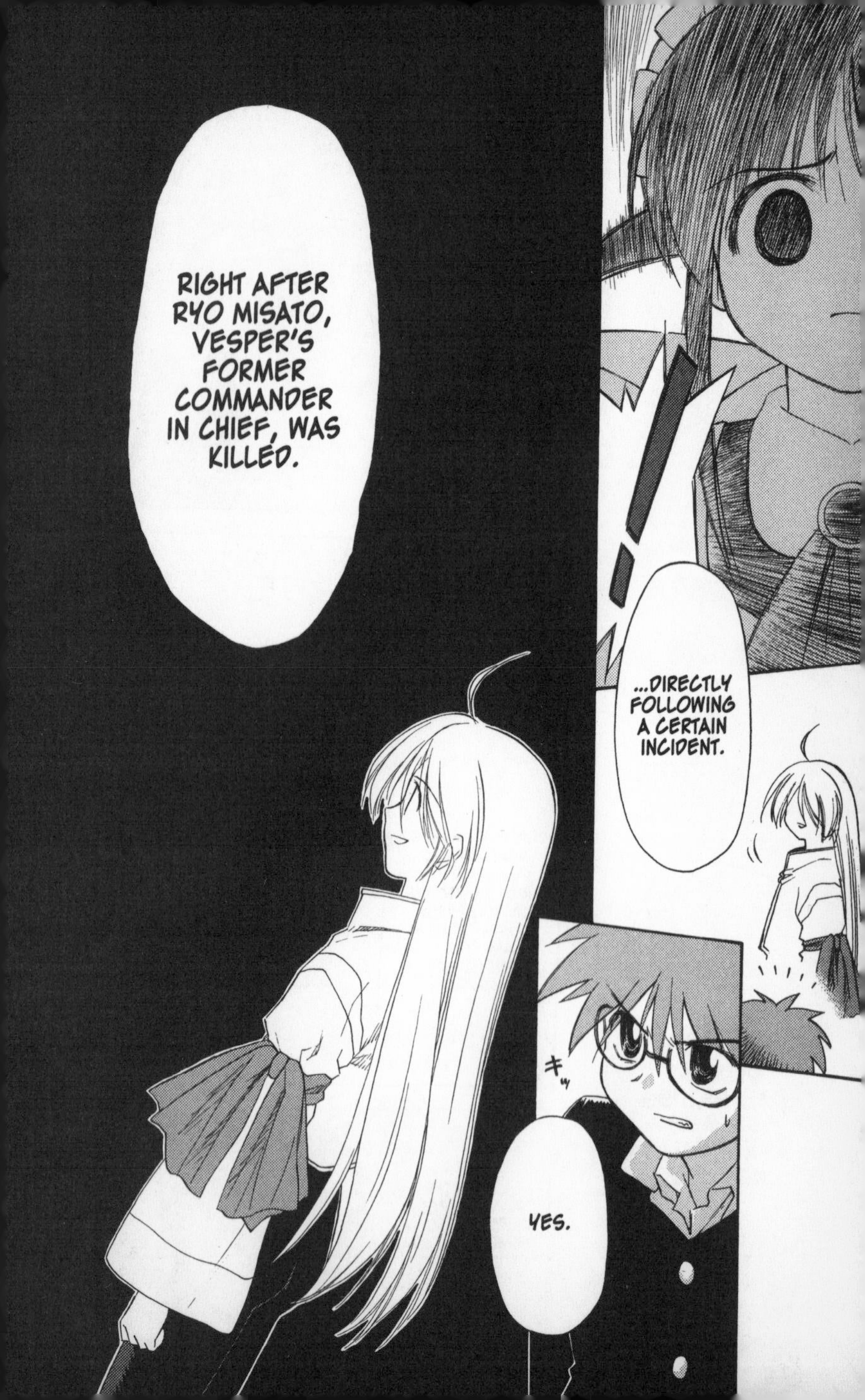
...DIRECTLY FOLLOWING A CERTAIN INCIDENT.
YES.
RIGHT AFTER RYO MISATO, VESPER'S FORMER COMMANDER IN CHIEF, WAS KILLED.

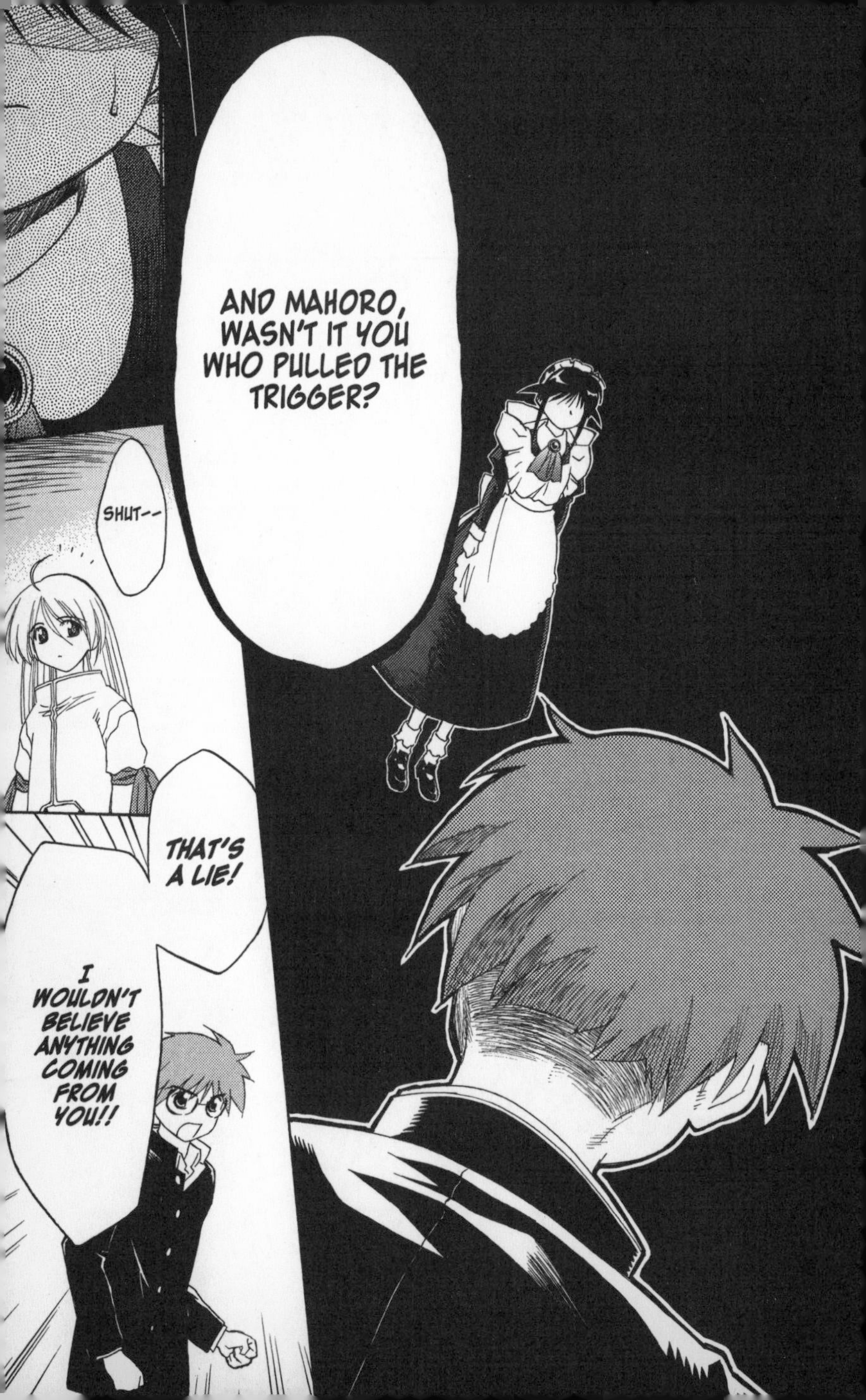
AND MAHORO, WASN'T IT YOU WHO PULLED THE TRIGGER?
SHUT--
THAT'S A LIE!
I WOULDN'T BELIEVE ANYTHING COMING FROM YOU!!

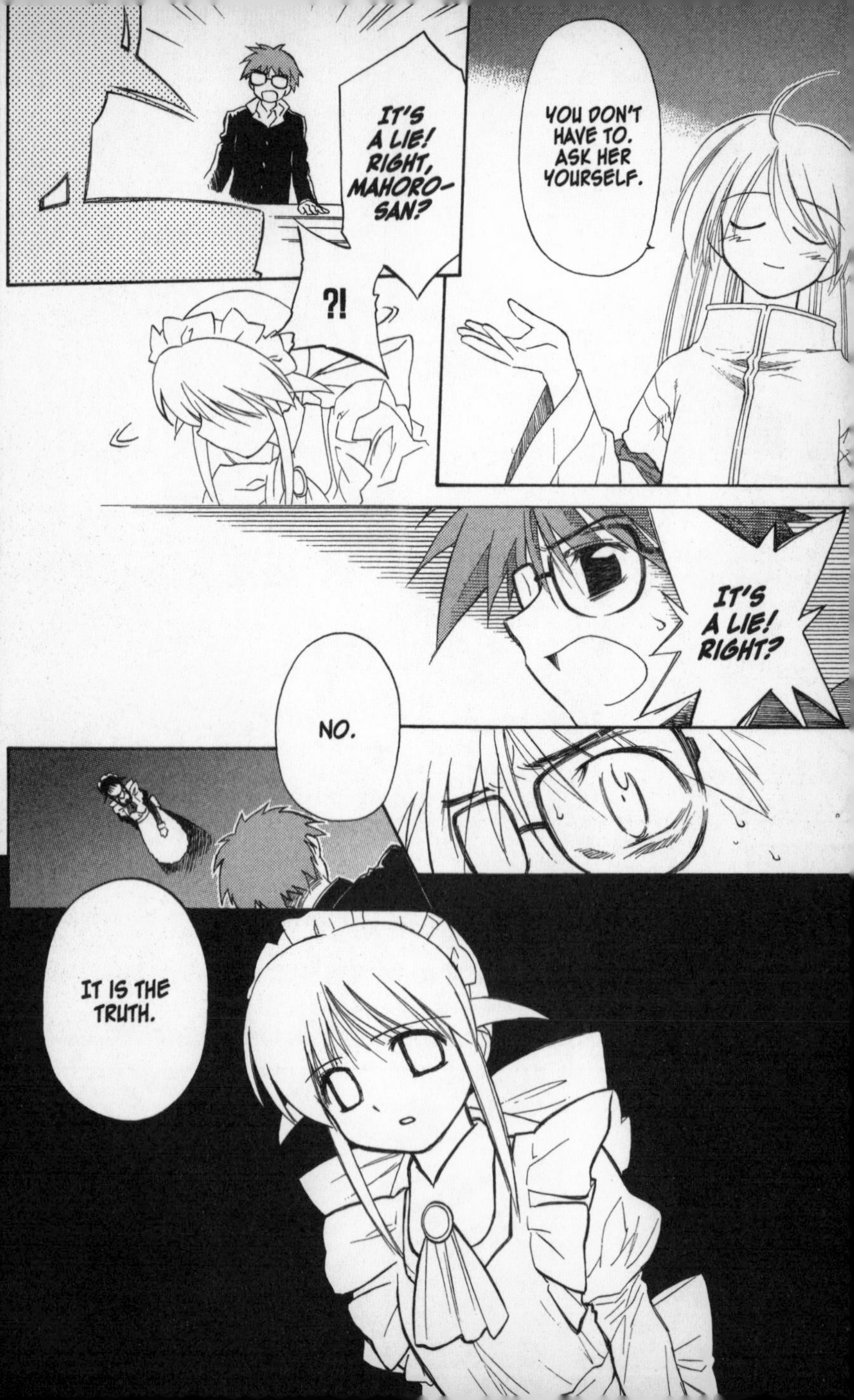
YOU DON'T HAVE TO. ASK HER YOURSELF.
IT'S A LIE! RIGHT, MAHORO-SAN?
?!
IT'S A LIE! RIGHT?
NO.
IT IS THE TRUTH.

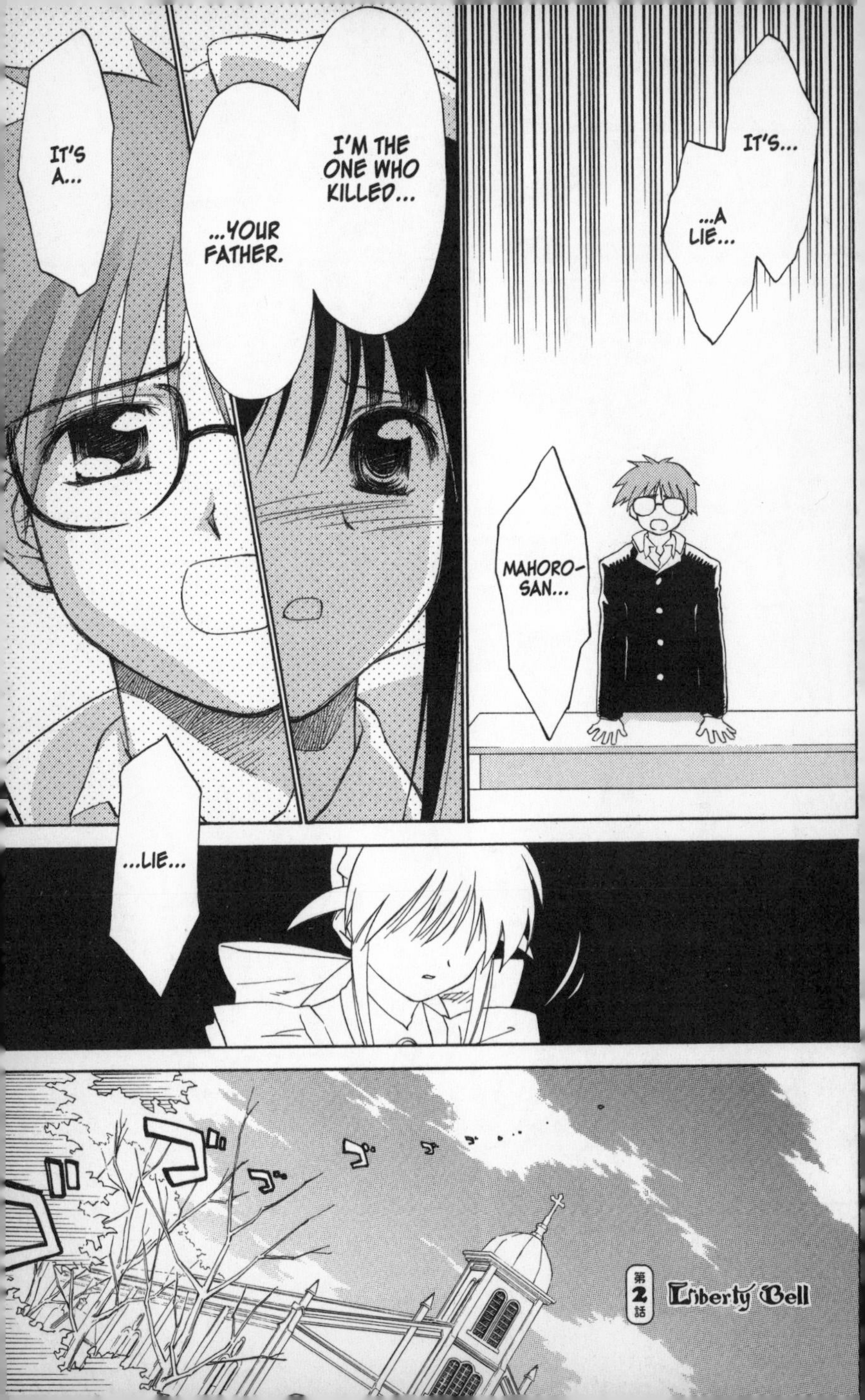
IT'S...
...A LIE...
MAHORO-SAN...
I'M THE ONE WHO KILLED...
...YOUR FATHER.
IT'S A...
...LIE...
第2話
Liberty Bell

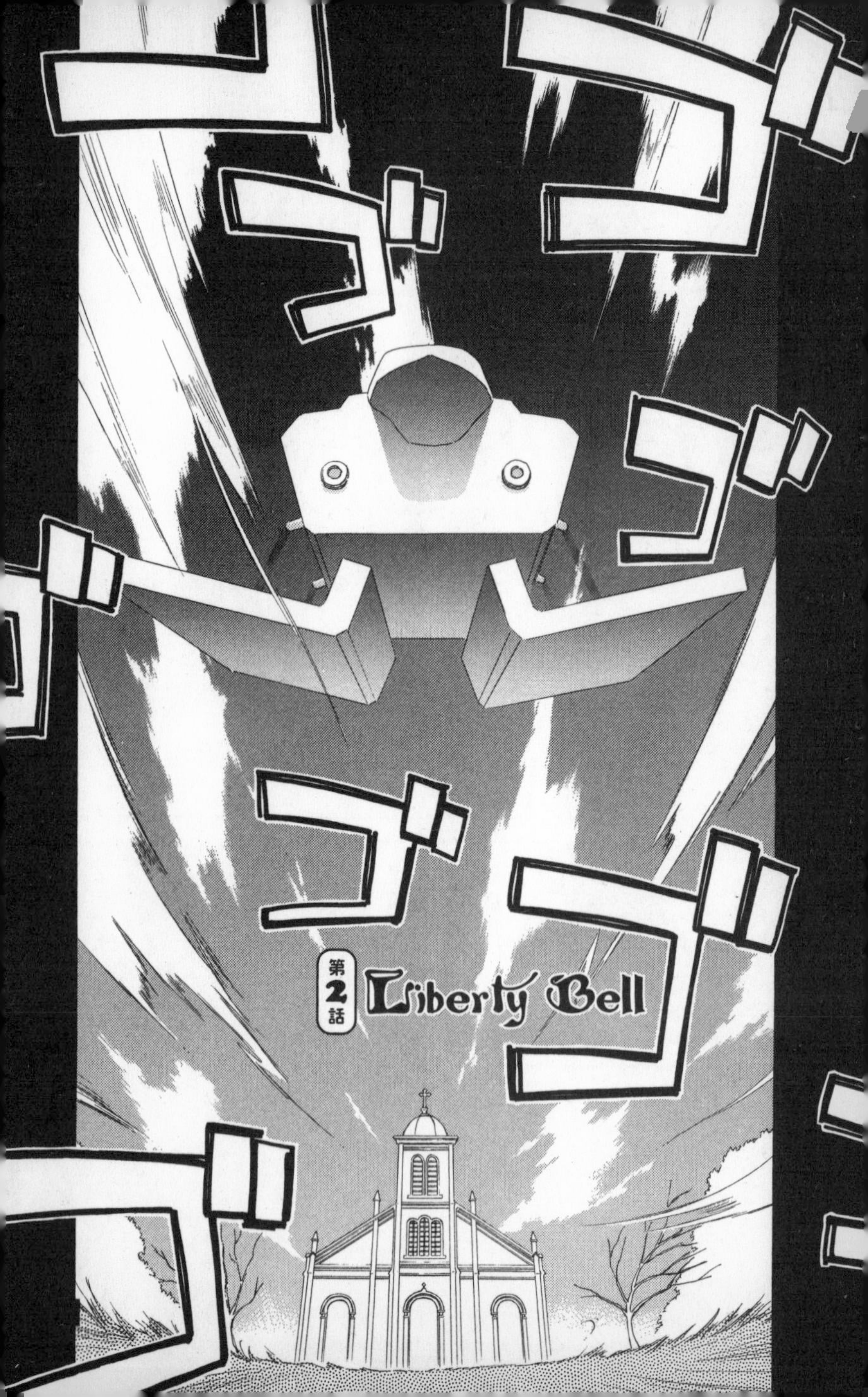
ゴゴゴゴゴゴゴ
第2話 Liberty Bell

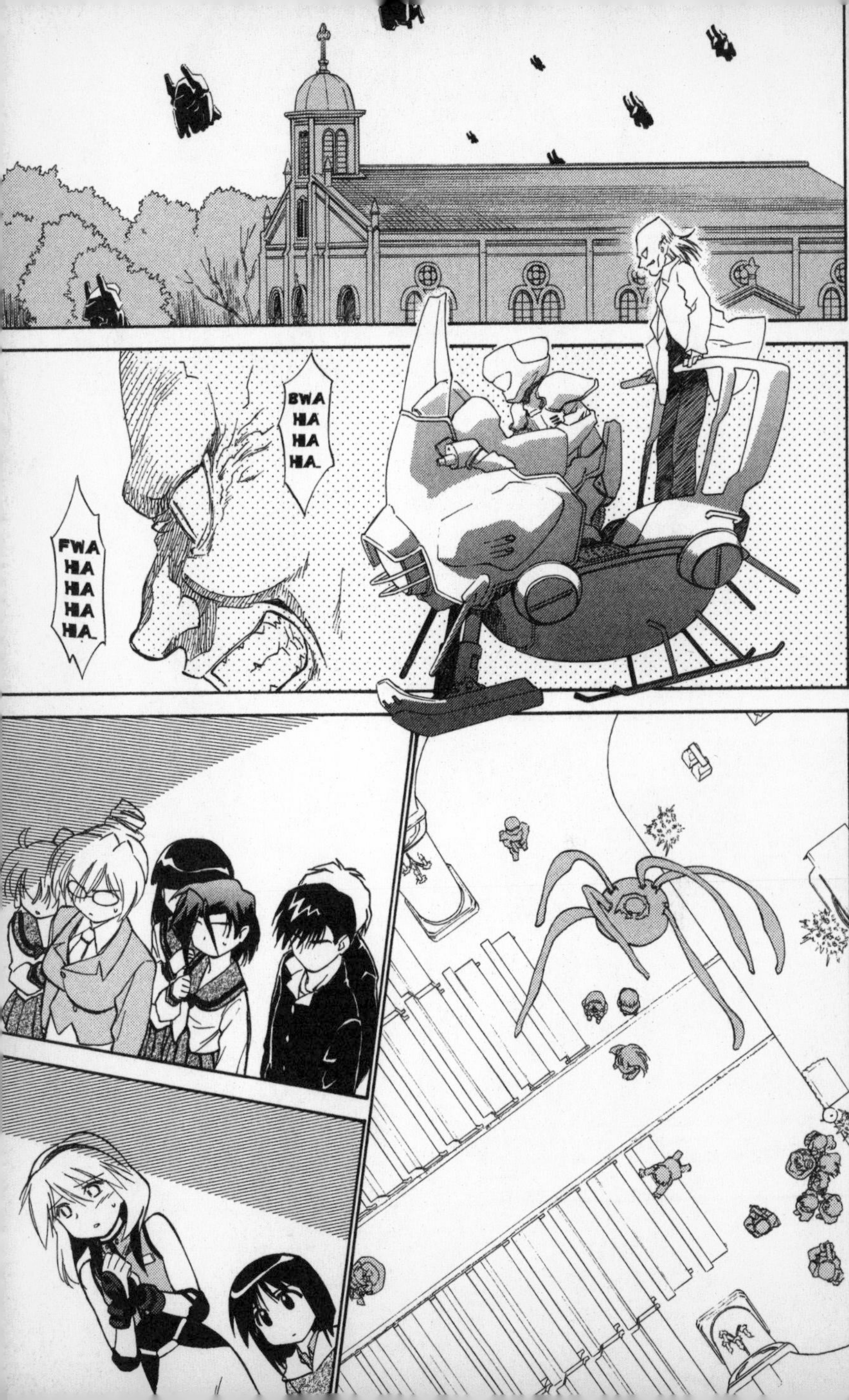
BWA HA HA HA...
FWA HA HA HA HA HA...

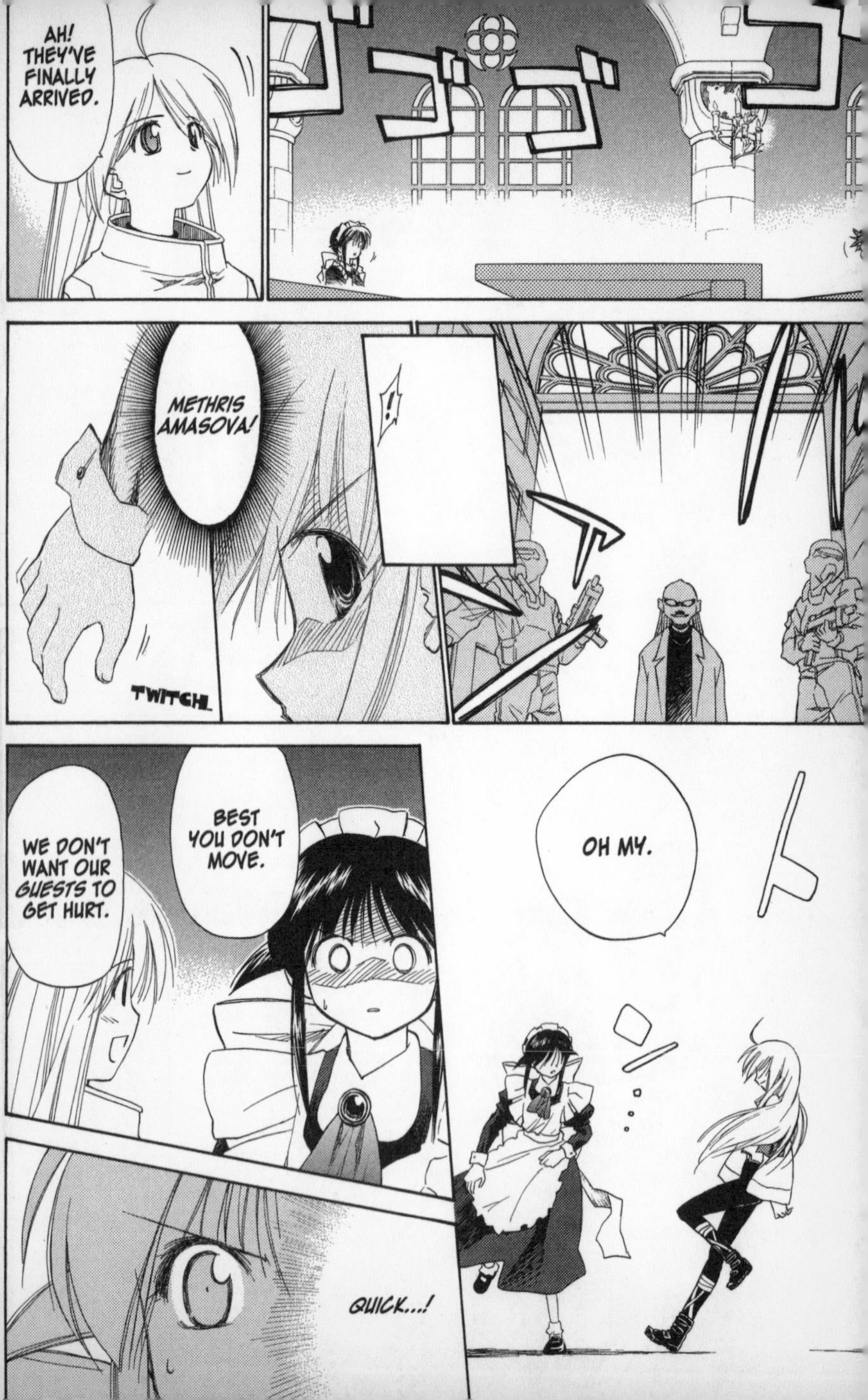
AH! THEY'VE FINALLY ARRIVED.
!
METHRIS AMASOVA!
TWITCH
OH MY.
QUICK...!
BEST YOU DON'T MOVE.
WE DON'T WANT OUR GUESTS TO GET HURT.

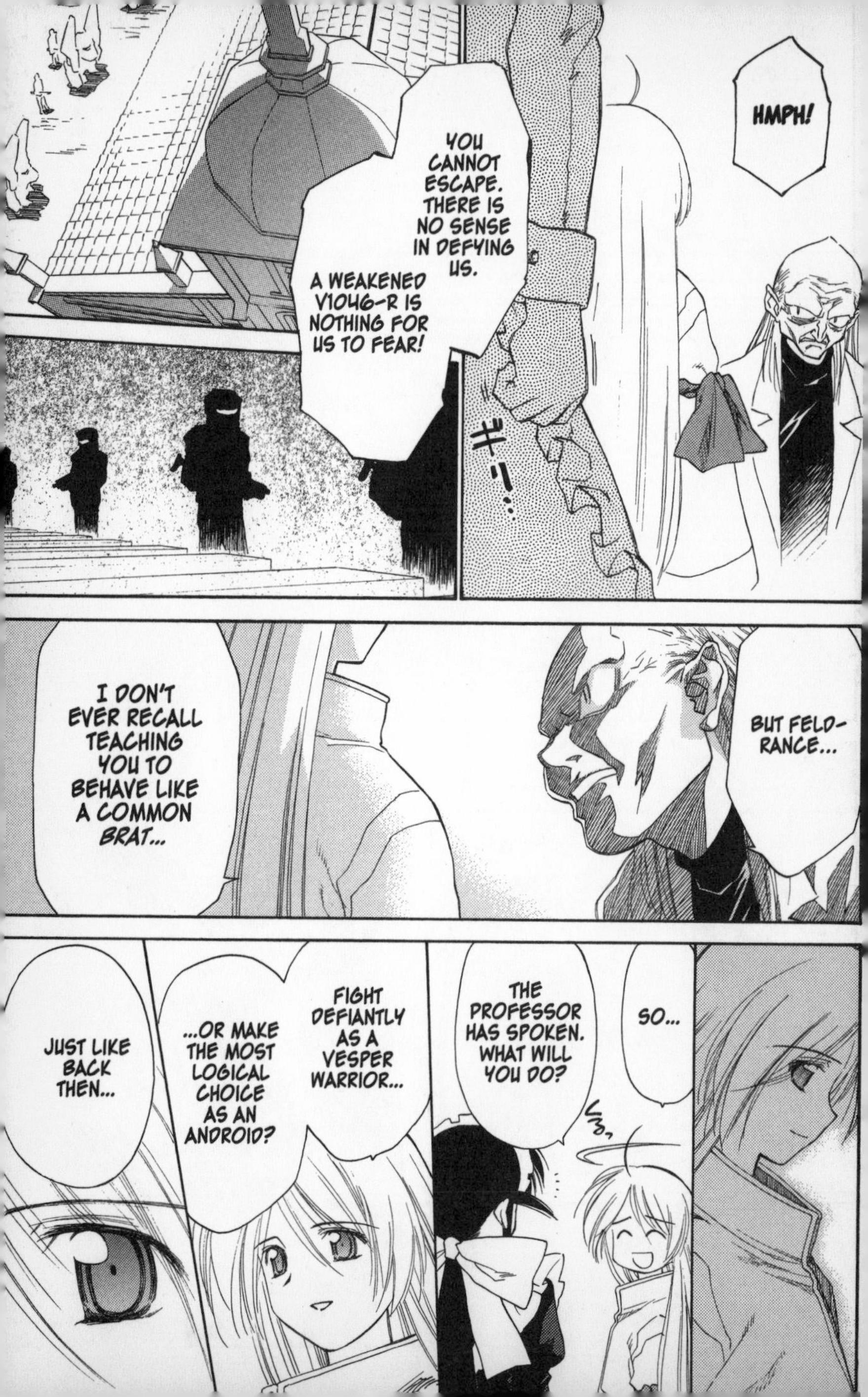
HMPH!
ギリ…
YOU CANNOT ESCAPE. THERE IS NO SENSE IN DEFYING US.
A WEAKENED V1046-R IS NOTHING FOR US TO FEAR!
BUT FELD-RANCE...
I DON'T EVER RECALL TEACHING YOU TO BEHAVE LIKE A COMMON BRAT...
SO...
THE PROFESSOR HAS SPOKEN. WHAT WILL YOU DO?
FIGHT DEFIANTLY AS A VESPER WARRIOR...
...OR MAKE THE MOST LOGICAL CHOICE AS AN ANDROID?
JUST LIKE BACK THEN...

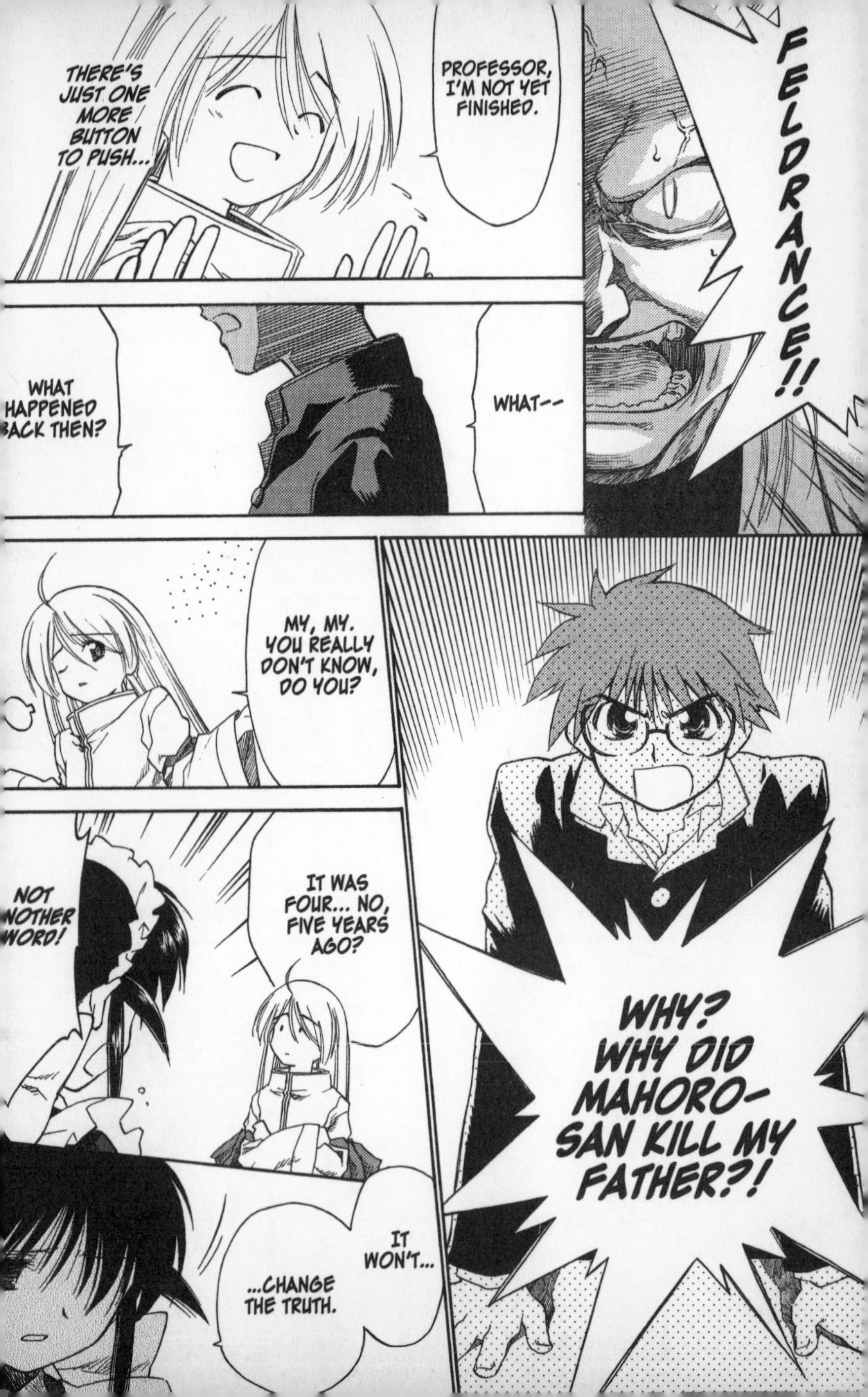
FELDRANCE!!
PROFESSOR, I'M NOT YET FINISHED.
THERE'S JUST ONE MORE BUTTON TO PUSH...
WHAT--
WHAT HAPPENED BACK THEN?
WHY? WHY DID MAHORO-SAN KILL MY FATHER?!
MY, MY. YOU REALLY DON'T KNOW, DO YOU?
IT WAS FOUR... NO, FIVE YEARS AGO?
NOT NOTHER WORD!
IT WON'T...
...CHANGE THE TRUTH.

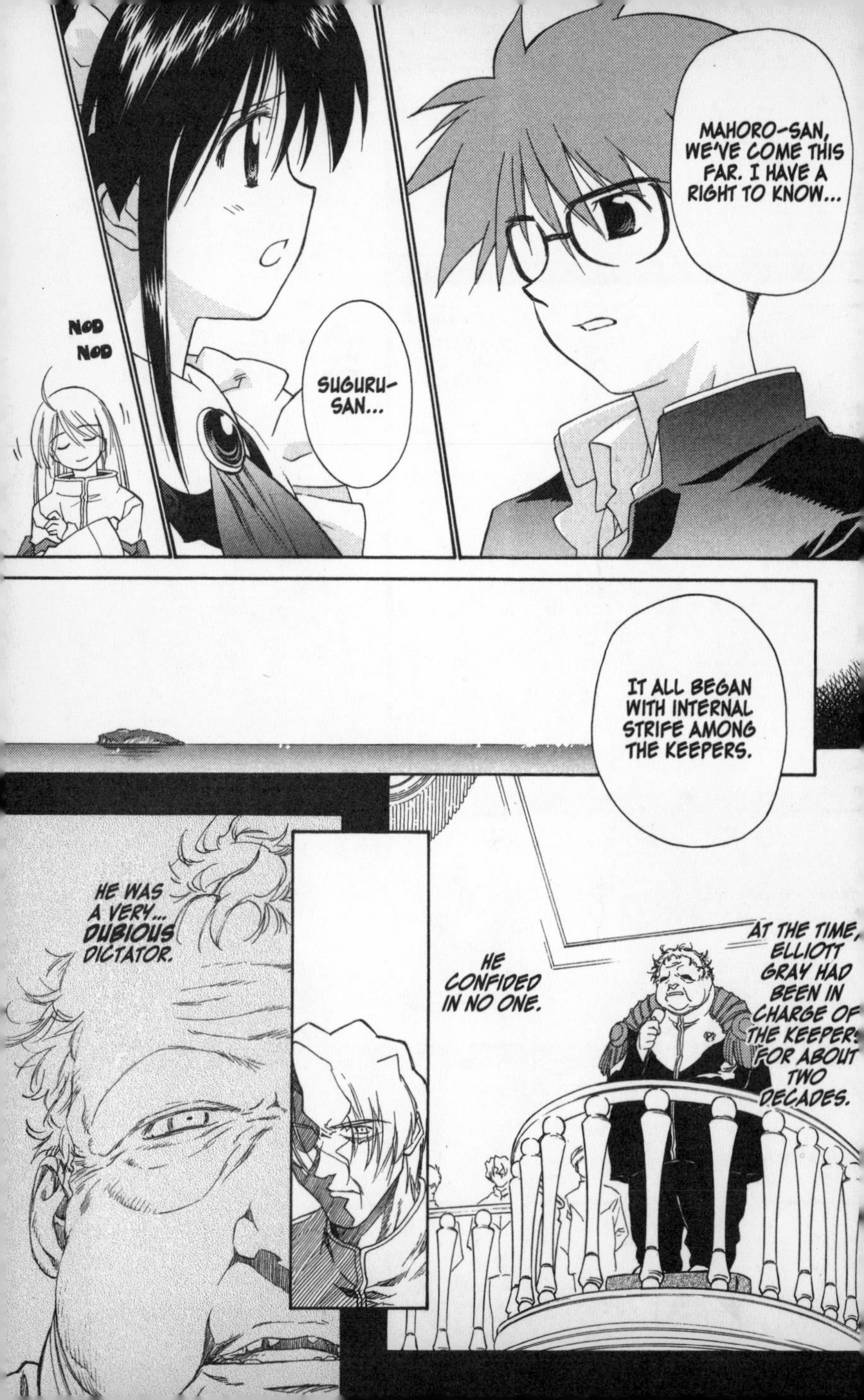
MAHORO-SAN, WE'VE COME THIS FAR. I HAVE A RIGHT TO KNOW...
SUGURU-SAN...
NOD NOD
IT ALL BEGAN WITH INTERNAL STRIFE AMONG THE KEEPERS.
AT THE TIME, ELLIOTT GRAY HAD BEEN IN CHARGE OF THE KEEPERS FOR ABOUT TWO DECADES.
HE CONFIDED IN NO ONE.
HE WAS A VERY... DUBIOUS DICTATOR.

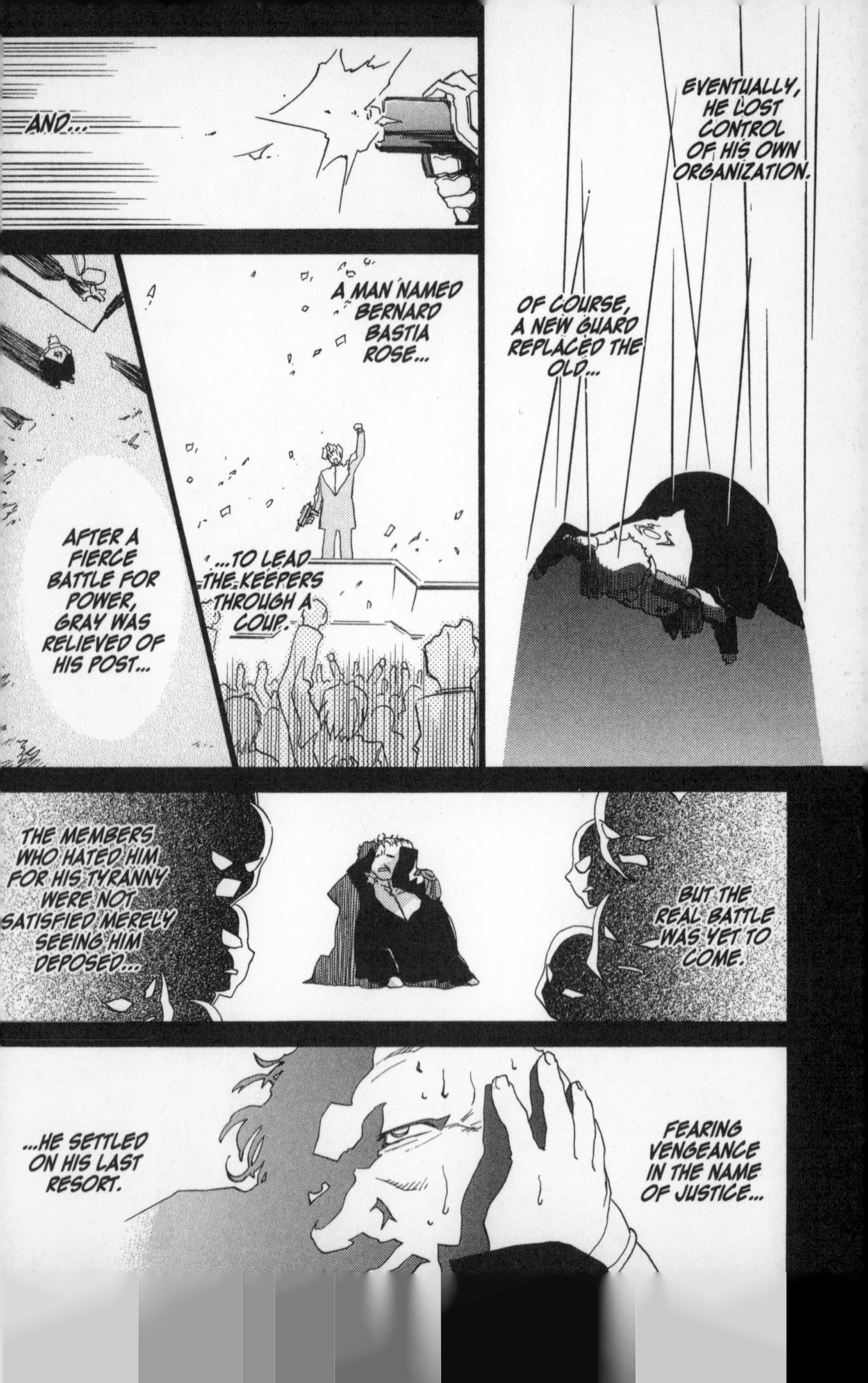
EVENTUALLY, HE LOST CONTROL OF HIS OWN ORGANIZATION.
OF COURSE, A NEW GUARD REPLACED THE OLD...
AND...
A MAN NAMED BERNARD BASTIA ROSE...
...TO LEAD THE KEEPERS THROUGH A COUP.
AFTER A FIERCE BATTLE FOR POWER, GRAY WAS RELIEVED OF HIS POST...
BUT THE REAL BATTLE WAS YET TO COME.
THE MEMBERS WHO HATED HIM FOR HIS TYRANNY WERE NOT SATISFIED MERELY SEEING HIM DEPOSED...
FEARING VENGEANCE IN THE NAME OF JUSTICE...
...HE SETTLED ON HIS LAST RESORT.

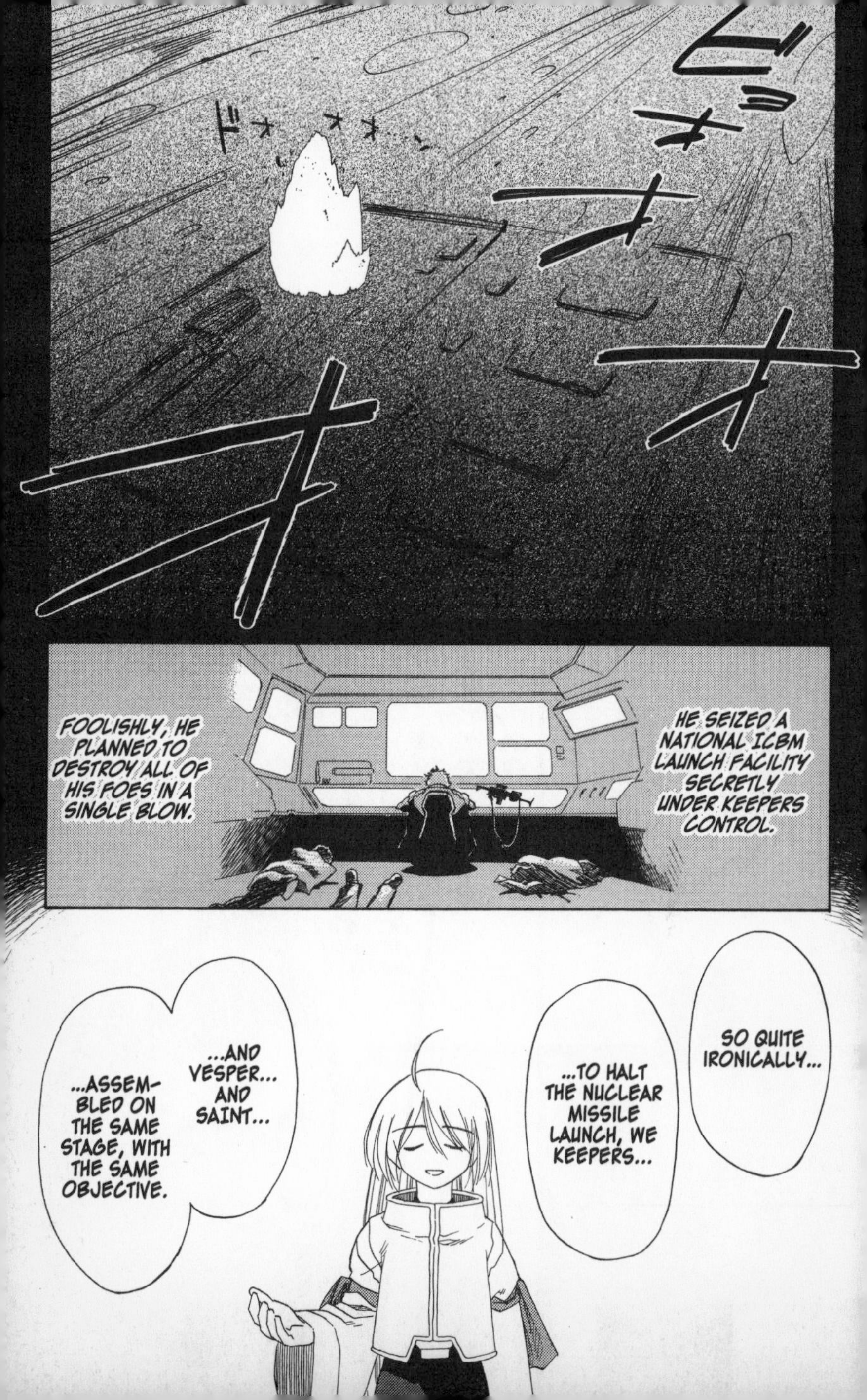
HE SEIZED A NATIONAL ICBM LAUNCH FACILITY SECRETLY UNDER KEEPERS CONTROL.
FOOLISHLY, HE PLANNED TO DESTROY ALL OF HIS FOES IN A SINGLE BLOW.
SO QUITE IRONICALLY...
...TO HALT THE NUCLEAR MISSILE LAUNCH, WE KEEPERS...
...AND VESPER... AND SAINT...
...ASSEM-BLED ON THE SAME STAGE, WITH THE SAME OBJECTIVE.

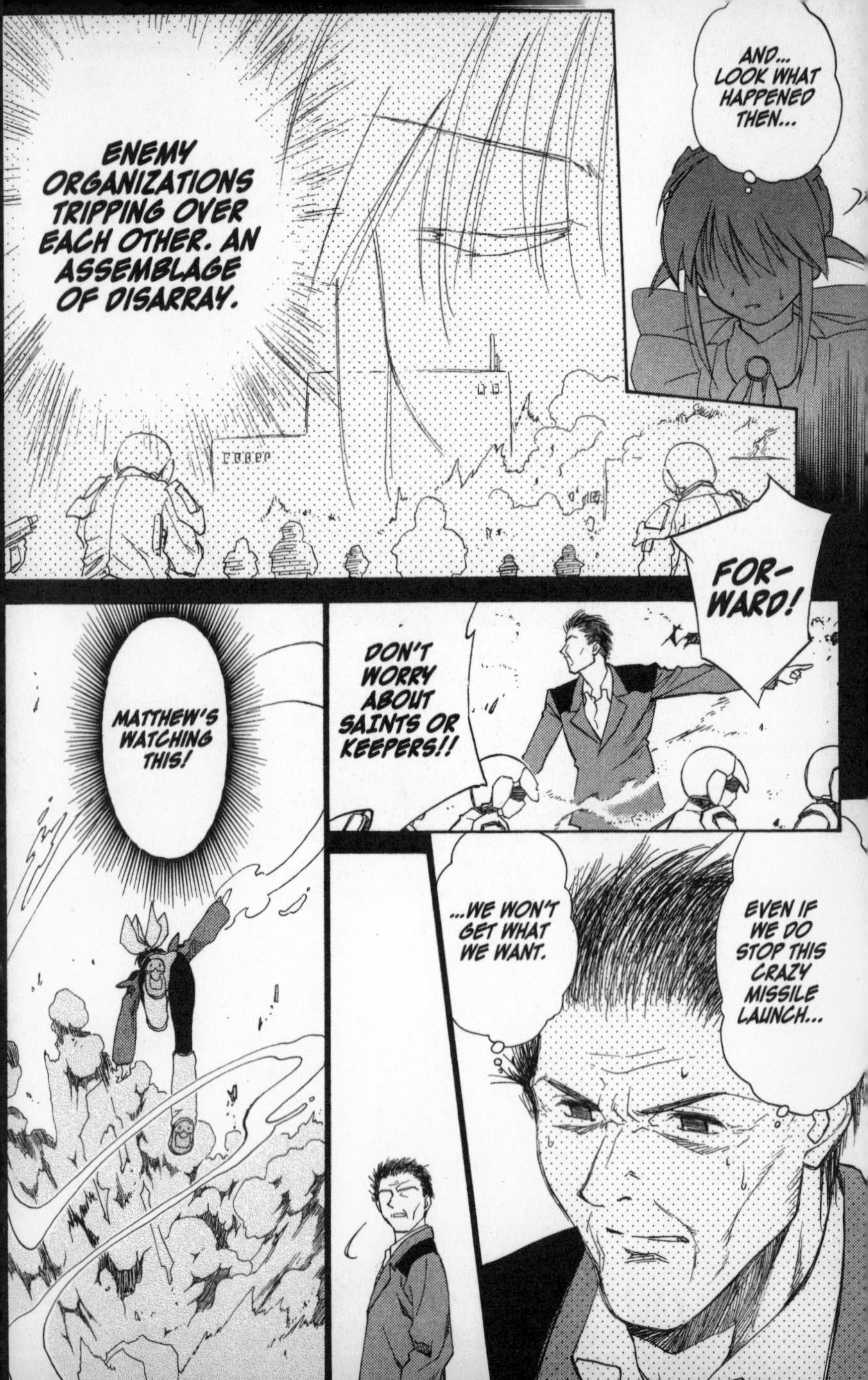
AND... LOOK WHAT HAPPENED THEN...
ENEMY ORGANIZATIONS TRIPPING OVER EACH OTHER. AN ASSEMBLAGE OF DISARRAY.
FOR-WARD!
DON'T WORRY ABOUT SAINTS OR KEEPERS!!
EVEN IF WE DO STOP THIS CRAZY MISSILE LAUNCH...
...WE WON'T GET WHAT WE WANT.
MATTHEW'S WATCHING THIS!

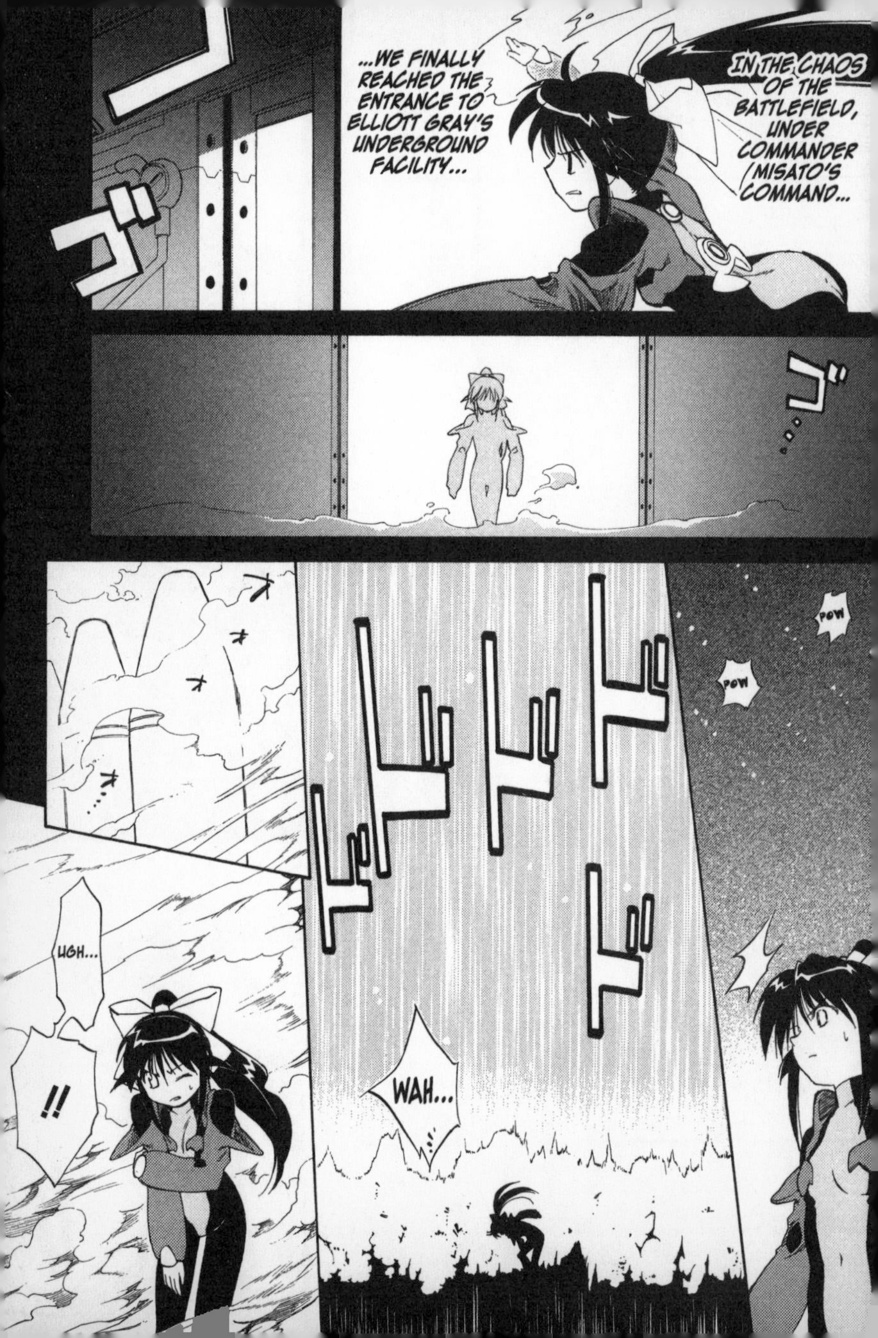
IN THE CHAOS OF THE BATTLEFIELD, UNDER COMMANDER MISATO'S COMMAND...
...WE FINALLY REACHED THE ENTRANCE TO ELLIOTT GRAY'S UNDERGROUND FACILITY...
POW
POW
WAH...
UGH...
!!

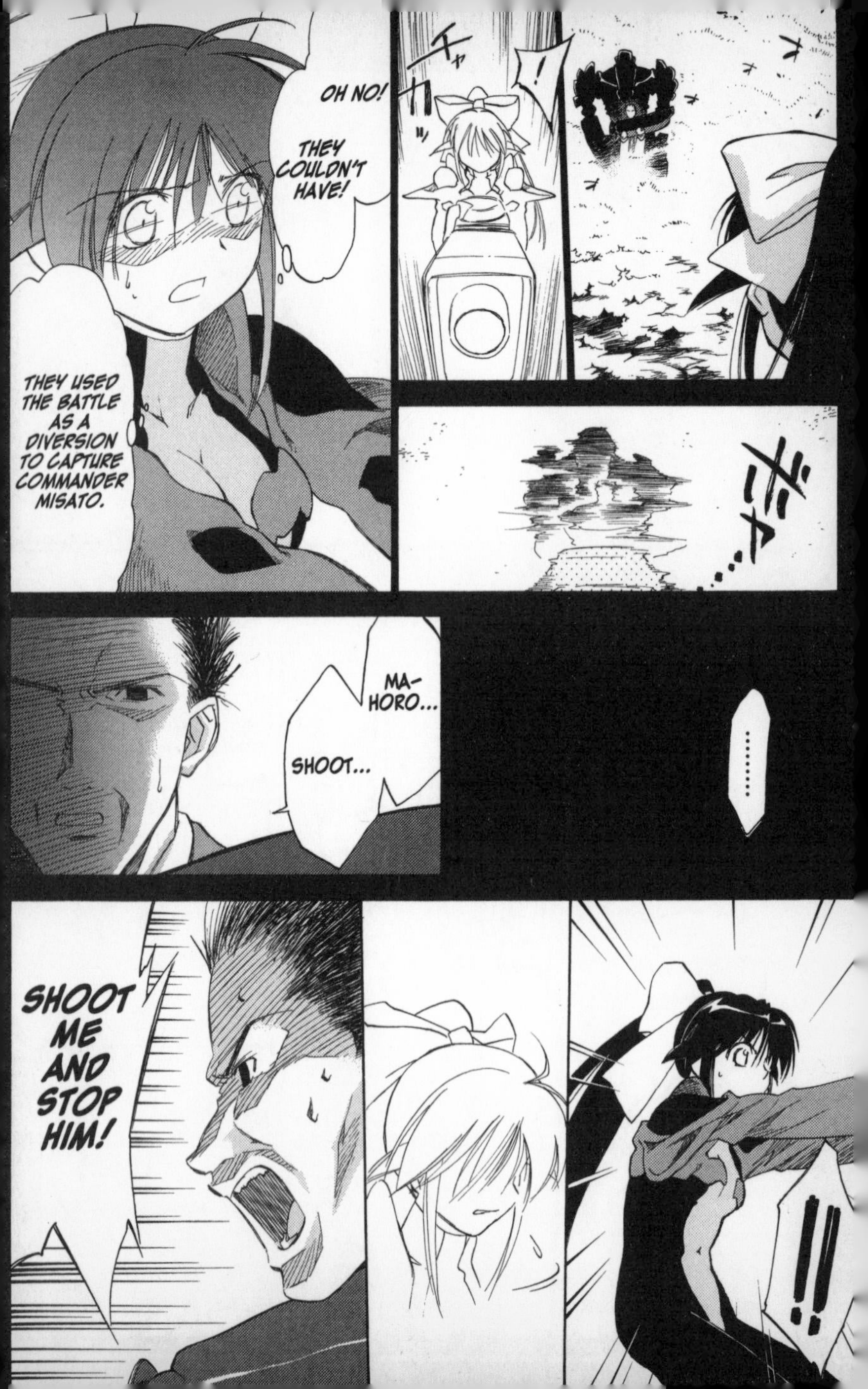
!
OH NO!
THEY COULDN'T HAVE!
THEY USED THE BATTLE AS A DIVERSION TO CAPTURE COMMANDER MISATO.
......
MA-HORO...
SHOOT...
!!
SHOOT ME AND STOP HIM!

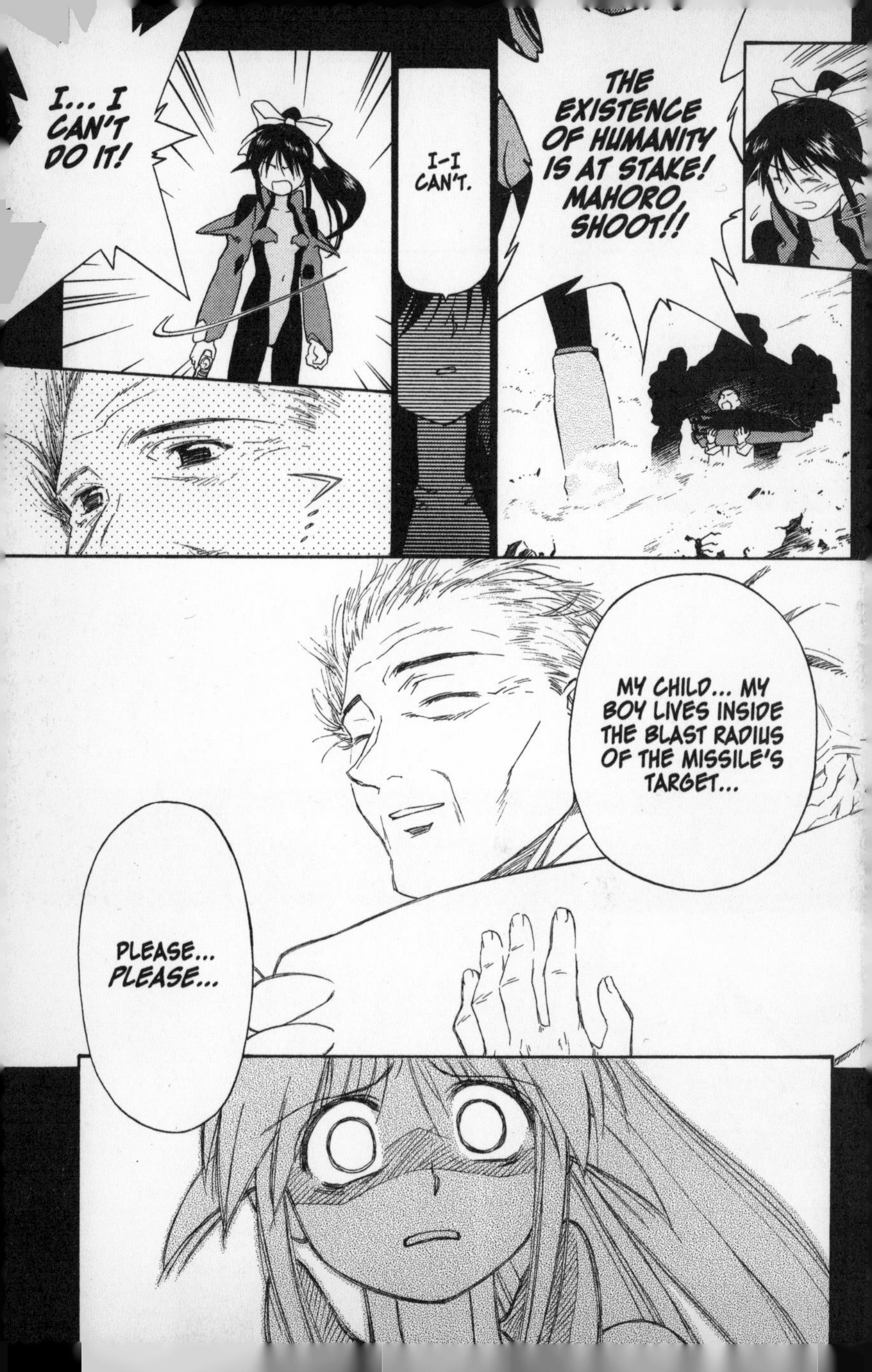
THE EXISTENCE OF HUMANITY IS AT STAKE! MAHORO, SHOOT!!
I-I CAN'T.
I... I CAN'T DO IT!
MY CHILD... MY BOY LIVES INSIDE THE BLAST RADIUS OF THE MISSILE'S TARGET...
PLEASE... PLEASE...

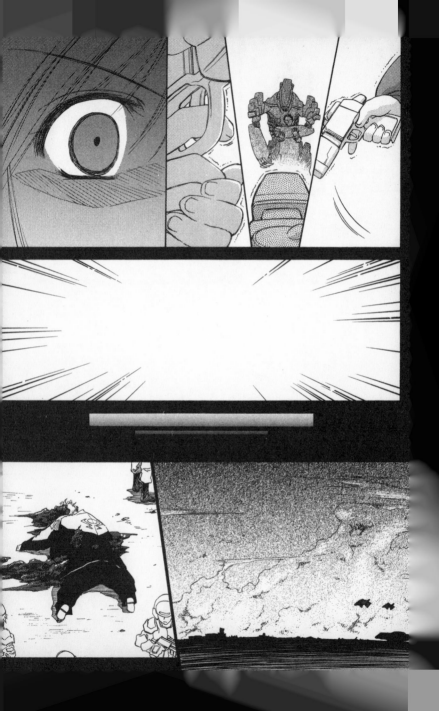

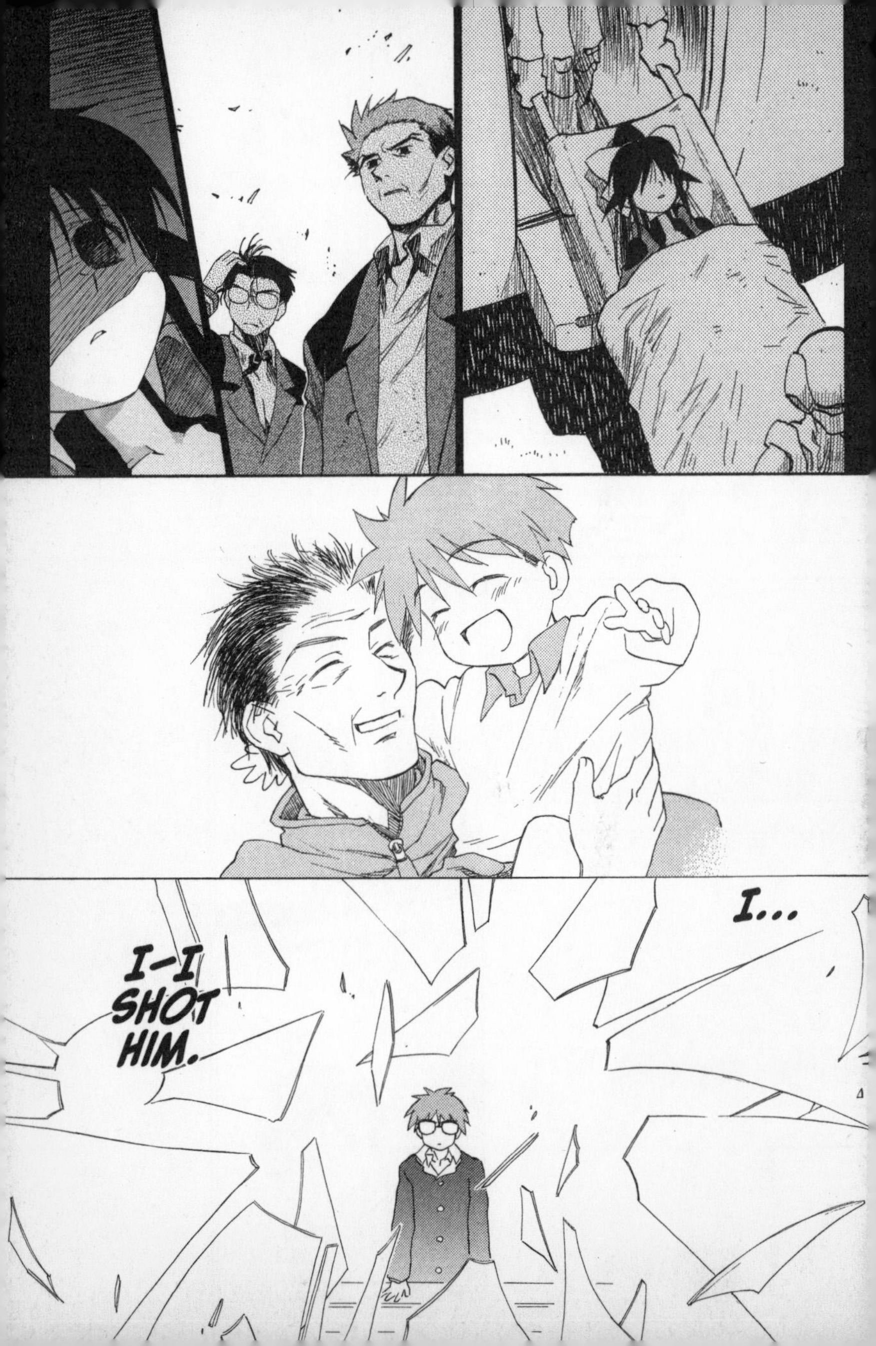
I...
I-I SHOT HIM.

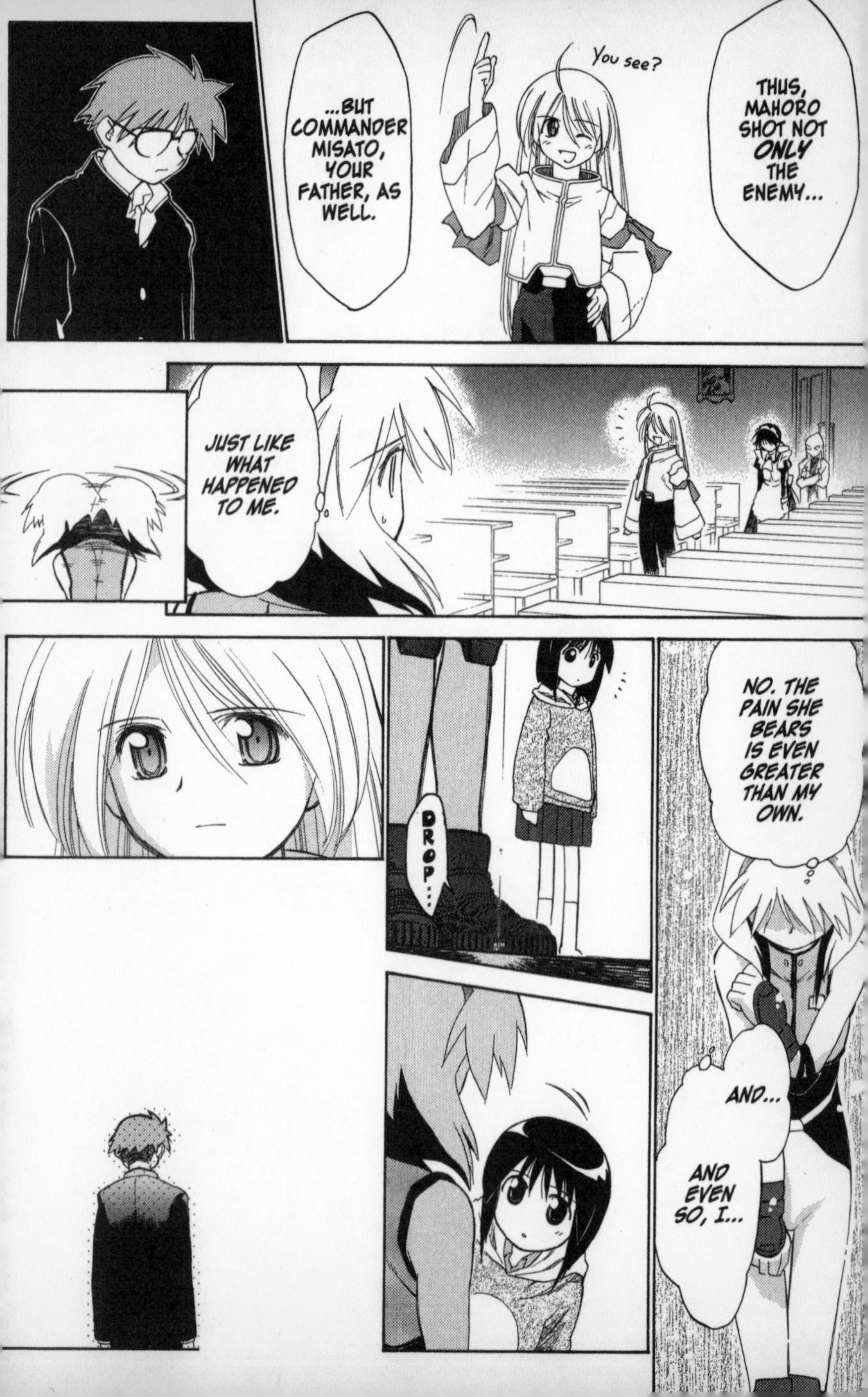
THUS, MAHORO SHOT NOT ONLY THE ENEMY...
You see?
...BUT COMMANDER MISATO, YOUR FATHER, AS WELL.
JUST LIKE WHAT HAPPENED TO ME.
NO. THE PAIN SHE BEARS IS EVEN GREATER THAN MY OWN.
AND...
AND EVEN SO, I...
DROP...

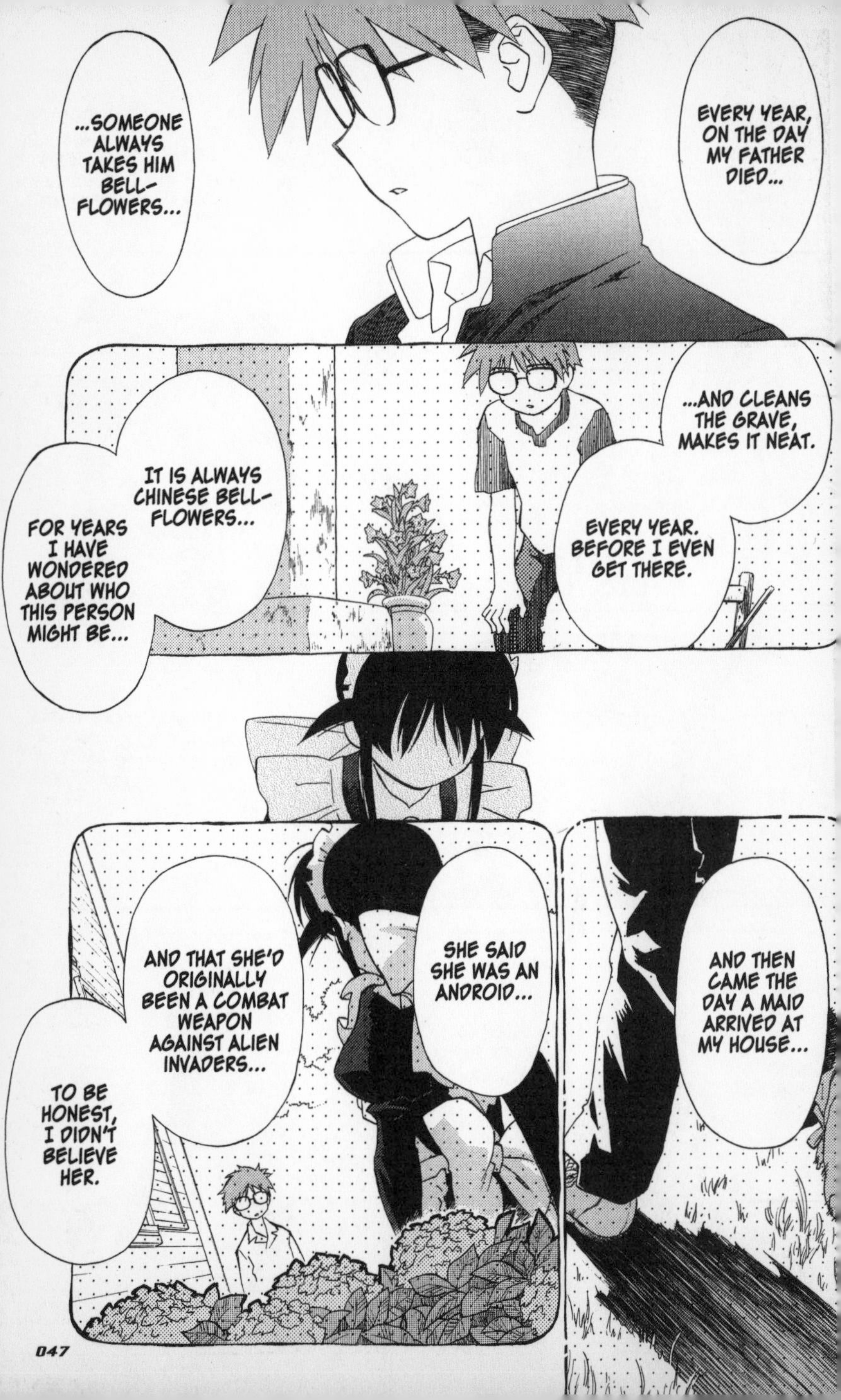
EVERY YEAR, ON THE DAY MY FATHER DIED...
...SOMEONE ALWAYS TAKES HIM BELL-FLOWERS...
...AND CLEANS THE GRAVE, MAKES IT NEAT.
EVERY YEAR. BEFORE I EVEN GET THERE.
IT IS ALWAYS CHINESE BELL-FLOWERS...
FOR YEARS I HAVE WONDERED ABOUT WHO THIS PERSON MIGHT BE...
AND THEN CAME THE DAY A MAID ARRIVED AT MY HOUSE...
SHE SAID SHE WAS AN ANDROID...
AND THAT SHE'D ORIGINALLY BEEN A COMBAT WEAPON AGAINST ALIEN INVADERS...
TO BE HONEST, I DIDN'T BELIEVE HER.

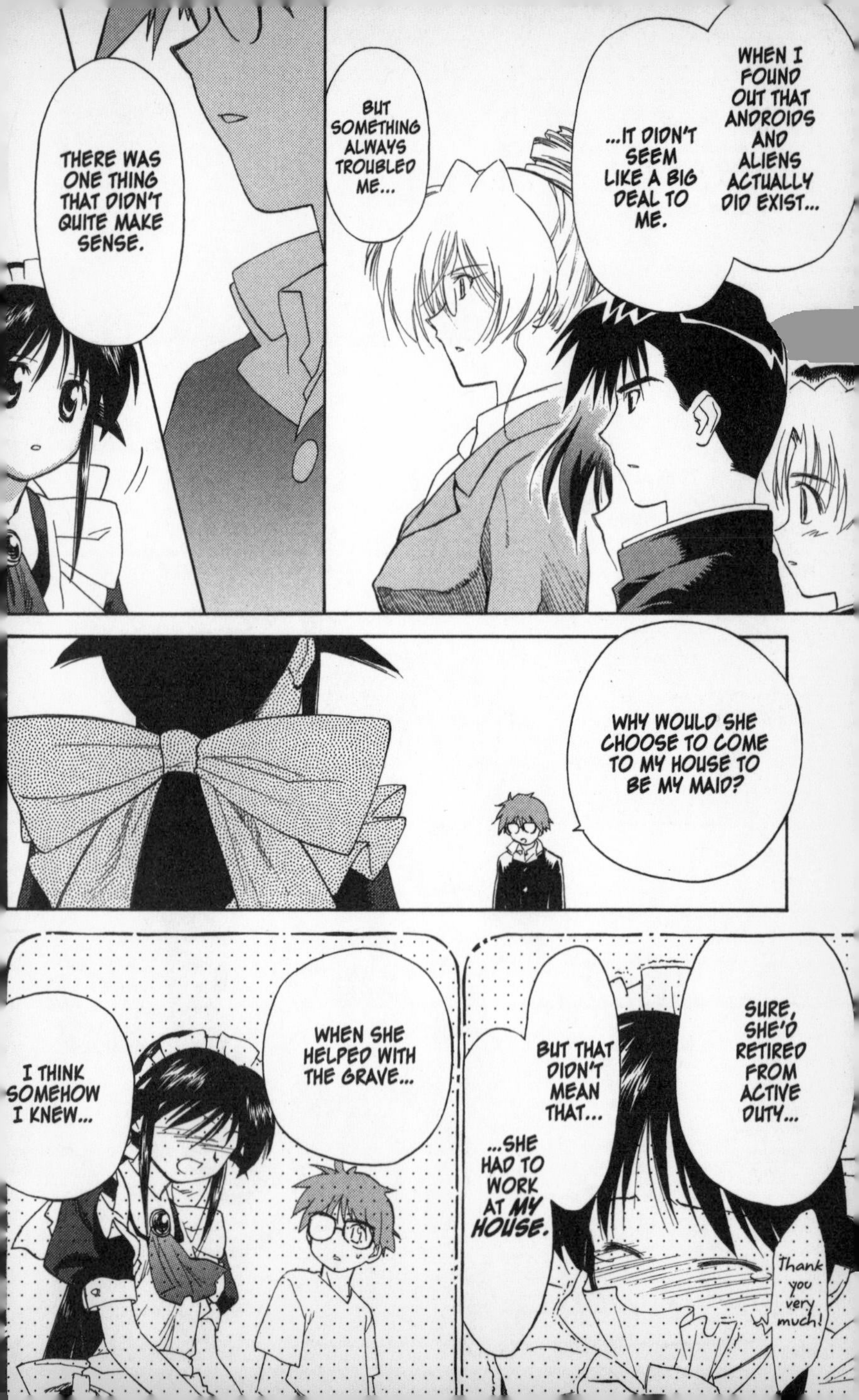
WHEN I FOUND OUT THAT ANDROIDS AND ALIENS ACTUALLY DID EXIST...
...IT DIDN'T SEEM LIKE A BIG DEAL TO ME.
BUT SOMETHING ALWAYS TROUBLED ME...
THERE WAS ONE THING THAT DIDN'T QUITE MAKE SENSE.
WHY WOULD SHE CHOOSE TO COME TO MY HOUSE TO BE MY MAID?
SURE, SHE'D RETIRED FROM ACTIVE DUTY...
BUT THAT DIDN'T MEAN THAT...
...SHE HAD TO WORK AT *MY HOUSE*.
Thank you very much!
WHEN SHE HELPED WITH THE GRAVE...
I THINK SOMEHOW I KNEW...

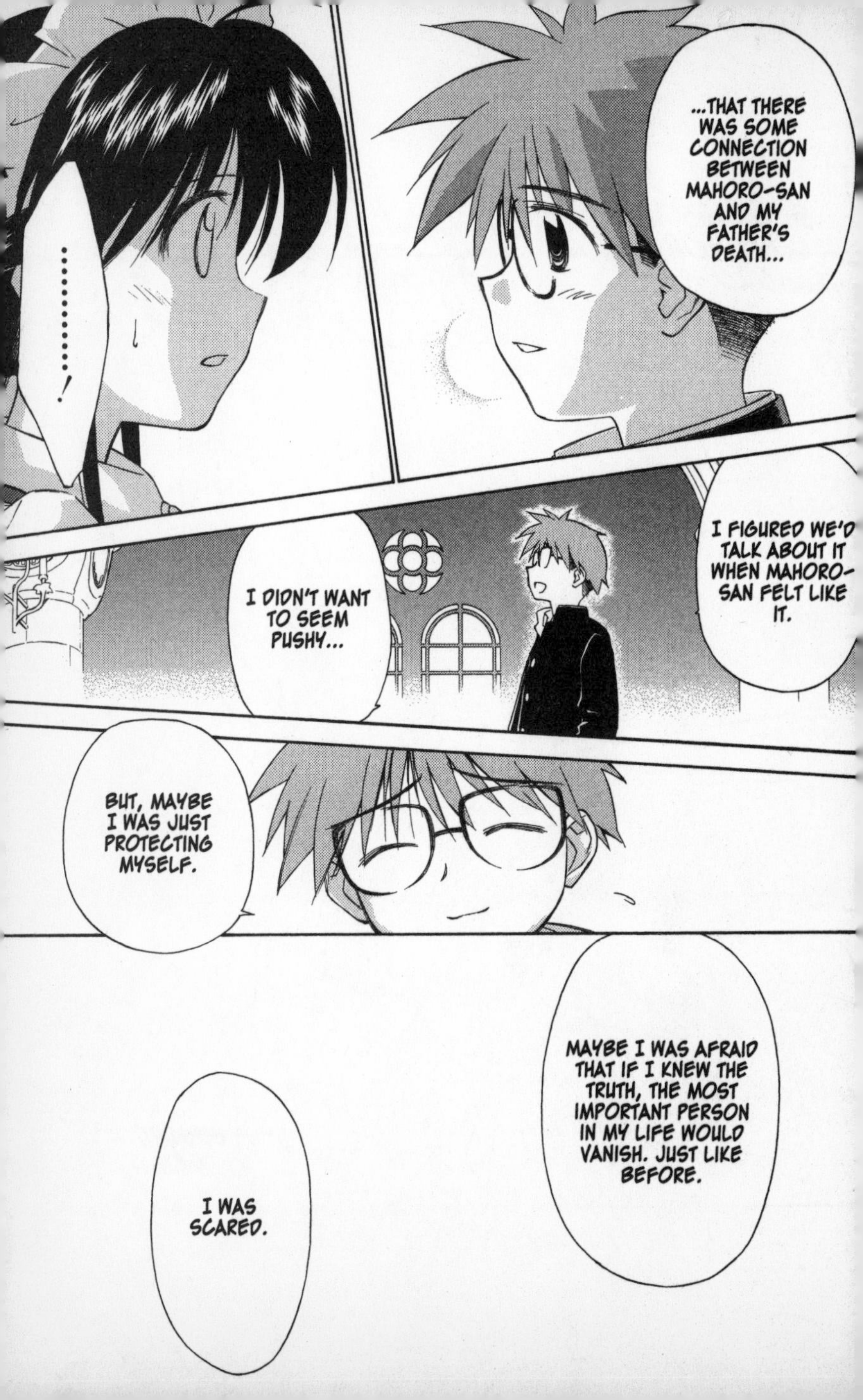
...THAT THERE WAS SOME CONNECTION BETWEEN MAHORO-SAN AND MY FATHER'S DEATH...
.........!
I FIGURED WE'D TALK ABOUT IT WHEN MAHORO-SAN FELT LIKE IT.
I DIDN'T WANT TO SEEM PUSHY...
BUT, MAYBE I WAS JUST PROTECTING MYSELF.
MAYBE I WAS AFRAID THAT IF I KNEW THE TRUTH, THE MOST IMPORTANT PERSON IN MY LIFE WOULD VANISH. JUST LIKE BEFORE.
I WAS SCARED.

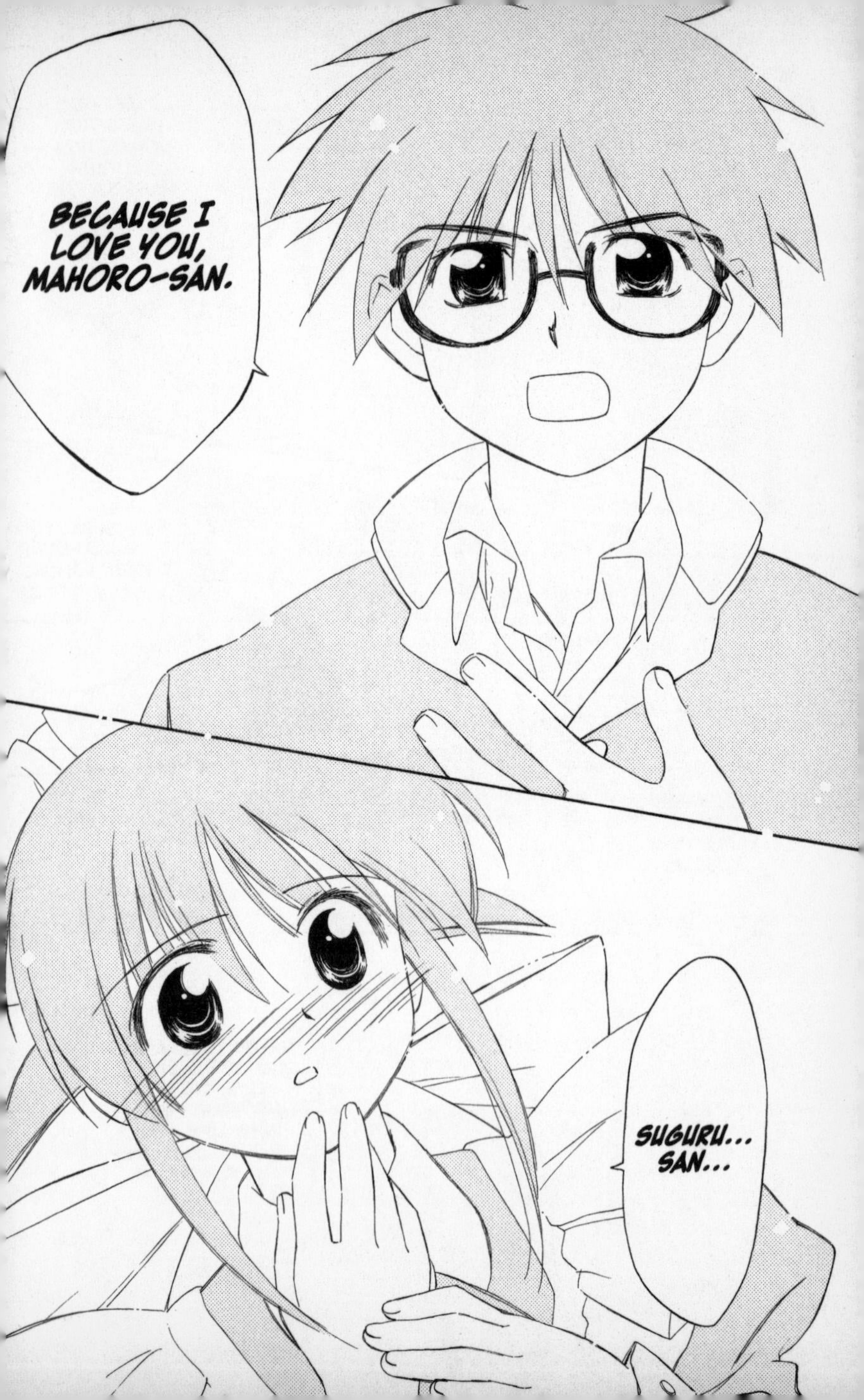
BECAUSE I LOVE YOU, MAHORO-SAN.
SUGURU... SAN...

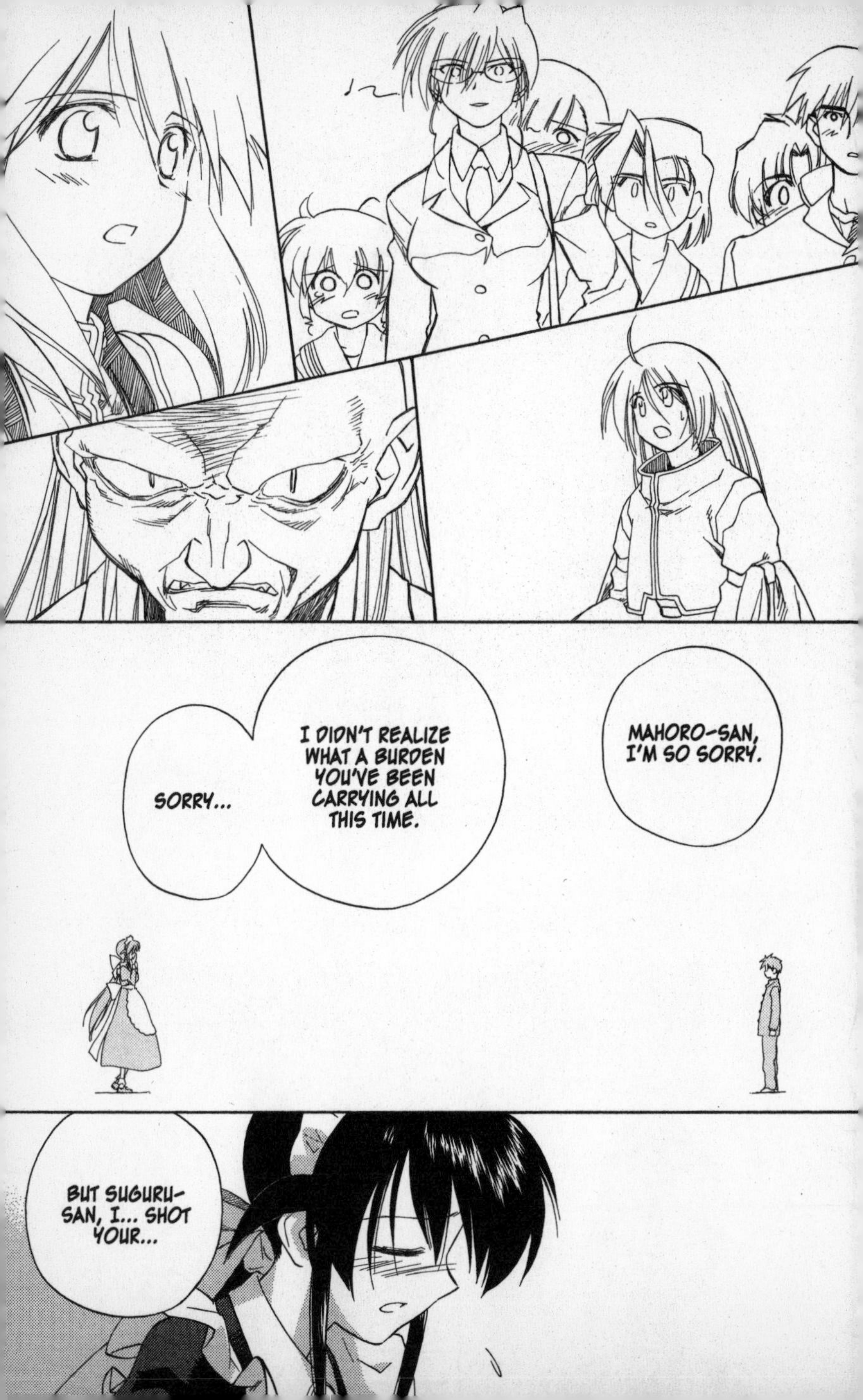
MAHORO-SAN, I'M SO SORRY.
I DIDN'T REALIZE WHAT A BURDEN YOU'VE BEEN CARRYING ALL THIS TIME.
SORRY...
BUT SUGURU-SAN, I... SHOT YOUR...

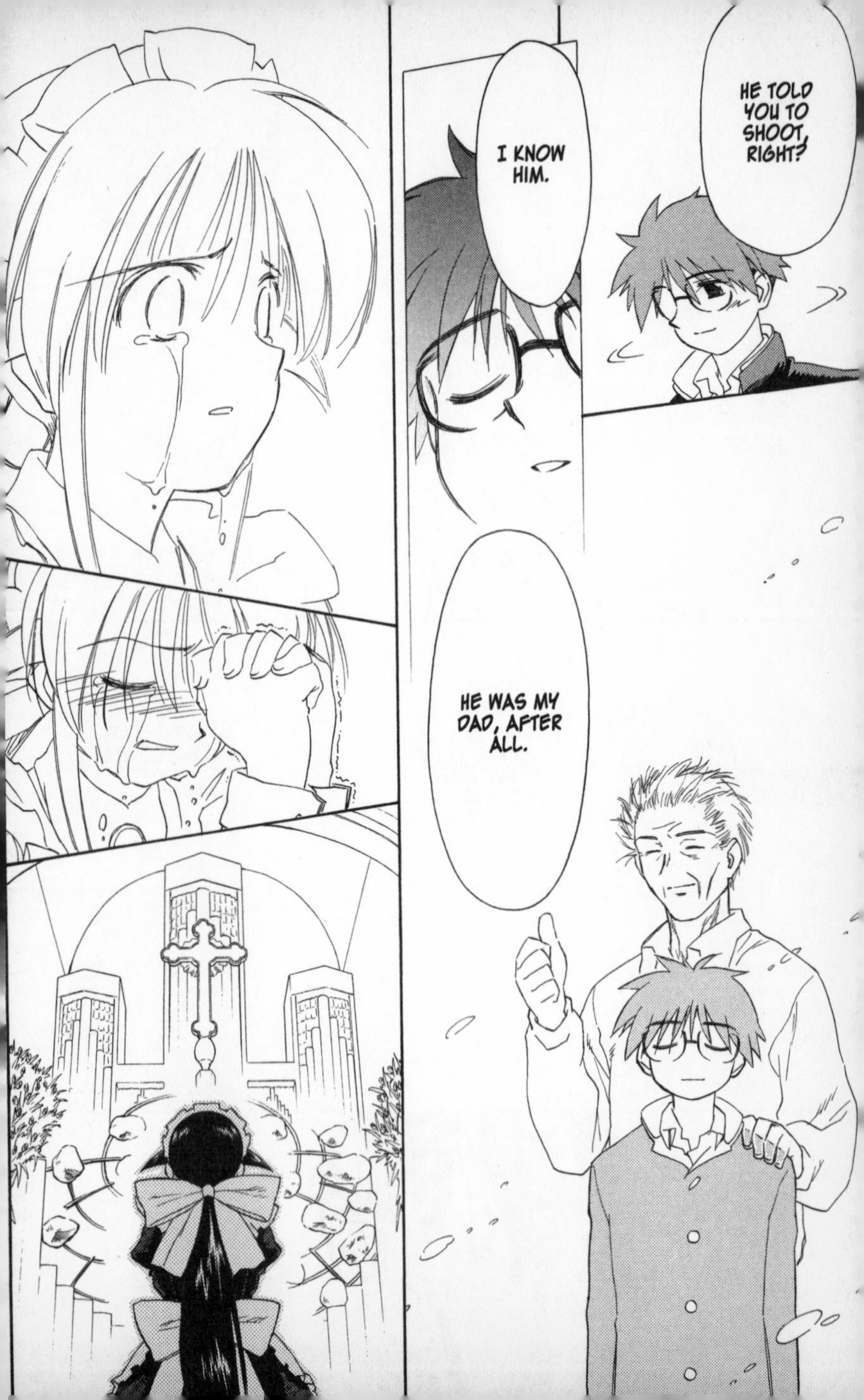
HE TOLD YOU TO SHOOT, RIGHT?
I KNOW HIM.
HE WAS MY DAD, AFTER ALL.

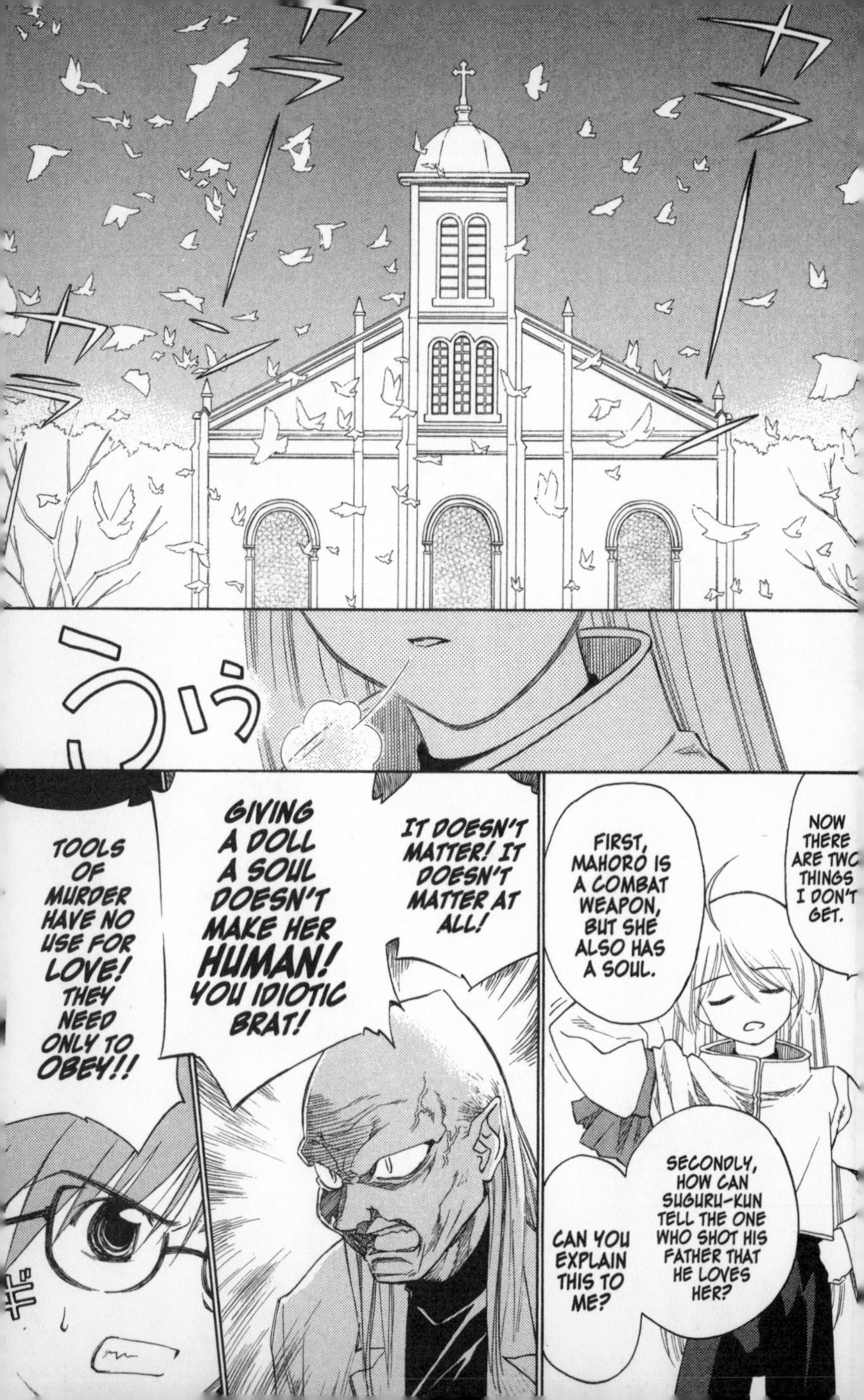
NOW THERE ARE TWO THINGS I DON'T GET.
FIRST, MAHORO IS A COMBAT WEAPON, BUT SHE ALSO HAS A SOUL.
SECONDLY, HOW CAN SUGURU-KUN TELL THE ONE WHO SHOT HIS FATHER THAT HE LOVES HER?
CAN YOU EXPLAIN THIS TO ME?
IT DOESN'T MATTER! IT DOESN'T MATTER AT ALL!
GIVING A DOLL A SOUL DOESN'T MAKE HER HUMAN! YOU IDIOTIC BRAT!
TOOLS OF MURDER HAVE NO USE FOR LOVE! THEY NEED ONLY TO OBEY!!

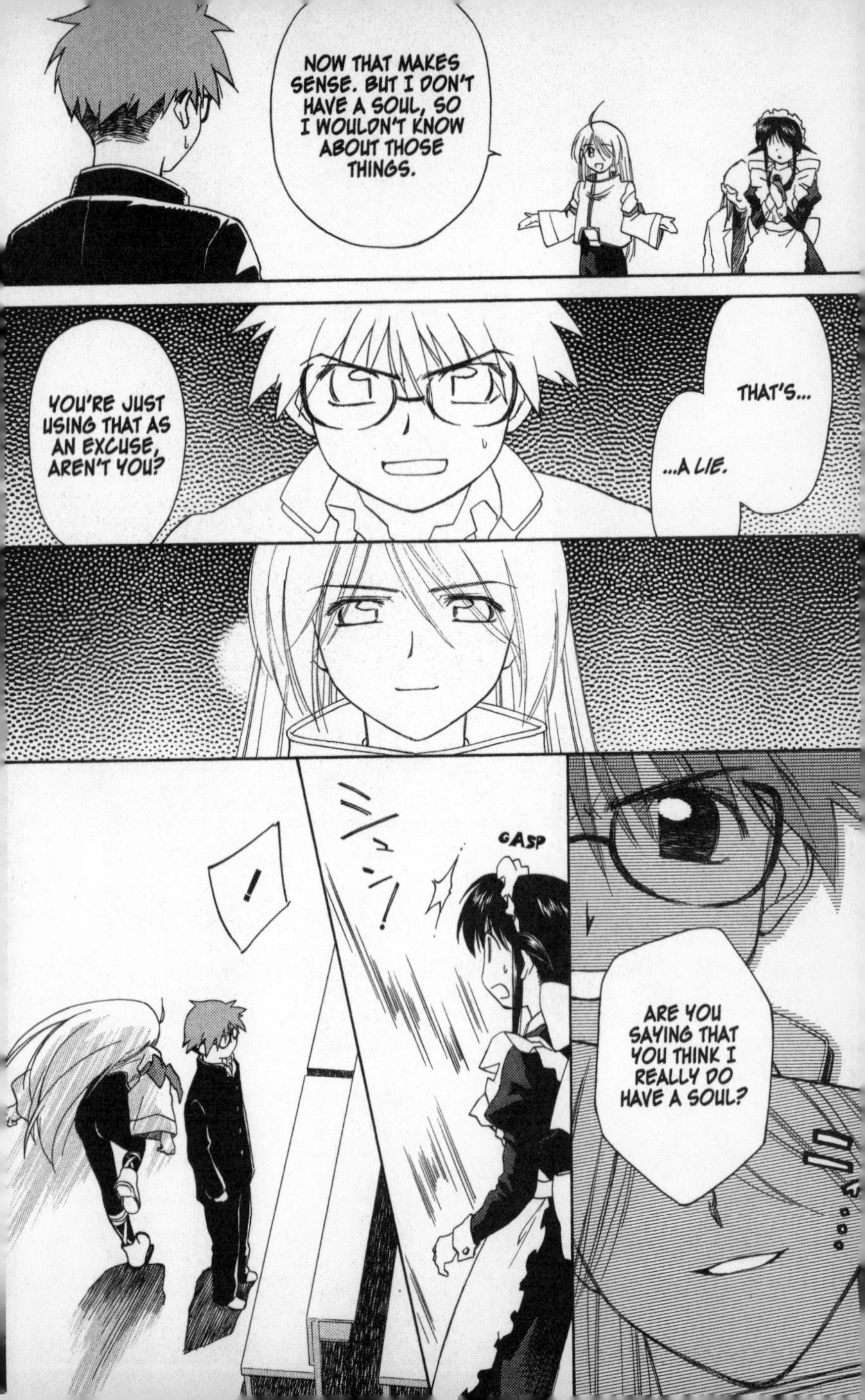
NOW THAT MAKES SENSE. BUT I DON'T HAVE A SOUL, SO I WOULDN'T KNOW ABOUT THOSE THINGS.
THAT'S...
...A LIE.
YOU'RE JUST USING THAT AS AN EXCUSE, AREN'T YOU?
ARE YOU SAYING THAT YOU THINK I REALLY DO HAVE A SOUL?
...
GASP
!
!

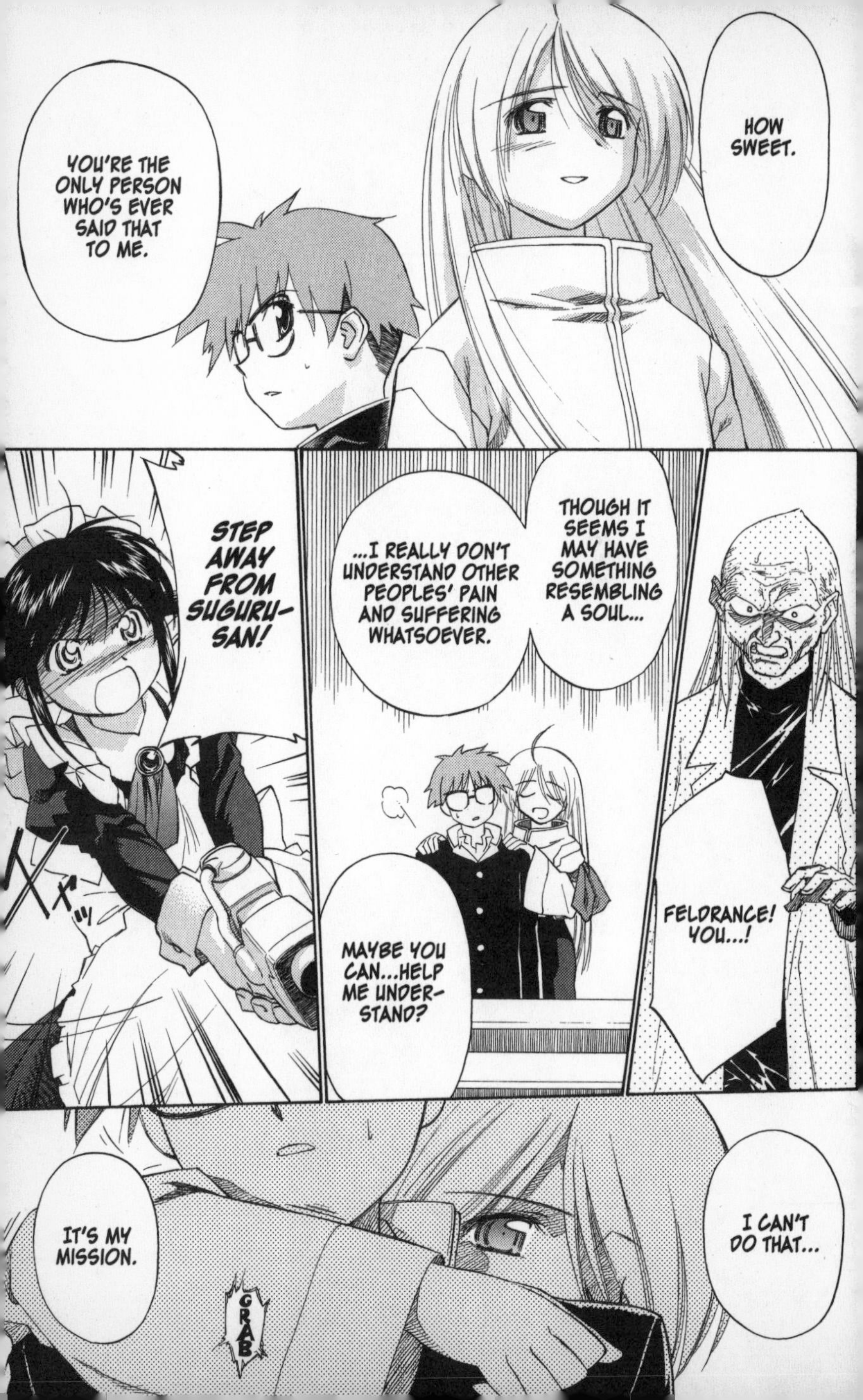
HOW SWEET.
YOU'RE THE ONLY PERSON WHO'S EVER SAID THAT TO ME.
FELDRANCE! YOU...!
THOUGH IT SEEMS I MAY HAVE SOMETHING RESEMBLING A SOUL...
...I REALLY DON'T UNDERSTAND OTHER PEOPLES' PAIN AND SUFFERING WHATSOEVER.
MAYBE YOU CAN...HELP ME UNDERSTAND?
STEP AWAY FROM SUGURU-SAN!
I CAN'T DO THAT...
GRAB
IT'S MY MISSION.

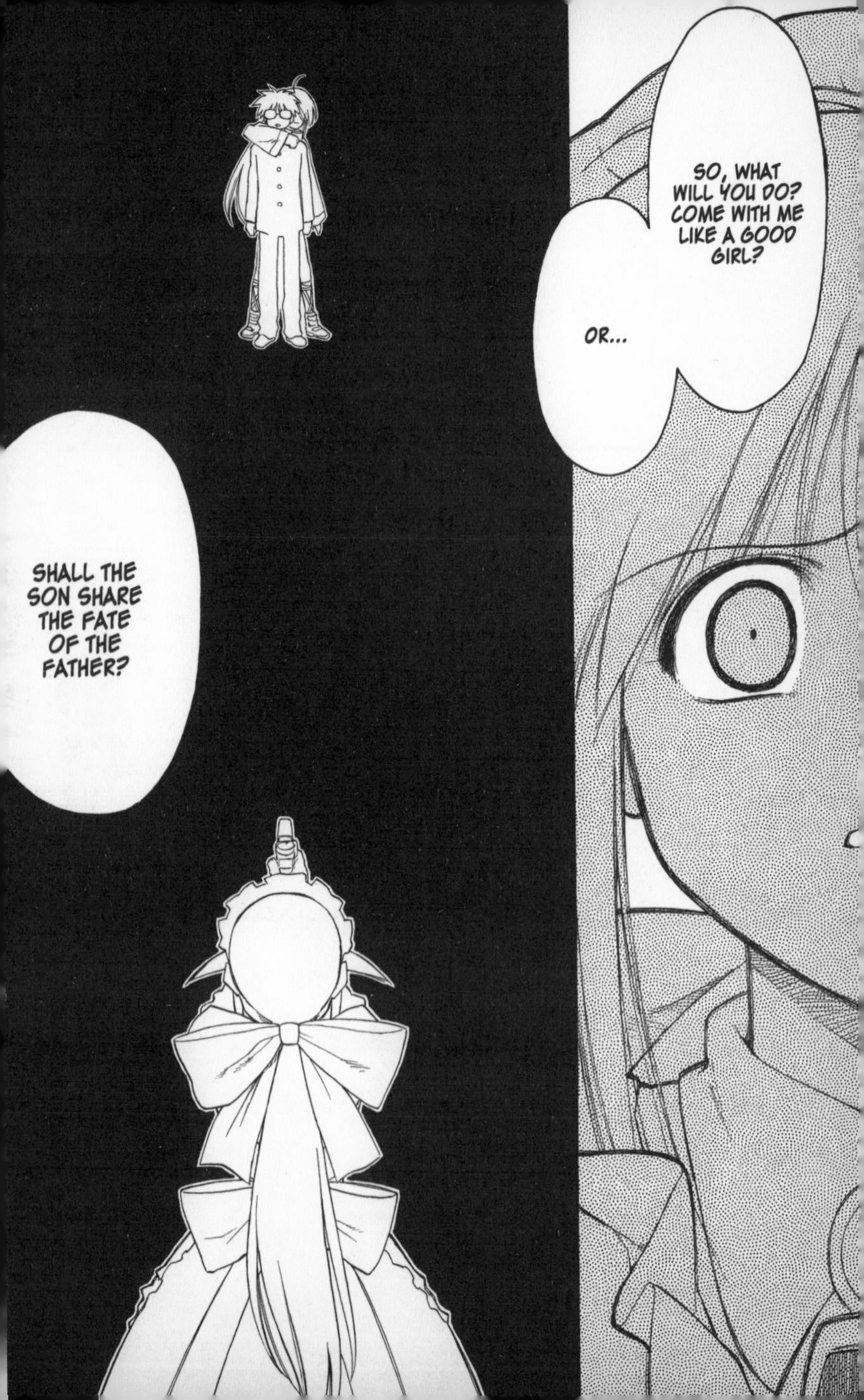
SO, WHAT WILL YOU DO? COME WITH ME LIKE A GOOD GIRL?
OR...
SHALL THE SON SHARE THE FATE OF THE FATHER?

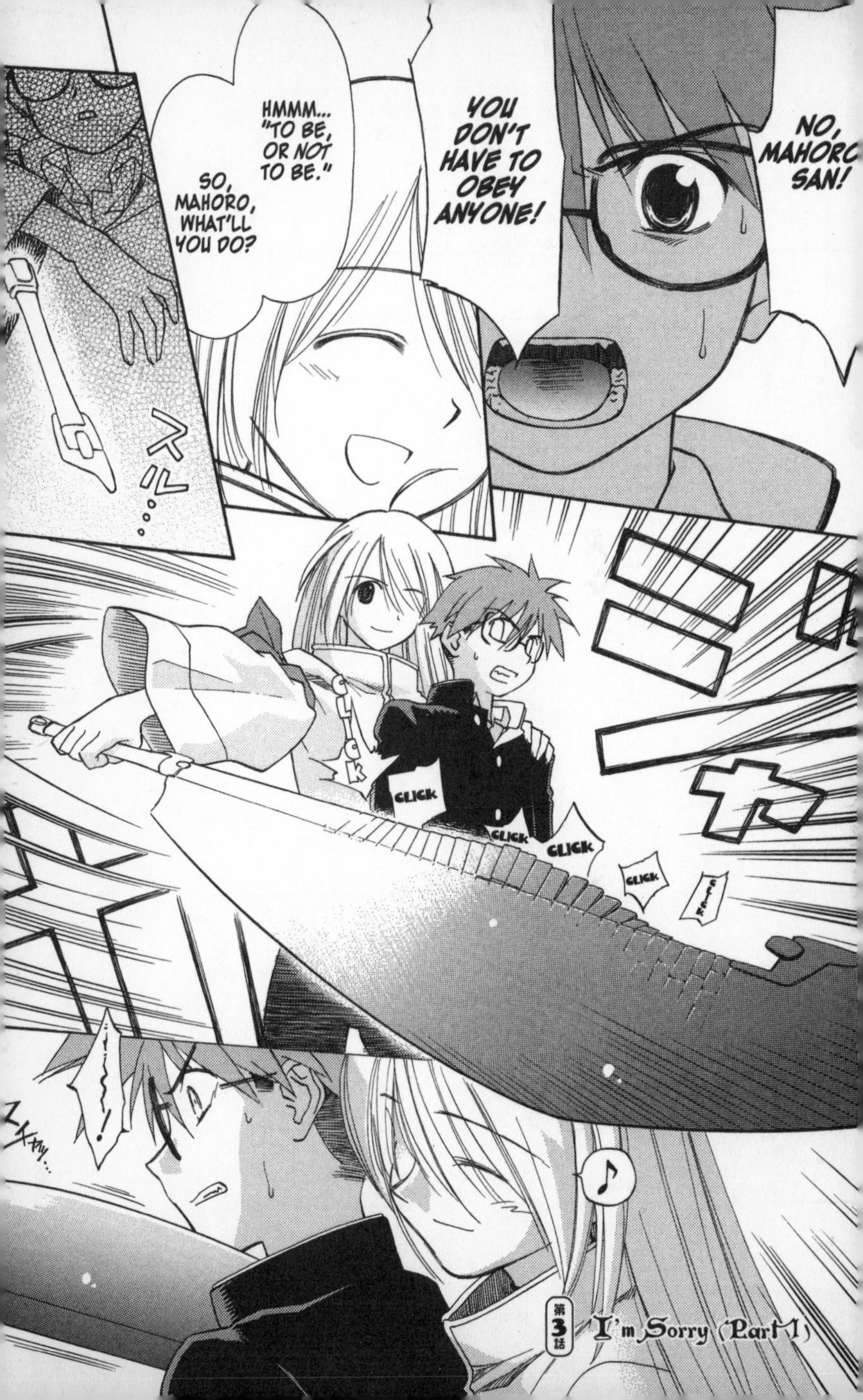

NO, MAHORO SAN!
YOU DON'T HAVE TO OBEY ANYONE!
HMMM... "TO BE, OR NOT TO BE."
SO, MAHORO, WHAT'LL YOU DO?
スル...
CLICK
CLICK
CLICK
CLICK
CLICK
CLICK
CLICK
!
♪
ムスッ...
第3話 I'm Sorry (Part 1)

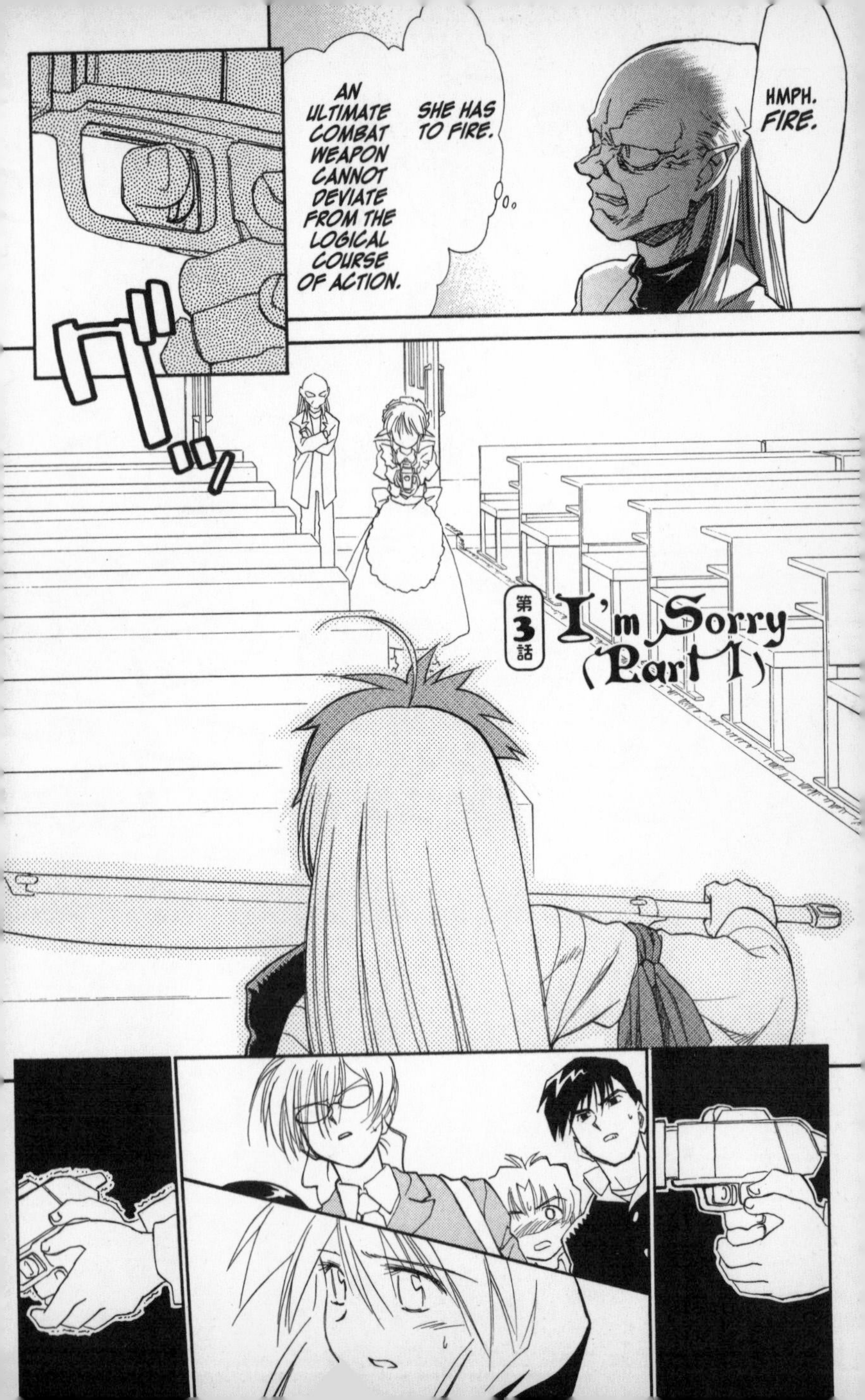
HMPH. FIRE.
SHE HAS TO FIRE.
AN ULTIMATE COMBAT WEAPON CANNOT DEVIATE FROM THE LOGICAL COURSE OF ACTION.
第3話
I'm Sorry (Part 1)

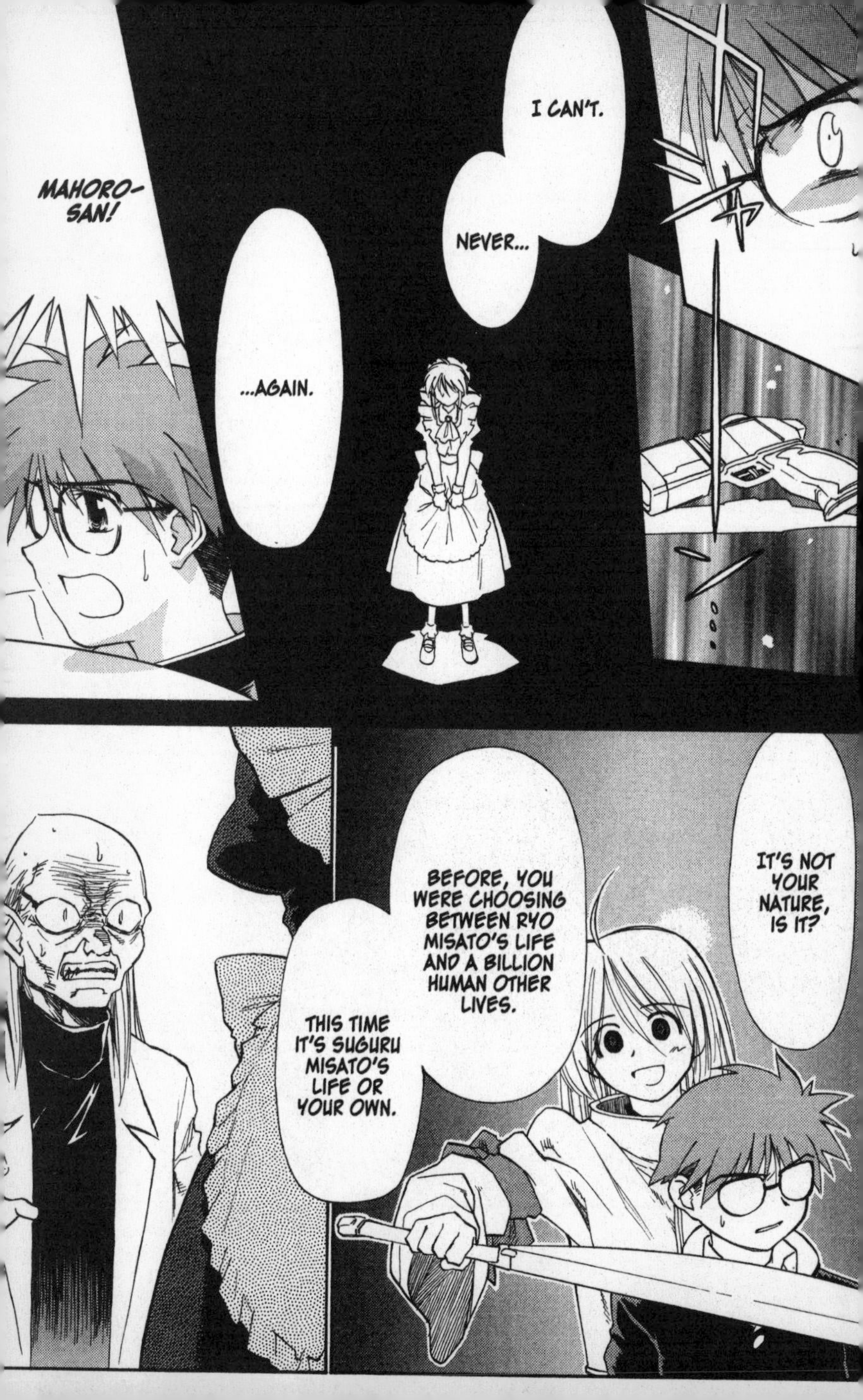
I CAN'T.
NEVER...
...AGAIN.
MAHORO-SAN!
IT'S NOT YOUR NATURE, IS IT?
BEFORE, YOU WERE CHOOSING BETWEEN RYO MISATO'S LIFE AND A BILLION HUMAN OTHER LIVES.
THIS TIME IT'S SUGURU MISATO'S LIFE OR YOUR OWN.

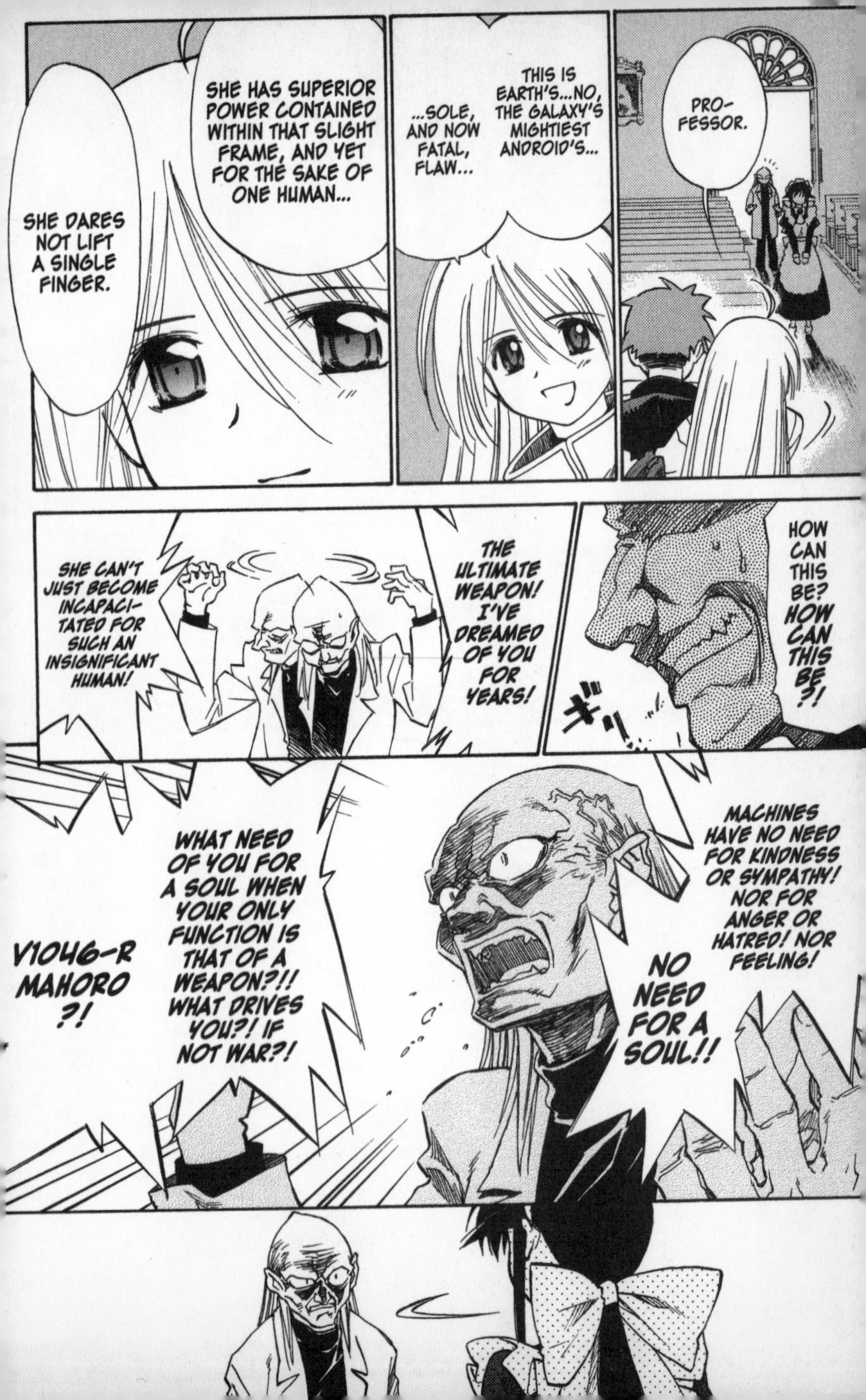
PRO-FESSOR.
THIS IS EARTH'S...NO, THE GALAXY'S MIGHTIEST ANDROID'S...
...SOLE, AND NOW FATAL, FLAW...
SHE HAS SUPERIOR POWER CONTAINED WITHIN THAT SLIGHT FRAME, AND YET FOR THE SAKE OF ONE HUMAN...
SHE DARES NOT LIFT A SINGLE FINGER.
HOW CAN THIS BE? HOW CAN THIS BE?!
THE ULTIMATE WEAPON! I'VE DREAMED OF YOU FOR YEARS!
SHE CAN'T JUST BECOME INCAPACITATED FOR SUCH AN INSIGNIFICANT HUMAN!
MACHINES HAVE NO NEED FOR KINDNESS OR SYMPATHY! NOR FOR ANGER OR HATRED! NOR FEELING!
NO NEED FOR A SOUL!!
WHAT NEED OF YOU FOR A SOUL WHEN YOUR ONLY FUNCTION IS THAT OF A WEAPON?!! WHAT DRIVES YOU?! IF NOT WAR?!
V1046-R MAHORO ?!

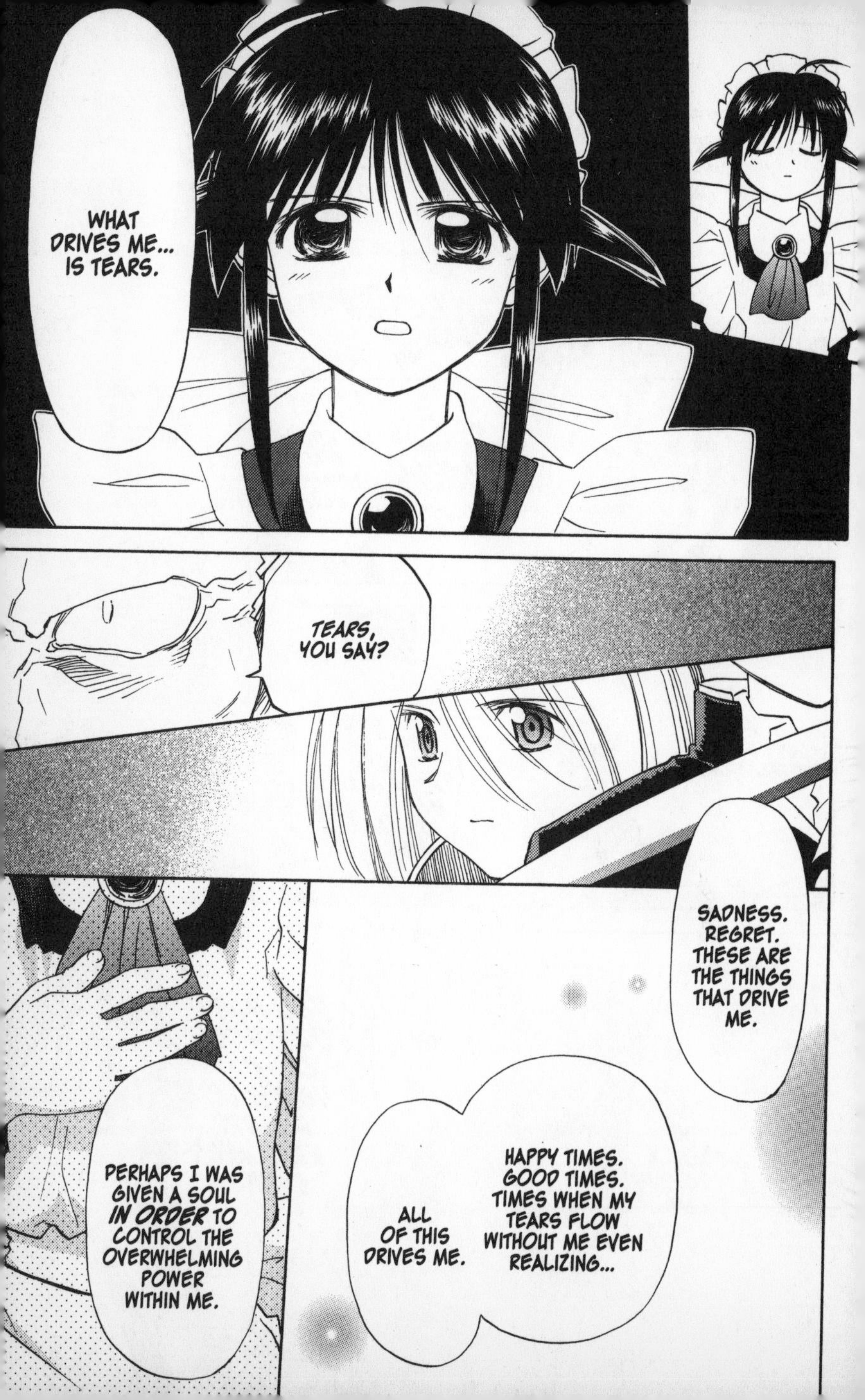

WHAT DRIVES ME... IS TEARS.
TEARS, YOU SAY?
SADNESS. REGRET. THESE ARE THE THINGS THAT DRIVE ME.
HAPPY TIMES. GOOD TIMES. TIMES WHEN MY TEARS FLOW WITHOUT ME EVEN REALIZING...
ALL OF THIS DRIVES ME.
PERHAPS I WAS GIVEN A SOUL *IN ORDER* TO CONTROL THE OVERWHELMING POWER WITHIN ME.

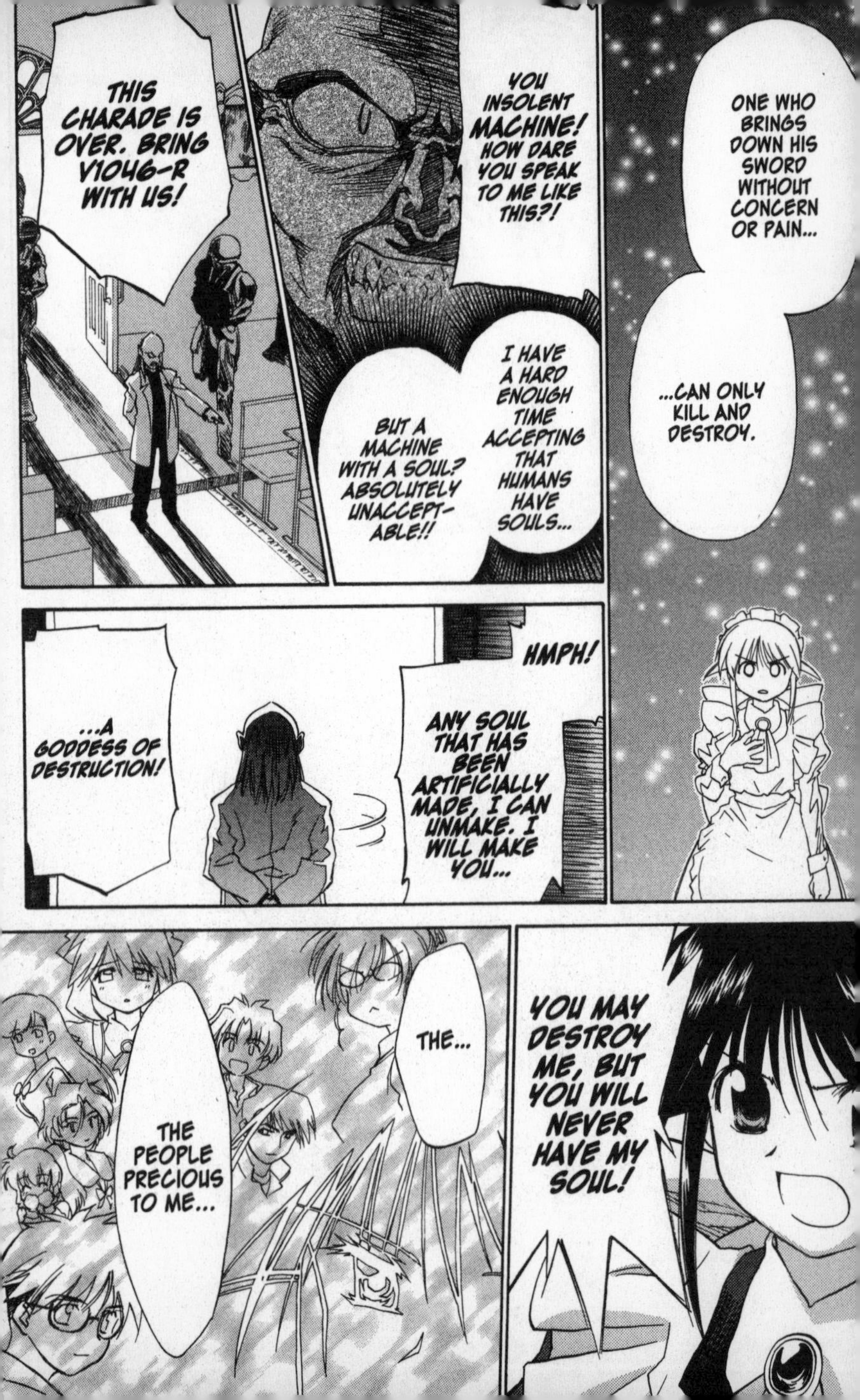
ONE WHO BRINGS DOWN HIS SWORD WITHOUT CONCERN OR PAIN...
...CAN ONLY KILL AND DESTROY.
YOU INSOLENT MACHINE! HOW DARE YOU SPEAK TO ME LIKE THIS?!
I HAVE A HARD ENOUGH TIME ACCEPTING THAT HUMANS HAVE SOULS...
BUT A MACHINE WITH A SOUL? ABSOLUTELY UNACCEPT-ABLE!!
THIS CHARADE IS OVER. BRING V1046-R WITH US!
HMPH!
ANY SOUL THAT HAS BEEN ARTIFICIALLY MADE, I CAN UNMAKE. I WILL MAKE YOU...
...A GODDESS OF DESTRUCTION!
YOU MAY DESTROY ME, BUT YOU WILL NEVER HAVE MY SOUL!
THE...
THE PEOPLE PRECIOUS TO ME...

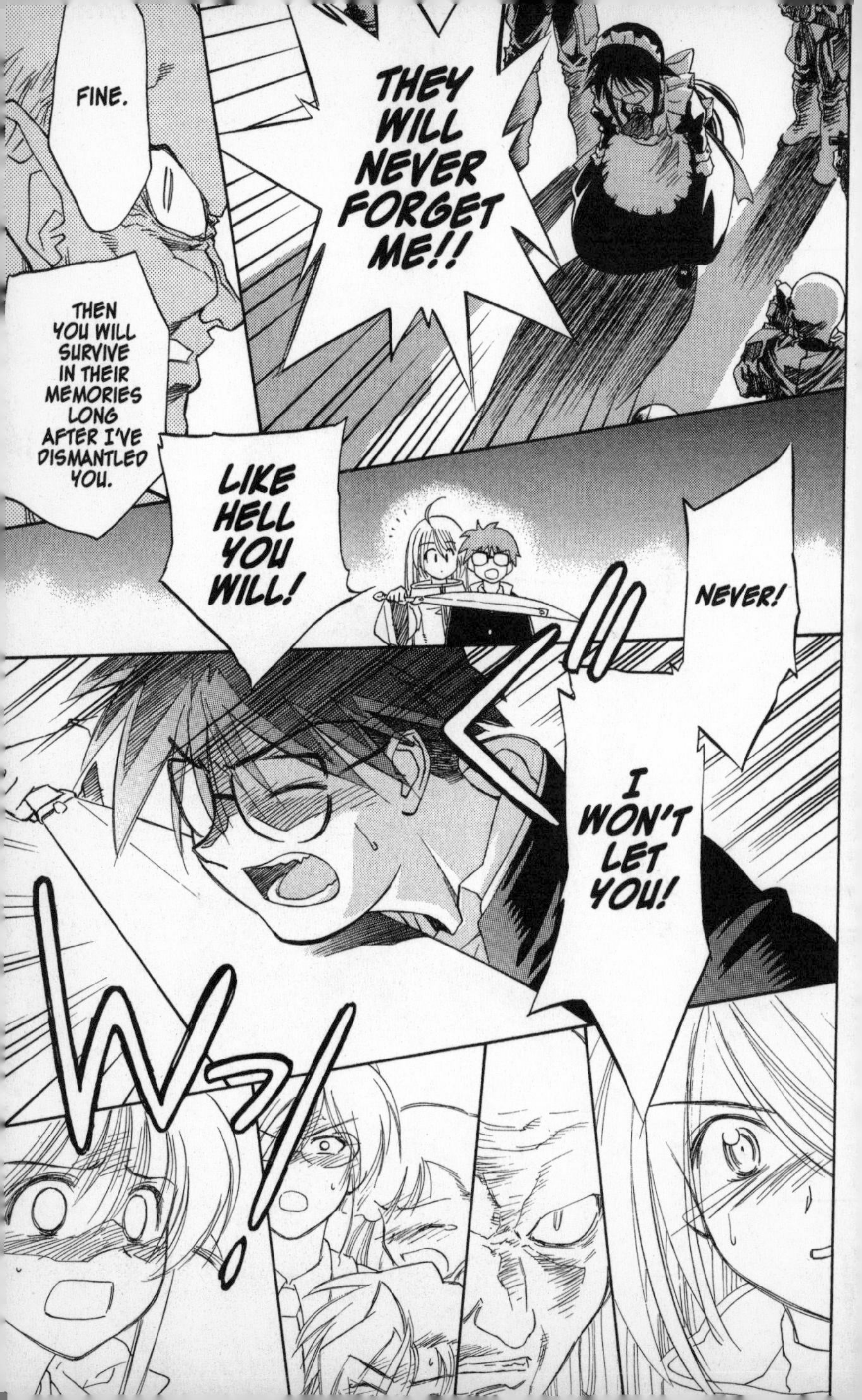
THEY WILL NEVER FORGET ME!!
FINE.
THEN YOU WILL SURVIVE IN THEIR MEMORIES LONG AFTER I'VE DISMANTLED YOU.
LIKE HELL YOU WILL!
NEVER!
I WON'T LET YOU!
WA!

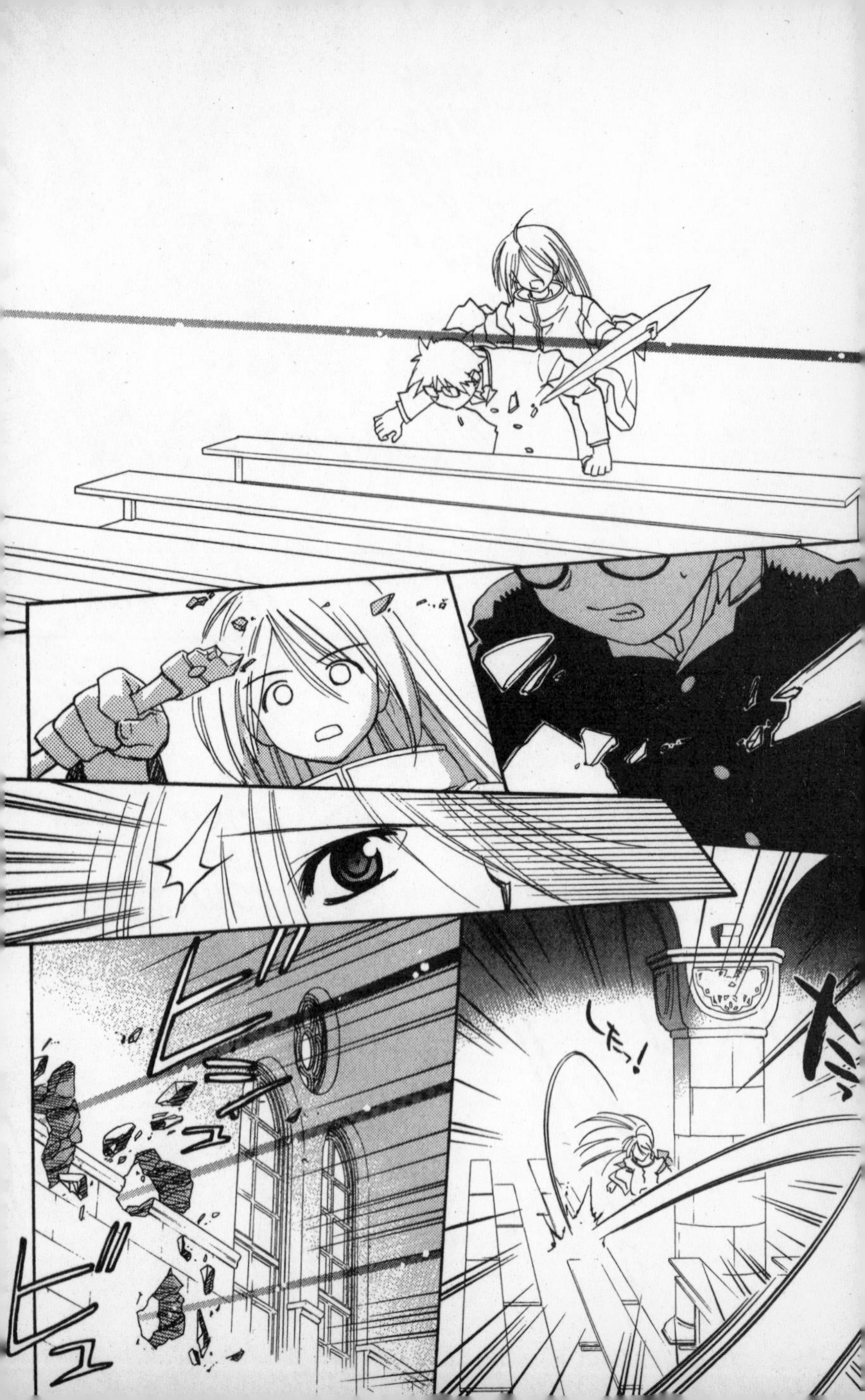
メシッ
したっ!
ビュ
ビュ

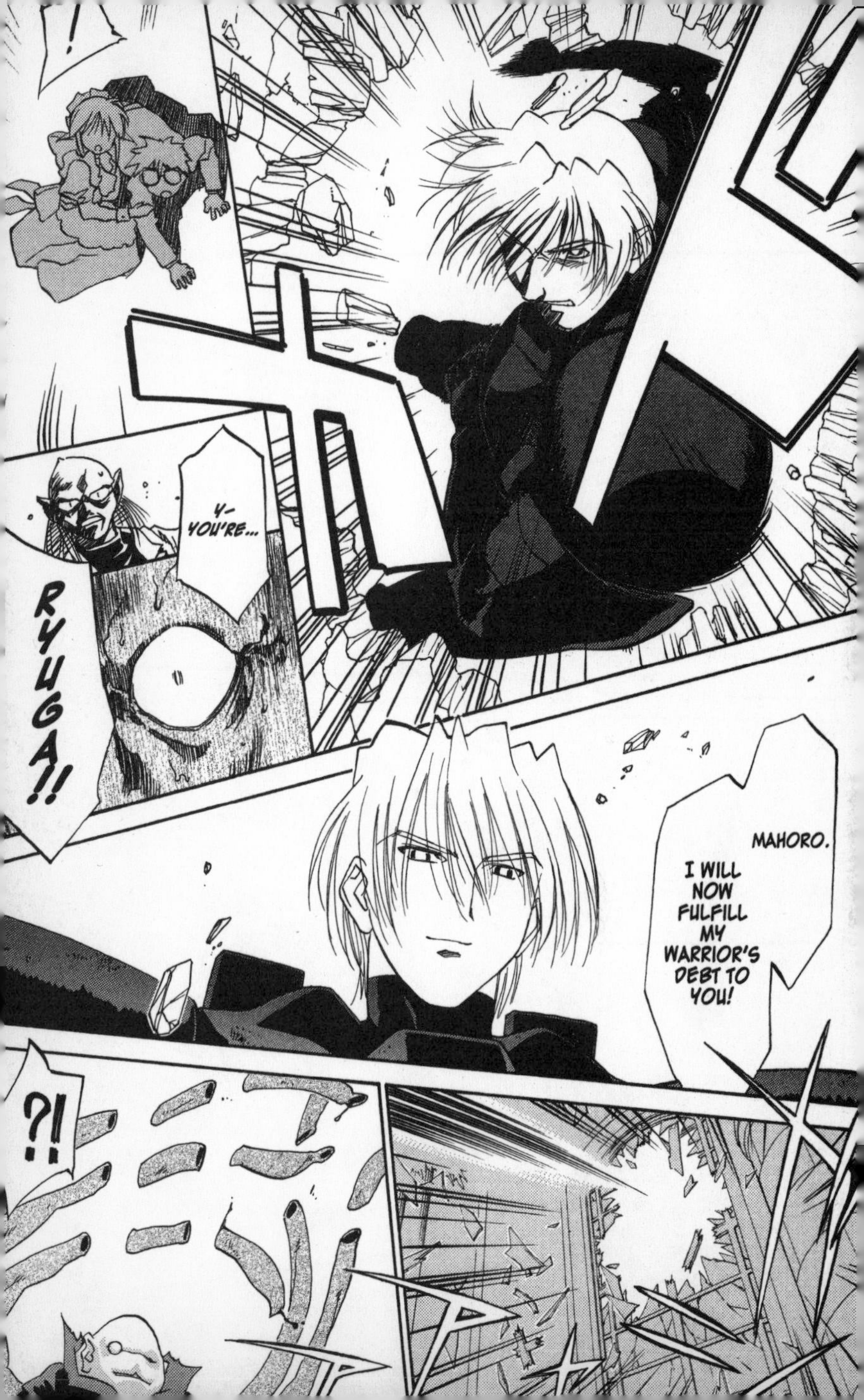
!
Y-YOU'RE...
RYUGA!!
MAHORO.
I WILL NOW FULFILL MY WARRIOR'S DEBT TO YOU!
?!

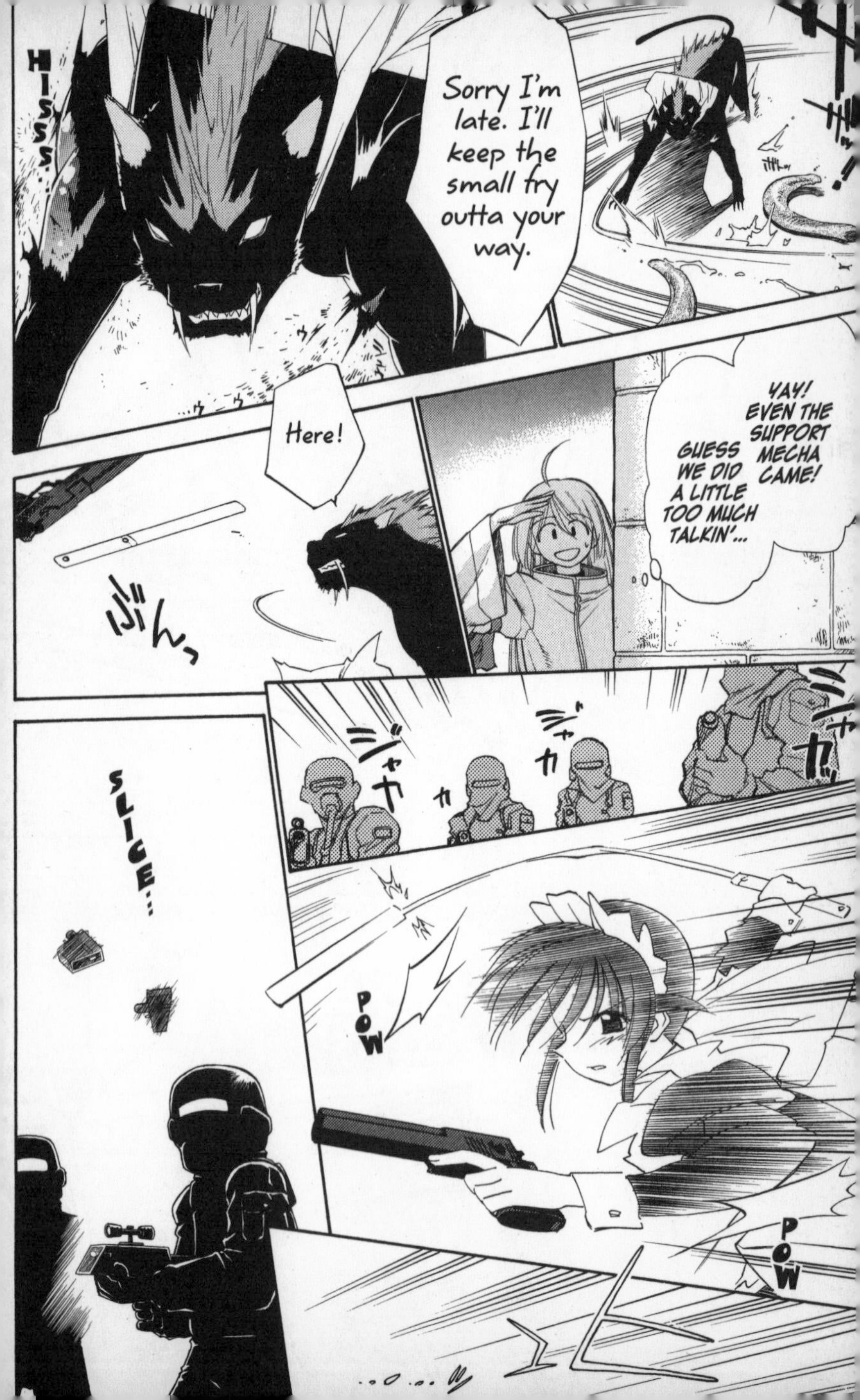
Sorry I'm late. I'll keep the small fry outta your way.
HISS...
YAY! EVEN THE SUPPORT MECHA CAME!
GUESS WE DID A LITTLE TOO MUCH TALKIN'...
Here!
POW
POW
SLICE...

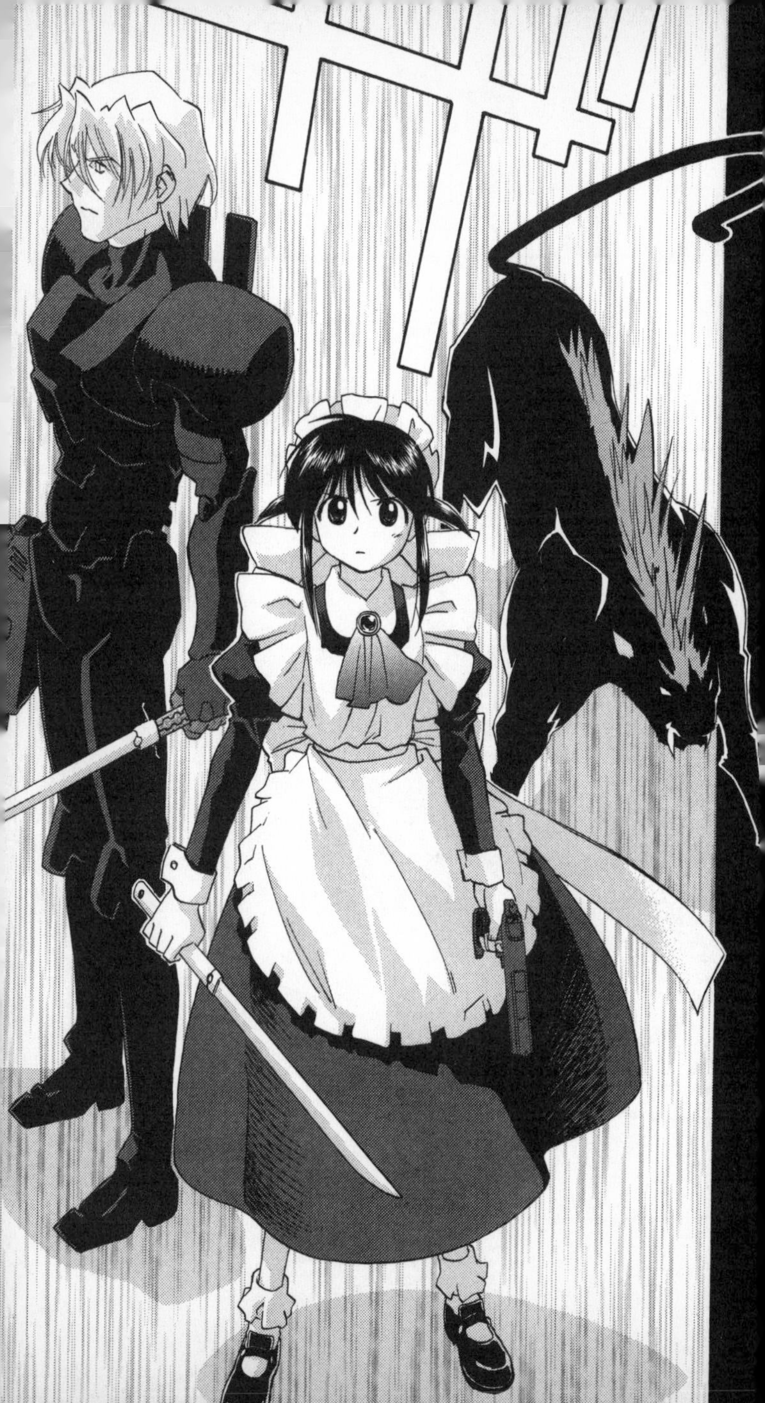

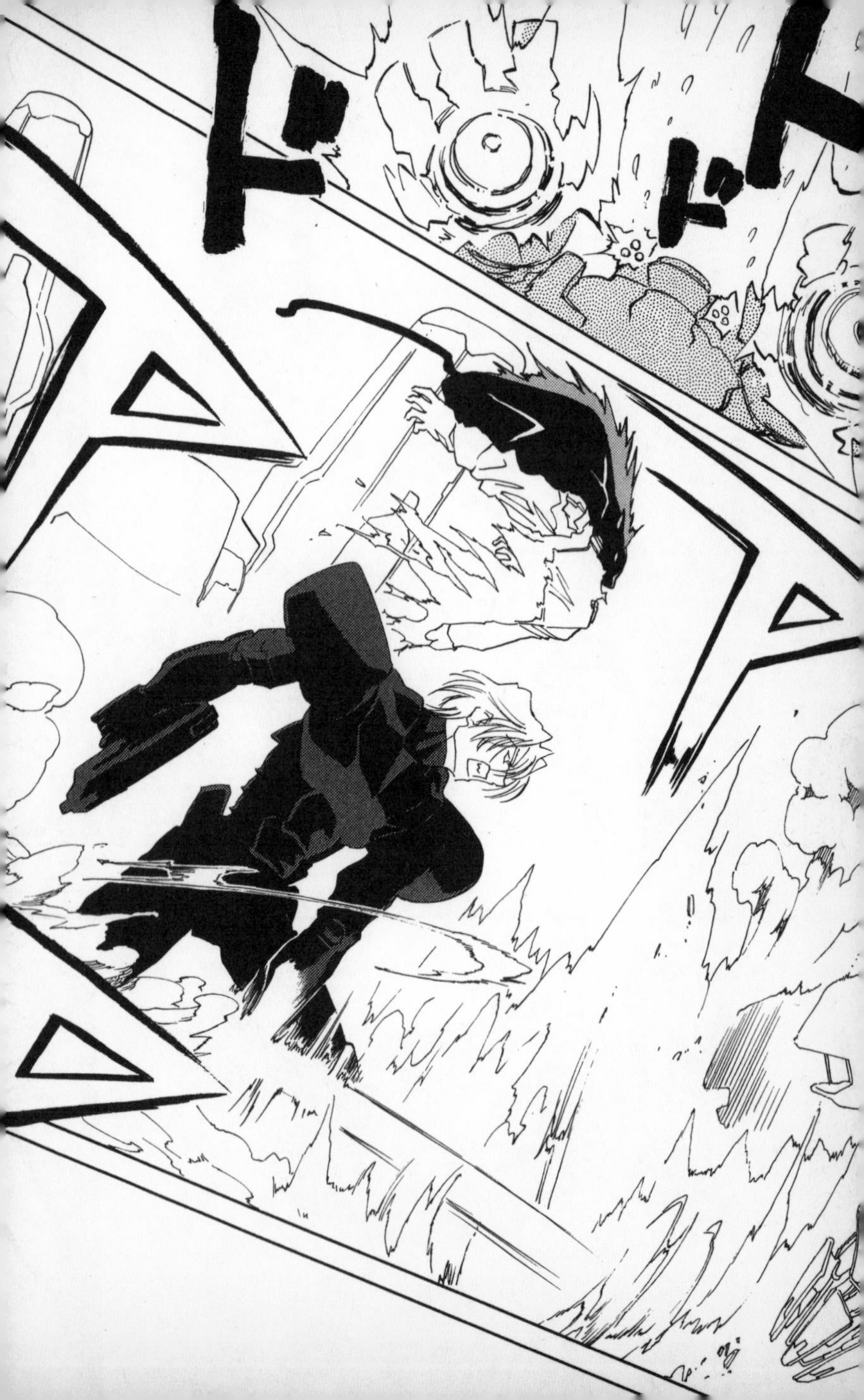
ド
ドッ
ド

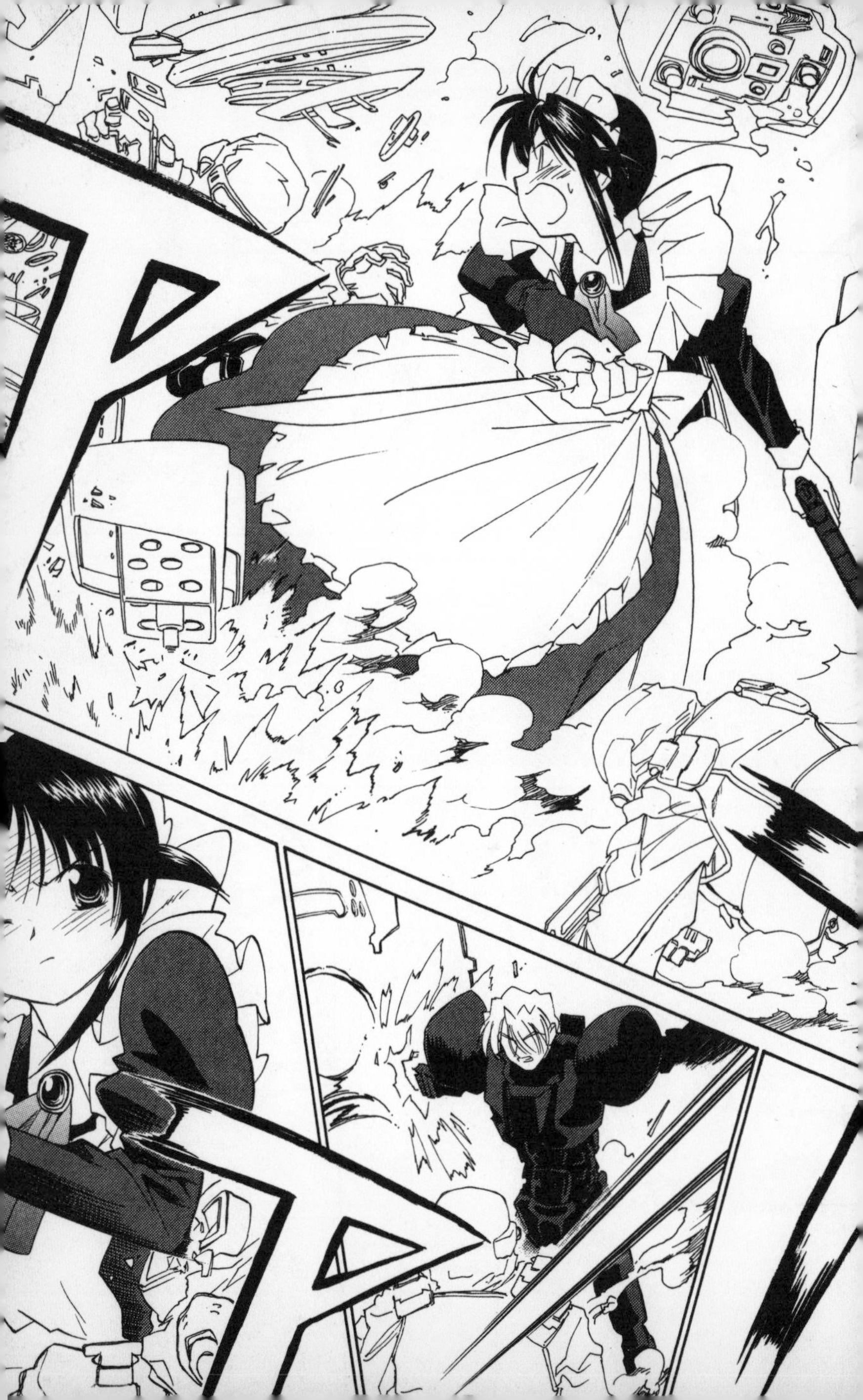

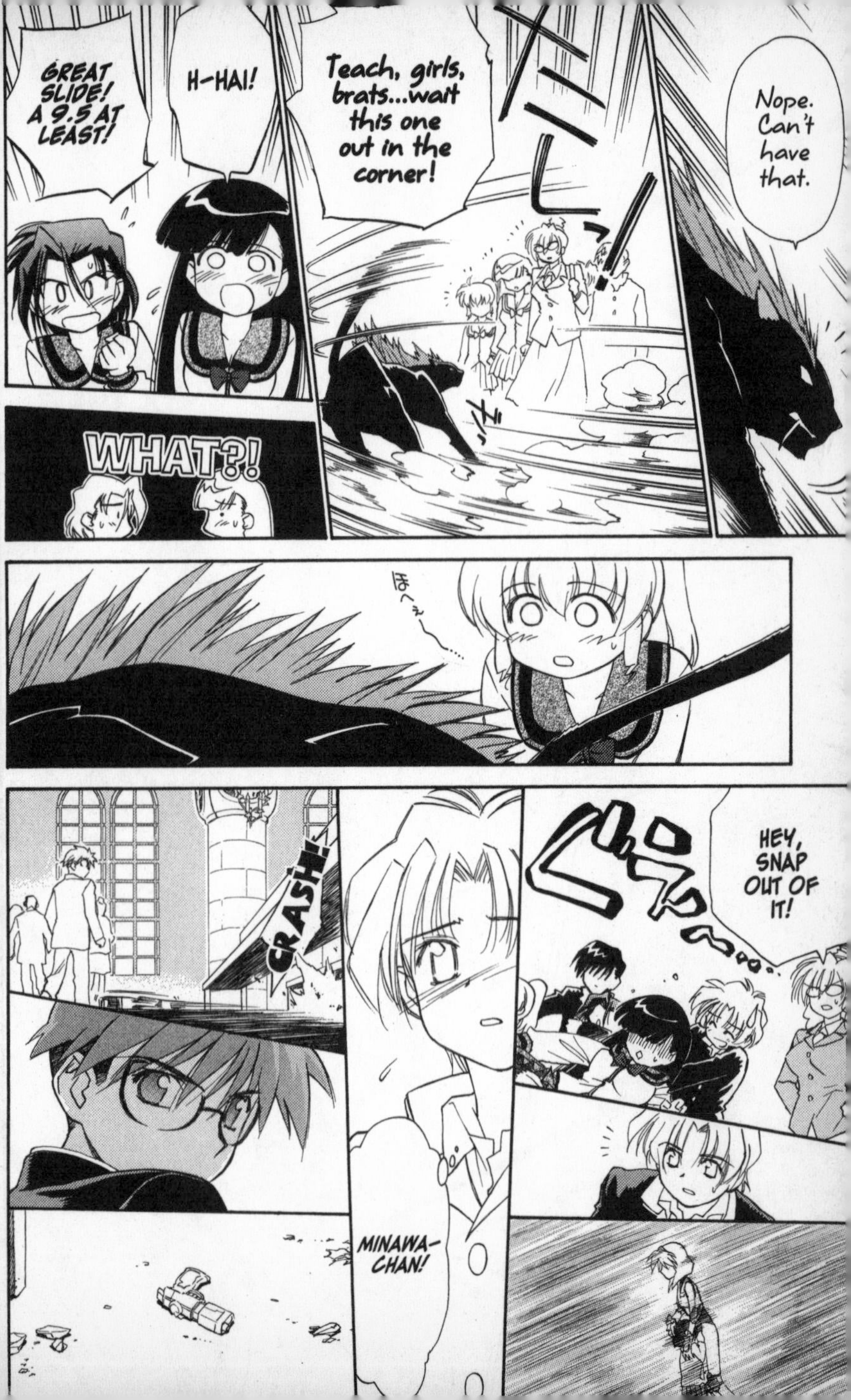
Nope. Can't have that.
Teach, girls, brats...wait this one out in the corner!
H-HAI!
GREAT SLIDE! A 9.5 AT LEAST!
WHAT?!
ほへぇ〜……
HEY, SNAP OUT OF IT!
MINAWA-CHAN!
CRASH!

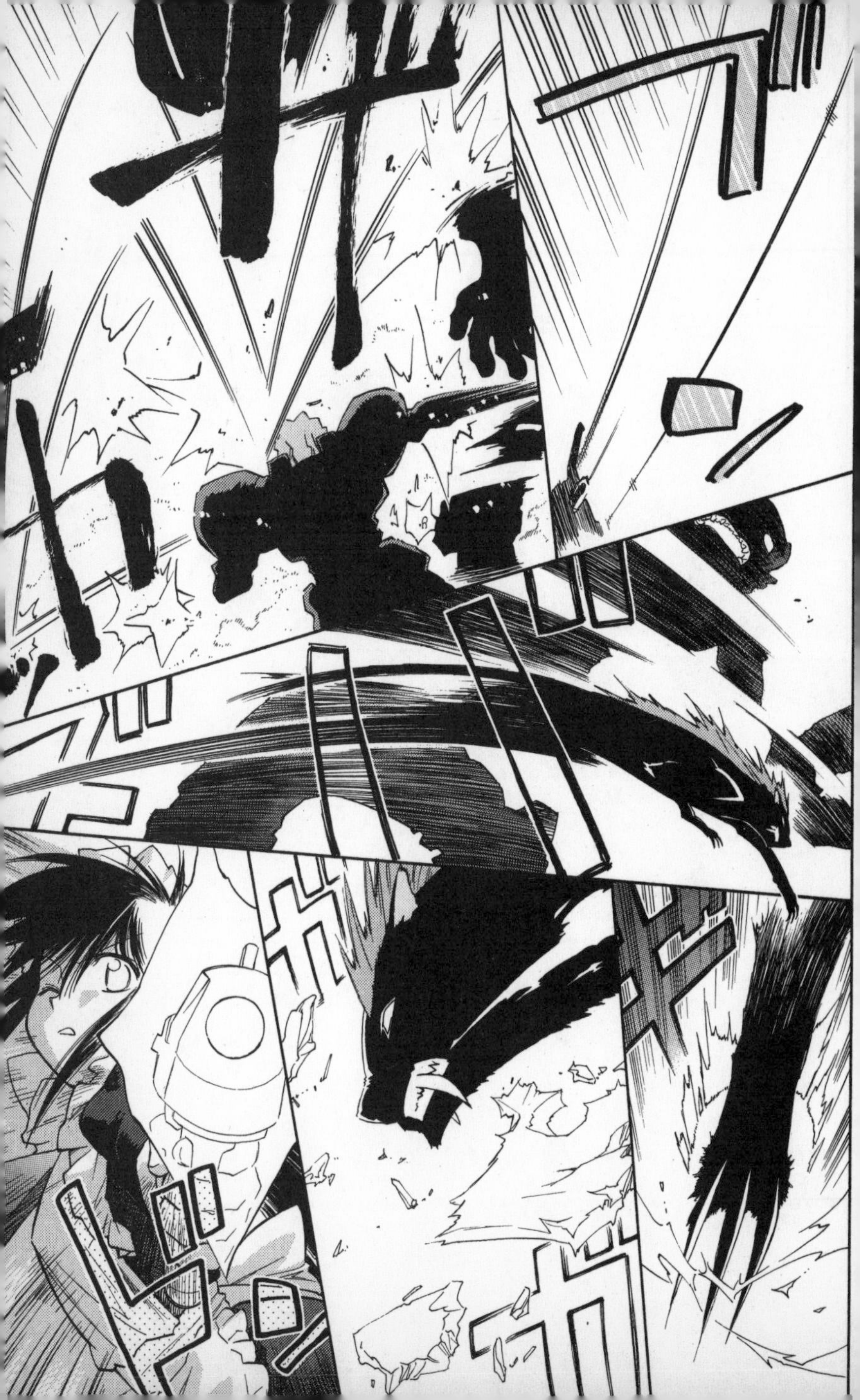

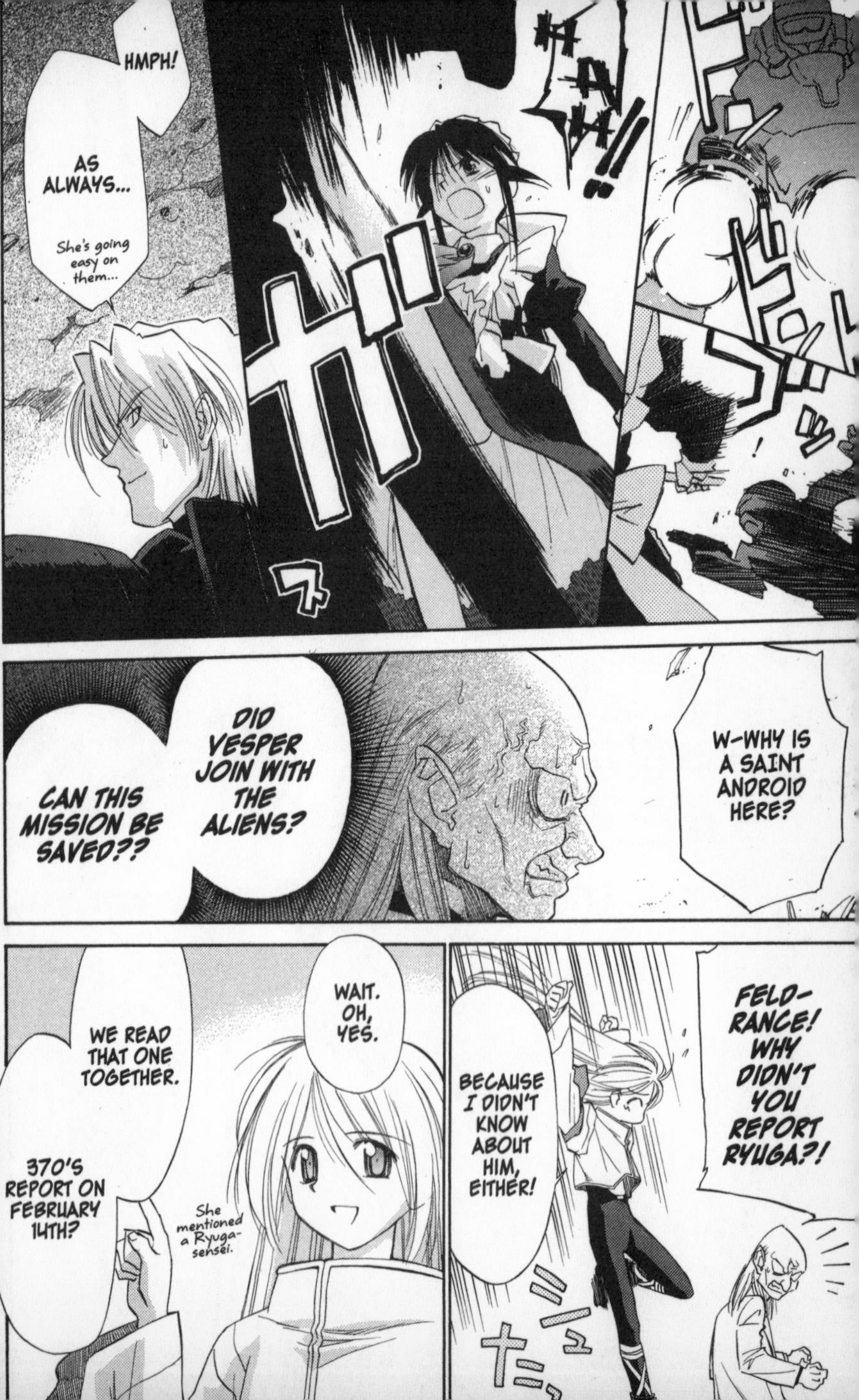
HMPH!
AS ALWAYS...
She's going easy on them...
W-WHY IS A SAINT ANDROID HERE?
DID VESPER JOIN WITH THE ALIENS?
CAN THIS MISSION BE SAVED??
FELD-RANCE! WHY DIDN'T YOU REPORT RYUGA?!
BECAUSE I DIDN'T KNOW ABOUT HIM, EITHER!
WAIT. OH, YES.
WE READ THAT ONE TOGETHER.
370'S REPORT ON FEBRUARY 14TH?
She mentioned a Ryuga-sensei.

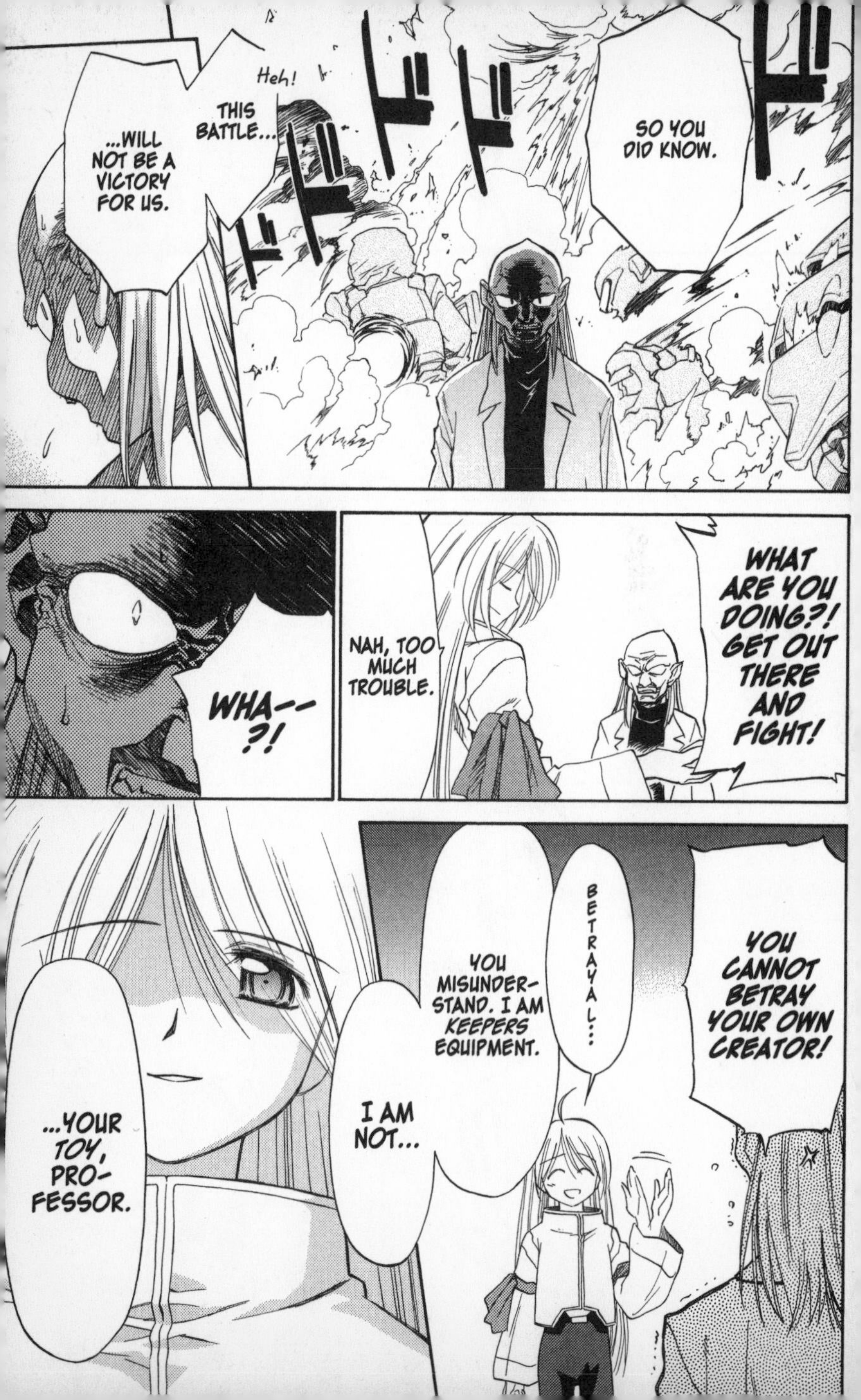
SO YOU DID KNOW.
Heh!
THIS BATTLE...
...WILL NOT BE A VICTORY FOR US.
WHAT ARE YOU DOING?! GET OUT THERE AND FIGHT!
NAH, TOO MUCH TROUBLE.
WHA--?!
YOU CANNOT BETRAY YOUR OWN CREATOR!
BETRAYAL...
YOU MISUNDER-STAND. I AM KEEPERS EQUIPMENT.
I AM NOT...
...YOUR TOY, PRO-FESSOR.

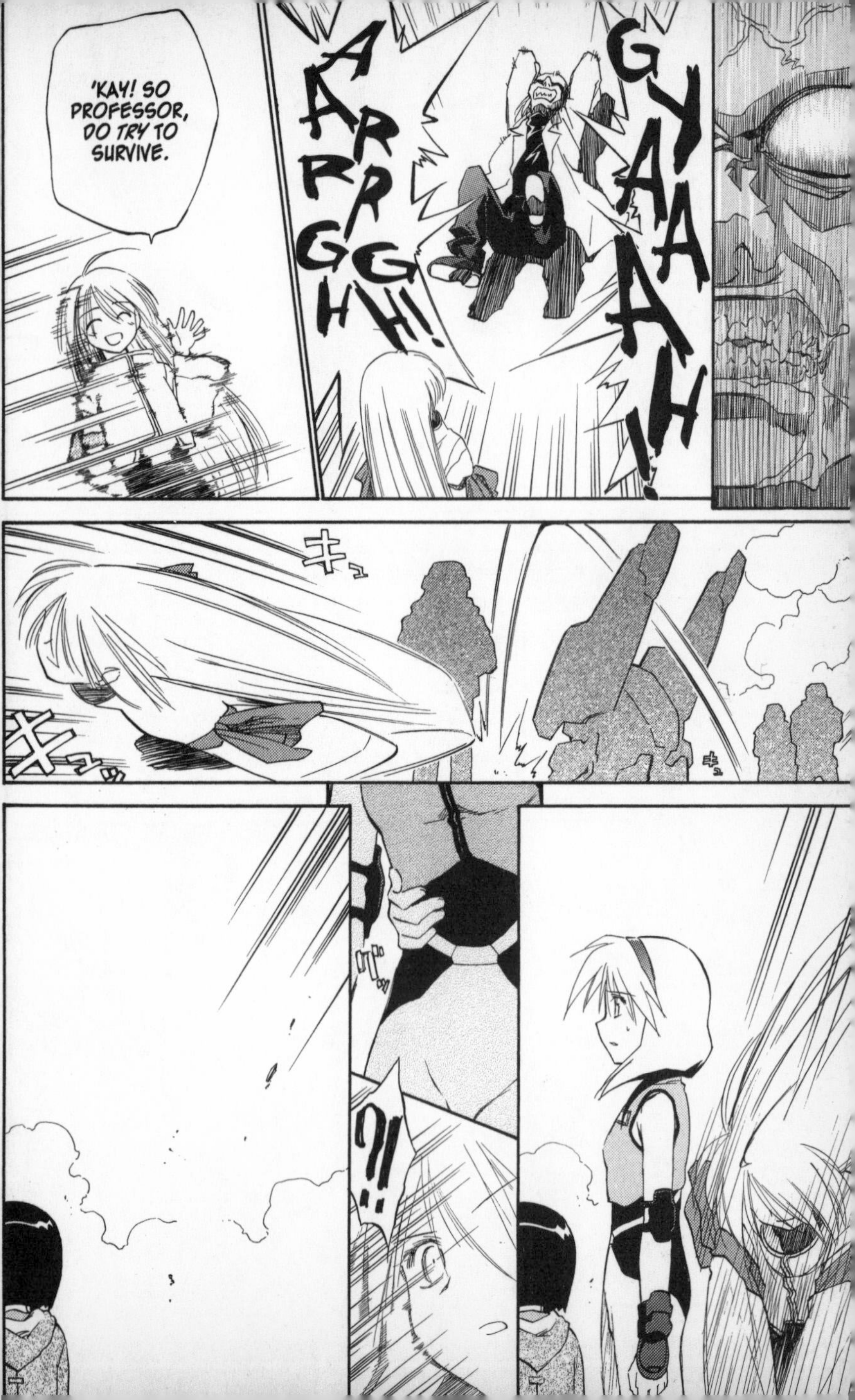
GYAAAAH!!
AARRRGGHH!
'KAY! SO PROFESSOR, DO TRY TO SURVIVE.
キュ
?!!

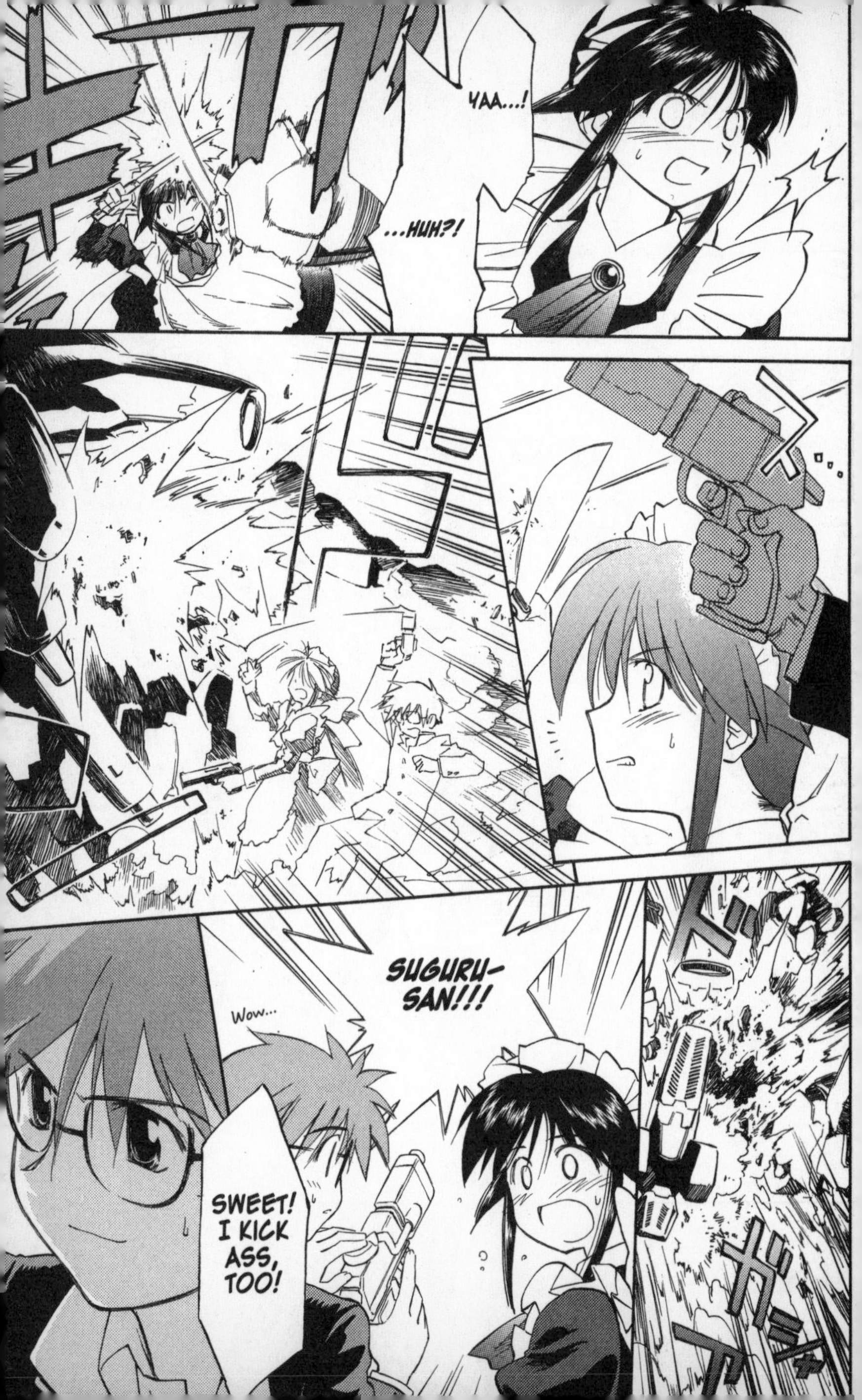
YAA...!
...HUH?!
SUGURU-SAN!!!
Wow...
SWEET! I KICK ASS, TOO!

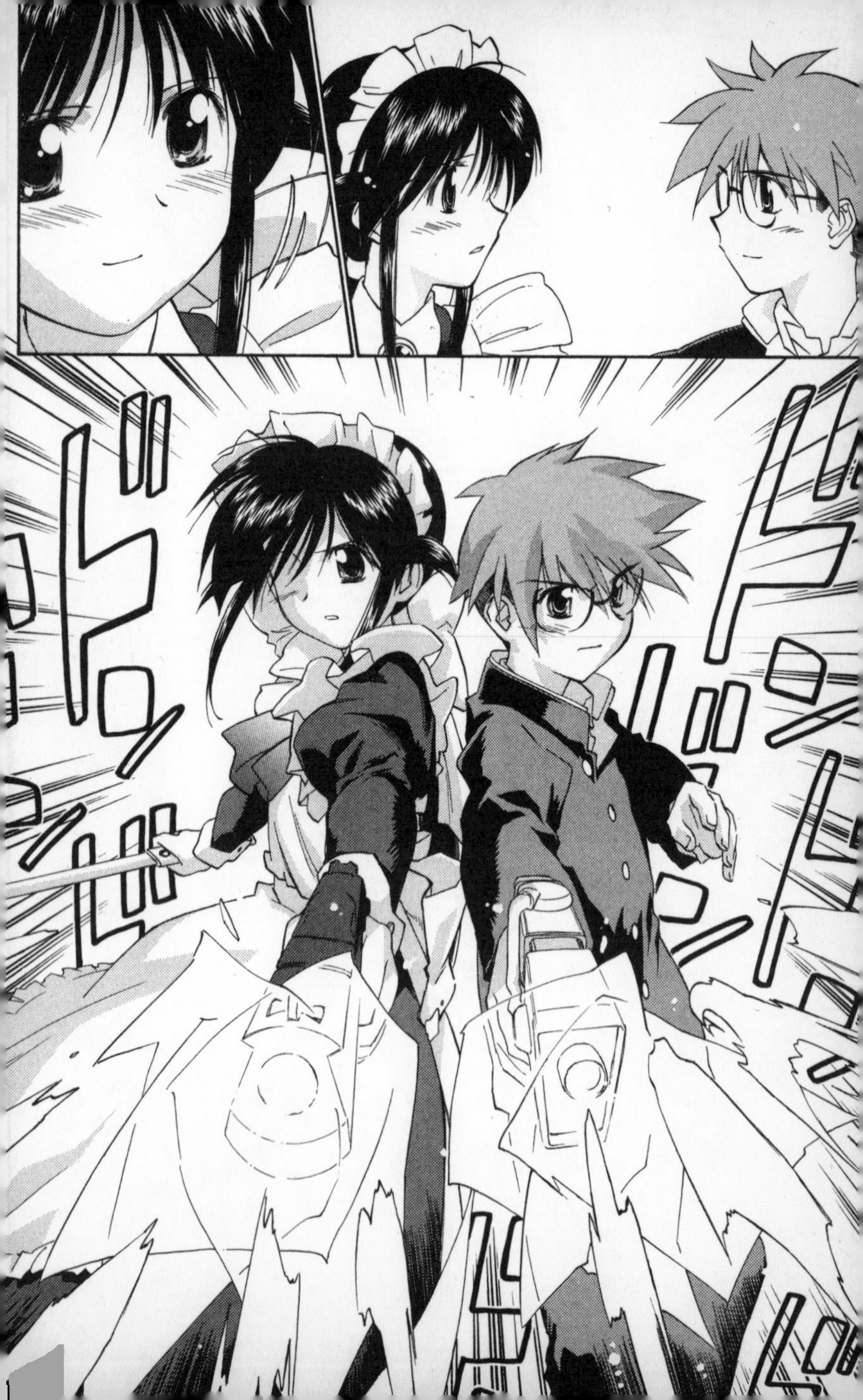

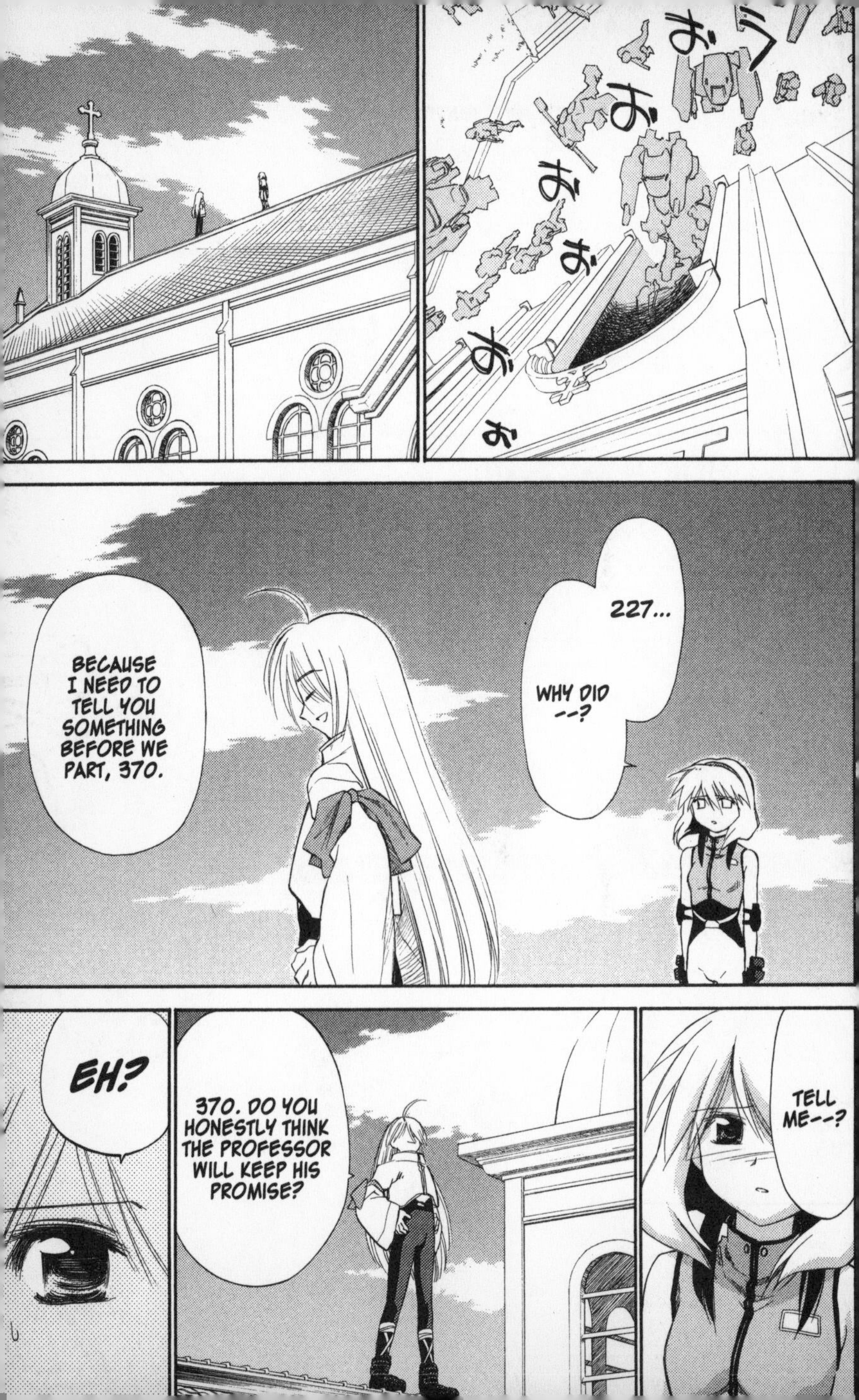
おおおおお
227...
WHY DID --?
BECAUSE I NEED TO TELL YOU SOMETHING BEFORE WE PART, 370.
TELL ME--?
370. DO YOU HONESTLY THINK THE PROFESSOR WILL KEEP HIS PROMISE?
EH?

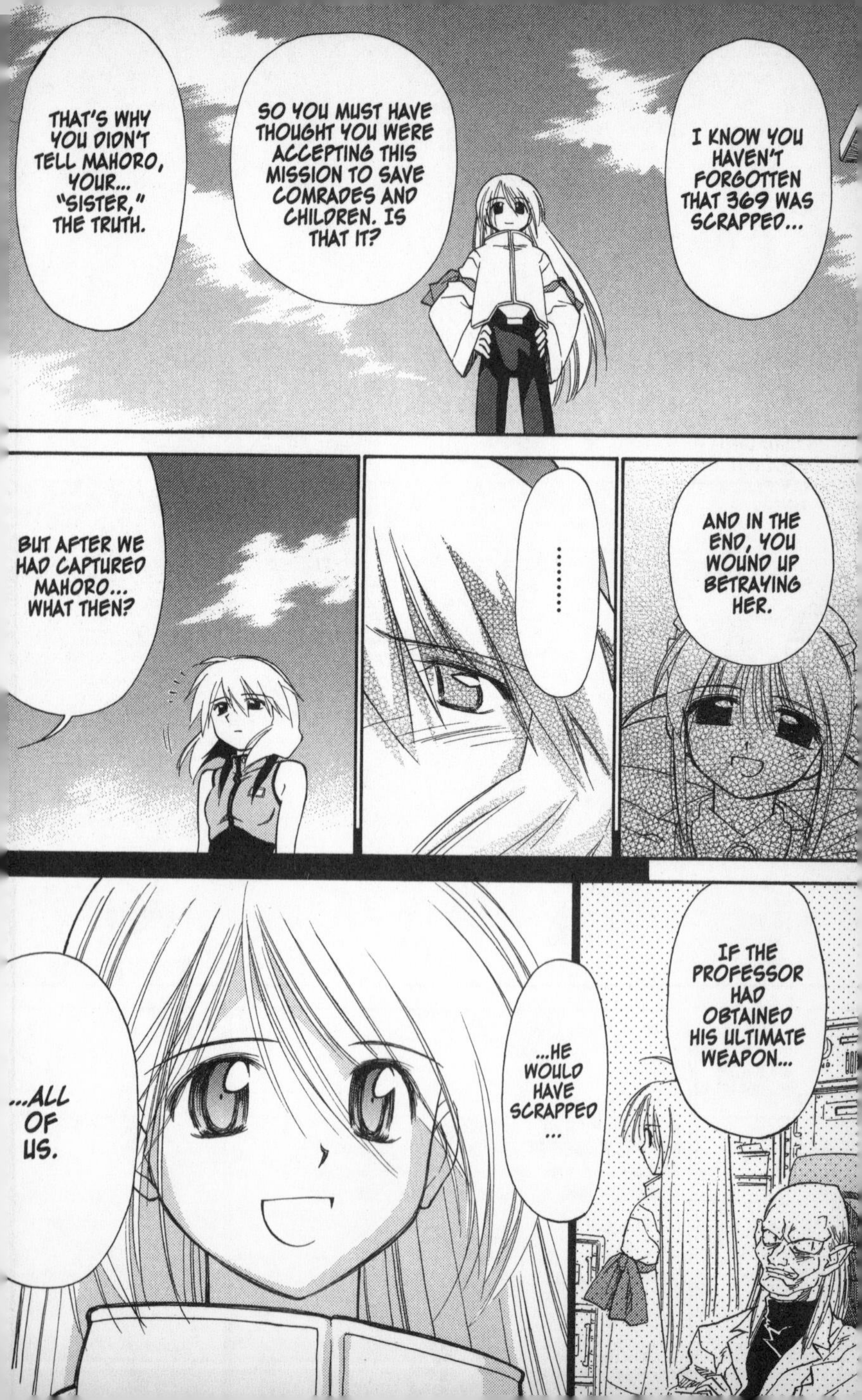
I KNOW YOU HAVEN'T FORGOTTEN THAT 369 WAS SCRAPPED...
SO YOU MUST HAVE THOUGHT YOU WERE ACCEPTING THIS MISSION TO SAVE COMRADES AND CHILDREN. IS THAT IT?
THAT'S WHY YOU DIDN'T TELL MAHORO, YOUR... "SISTER," THE TRUTH.
AND IN THE END, YOU WOUND UP BETRAYING HER.
....
BUT AFTER WE HAD CAPTURED MAHORO... WHAT THEN?
IF THE PROFESSOR HAD OBTAINED HIS ULTIMATE WEAPON...
...HE WOULD HAVE SCRAPPED ...
...ALL OF US.

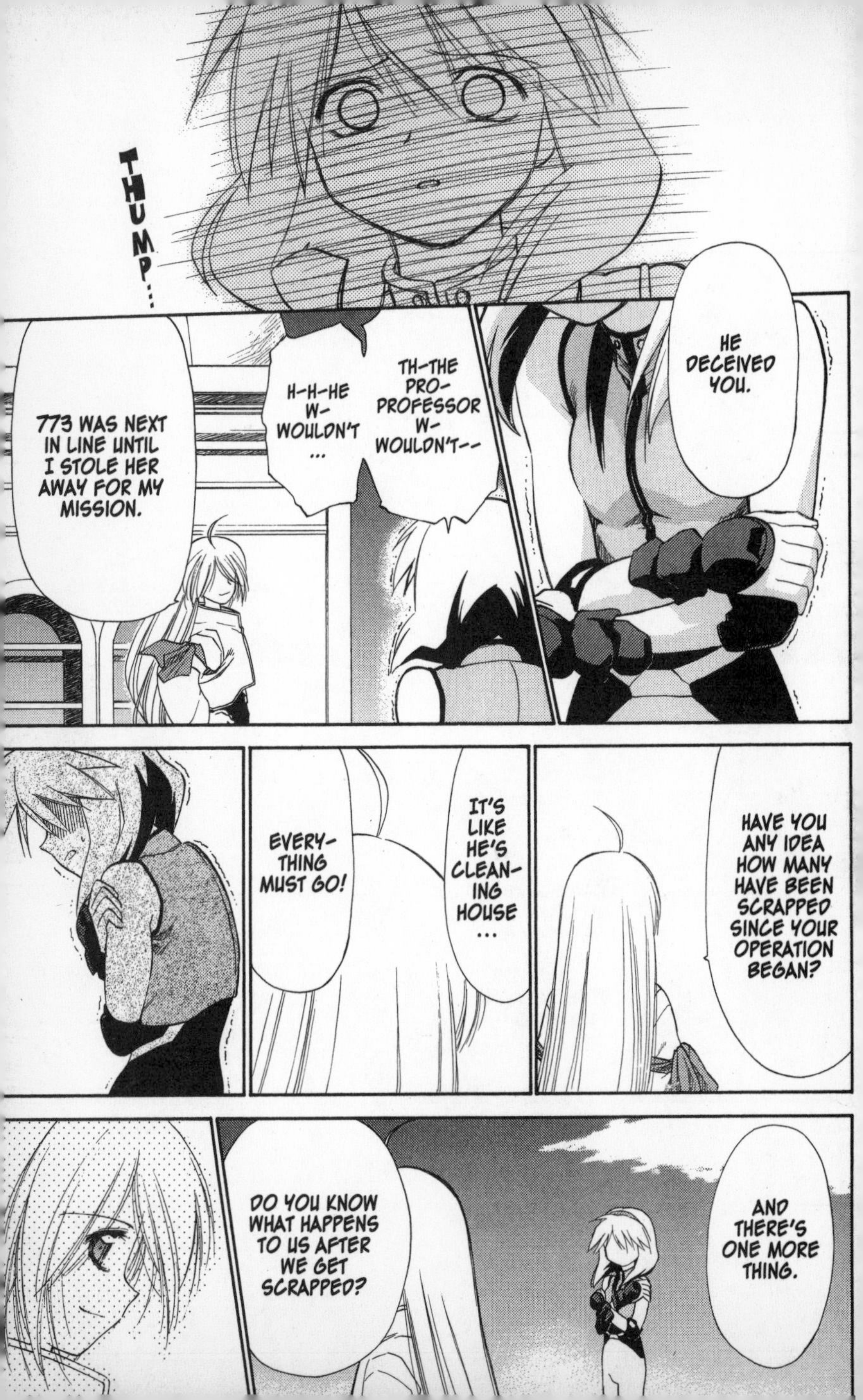
THUMP...
HE DECEIVED YOU.
TH-THE PRO-PROFESSOR W-WOULDN'T--
H-H-HE W-WOULDN'T ...
773 WAS NEXT IN LINE UNTIL I STOLE HER AWAY FOR MY MISSION.
HAVE YOU ANY IDEA HOW MANY HAVE BEEN SCRAPPED SINCE YOUR OPERATION BEGAN?
IT'S LIKE HE'S CLEAN-ING HOUSE ...
EVERY-THING MUST GO!
AND THERE'S ONE MORE THING.
DO YOU KNOW WHAT HAPPENS TO US AFTER WE GET SCRAPPED?

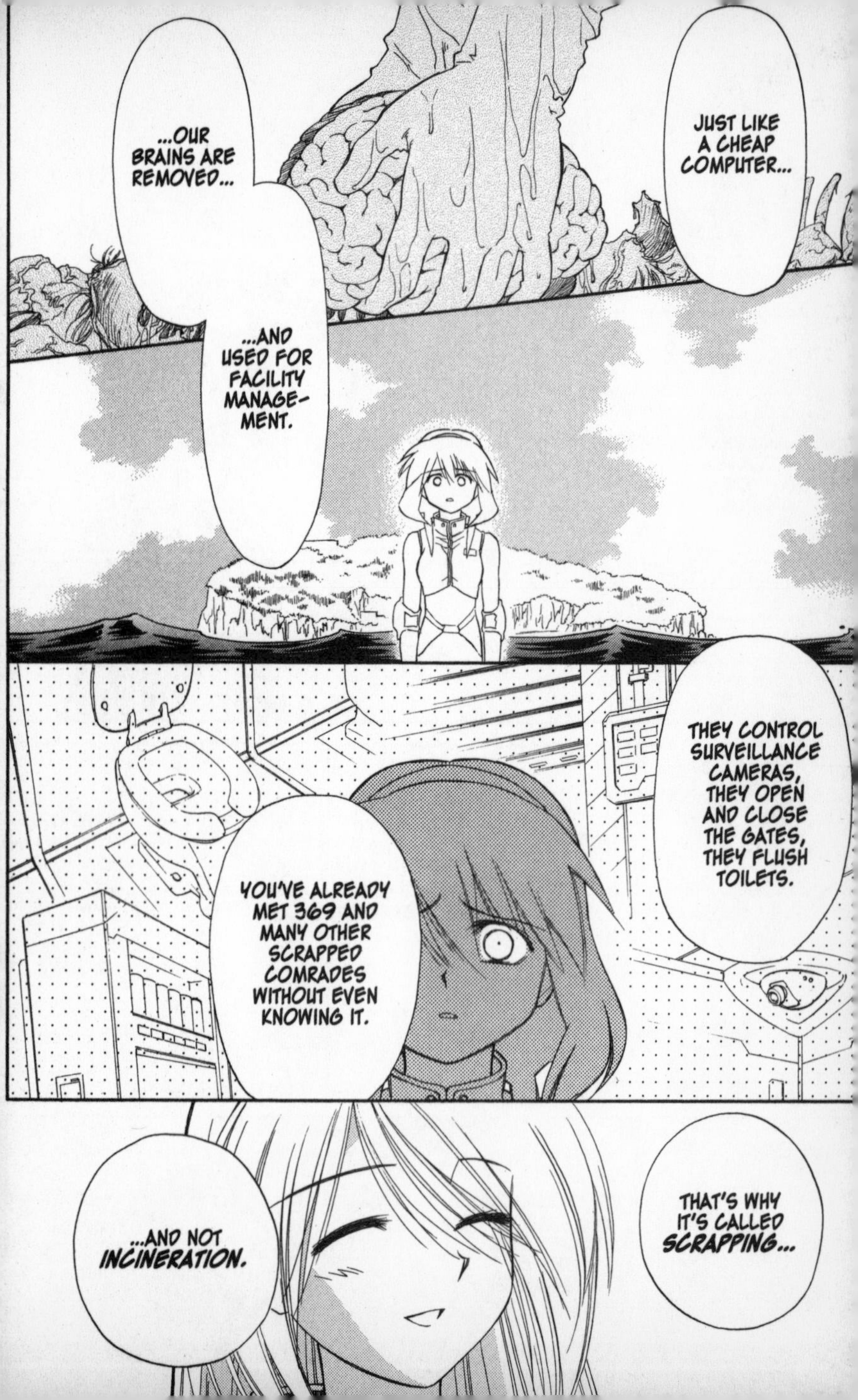
JUST LIKE A CHEAP COMPUTER...
...OUR BRAINS ARE REMOVED...
...AND USED FOR FACILITY MANAGE-MENT.
THEY CONTROL SURVEILLANCE CAMERAS, THEY OPEN AND CLOSE THE GATES, THEY FLUSH TOILETS.
YOU'VE ALREADY MET 369 AND MANY OTHER SCRAPPED COMRADES WITHOUT EVEN KNOWING IT.
THAT'S WHY IT'S CALLED *SCRAPPING*...
...AND NOT *INCINERATION*.

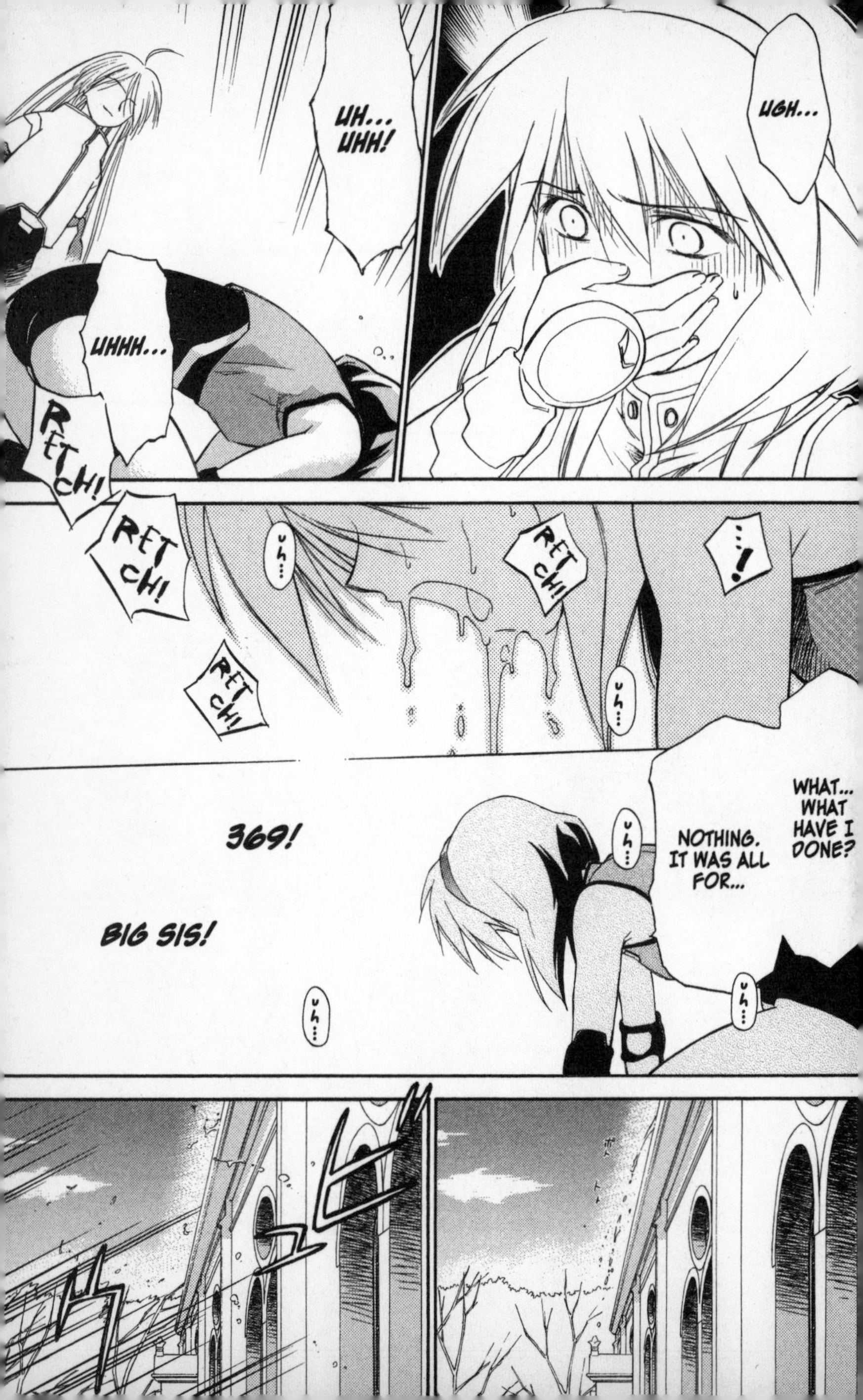

UGH...
UH... UHH!
UHHH...
RETCH!
...!
uh...
RETCH!
uh...
RETCH!
RETCH!
WHAT... WHAT HAVE I DONE?
NOTHING. IT WAS ALL FOR...
uh...
uh...
369!
BIG SIS!
uh...

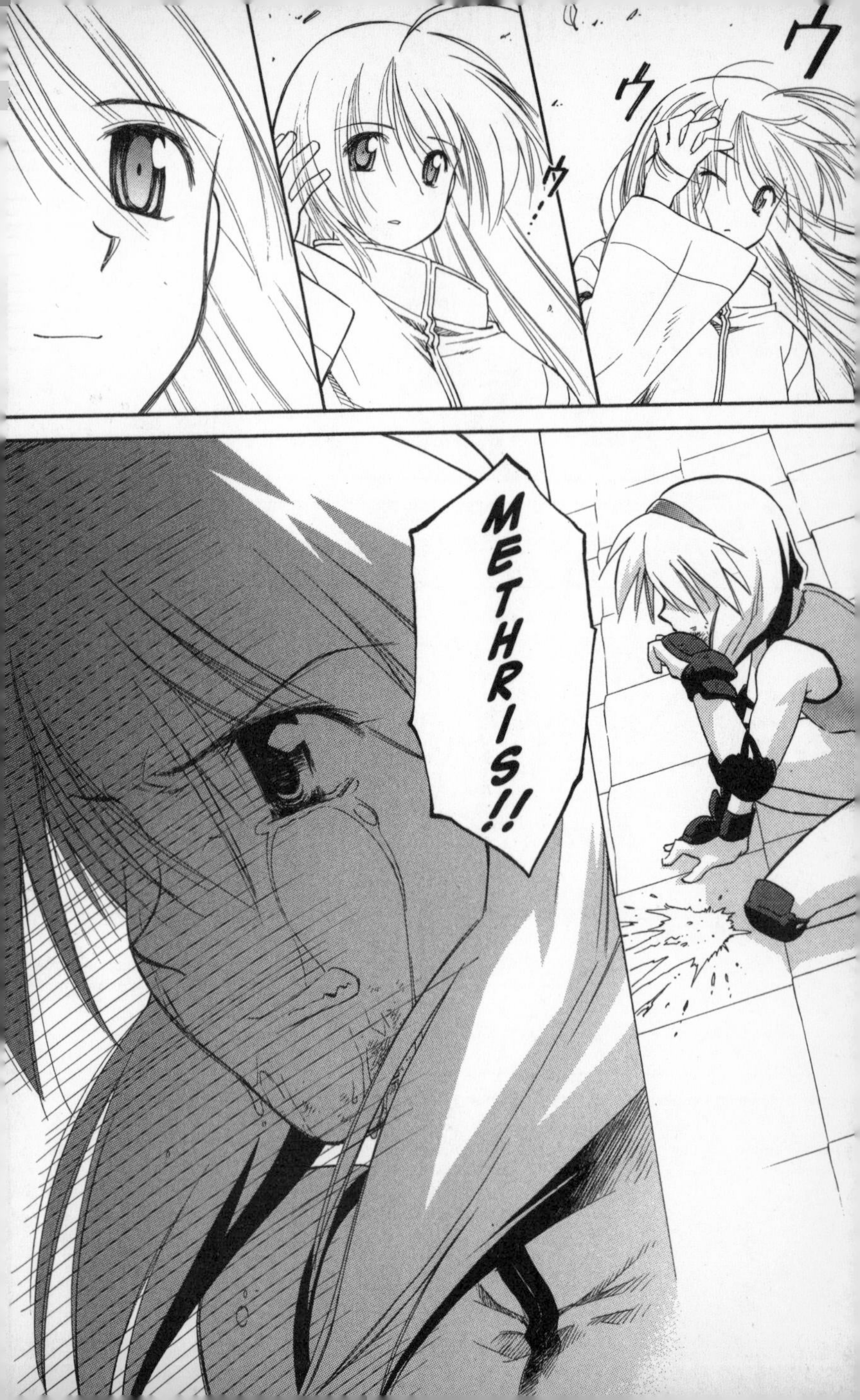
ウ
ウ
ウ…
METHRIS!!

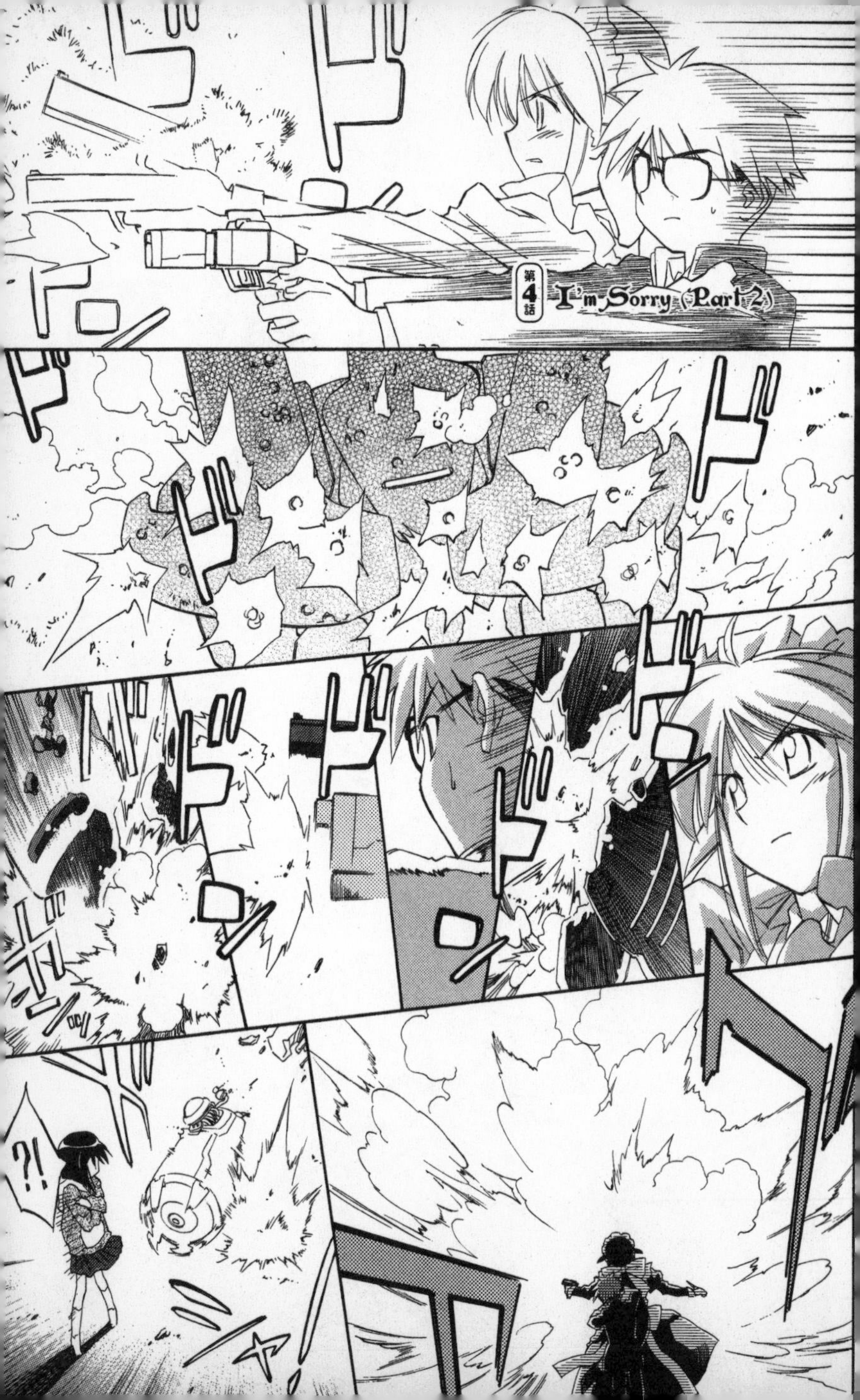
第4話
I'm Sorry (Part 2)
?!

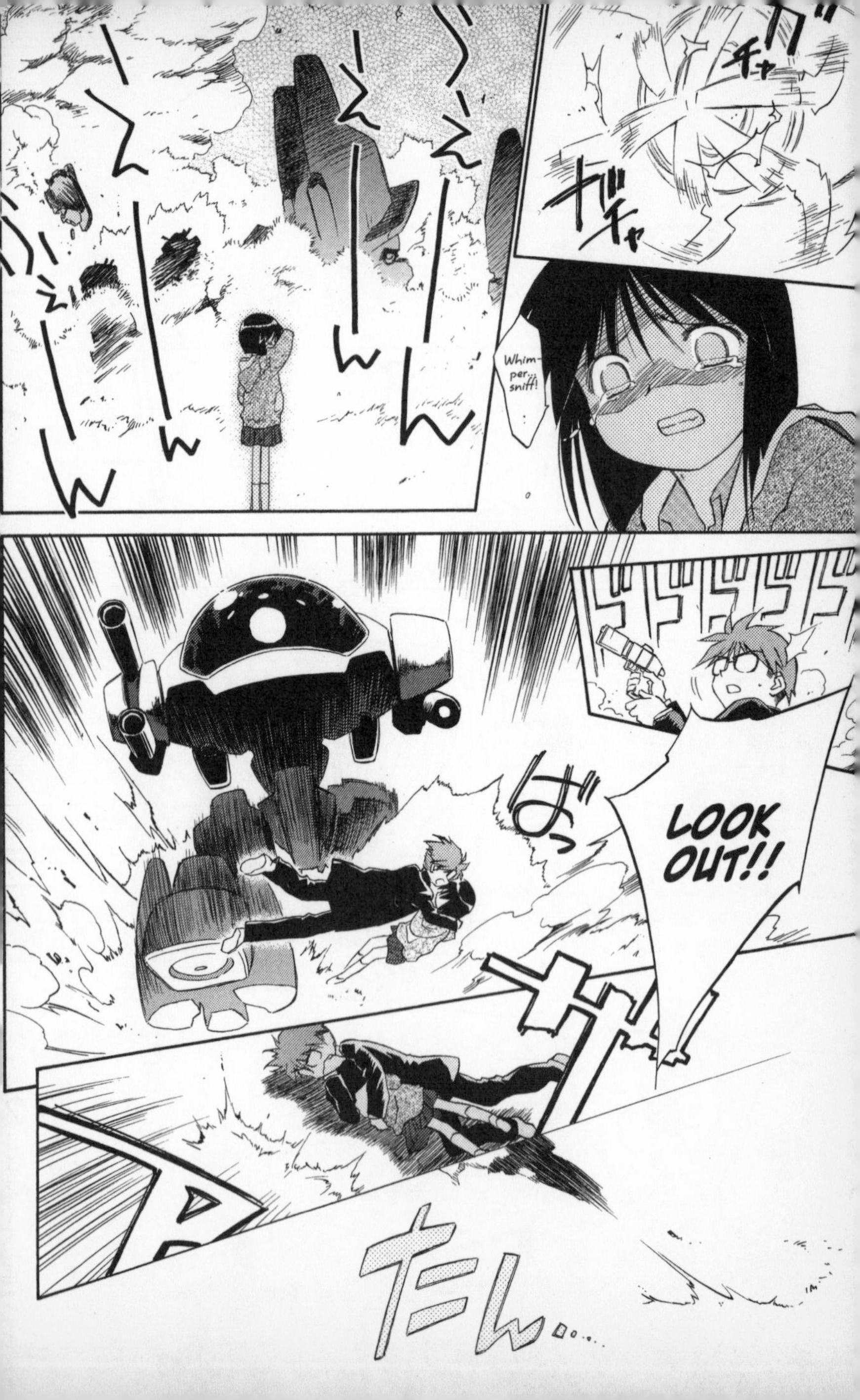
ガチャ
ガチャ
Whimper... sniff!
LOOK OUT!!
ばっ
たん。。。

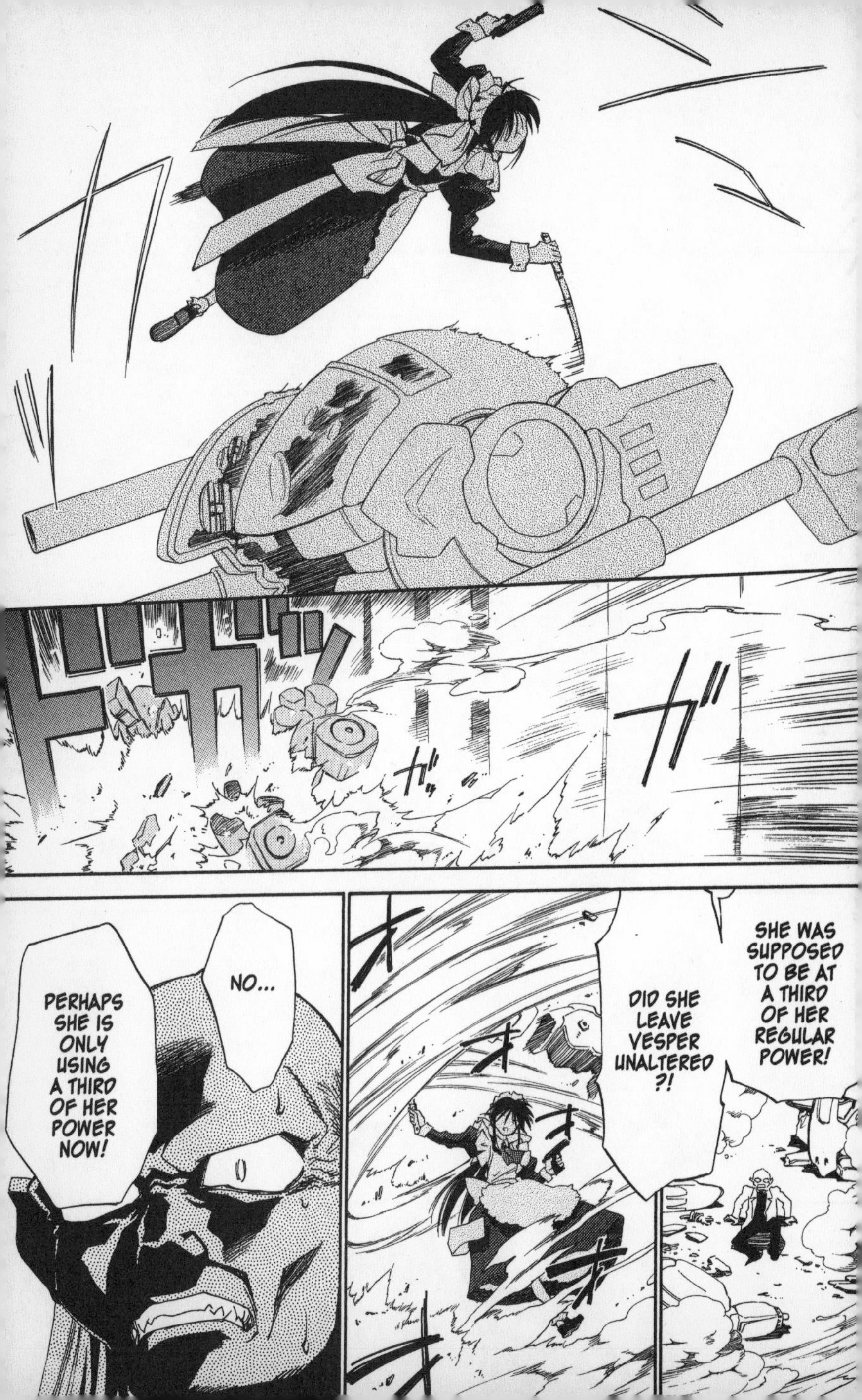
SHE WAS SUPPOSED TO BE AT A THIRD OF HER REGULAR POWER!
DID SHE LEAVE VESPER UNALTERED ?!
NO...
PERHAPS SHE IS ONLY USING A THIRD OF HER POWER NOW!

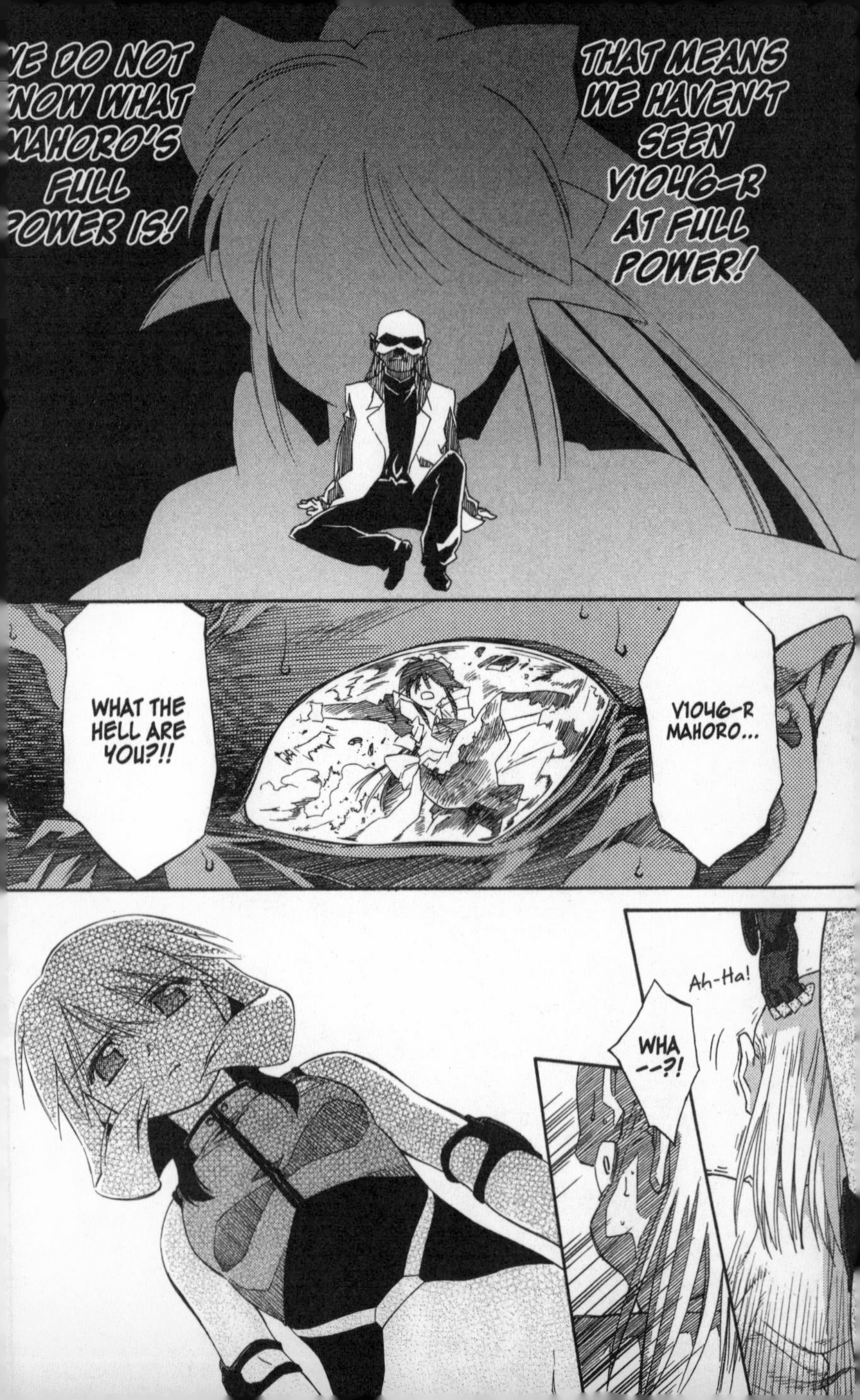
THAT MEANS WE HAVEN'T SEEN V1046-R AT FULL POWER!
WE DO NOT KNOW WHAT MAHORO'S FULL POWER IS!
V1046-R MAHORO...
WHAT THE HELL ARE YOU?!!
Ah-Ha!
WHA--?!

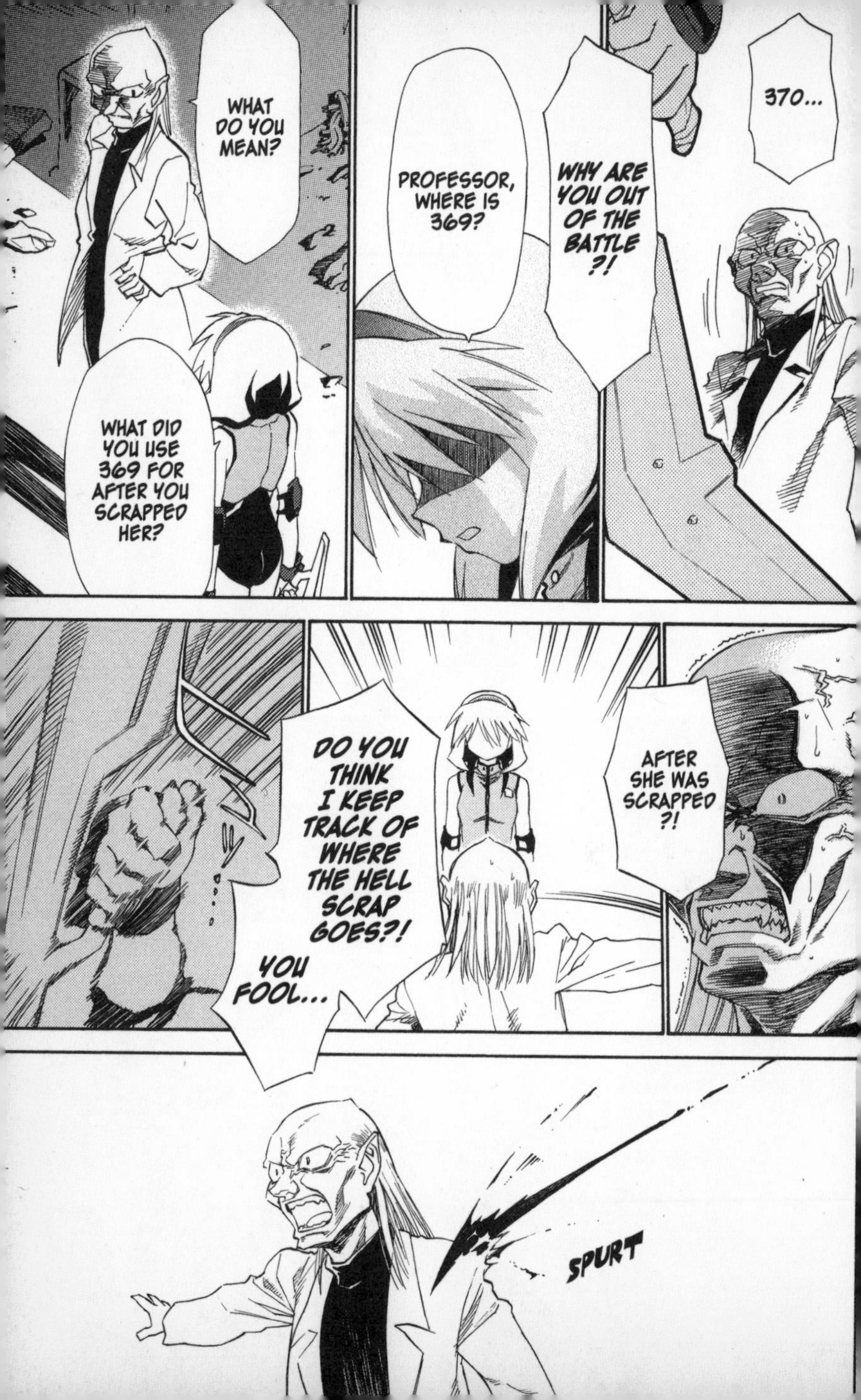
370...
WHY ARE YOU OUT OF THE BATTLE ?!
PROFESSOR, WHERE IS 369?
WHAT DO YOU MEAN?
WHAT DID YOU USE 369 FOR AFTER YOU SCRAPPED HER?
AFTER SHE WAS SCRAPPED ?!
DO YOU THINK I KEEP TRACK OF WHERE THE HELL SCRAP GOES?!
YOU FOOL...
SPURT

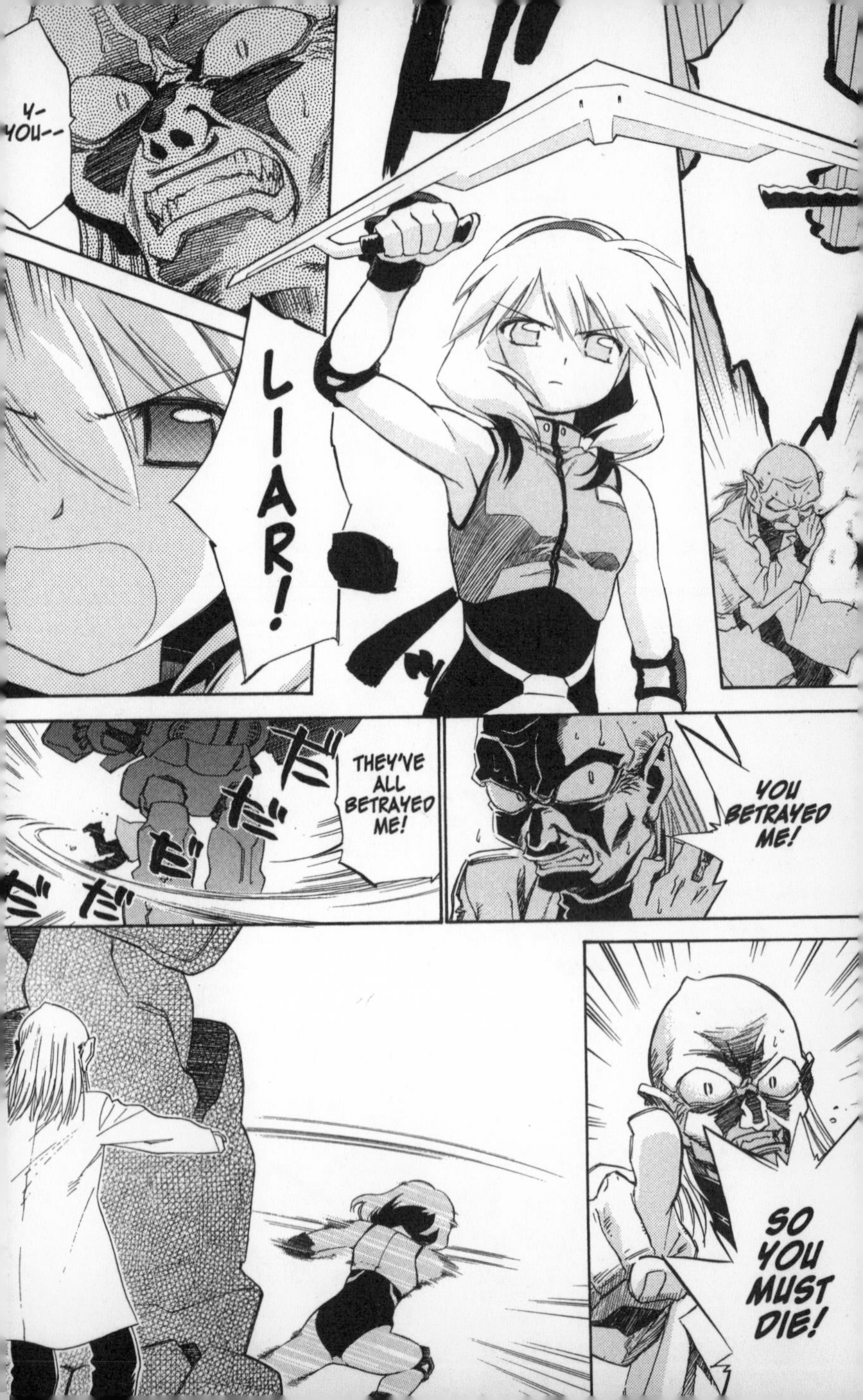
Y-YOU--
LIAR!
YOU BETRAYED ME!
THEY'VE ALL BETRAYED ME!
SO YOU MUST DIE!

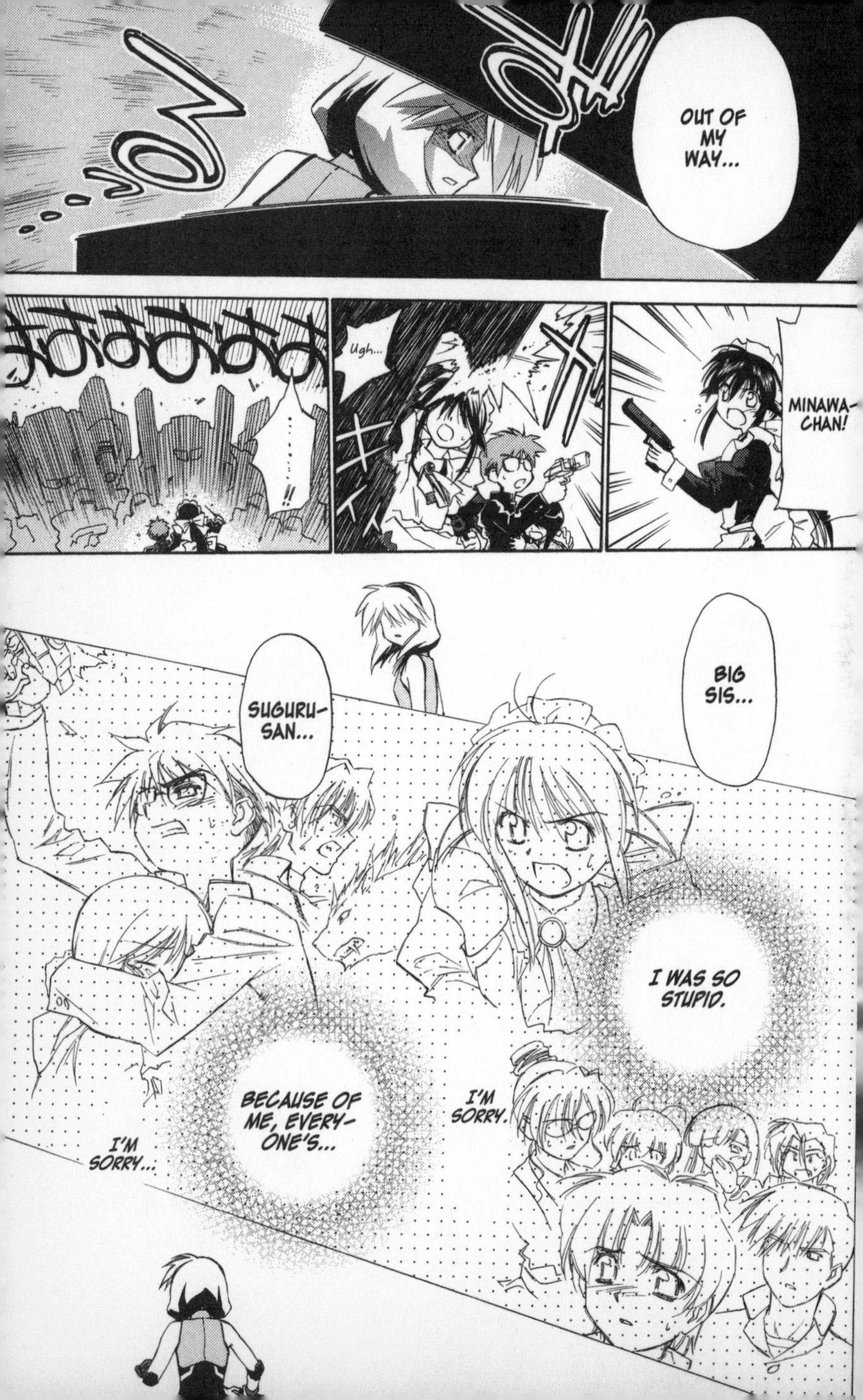
OUT OF MY WAY...
MINAWA-CHAN!
Ugh...
BIG SIS...
SUGURU-SAN...
I WAS SO STUPID.
I'M SORRY.
BECAUSE OF ME, EVERY-ONE'S...
I'M SORRY...

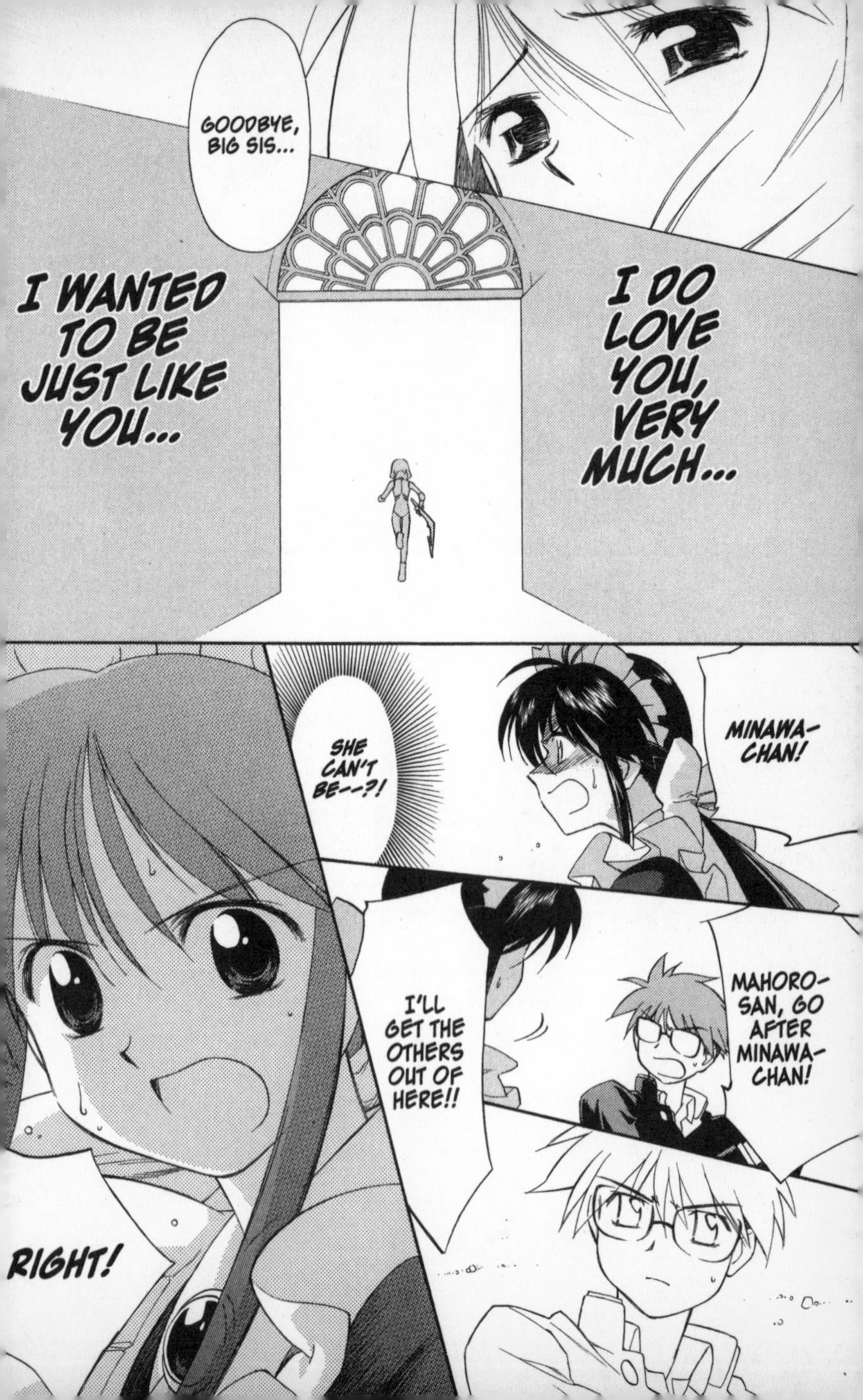
GOODBYE, BIG SIS...
I DO LOVE YOU, VERY MUCH...
I WANTED TO BE JUST LIKE YOU...
MINAWA-CHAN!
SHE CAN'T BE--?!
MAHORO-SAN, GO AFTER MINAWA-CHAN!
I'LL GET THE OTHERS OUT OF HERE!!
RIGHT!

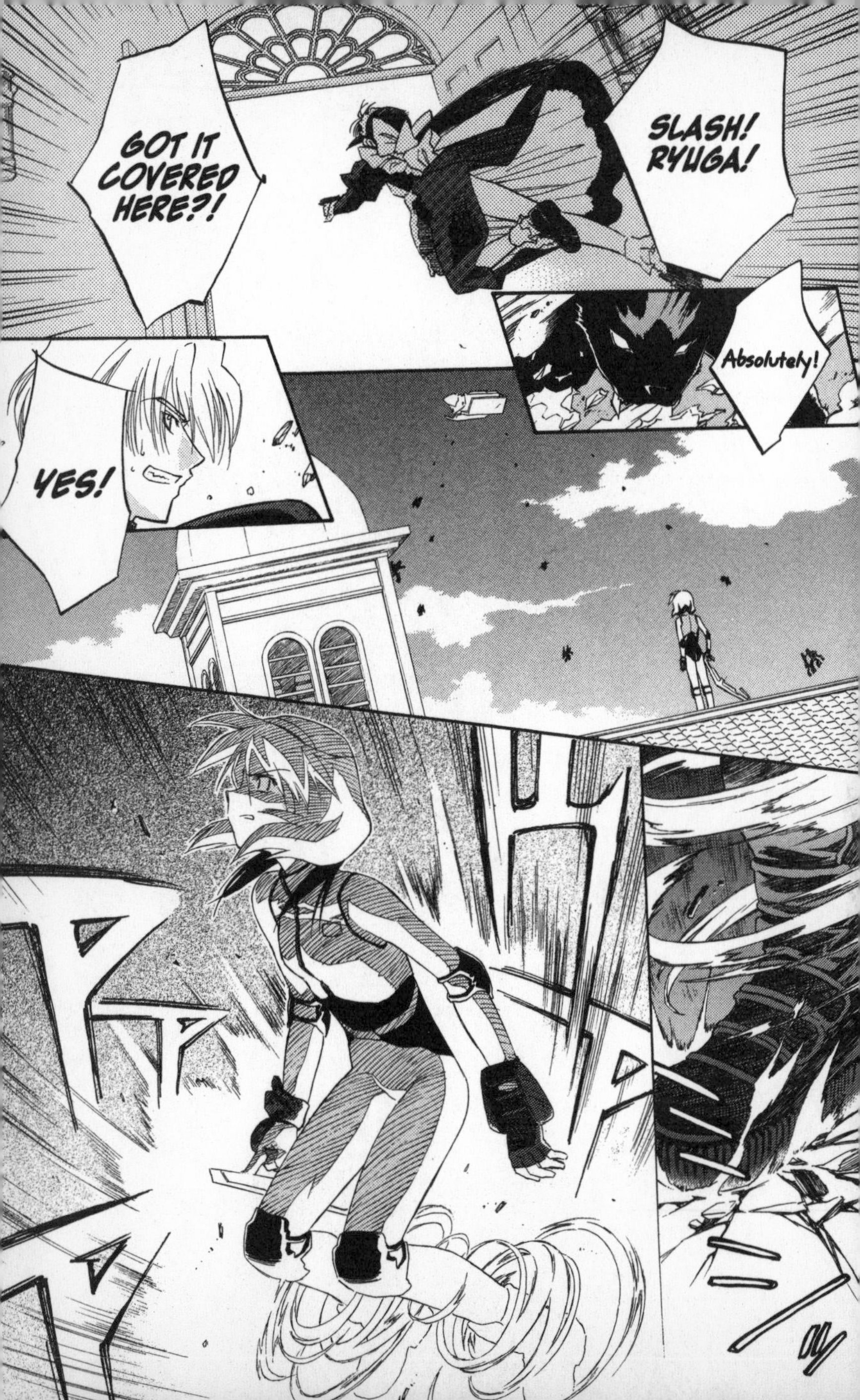
SLASH! RYUGA!
GOT IT COVERED HERE?!
Absolutely!
YES!

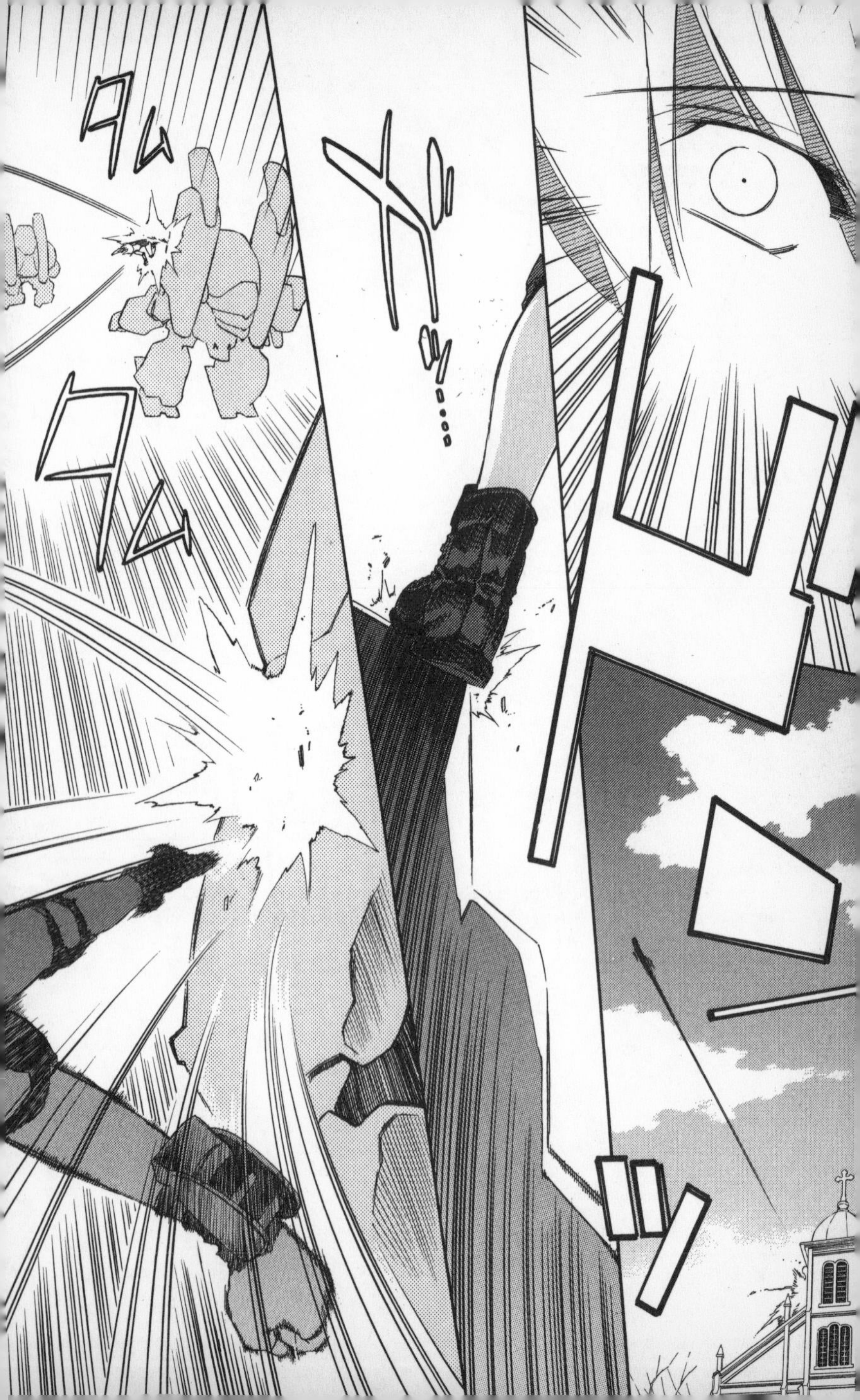

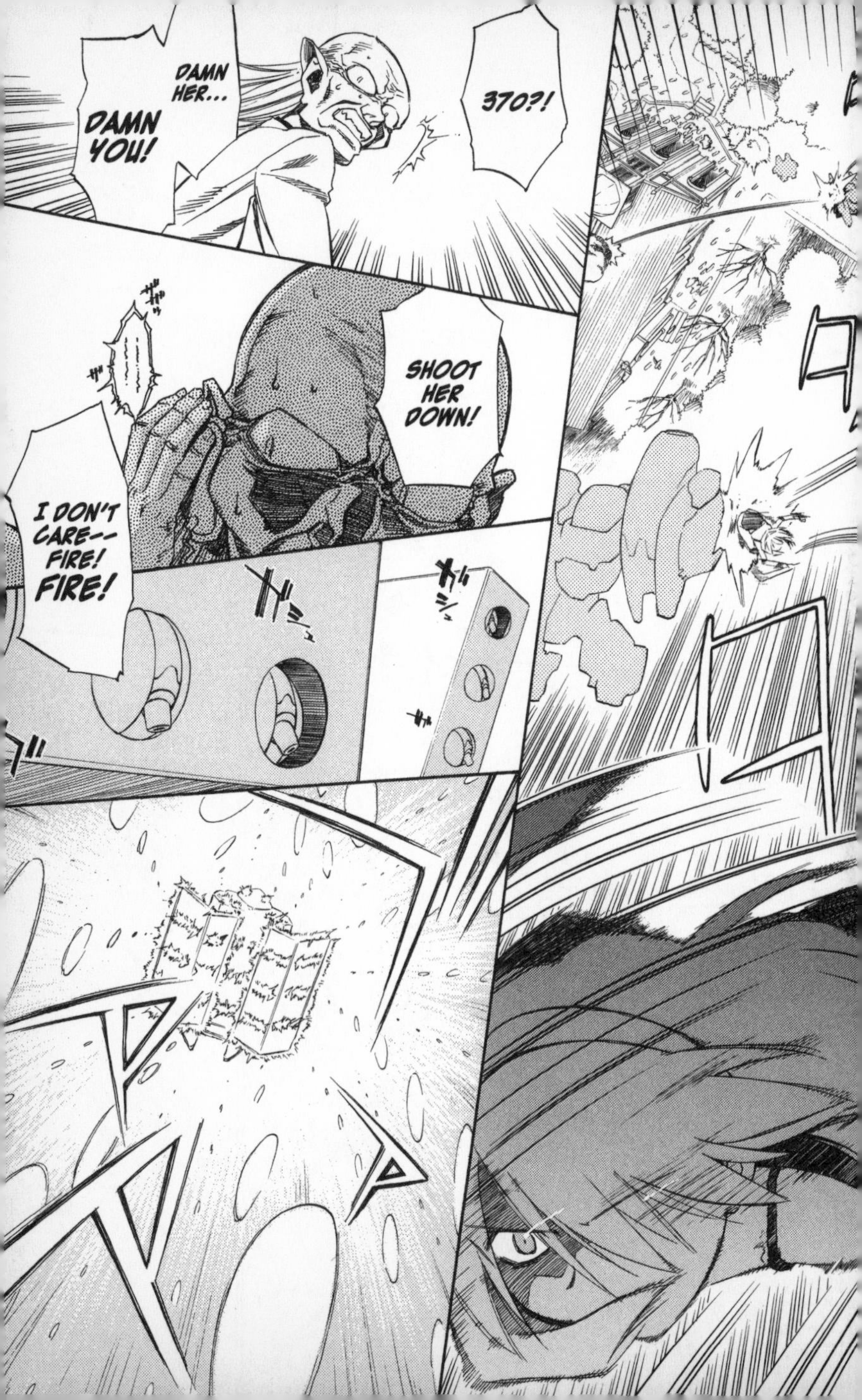
370?!
DAMN HER...
DAMN YOU!
SHOOT HER DOWN!
I DON'T CARE--FIRE! FIRE!

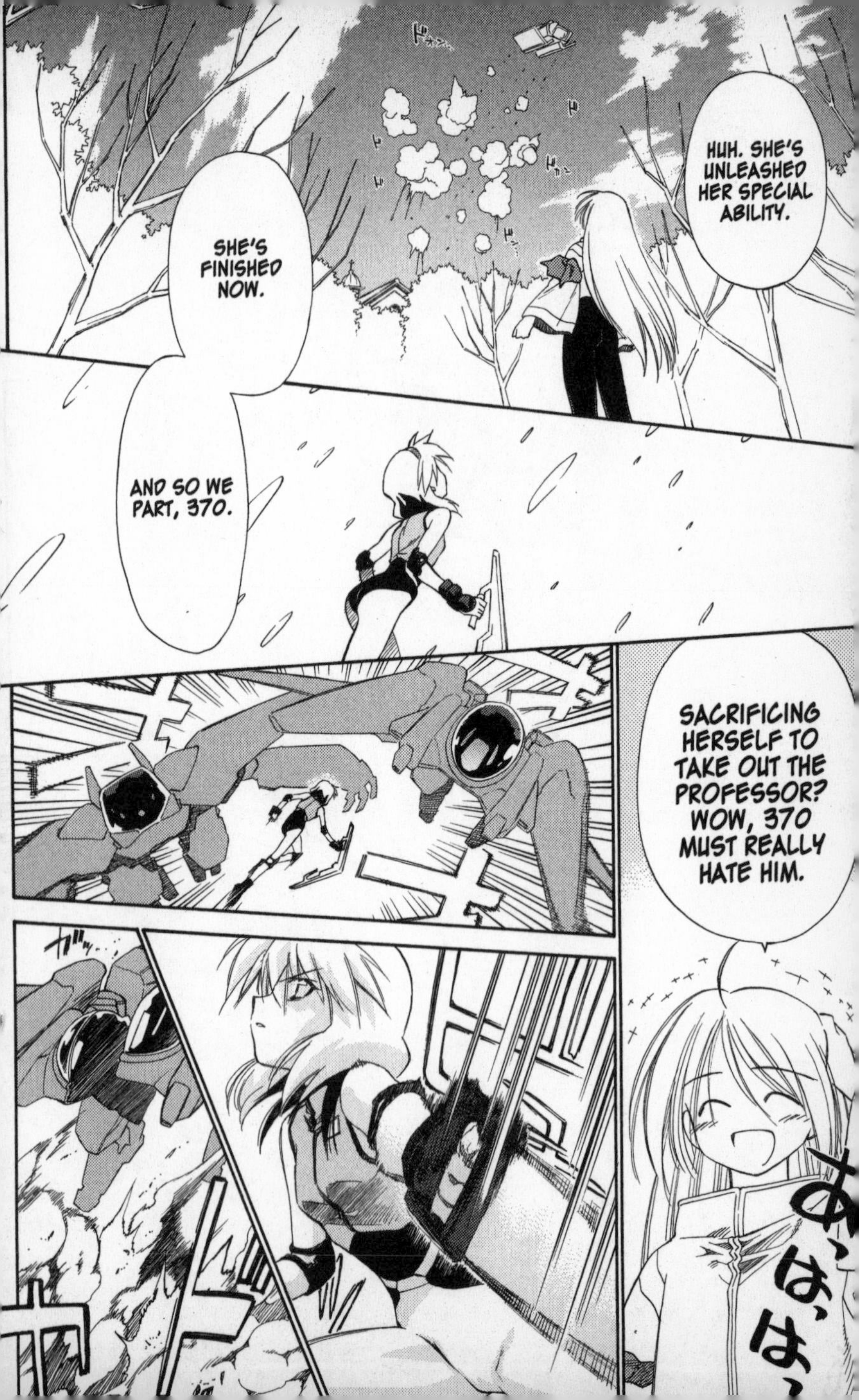
HUH. SHE'S UNLEASHED HER SPECIAL ABILITY.
SHE'S FINISHED NOW.
AND SO WE PART, 370.
SACRIFICING HERSELF TO TAKE OUT THE PROFESSOR? WOW, 370 MUST REALLY HATE HIM.
あはは

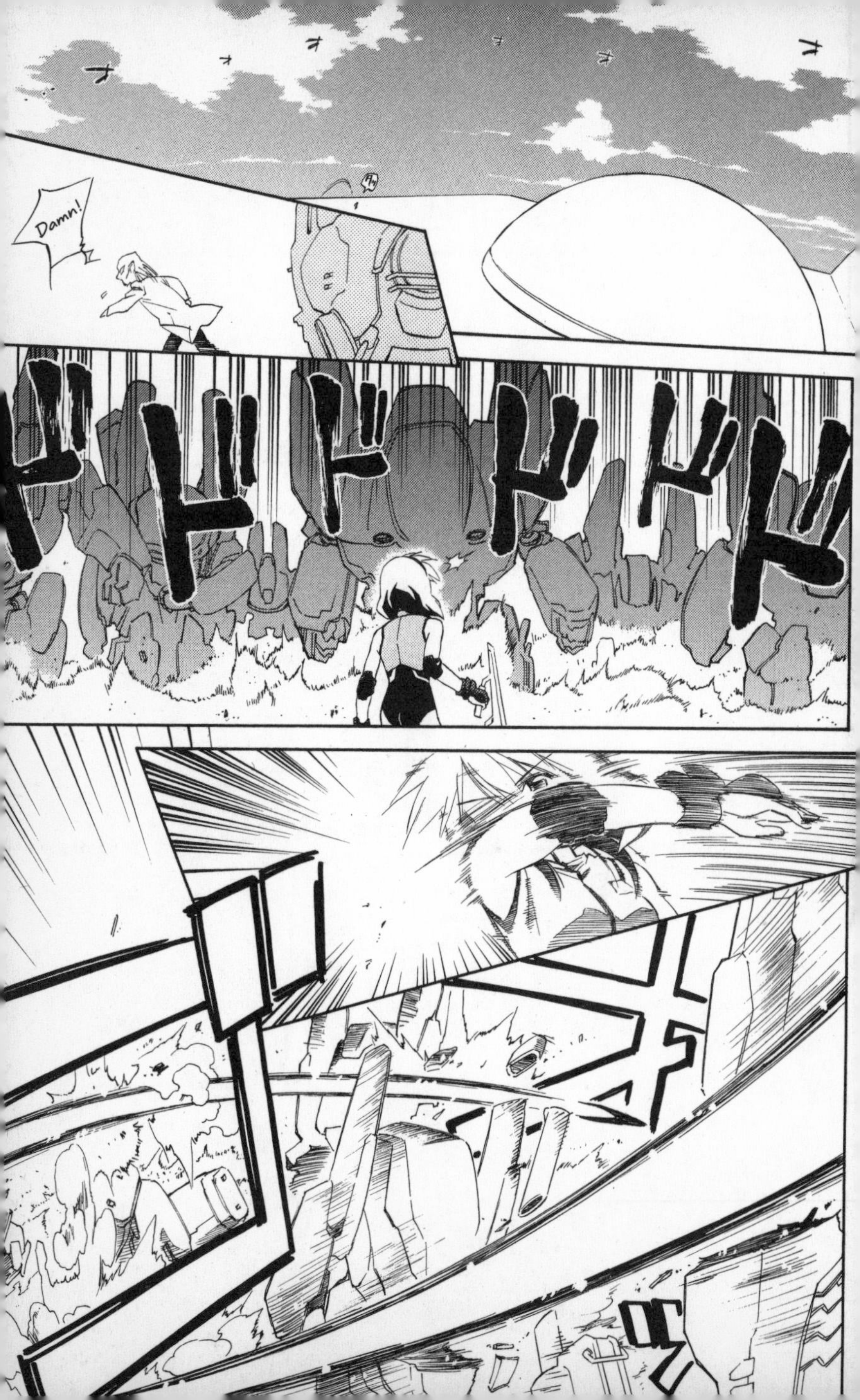

オ オ オ オ オ オ
Damn!
ドドドドドド

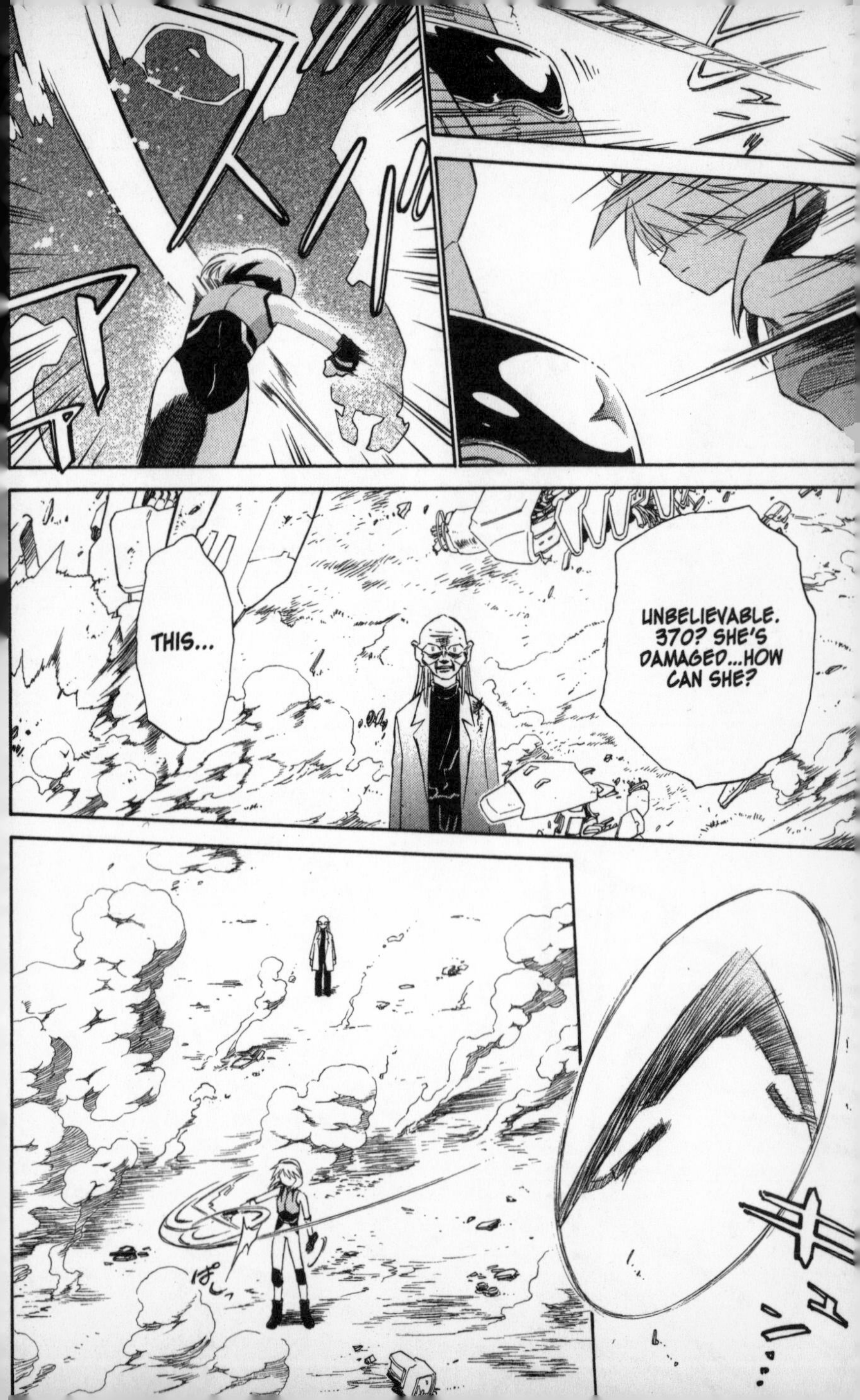
UNBELIEVABLE. 370? SHE'S DAMAGED...HOW CAN SHE?
THIS...
ぱしっ

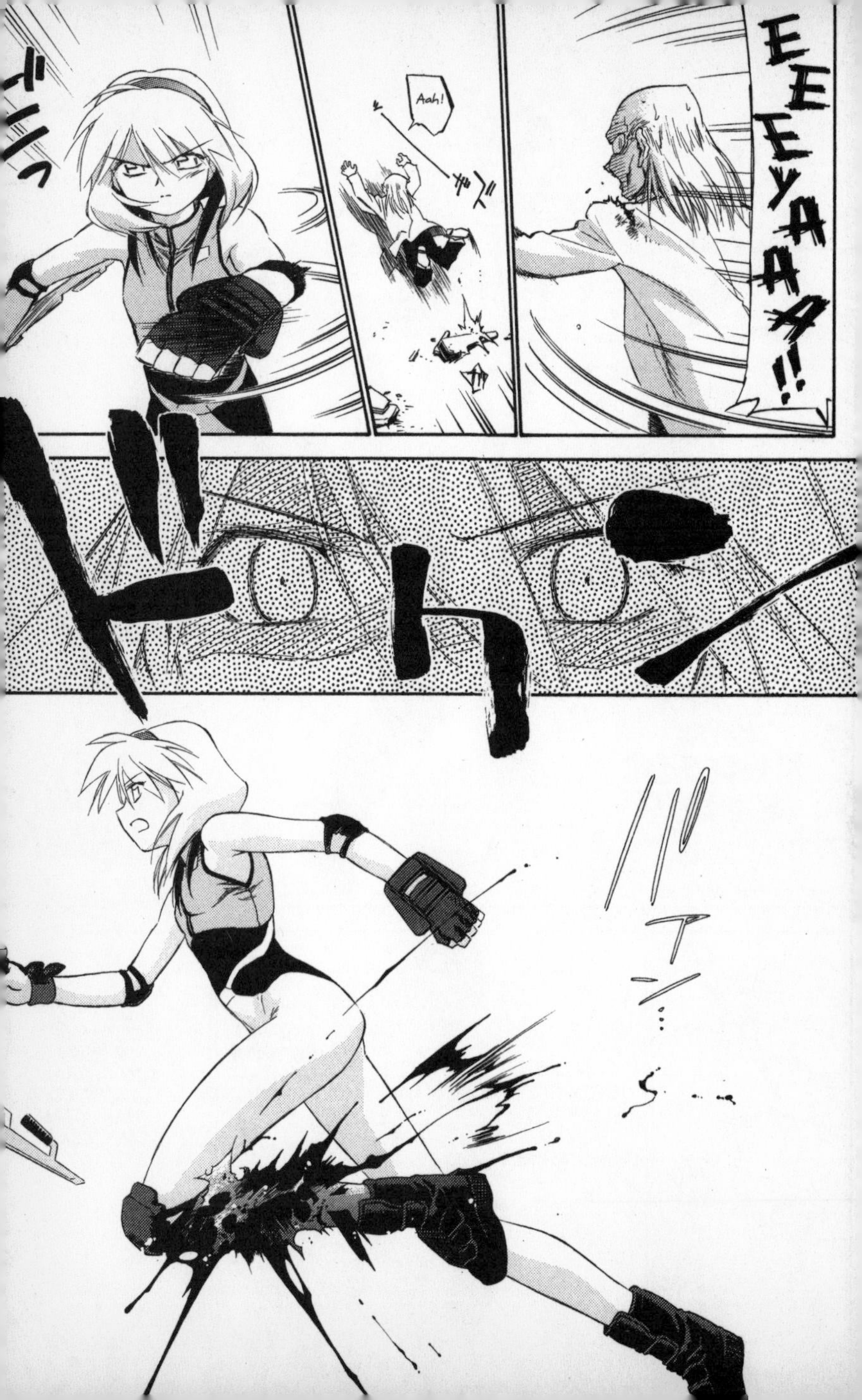
EEEYAAA!!
Aah!

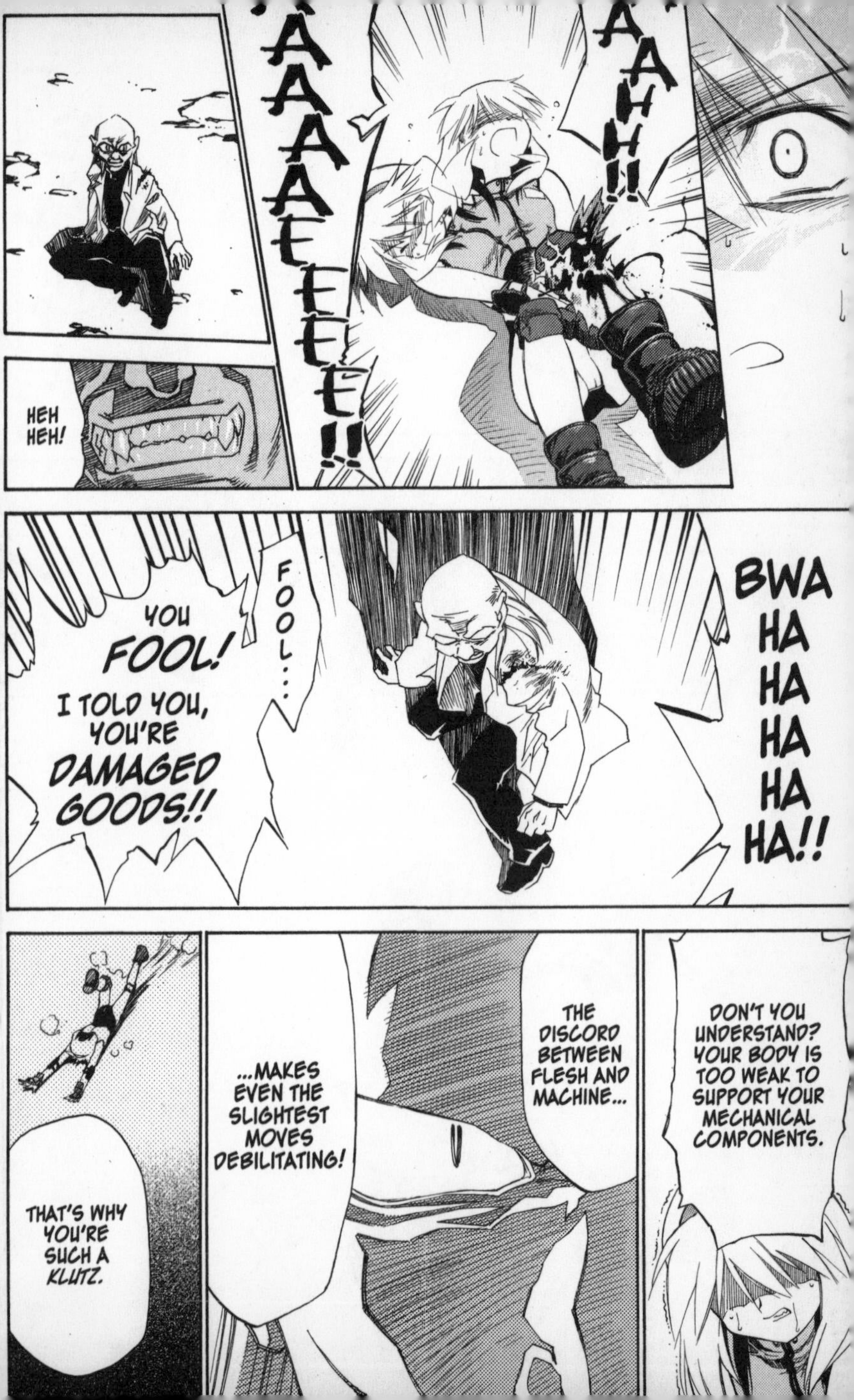
AAHH!!
AAAAEEEEE!!
HEH HEH!
BWA HA HA HA HA HA!!
FOOL...
YOU FOOL! I TOLD YOU, YOU'RE DAMAGED GOODS!!
DON'T YOU UNDERSTAND? YOUR BODY IS TOO WEAK TO SUPPORT YOUR MECHANICAL COMPONENTS.
THE DISCORD BETWEEN FLESH AND MACHINE...
...MAKES EVEN THE SLIGHTEST MOVES DEBILITATING!
THAT'S WHY YOU'RE SUCH A KLUTZ.

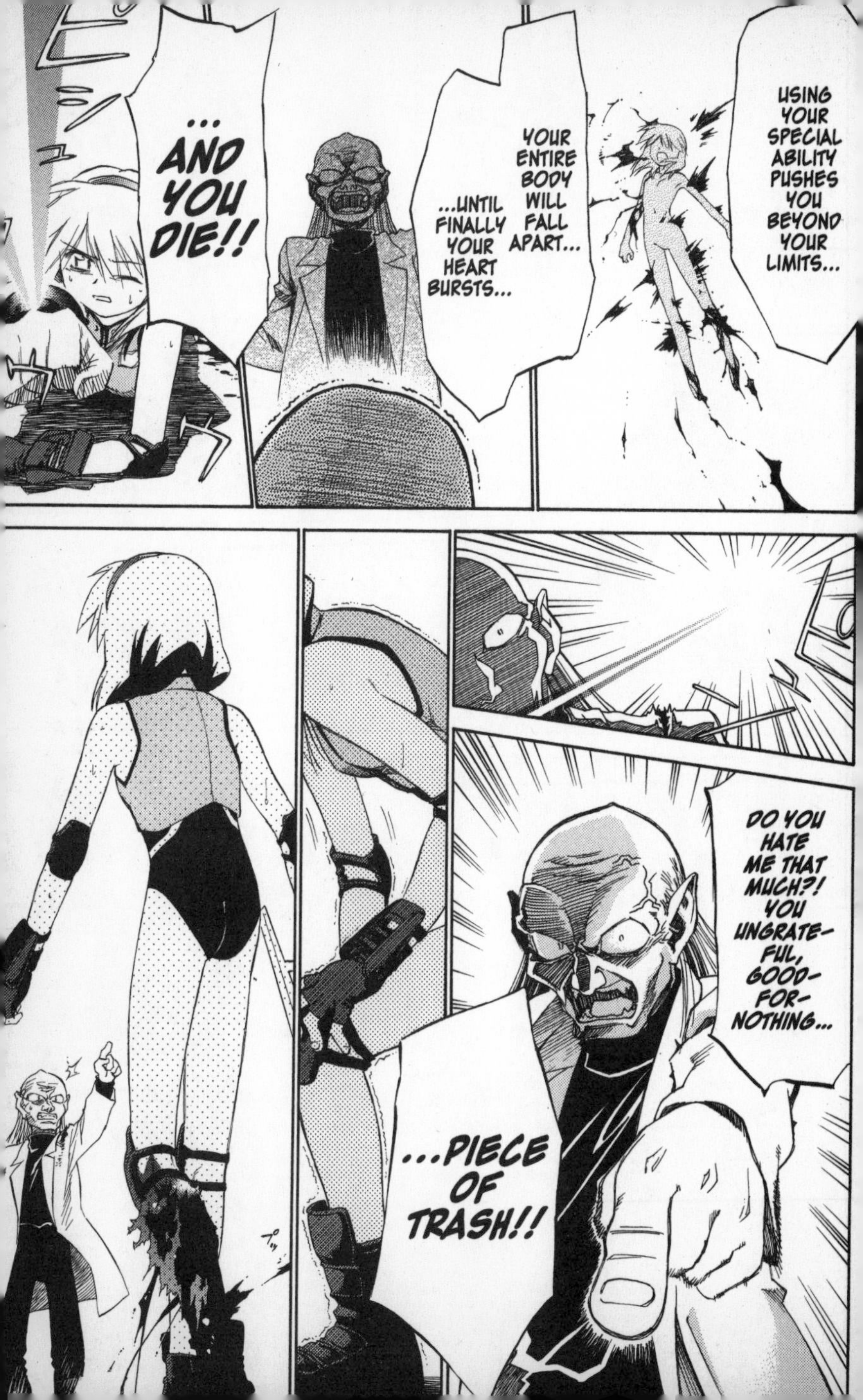
USING YOUR SPECIAL ABILITY PUSHES YOU BEYOND YOUR LIMITS...
YOUR ENTIRE BODY WILL FALL APART...
...UNTIL FINALLY YOUR HEART BURSTS...
...AND YOU DIE!!
DO YOU HATE ME THAT MUCH?! YOU UNGRATE-FUL, GOOD-FOR-NOTHING...
...PIECE OF TRASH!!

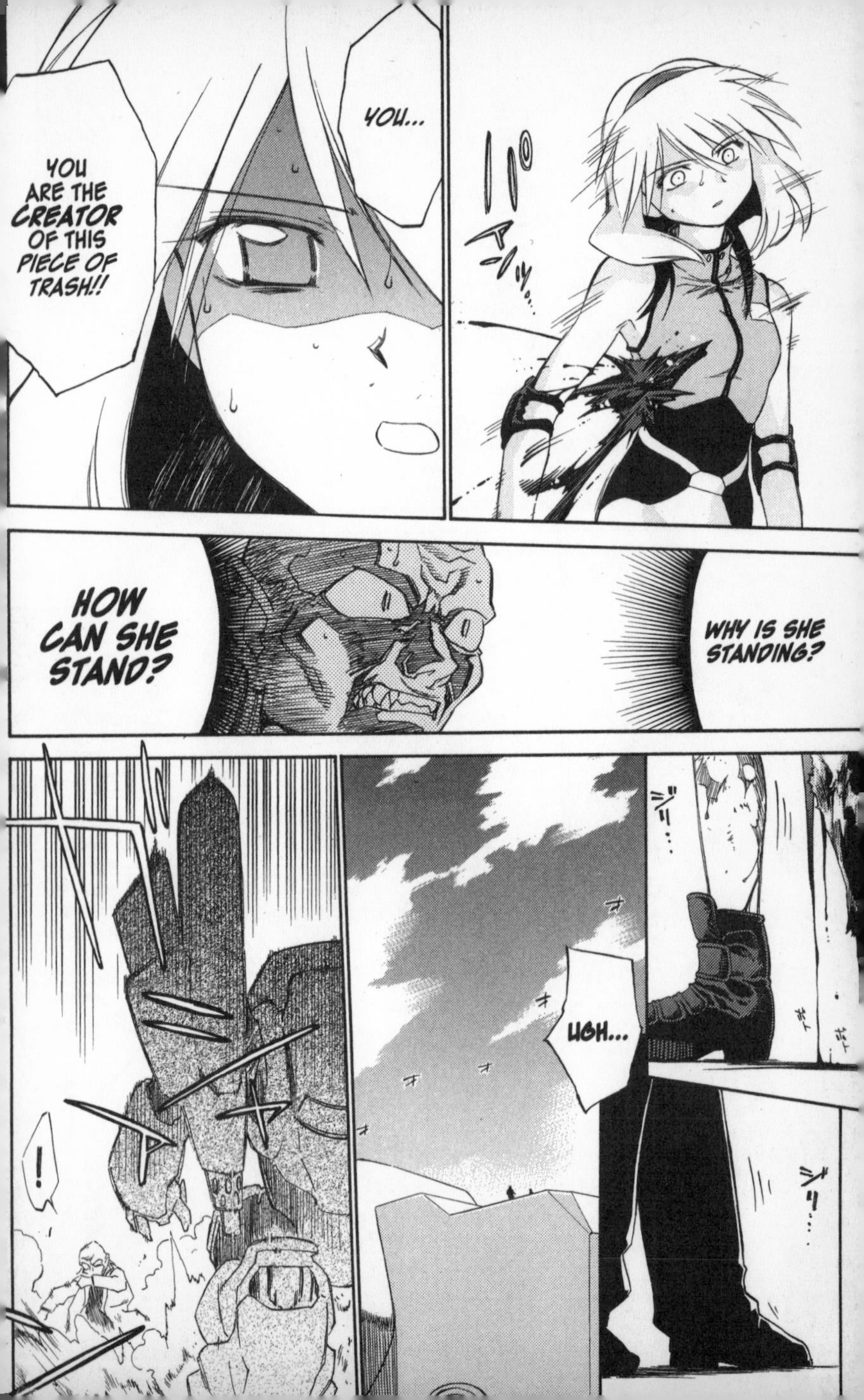
YOU...
YOU ARE THE CREATOR OF THIS PIECE OF TRASH!!
WHY IS SHE STANDING?
HOW CAN SHE STAND?
UGH...
!

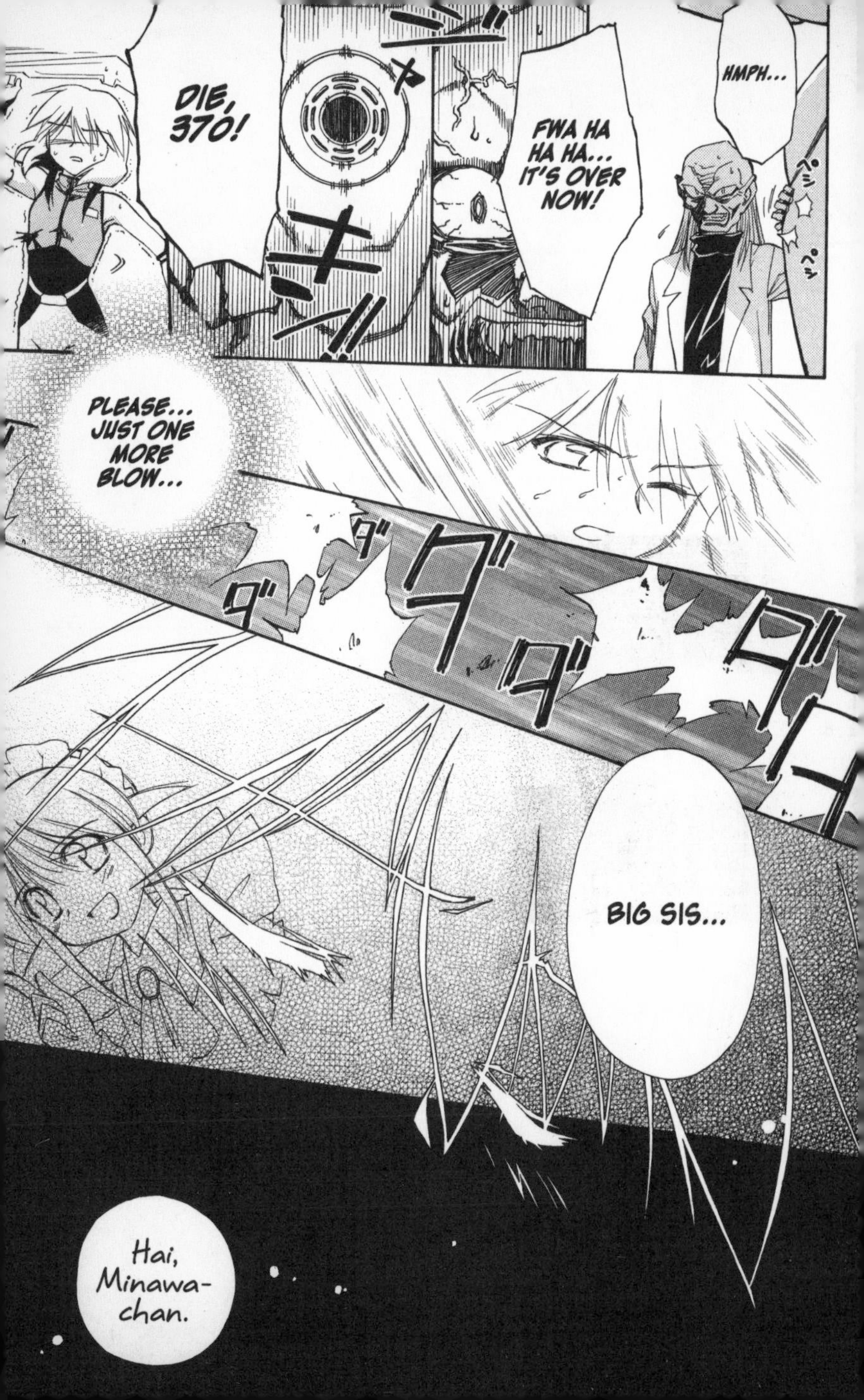
HMPH...
FWA HA HA HA... IT'S OVER NOW!
DIE, 370!
ジャキン!!
PLEASE... JUST ONE MORE BLOW...
BIG SIS...
Hai, Minawa-chan.

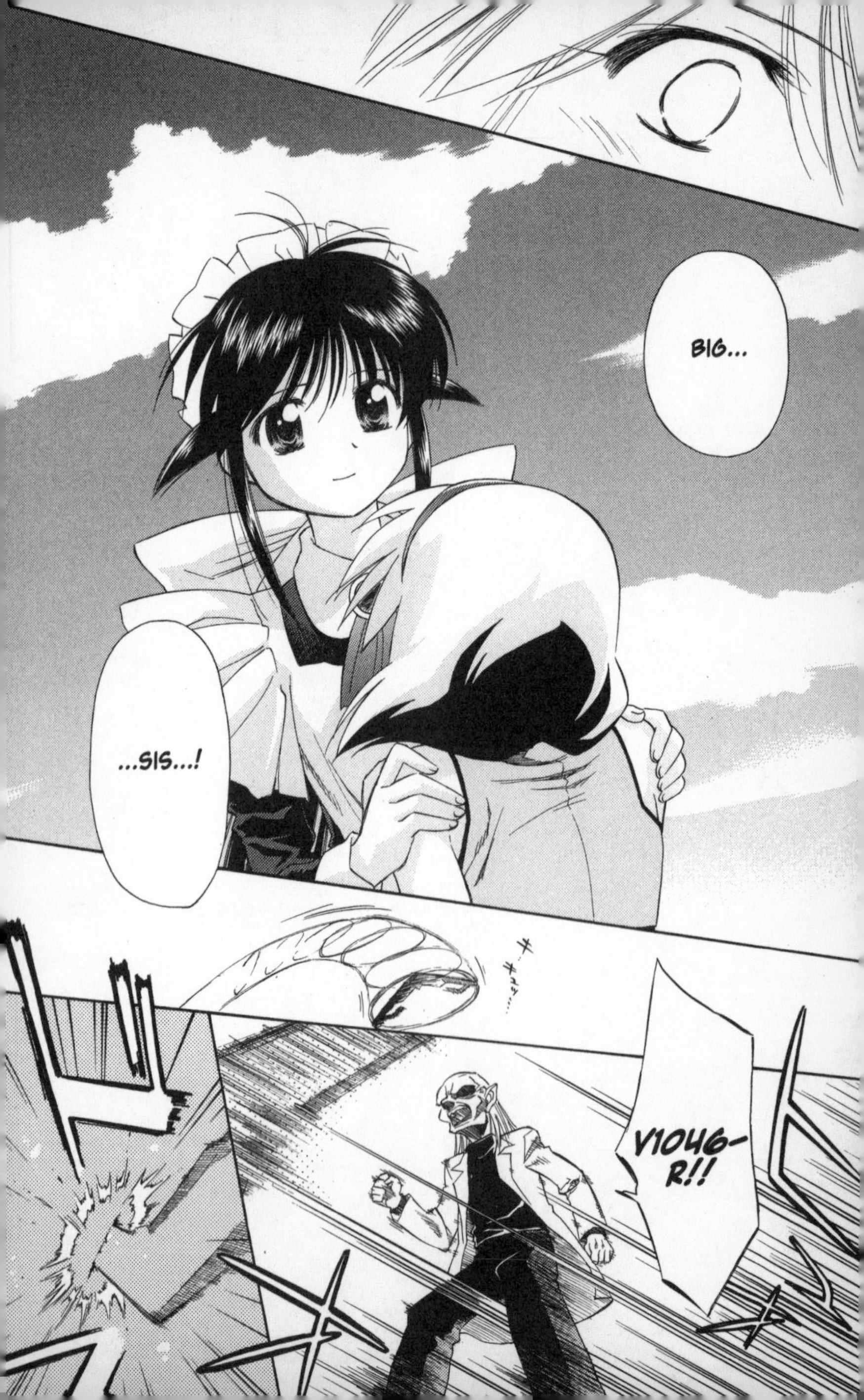
BIG...
...SIS...!
VIOUG-
R!!

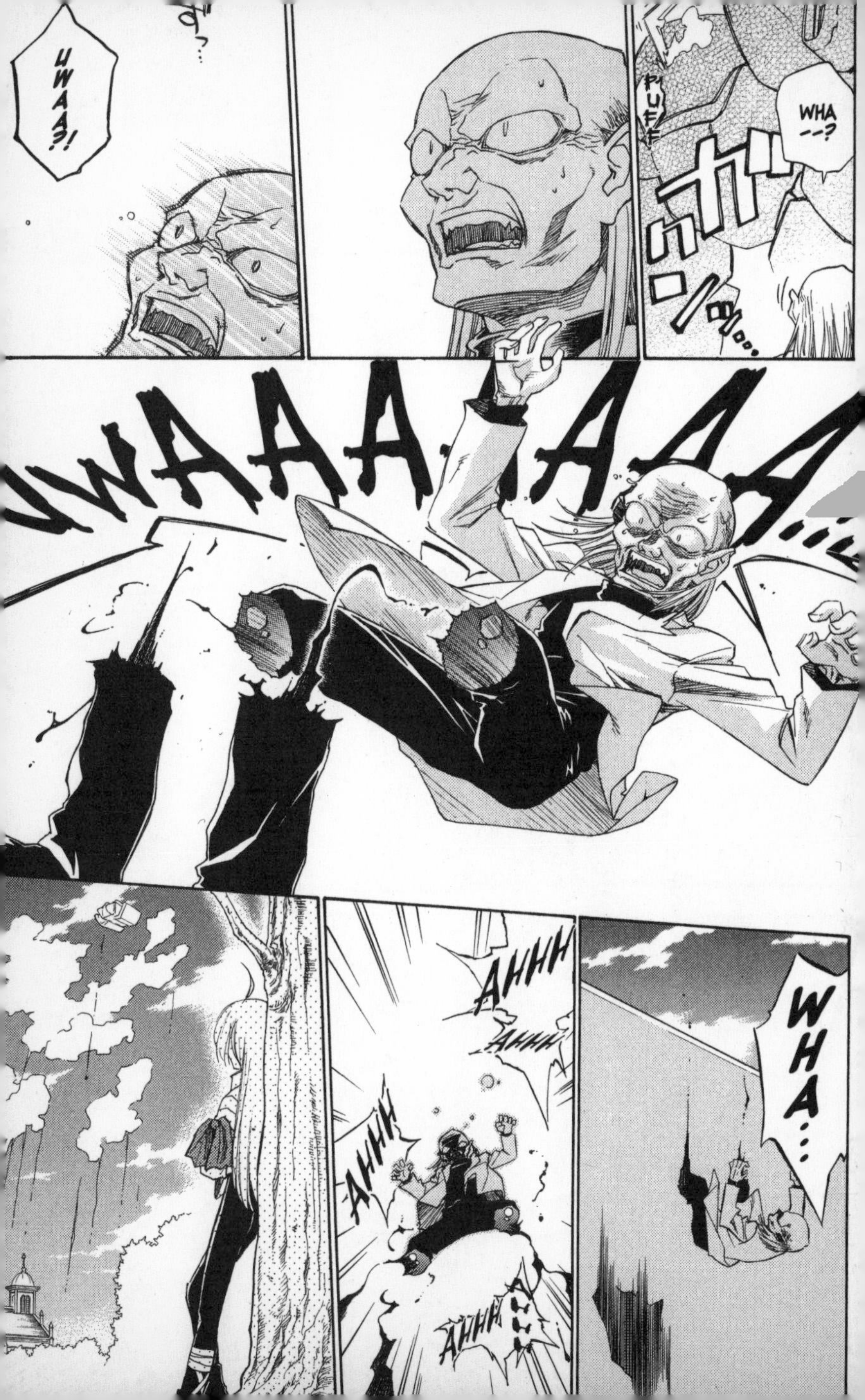
WHA--?
PUFF
UWAAA?!
UWAAAAAAAA...!!
WHA...
AHHH
AHHH
AHHH
AHHH...

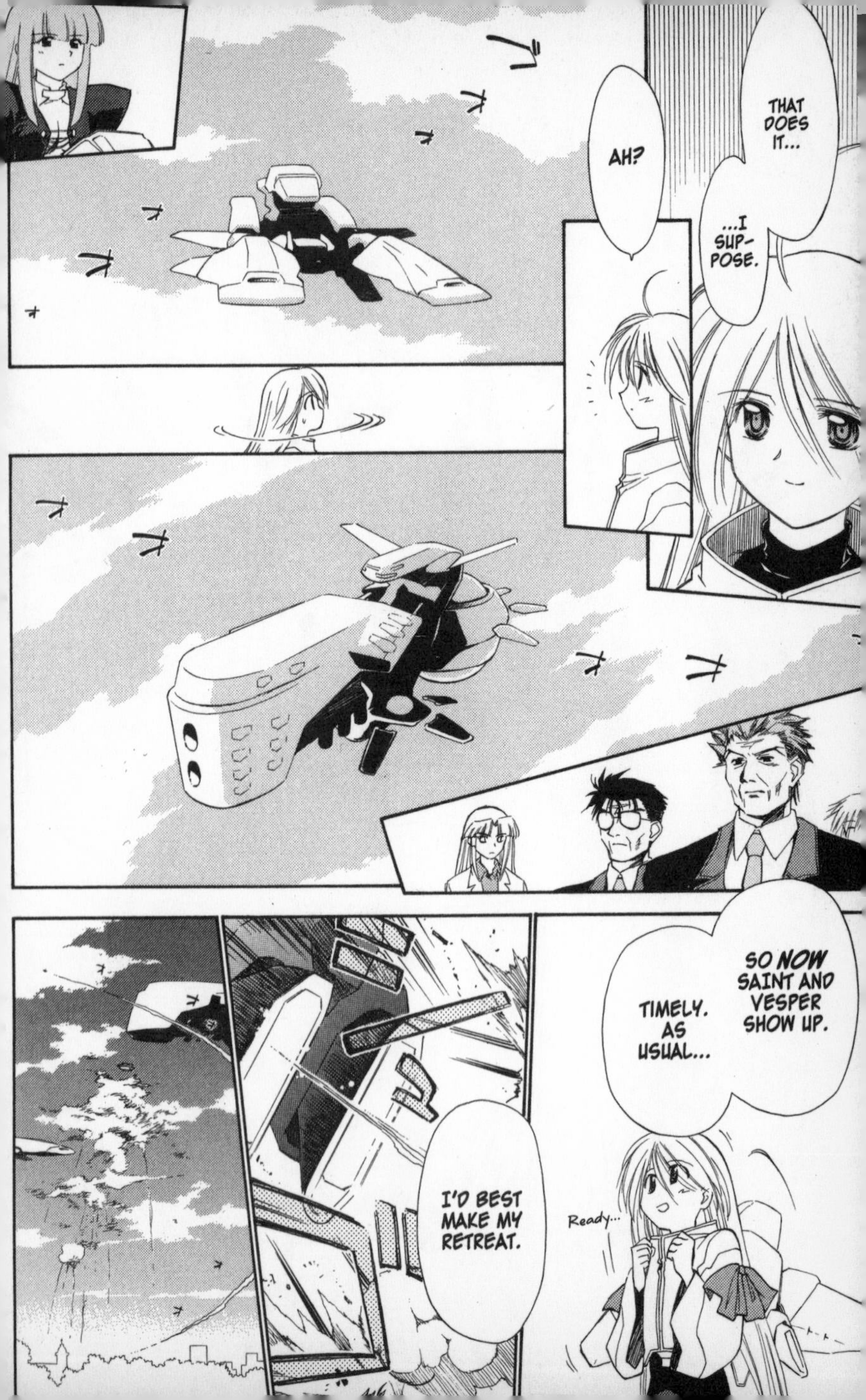
THAT DOES IT...
AH?
...I SUPPOSE.
SO NOW SAINT AND VESPER SHOW UP.
TIMELY. AS USUAL...
Ready...
I'D BEST MAKE MY RETREAT.

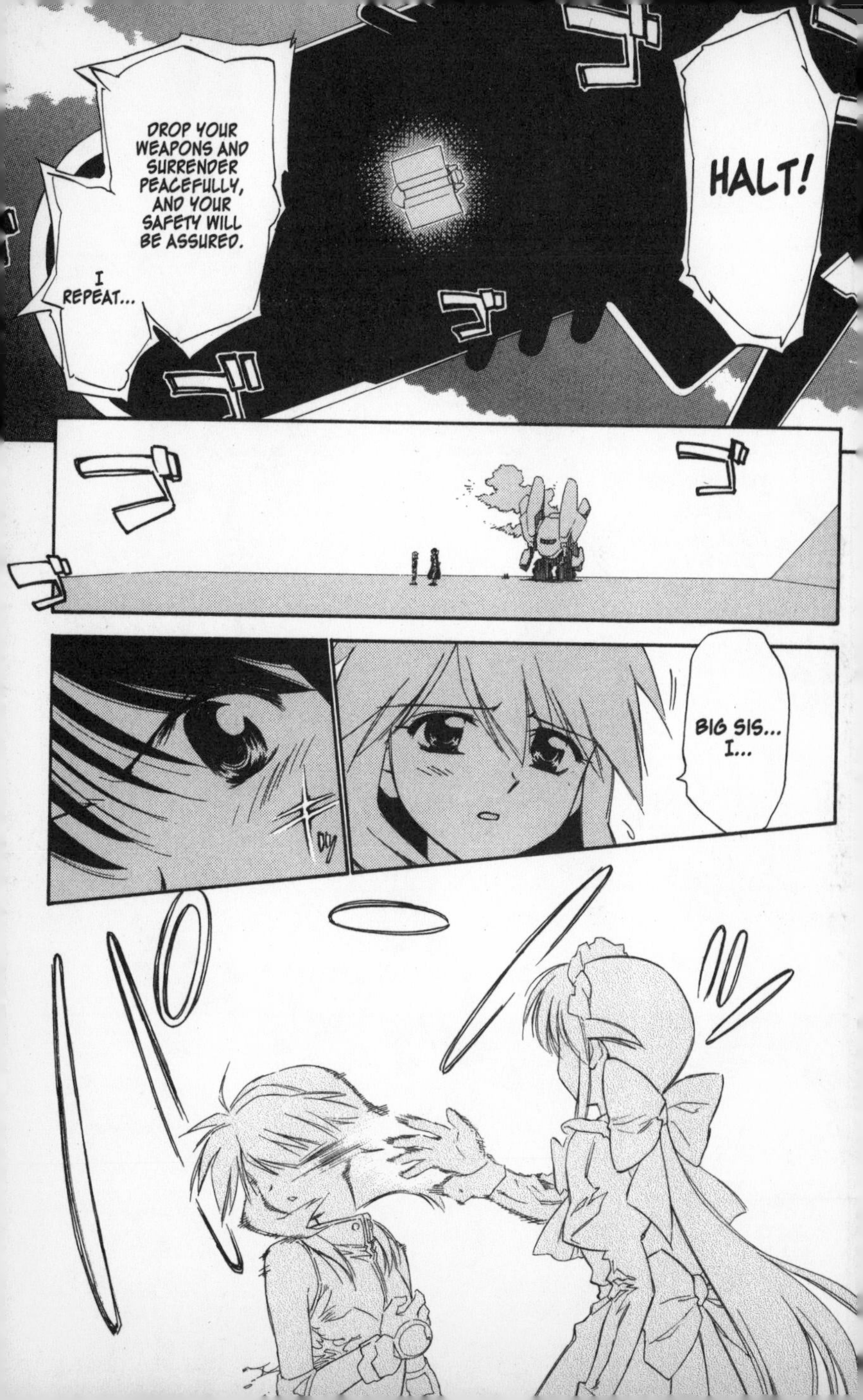
HALT!
DROP YOUR WEAPONS AND SURRENDER PEACEFULLY, AND YOUR SAFETY WILL BE ASSURED.
I REPEAT...
BIG SIS... I...

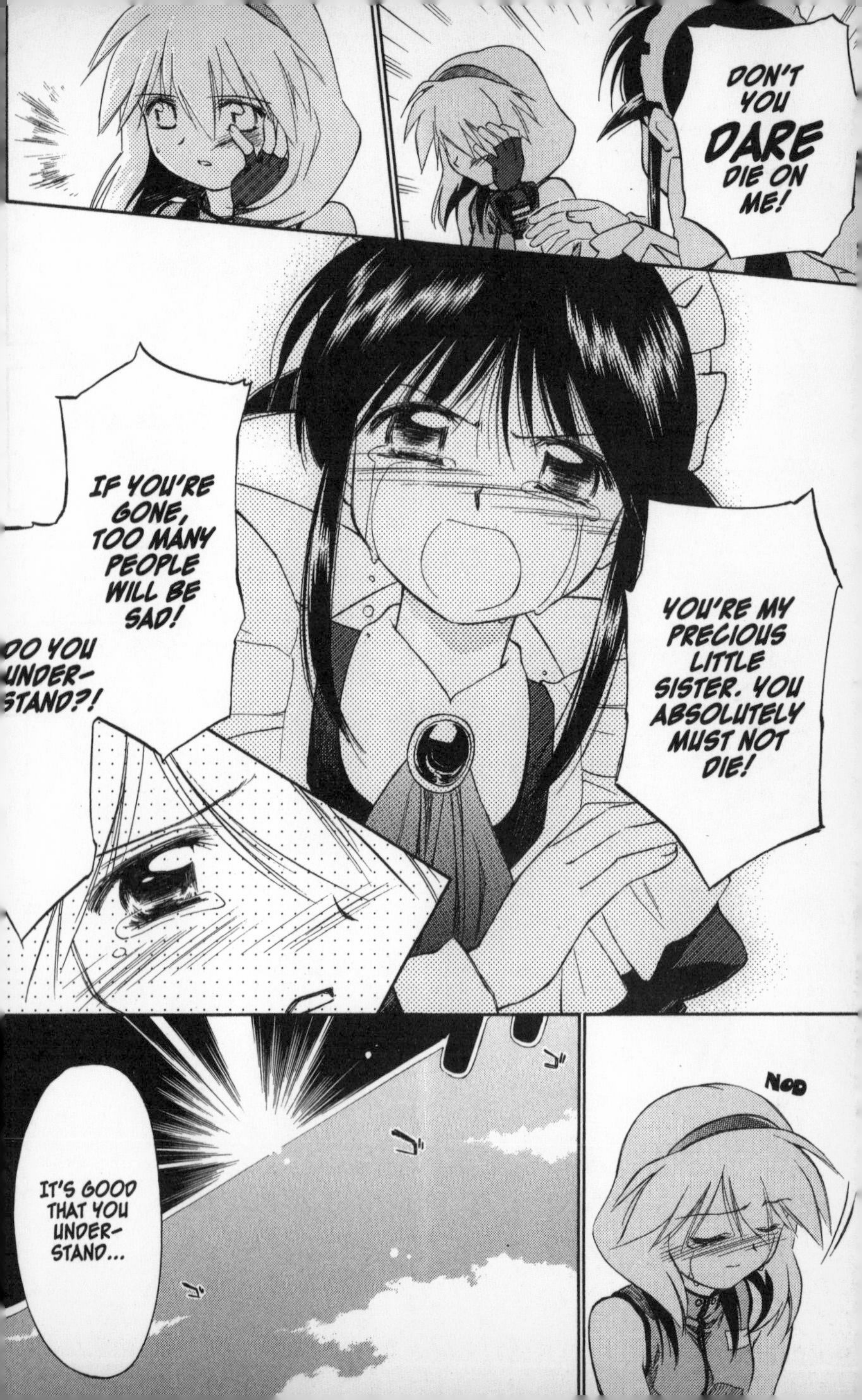

DON'T YOU DARE DIE ON ME!
YOU'RE MY PRECIOUS LITTLE SISTER. YOU ABSOLUTELY MUST NOT DIE!
IF YOU'RE GONE, TOO MANY PEOPLE WILL BE SAD!
DO YOU UNDER-STAND?!
NOD
IT'S GOOD THAT YOU UNDER-STAND...

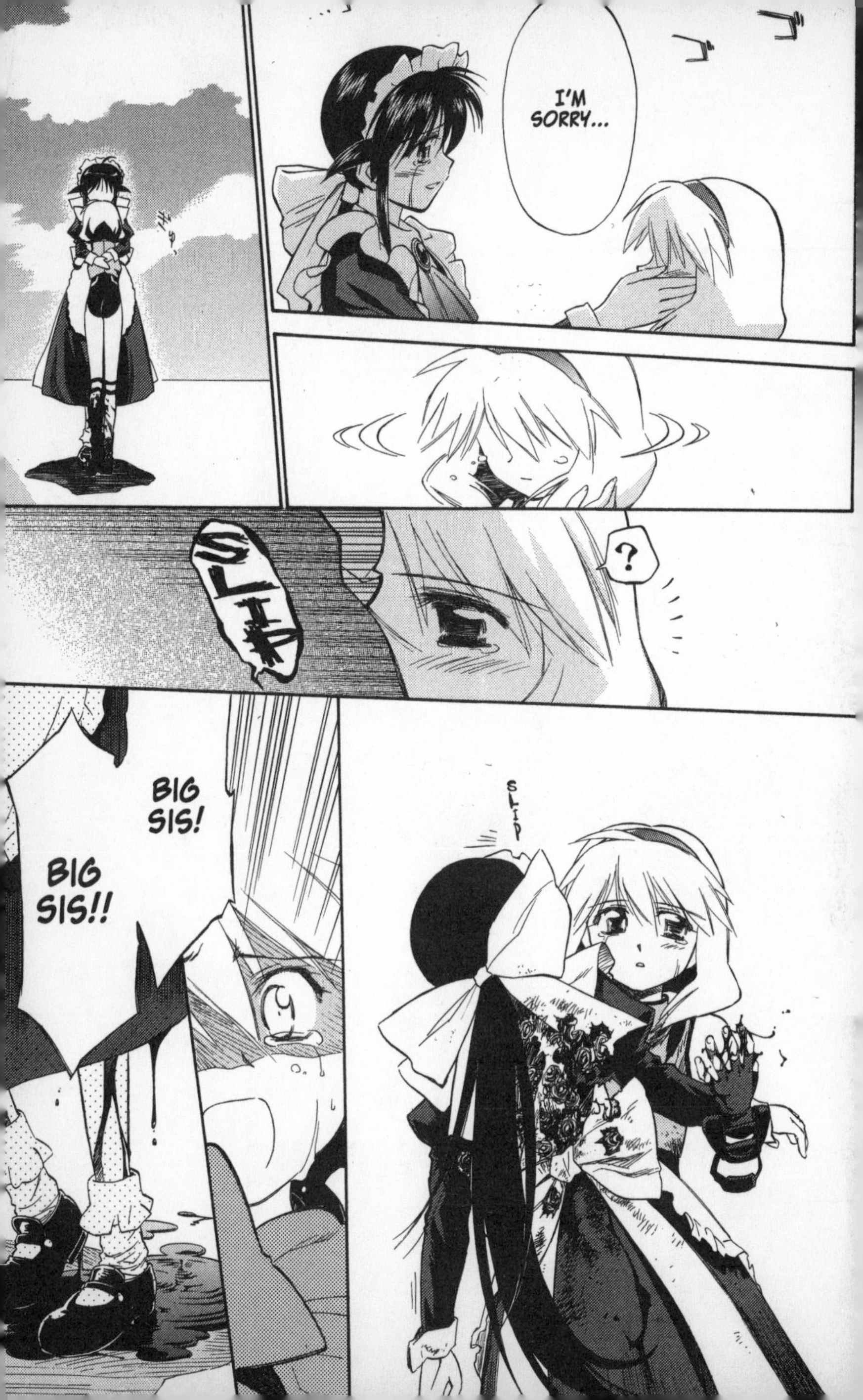
I'M SORRY...
?
SLIP
BIG SIS!
BIG SIS!!

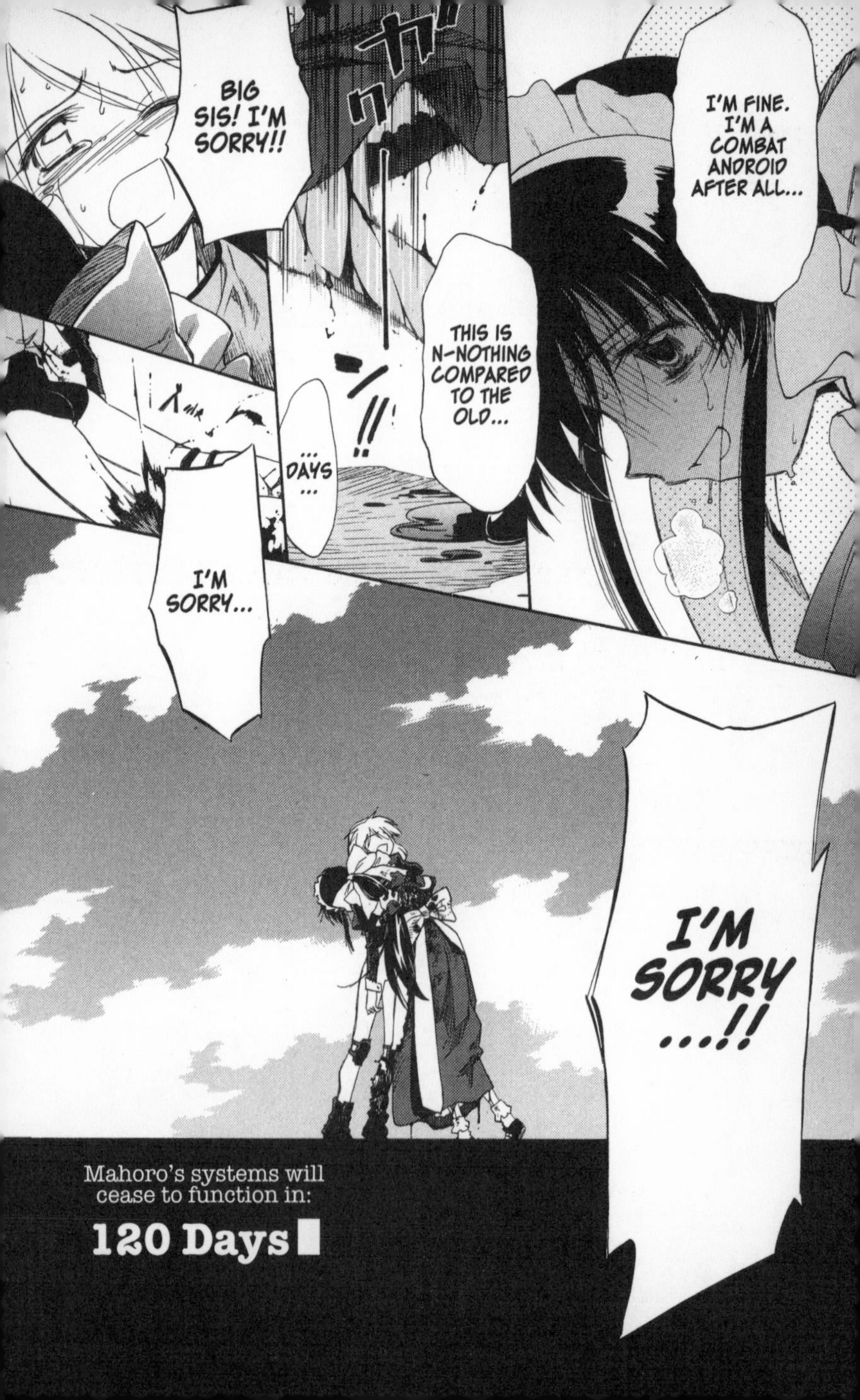
I'M FINE. I'M A COMBAT ANDROID AFTER ALL...
THIS IS N-NOTHING COMPARED TO THE OLD...
...DAYS...
BIG SIS! I'M SORRY!!
I'M SORRY...
I'M SORRY...!!
Mahoro's systems will cease to function in:
120 Days

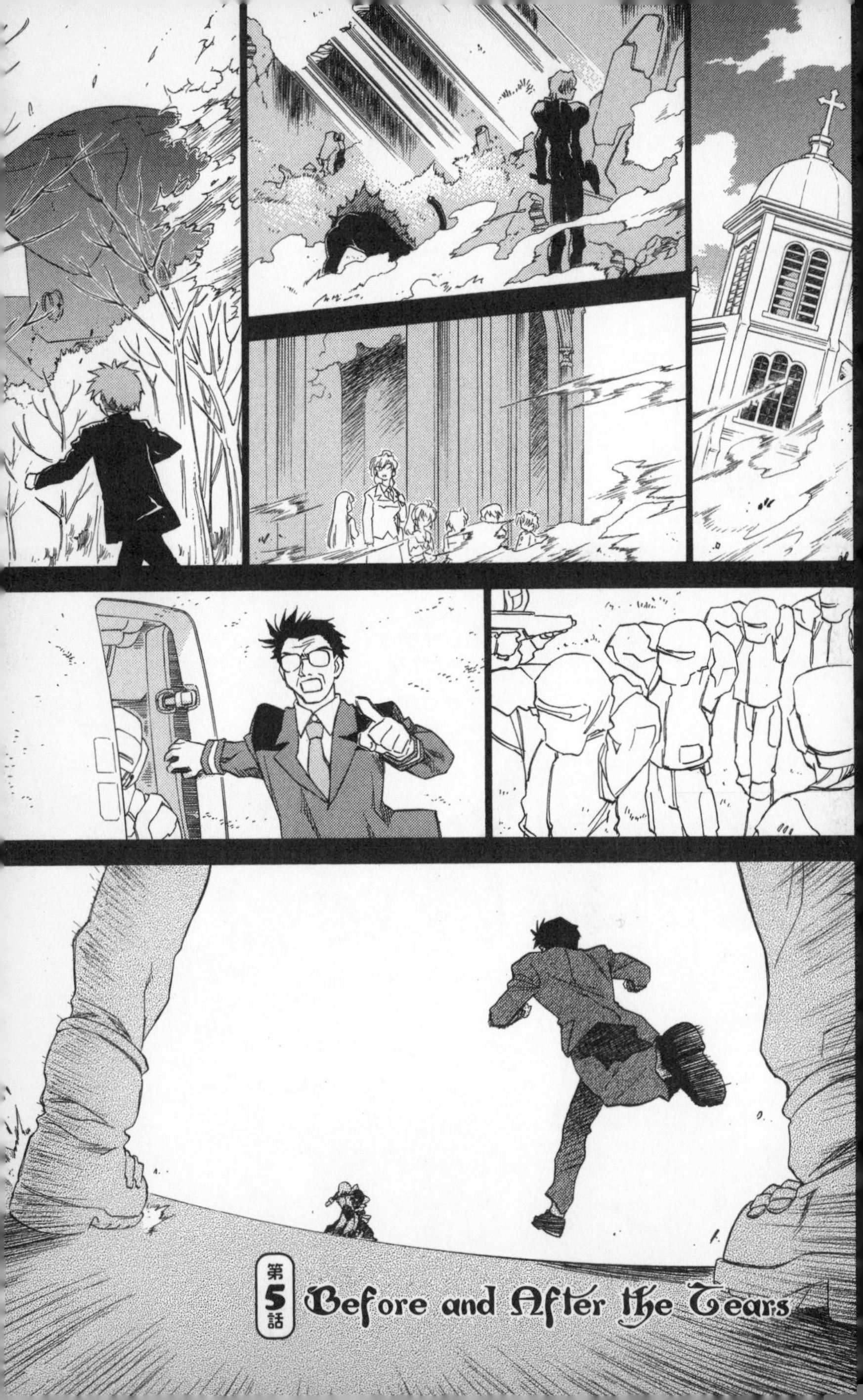
第5話 Before and After the Tears

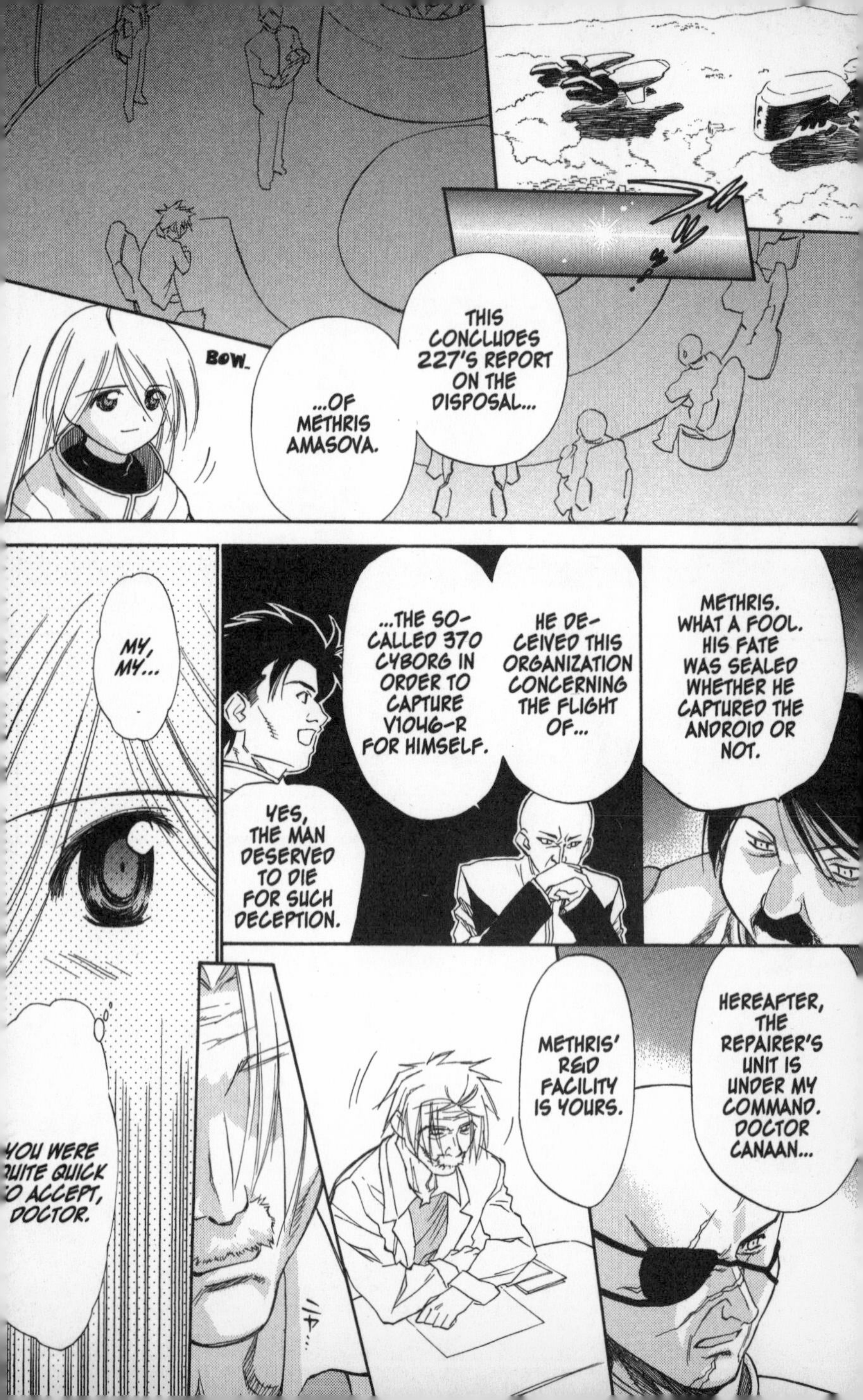
THIS CONCLUDES 227'S REPORT ON THE DISPOSAL...
...OF METHRIS AMASOVA.
BOW_
METHRIS. WHAT A FOOL. HIS FATE WAS SEALED WHETHER HE CAPTURED THE ANDROID OR NOT.
HE DE- CEIVED THIS ORGANIZATION CONCERNING THE FLIGHT OF...
...THE SO- CALLED 370 CYBORG IN ORDER TO CAPTURE V1046-R FOR HIMSELF.
YES, THE MAN DESERVED TO DIE FOR SUCH DECEPTION.
HEREAFTER, THE REPAIRER'S UNIT IS UNDER MY COMMAND. DOCTOR CANAAN...
METHRIS' R&D FACILITY IS YOURS.
MY, MY...
YOU WERE QUITE QUICK TO ACCEPT, DOCTOR.

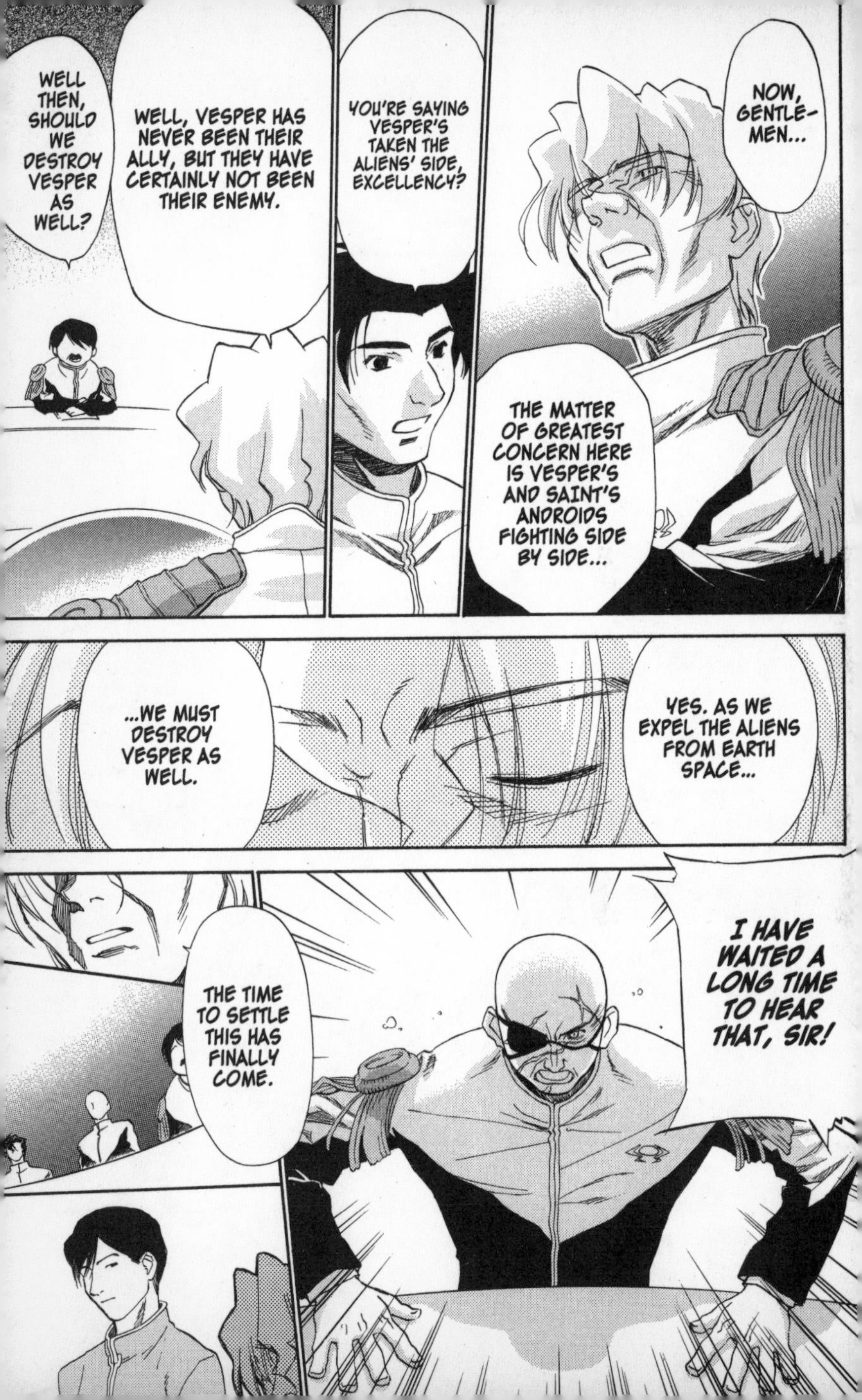
NOW, GENTLE-MEN...
THE MATTER OF GREATEST CONCERN HERE IS VESPER'S AND SAINT'S ANDROIDS FIGHTING SIDE BY SIDE...
YOU'RE SAYING VESPER'S TAKEN THE ALIENS' SIDE, EXCELLENCY?
WELL, VESPER HAS NEVER BEEN THEIR ALLY, BUT THEY HAVE CERTAINLY NOT BEEN THEIR ENEMY.
WELL THEN, SHOULD WE DESTROY VESPER AS WELL?
YES. AS WE EXPEL THE ALIENS FROM EARTH SPACE...
...WE MUST DESTROY VESPER AS WELL.
I HAVE WAITED A LONG TIME TO HEAR THAT, SIR!
THE TIME TO SETTLE THIS HAS FINALLY COME.

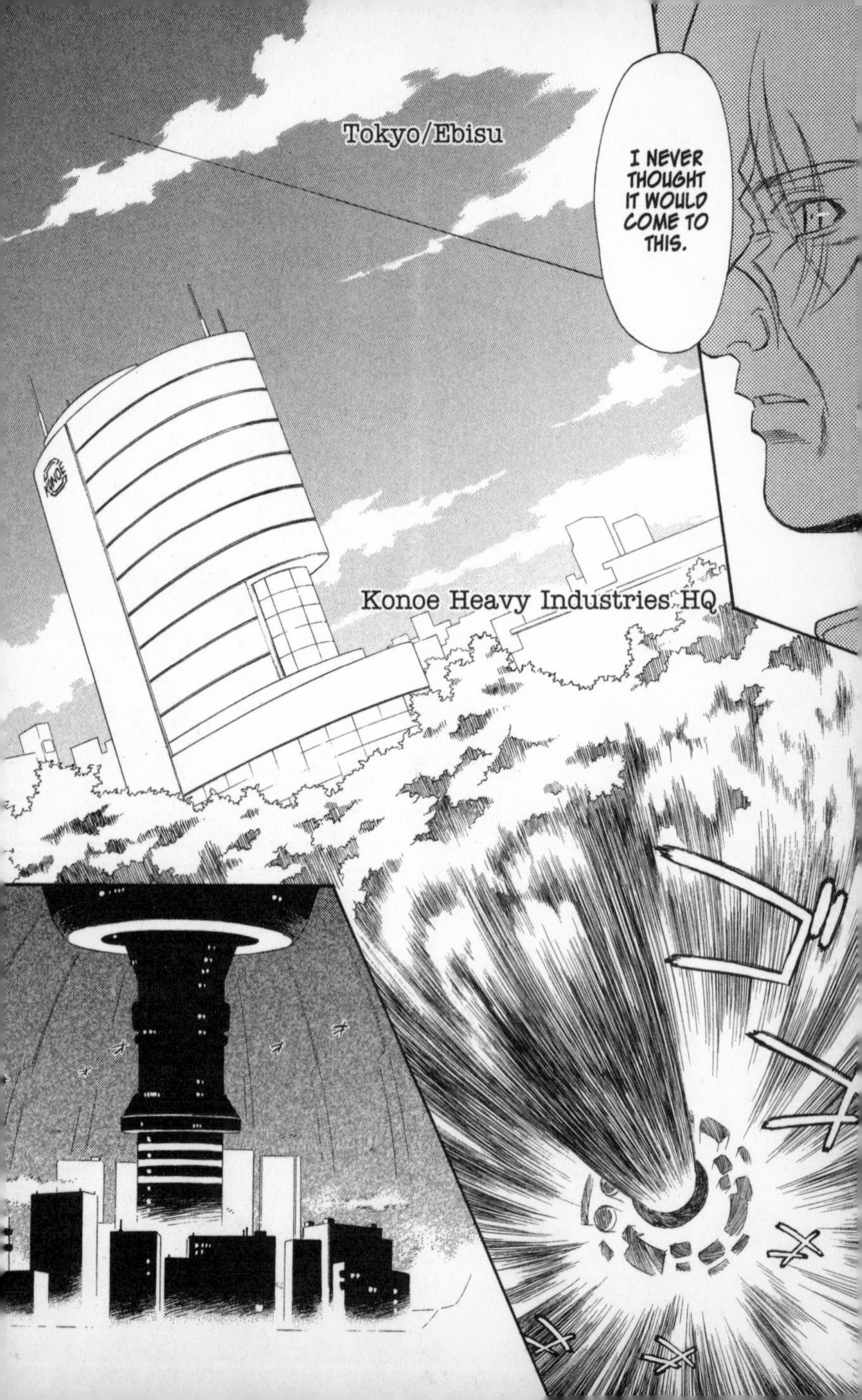
I NEVER THOUGHT IT WOULD COME TO THIS.
Tokyo/Ebisu
Konoe Heavy Industries HQ
KONOE

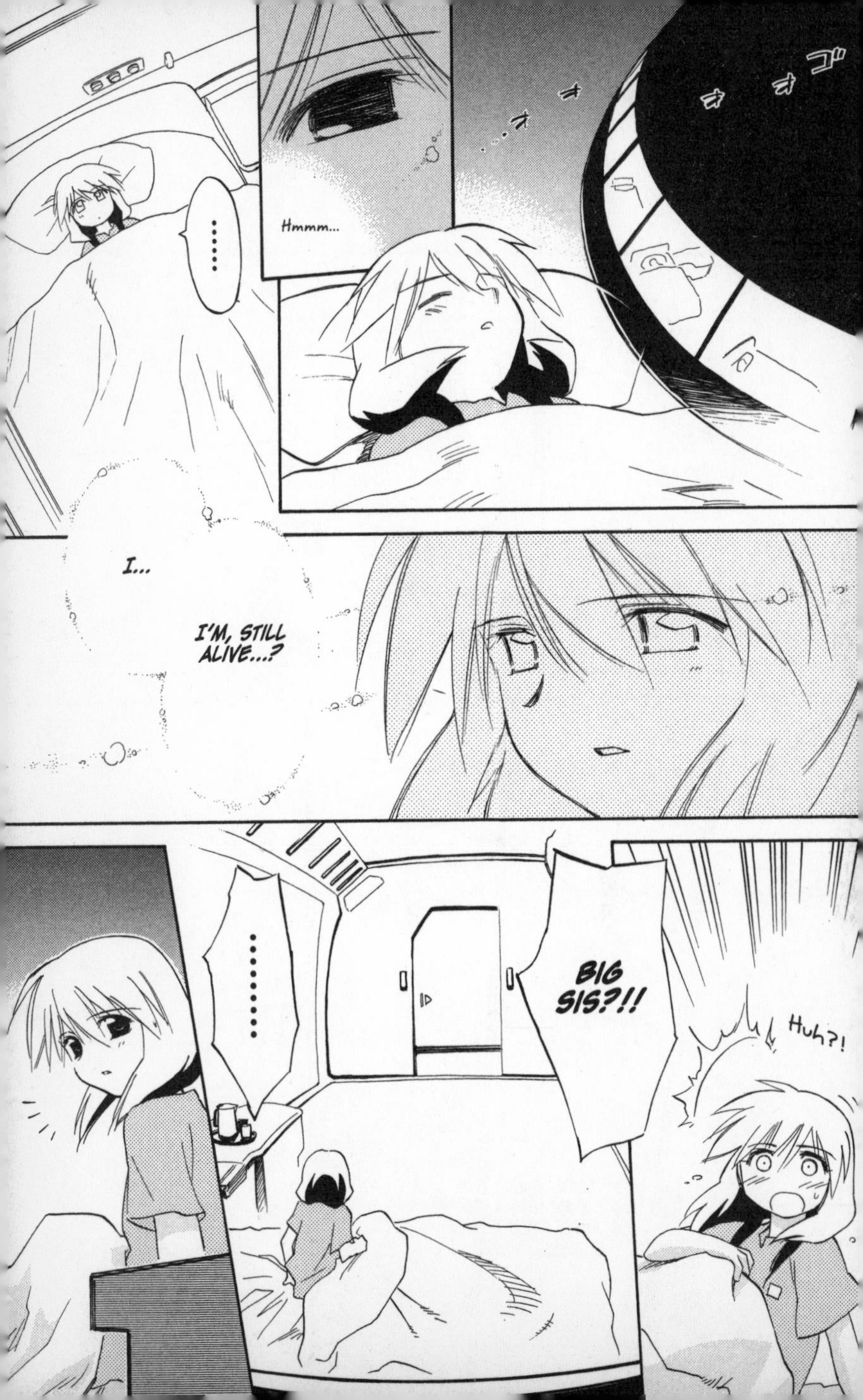

ゴオオ
オオ...
Hmmm...
......
I...
I'M, STILL ALIVE...?
Huh?!
BIG SIS?!!
....

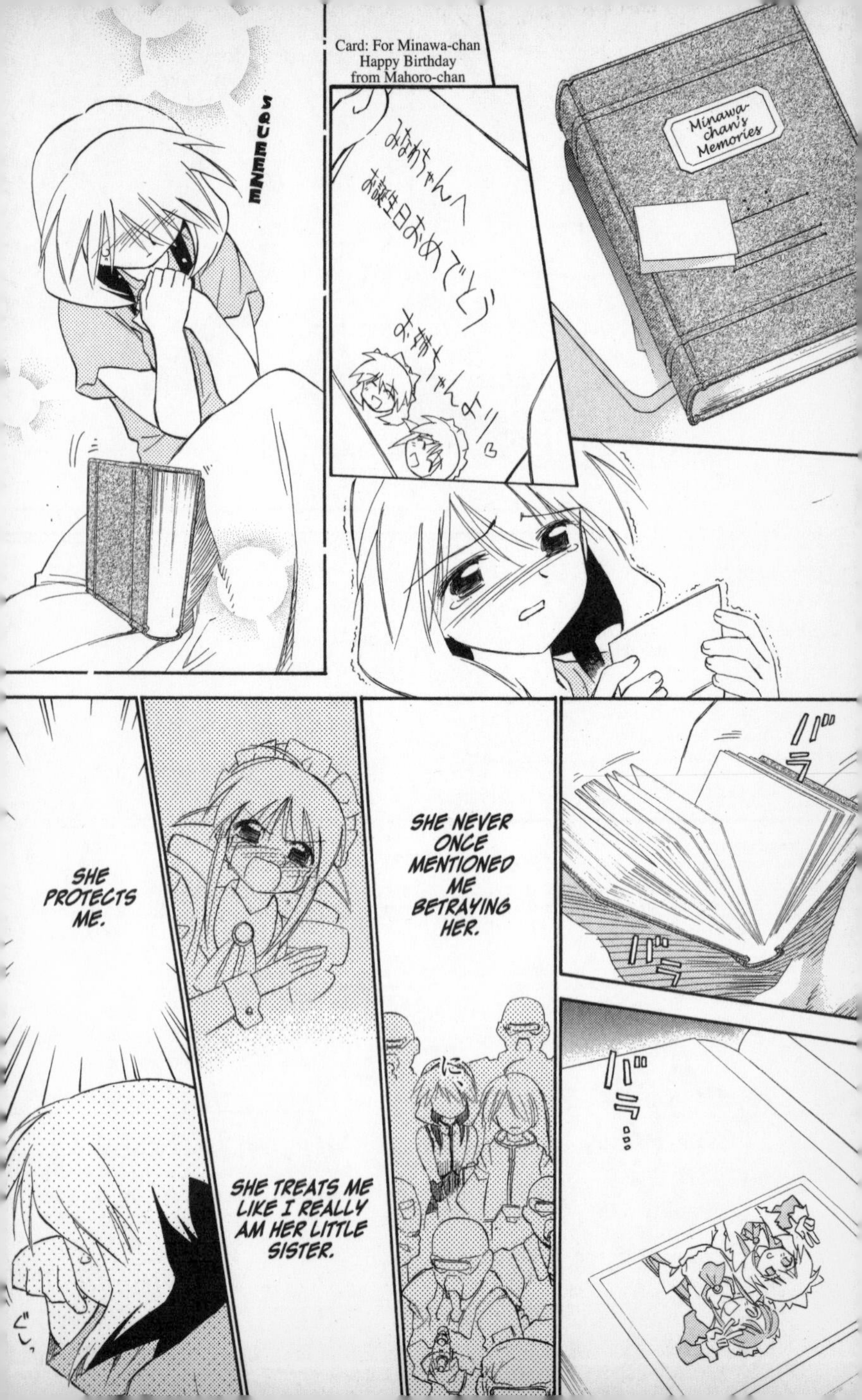
Minawa-chan's Memories
Card: For Minawa-chan
Happy Birthday
from Mahoro-chan
みなわちゃんへ
お誕生日おめでとう
お姉ちゃんより
SQUEEEEE
パラ
パラ
パラ…
SHE NEVER ONCE MENTIONED ME BETRAYING HER.
SHE TREATS ME LIKE I REALLY AM HER LITTLE SISTER.
SHE PROTECTS ME.
ぐしっ

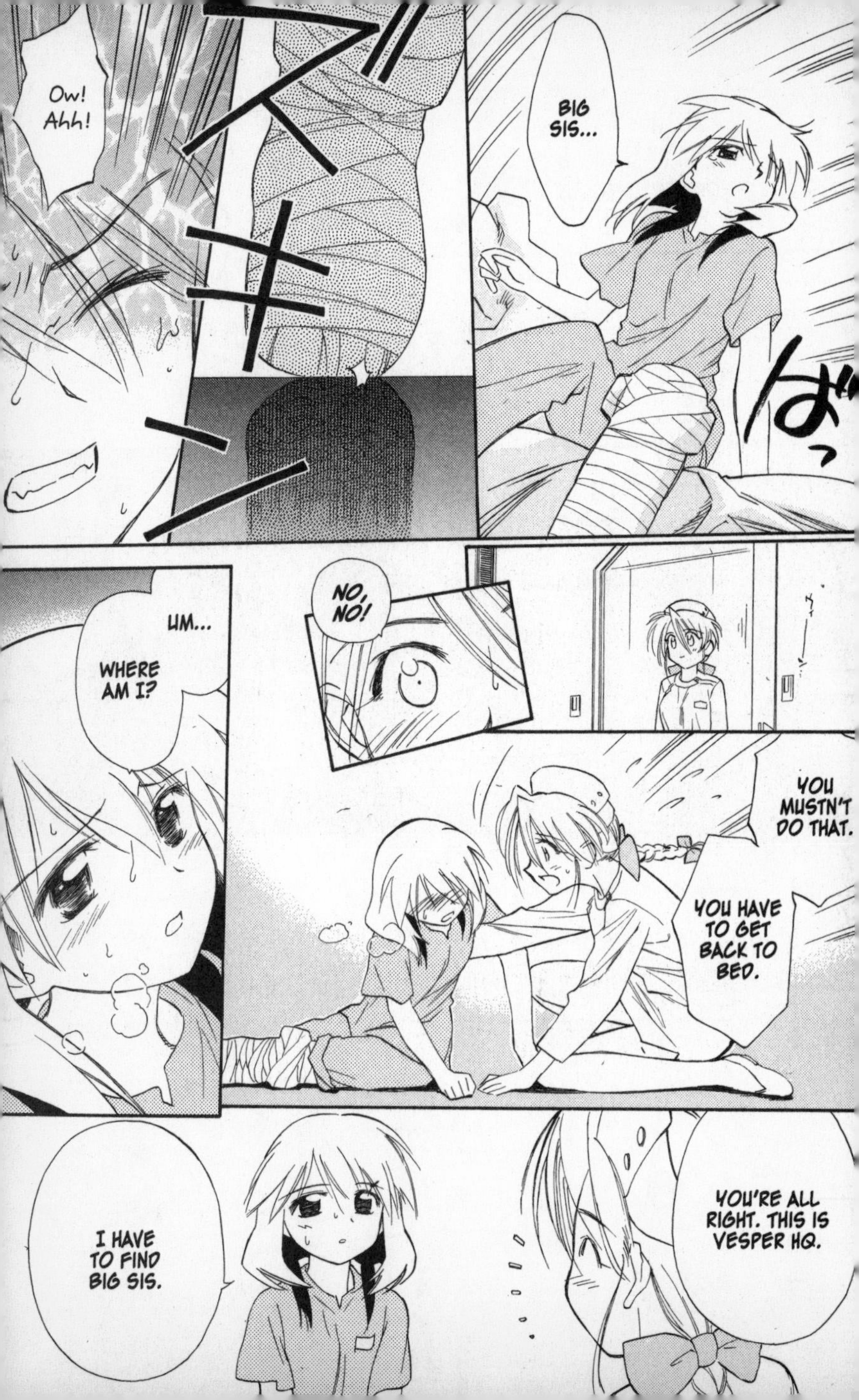
BIG SIS...
ぱっ
Ow! Ahh!
NO, NO!
YOU MUSTN'T DO THAT.
YOU HAVE TO GET BACK TO BED.
UM...
WHERE AM I?
YOU'RE ALL RIGHT. THIS IS VESPER HQ.
I HAVE TO FIND BIG SIS.

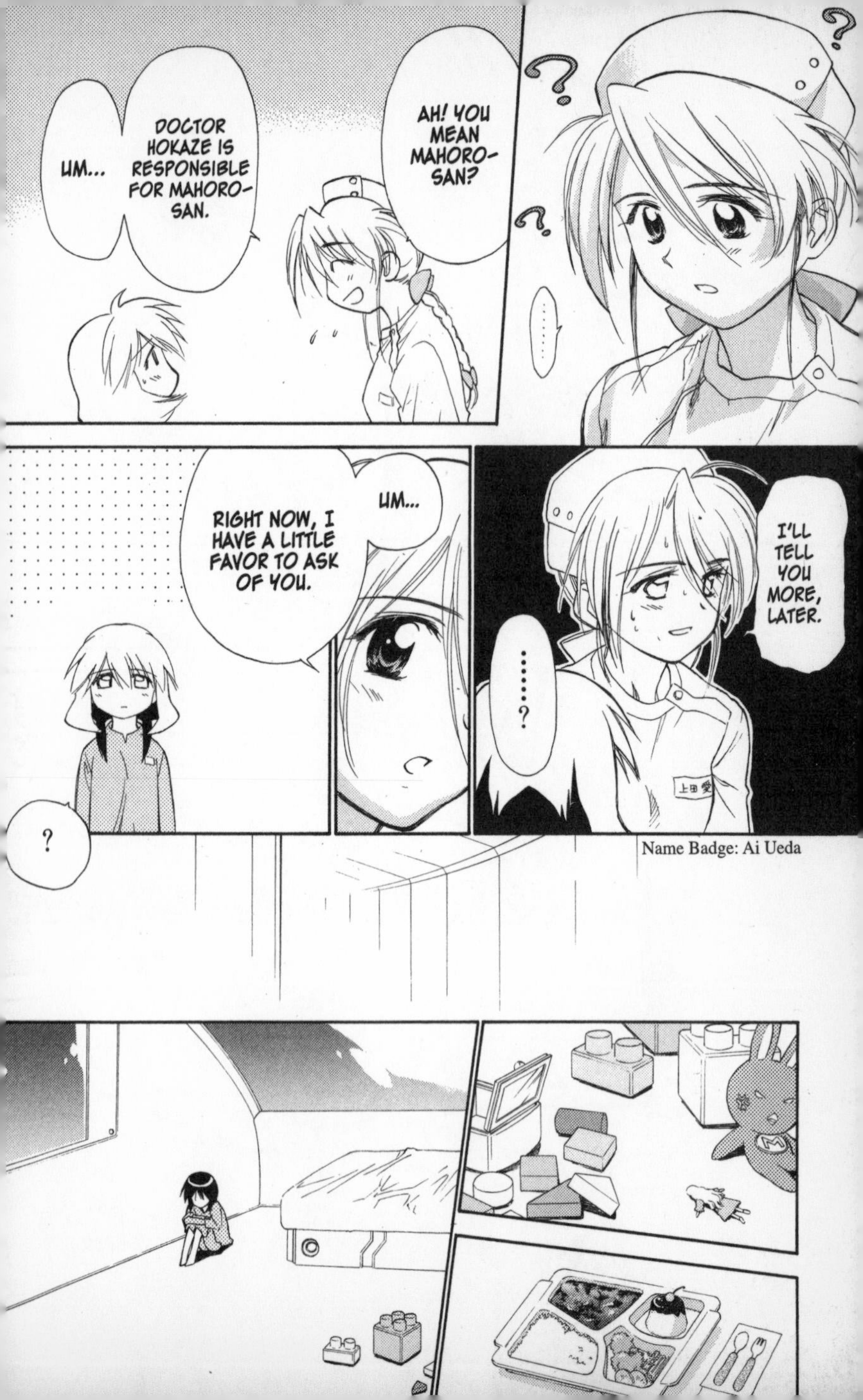

?
?
?
......
AH! YOU MEAN MAHORO-SAN?
UM...
DOCTOR HOKAZE IS RESPONSIBLE FOR MAHORO-SAN.
I'LL TELL YOU MORE, LATER.
......?
UM...
RIGHT NOW, I HAVE A LITTLE FAVOR TO ASK OF YOU.
?
上田愛

Name Badge: Ai Ueda

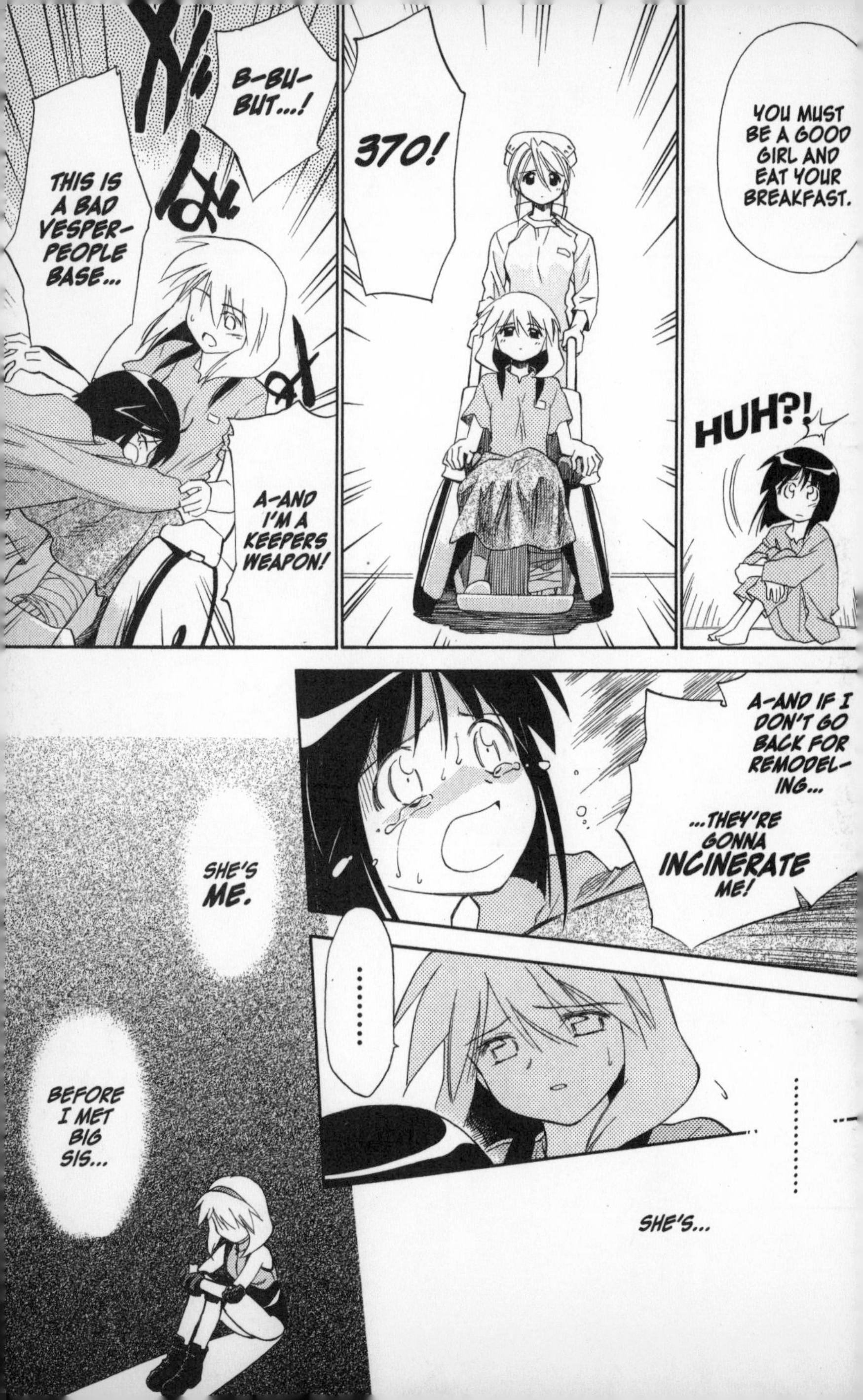
YOU MUST BE A GOOD GIRL AND EAT YOUR BREAKFAST.
HUH?!
370!
B-BU-BUT...!
THIS IS A BAD VESPER-PEOPLE BASE...
A-AND I'M A KEEPERS WEAPON!
A-AND IF I DON'T GO BACK FOR REMODEL-ING...
...THEY'RE GONNA INCINERATE ME!
......
......
SHE'S...
SHE'S ME.
BEFORE I MET BIG SIS...

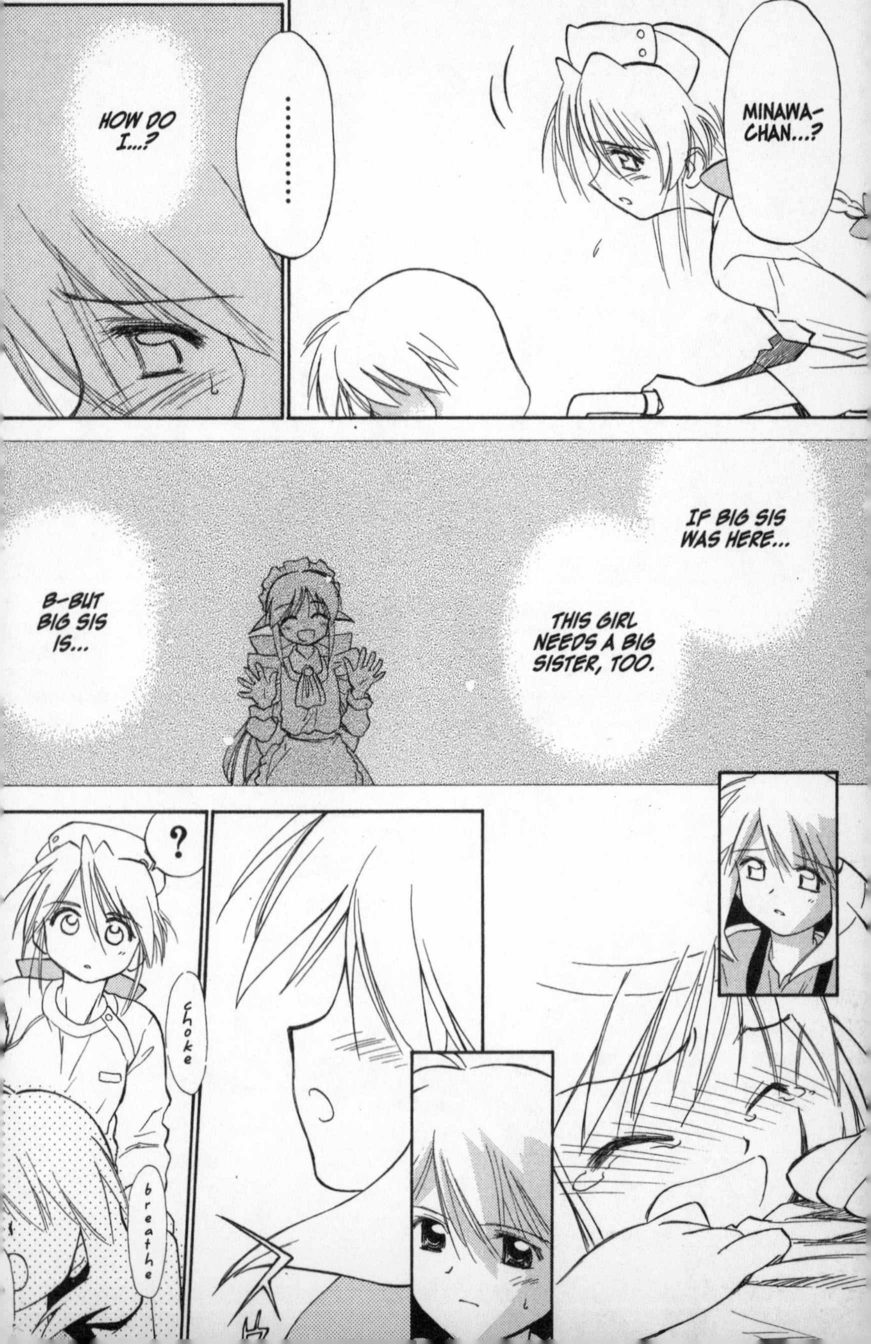
MINAWA-CHAN...?
......
HOW DO I...?
IF BIG SIS WAS HERE...
THIS GIRL NEEDS A BIG SISTER, TOO.
B-BUT BIG SIS IS...
?
choke
breathe

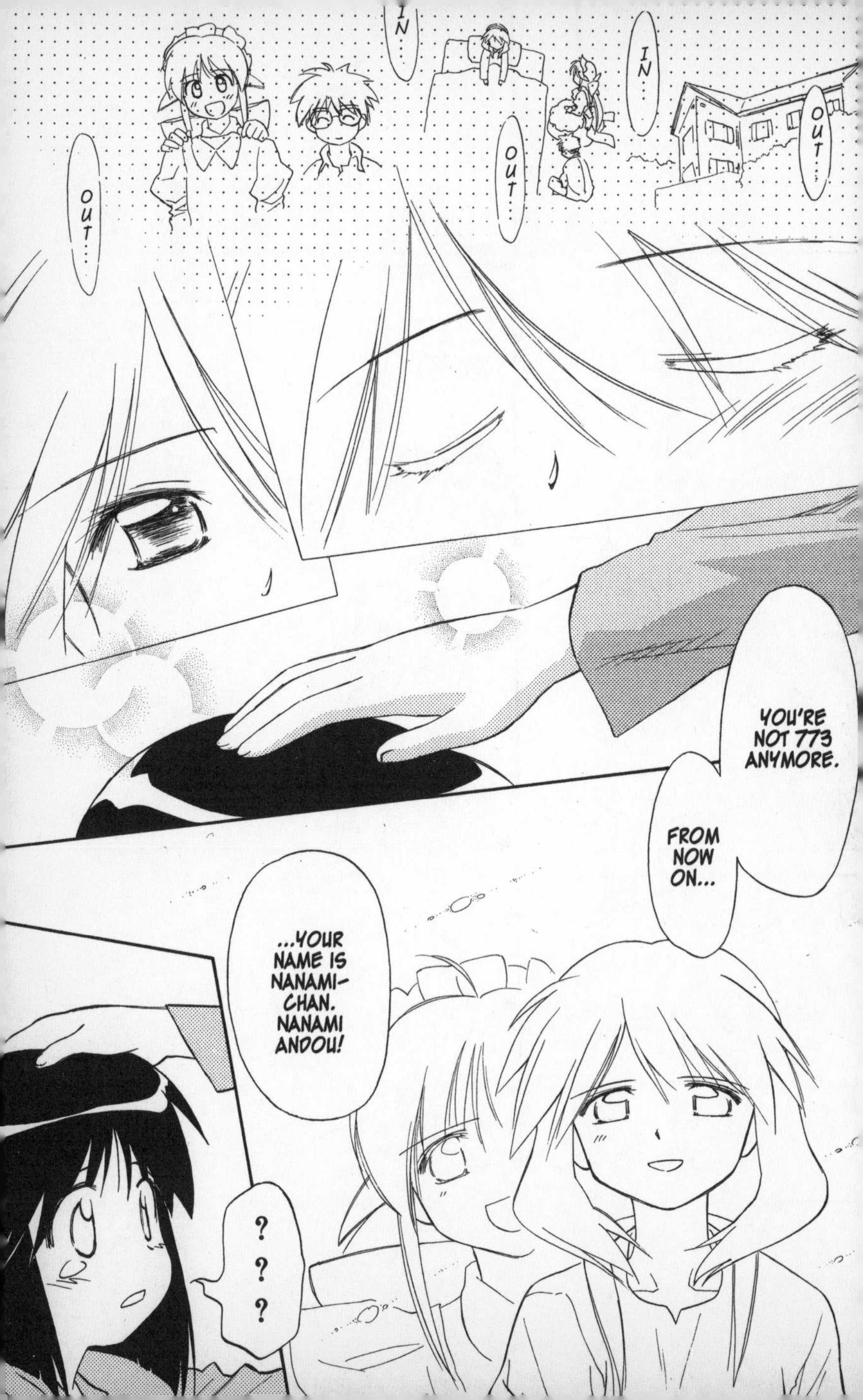
OUT...
IN...
OUT...
IN...
OUT...
YOU'RE NOT 773 ANYMORE.
FROM NOW ON...
...YOUR NAME IS NANAMI-CHAN. NANAMI ANDOU!
???

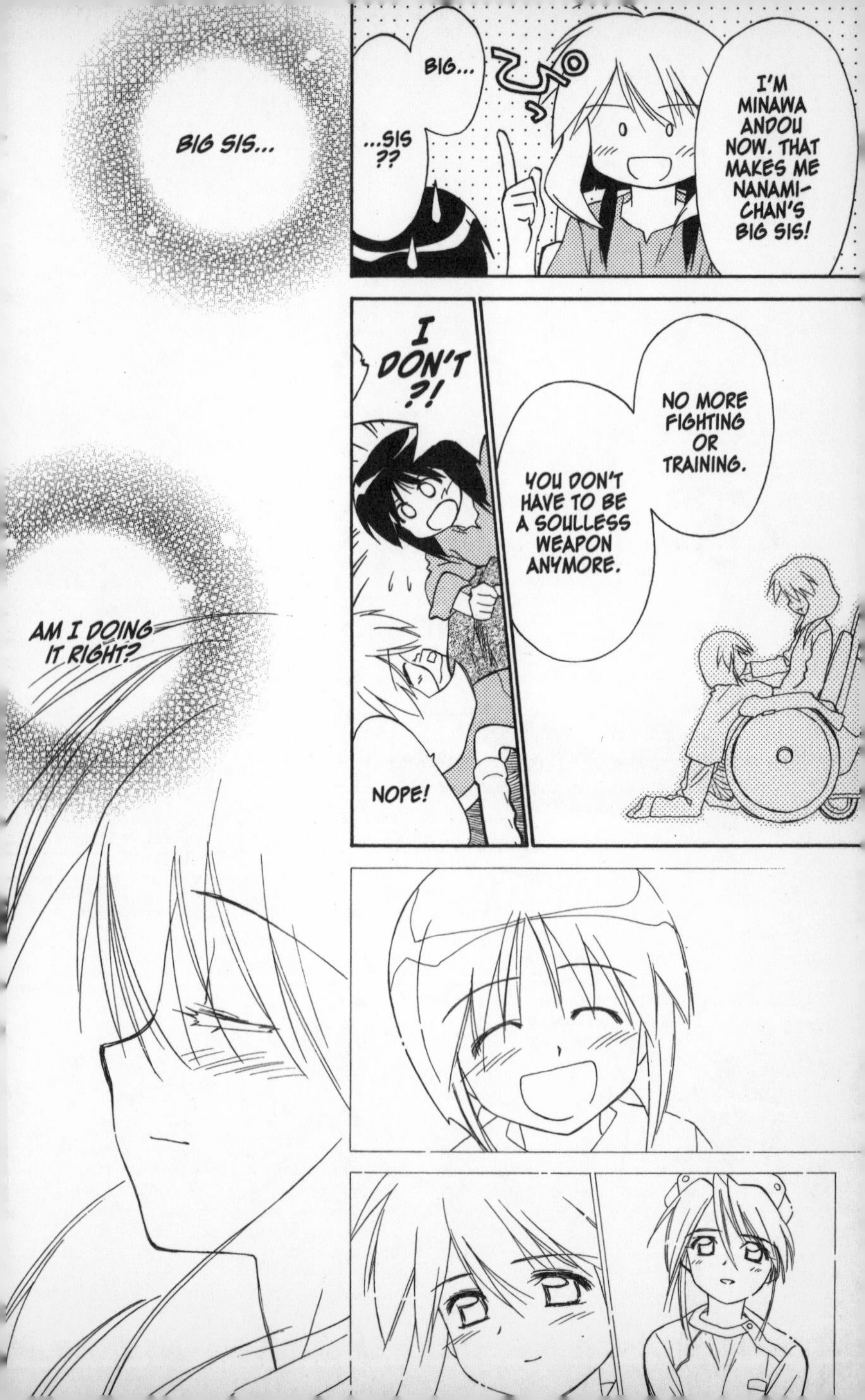
I'M MINAWA ANDOU NOW. THAT MAKES ME NANAMI-CHAN'S BIG SIS!
BIG...
...SIS ??
NO MORE FIGHTING OR TRAINING.
YOU DON'T HAVE TO BE A SOULLESS WEAPON ANYMORE.
I DON'T ?!
NOPE!
BIG SIS...
AM I DOING IT RIGHT?

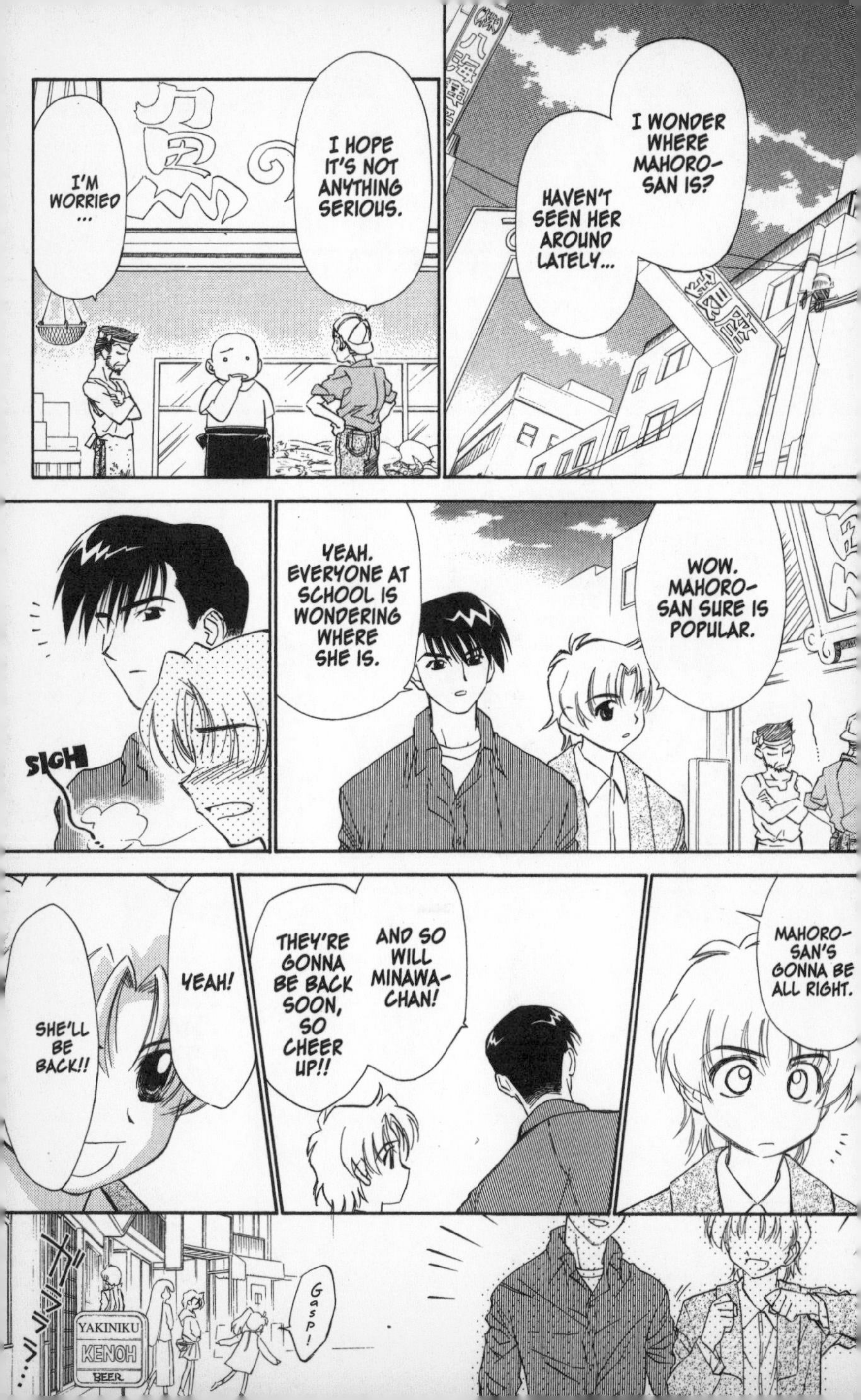
I WONDER WHERE MAHORO-SAN IS?
HAVEN'T SEEN HER AROUND LATELY...
I HOPE IT'S NOT ANYTHING SERIOUS.
I'M WORRIED ...
WOW. MAHORO-SAN SURE IS POPULAR.
YEAH. EVERYONE AT SCHOOL IS WONDERING WHERE SHE IS.
SIGH
MAHORO-SAN'S GONNA BE ALL RIGHT.
AND SO WILL MINAWA-CHAN!
THEY'RE GONNA BE BACK SOON, SO CHEER UP!!
YEAH!
SHE'LL BE BACK!!
Gasp!
YAKINIKU
KENOH
BEER

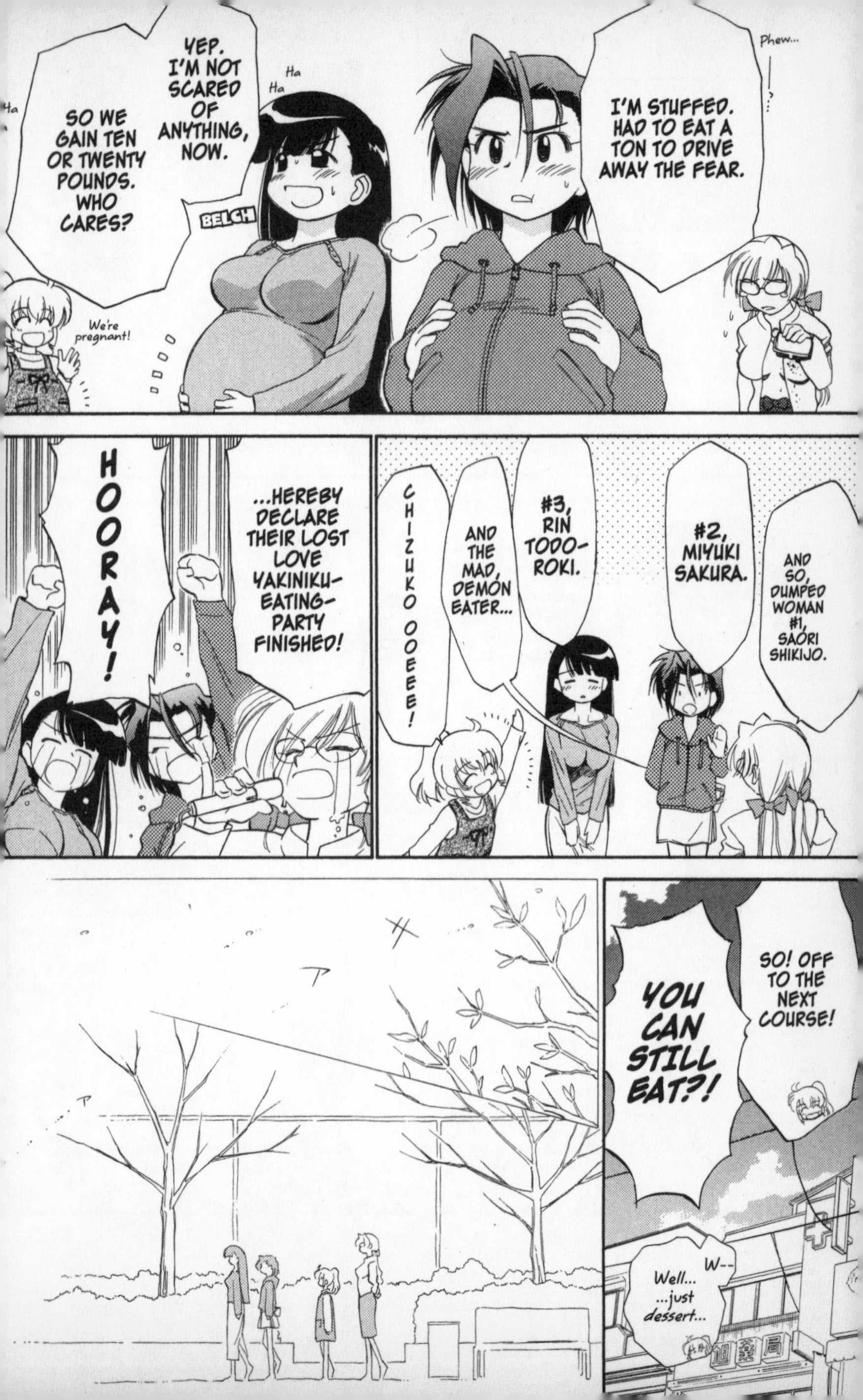
Phew...
I'M STUFFED. HAD TO EAT A TON TO DRIVE AWAY THE FEAR.
YEP. I'M NOT SCARED OF ANYTHING, NOW.
Ha
Ha
BELCH
SO WE GAIN TEN OR TWENTY POUNDS. WHO CARES?
Ha
We're pregnant!
AND SO, DUMPED WOMAN #1, SAORI SHIKIJO.
#2, MIYUKI SAKURA.
#3, RIN TODO-ROKI.
AND THE MAD, DEMON EATER...
CHIZUKO OOEEE!
...HEREBY DECLARE THEIR LOST LOVE YAKINIKU-EATING-PARTY FINISHED!
HOORAY!
SO! OFF TO THE NEXT COURSE!
YOU CAN STILL EAT?!
W--
Well... ...just dessert...

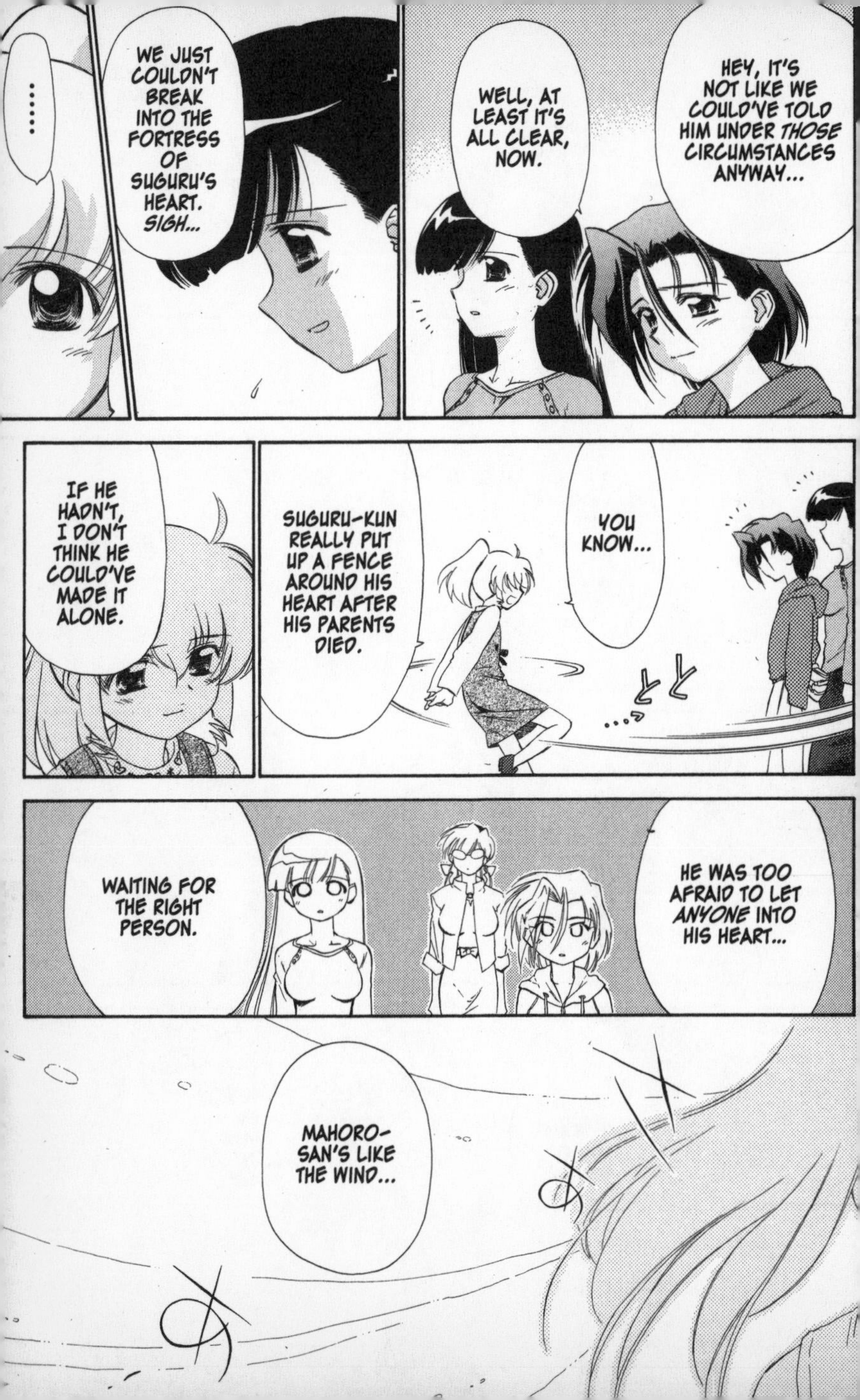
HEY, IT'S NOT LIKE WE COULD'VE TOLD HIM UNDER *THOSE* CIRCUMSTANCES ANYWAY...
WELL, AT LEAST IT'S ALL CLEAR, NOW.
WE JUST COULDN'T BREAK INTO THE FORTRESS OF SUGURU'S HEART. *SIGH...*
......
YOU KNOW...
とと
SUGURU-KUN REALLY PUT UP A FENCE AROUND HIS HEART AFTER HIS PARENTS DIED.
IF HE HADN'T, I DON'T THINK HE COULD'VE MADE IT ALONE.
HE WAS TOO AFRAID TO LET *ANYONE* INTO HIS HEART...
WAITING FOR THE RIGHT PERSON.
MAHORO-SAN'S LIKE THE WIND...

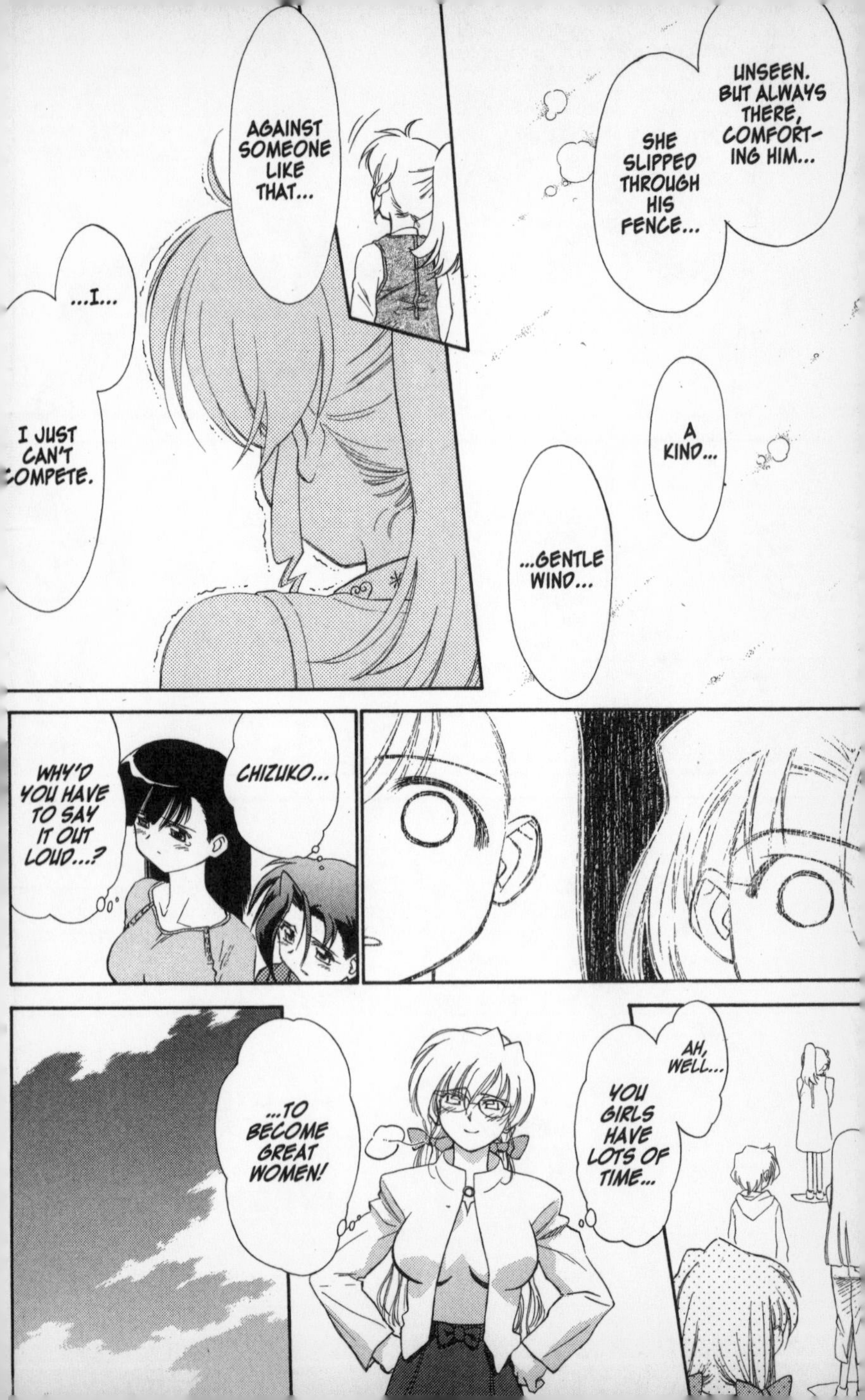

SHE SLIPPED THROUGH HIS FENCE...
UNSEEN. BUT ALWAYS THERE, COMFORTING HIM...
A KIND...
...GENTLE WIND...
AGAINST SOMEONE LIKE THAT...
...I...
I JUST CAN'T COMPETE.
CHIZUKO...
WHY'D YOU HAVE TO SAY IT OUT LOUD...?
AH, WELL...
YOU GIRLS HAVE LOTS OF TIME...
...TO BECOME GREAT WOMEN!

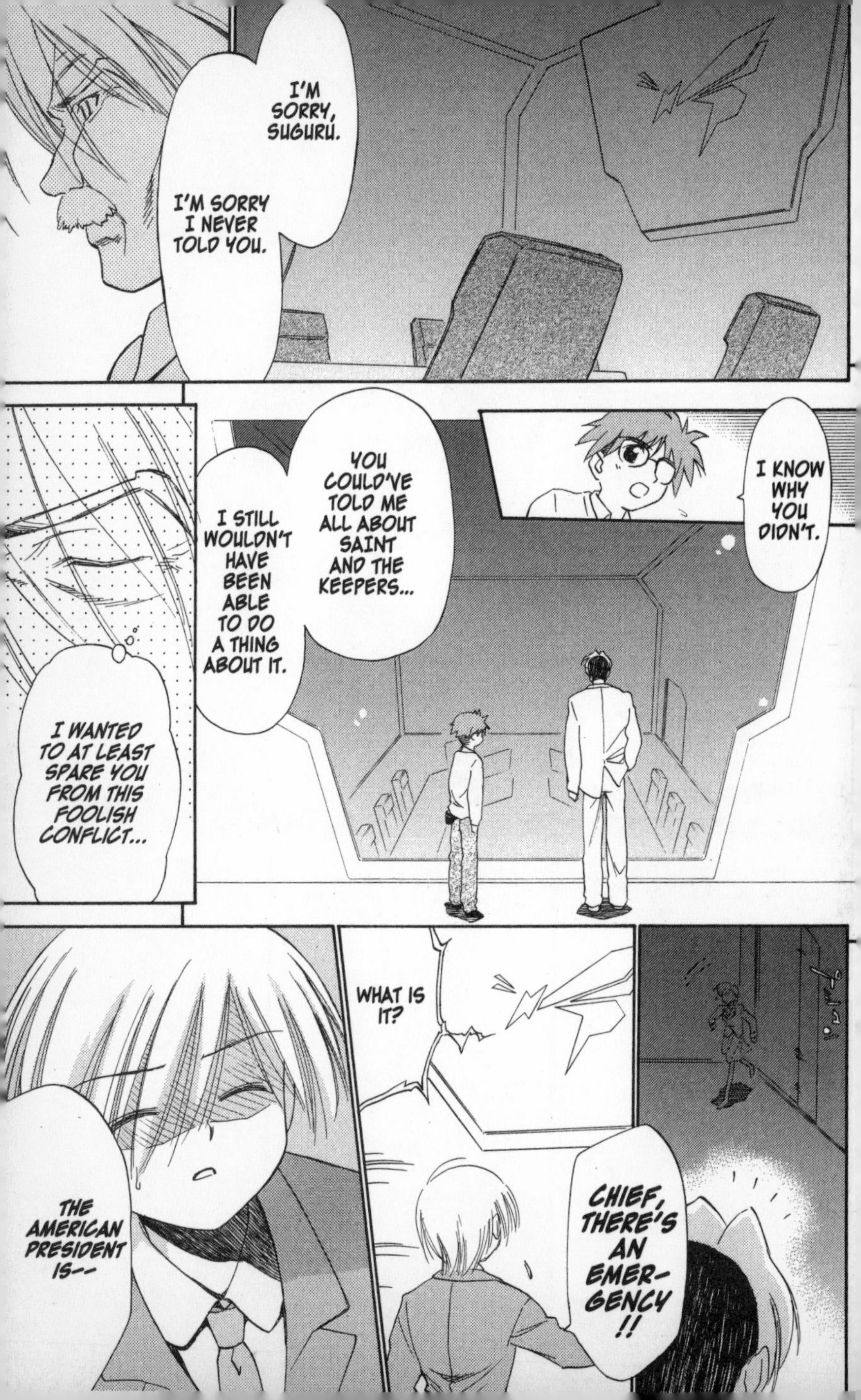
I'M SORRY, SUGURU.
I'M SORRY I NEVER TOLD YOU.
I KNOW WHY YOU DIDN'T.
YOU COULD'VE TOLD ME ALL ABOUT SAINT AND THE KEEPERS...
I STILL WOULDN'T HAVE BEEN ABLE TO DO A THING ABOUT IT.
I WANTED TO AT LEAST SPARE YOU FROM THIS FOOLISH CONFLICT...
CHIEF, THERE'S AN EMERGENCY!!
WHAT IS IT?
THE AMERICAN PRESIDENT IS--

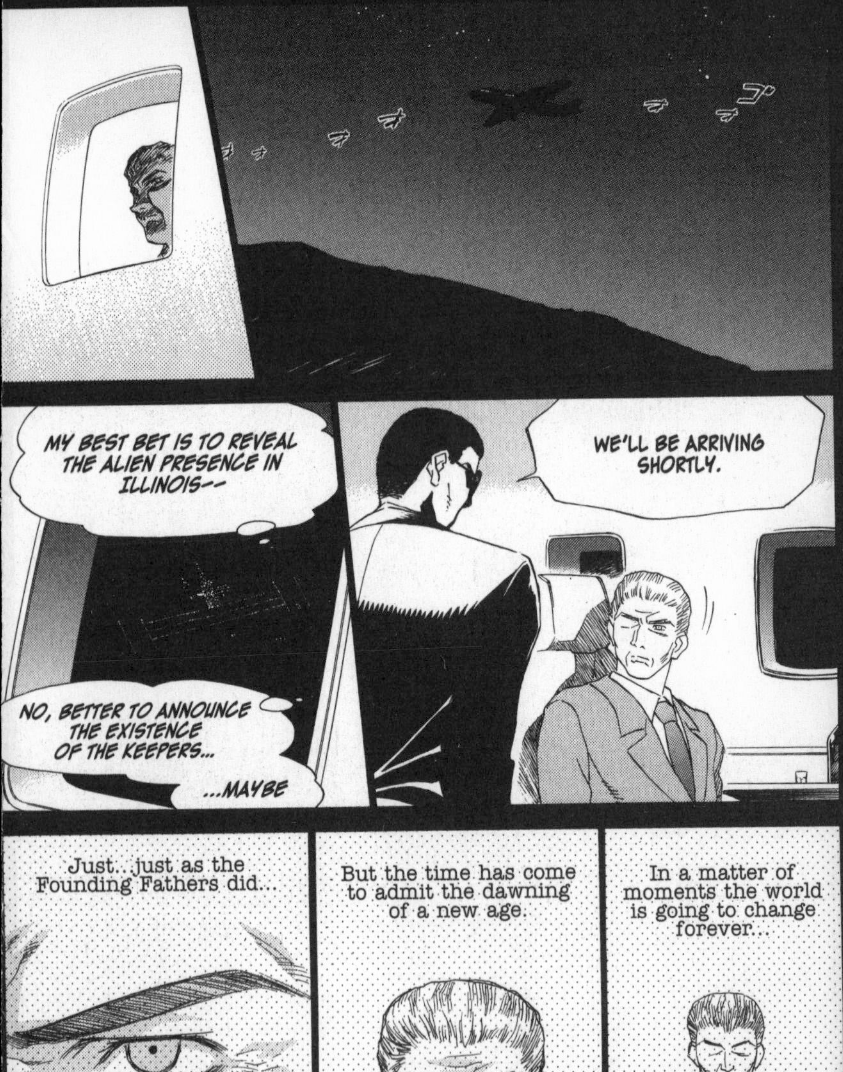
WE'LL BE ARRIVING SHORTLY.
MY BEST BET IS TO REVEAL THE ALIEN PRESENCE IN ILLINOIS--
NO, BETTER TO ANNOUNCE THE EXISTENCE OF THE KEEPERS...
...MAYBE
In a matter of moments the world is going to change forever...
Earth will be thrown into chaos!
But the time has come to admit the dawning of a new age.
Just... just as the Founding Fathers did...
I *must* lead the people into the future.

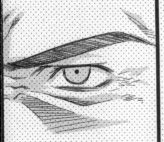

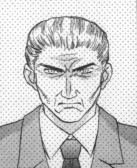

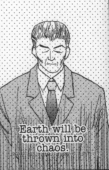

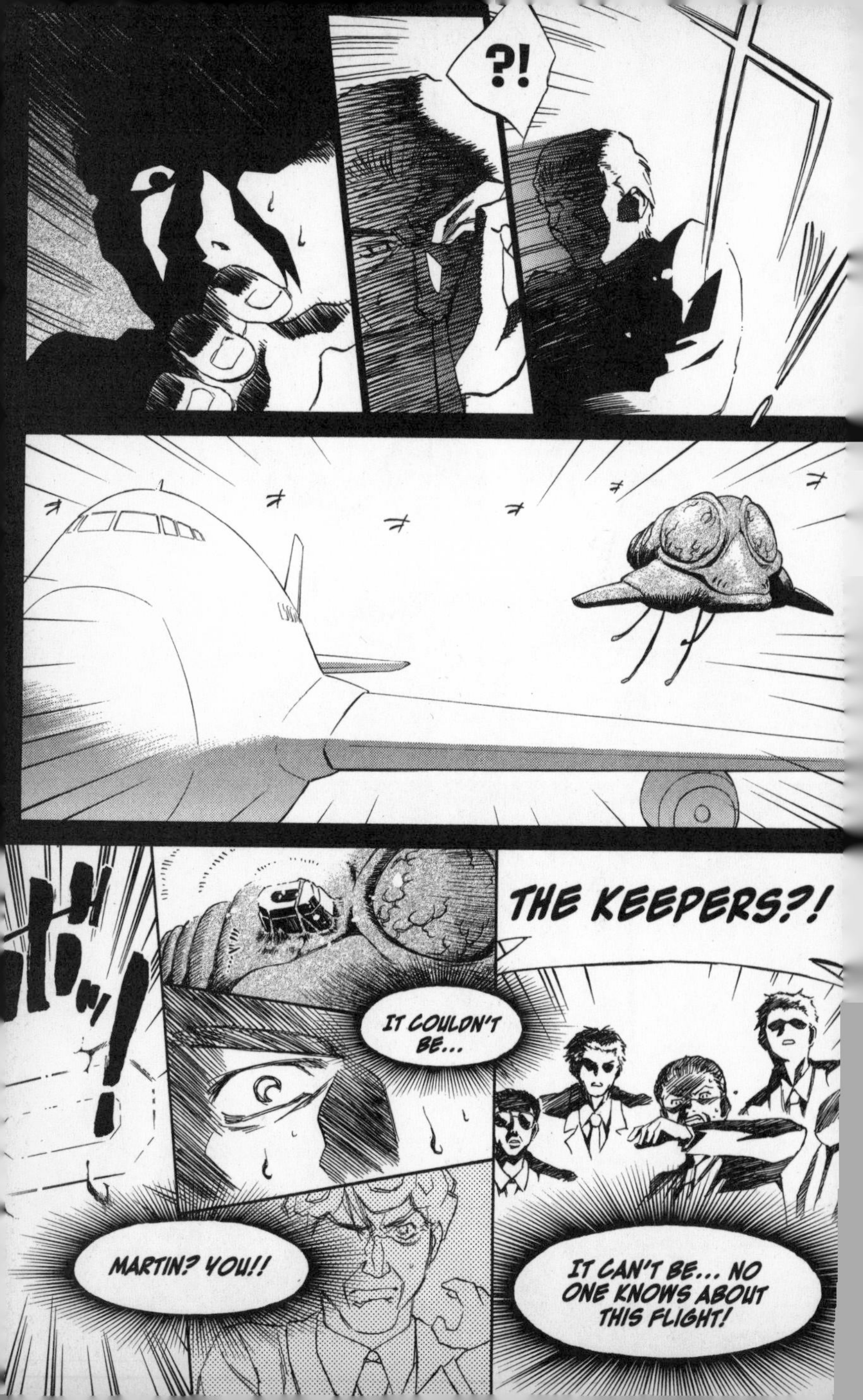
?!
THE KEEPERS?!
IT CAN'T BE... NO ONE KNOWS ABOUT THIS FLIGHT!
IT COULDN'T BE...
MARTIN? YOU!!

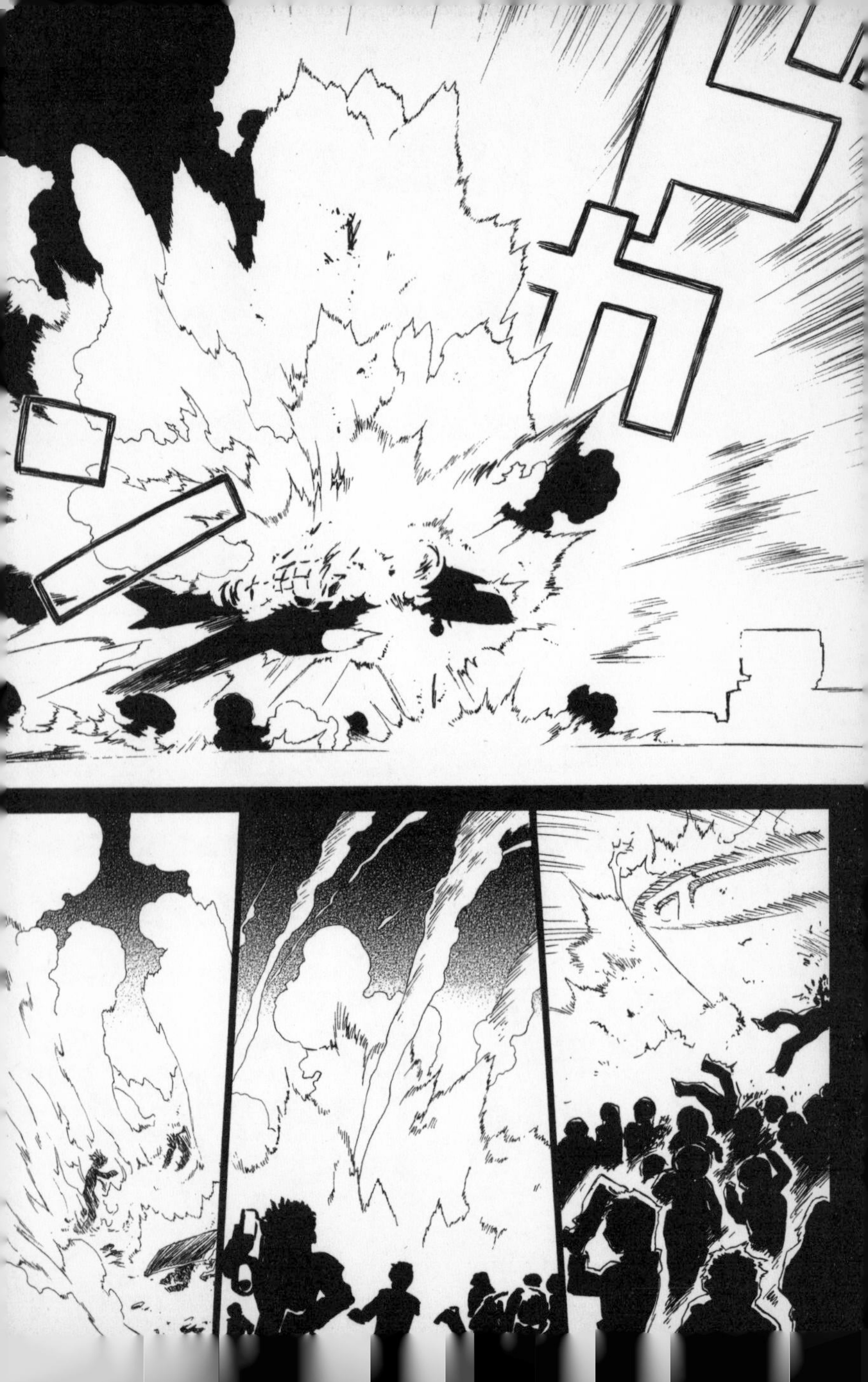

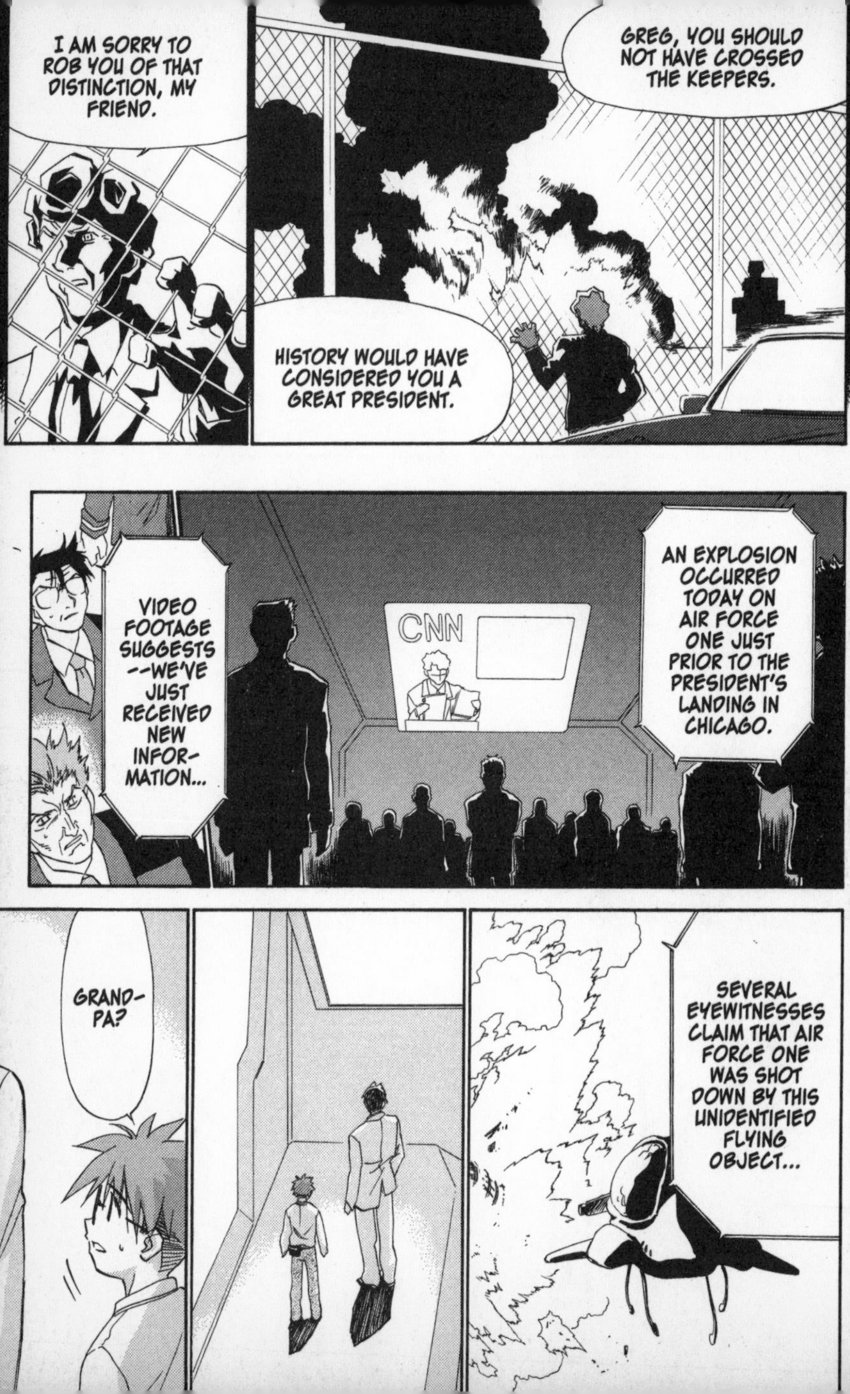
GREG, YOU SHOULD NOT HAVE CROSSED THE KEEPERS.
HISTORY WOULD HAVE CONSIDERED YOU A GREAT PRESIDENT.
I AM SORRY TO ROB YOU OF THAT DISTINCTION, MY FRIEND.
AN EXPLOSION OCCURRED TODAY ON AIR FORCE ONE JUST PRIOR TO THE PRESIDENT'S LANDING IN CHICAGO.
CNN
VIDEO FOOTAGE SUGGESTS --WE'VE JUST RECEIVED NEW INFOR-MATION...
SEVERAL EYEWITNESSES CLAIM THAT AIR FORCE ONE WAS SHOT DOWN BY THIS UNIDENTIFIED FLYING OBJECT...
GRAND-PA?

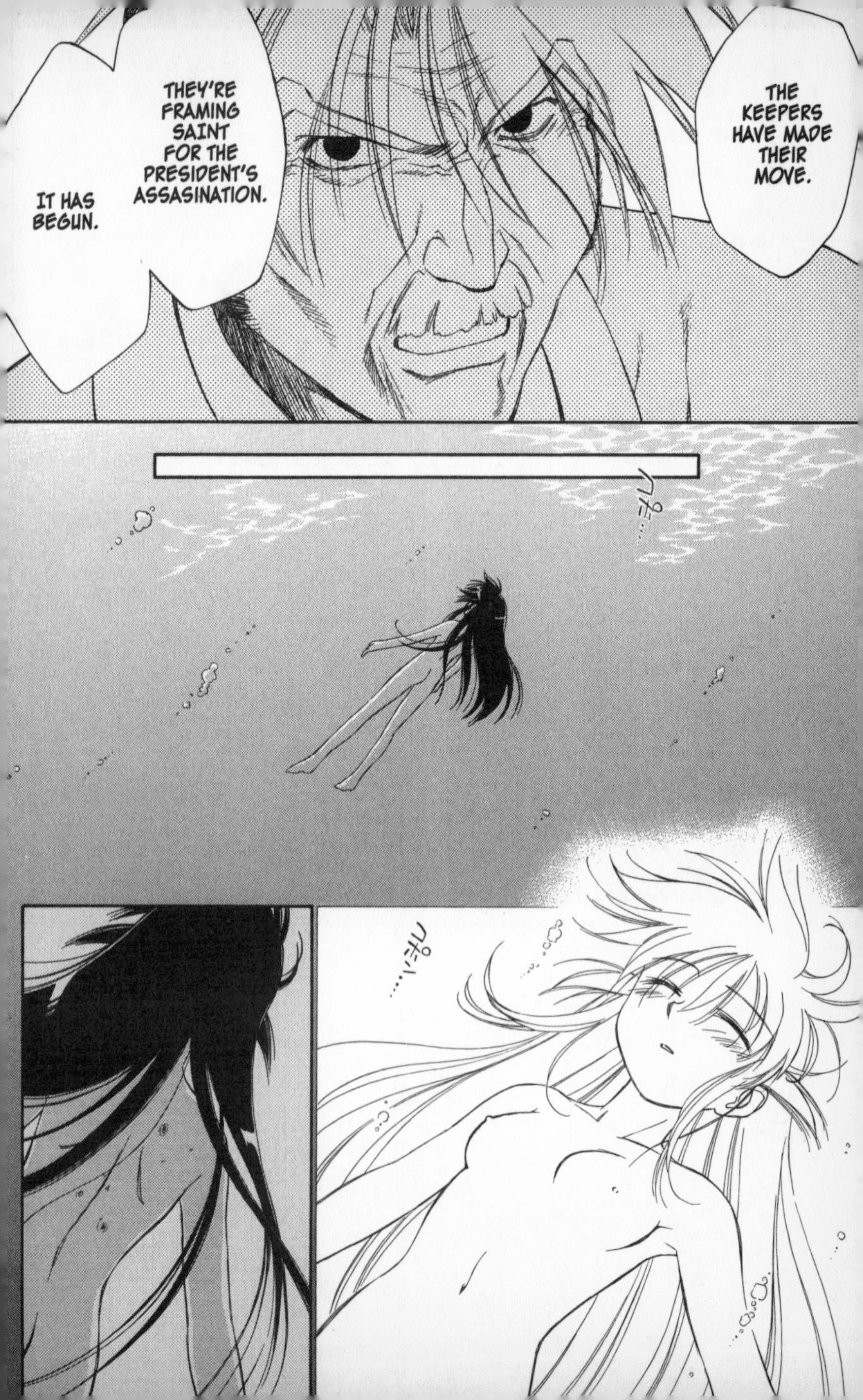
THE KEEPERS HAVE MADE THEIR MOVE.
THEY'RE FRAMING SAINT FOR THE PRESIDENT'S ASSASINATION.
IT HAS BEGUN.

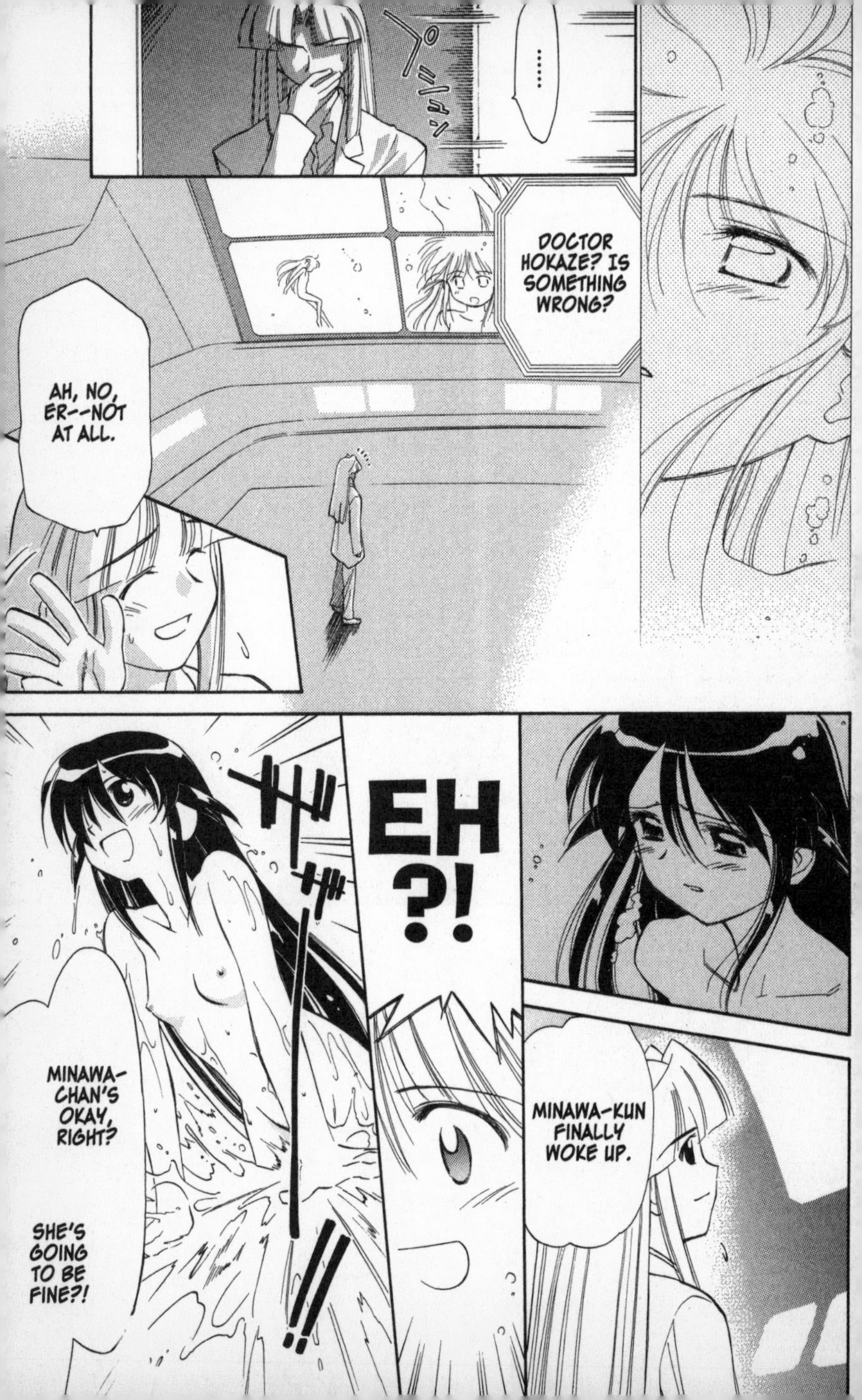
......
DOCTOR HOKAZE? IS SOMETHING WRONG?
AH, NO, ER--NOT AT ALL.
MINAWA-KUN FINALLY WOKE UP.
EH?!
MINAWA-CHAN'S OKAY, RIGHT?
SHE'S GOING TO BE FINE?!
!!

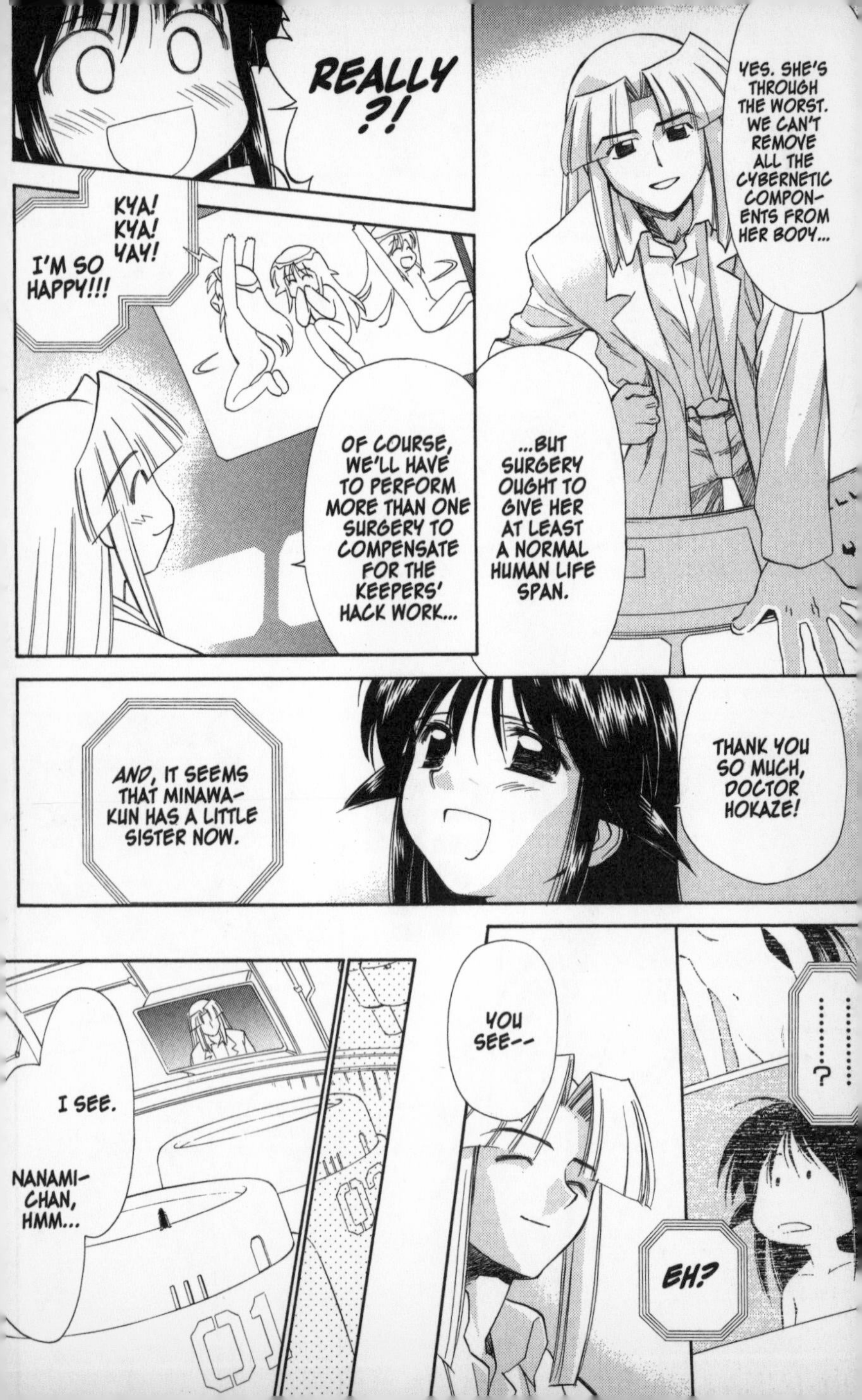
YES. SHE'S THROUGH THE WORST. WE CAN'T REMOVE ALL THE CYBERNETIC COMPON-ENTS FROM HER BODY...
...BUT SURGERY OUGHT TO GIVE HER AT LEAST A NORMAL HUMAN LIFE SPAN.
REALLY ?!
KYA! KYA! YAY!
I'M SO HAPPY!!!
OF COURSE, WE'LL HAVE TO PERFORM MORE THAN ONE SURGERY TO COMPENSATE FOR THE KEEPERS' HACK WORK...
THANK YOU SO MUCH, DOCTOR HOKAZE!
AND, IT SEEMS THAT MINAWA-KUN HAS A LITTLE SISTER NOW.
?......
EH?
YOU SEE--
I SEE.
NANAMI-CHAN, HMM...

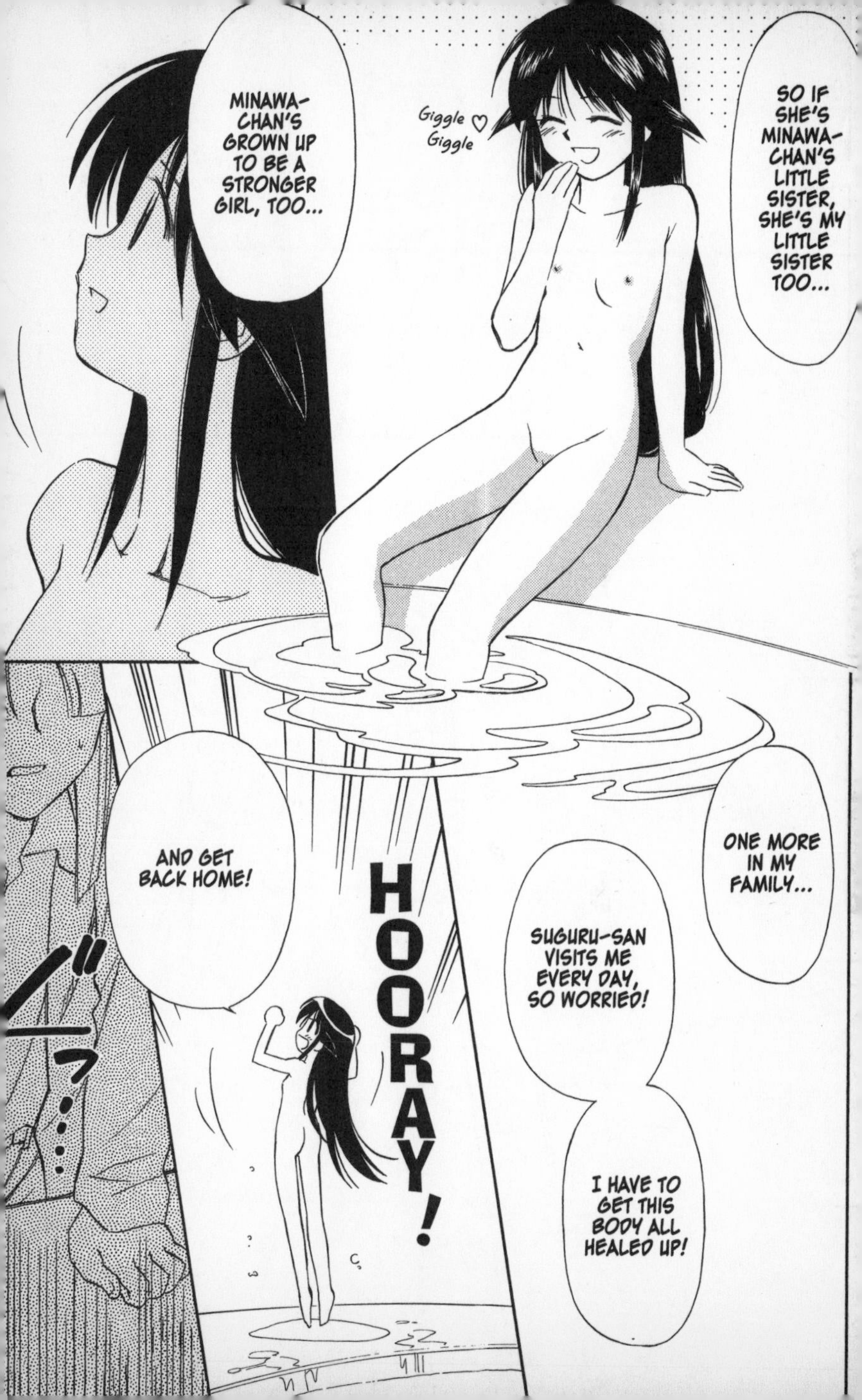
SO IF SHE'S MINAWA-CHAN'S LITTLE SISTER, SHE'S MY LITTLE SISTER TOO...
Giggle ♡ Giggle
MINAWA-CHAN'S GROWN UP TO BE A STRONGER GIRL, TOO...
ONE MORE IN MY FAMILY...
SUGURU-SAN VISITS ME EVERY DAY, SO WORRIED!
I HAVE TO GET THIS BODY ALL HEALED UP!
HOORAY!
AND GET BACK HOME!

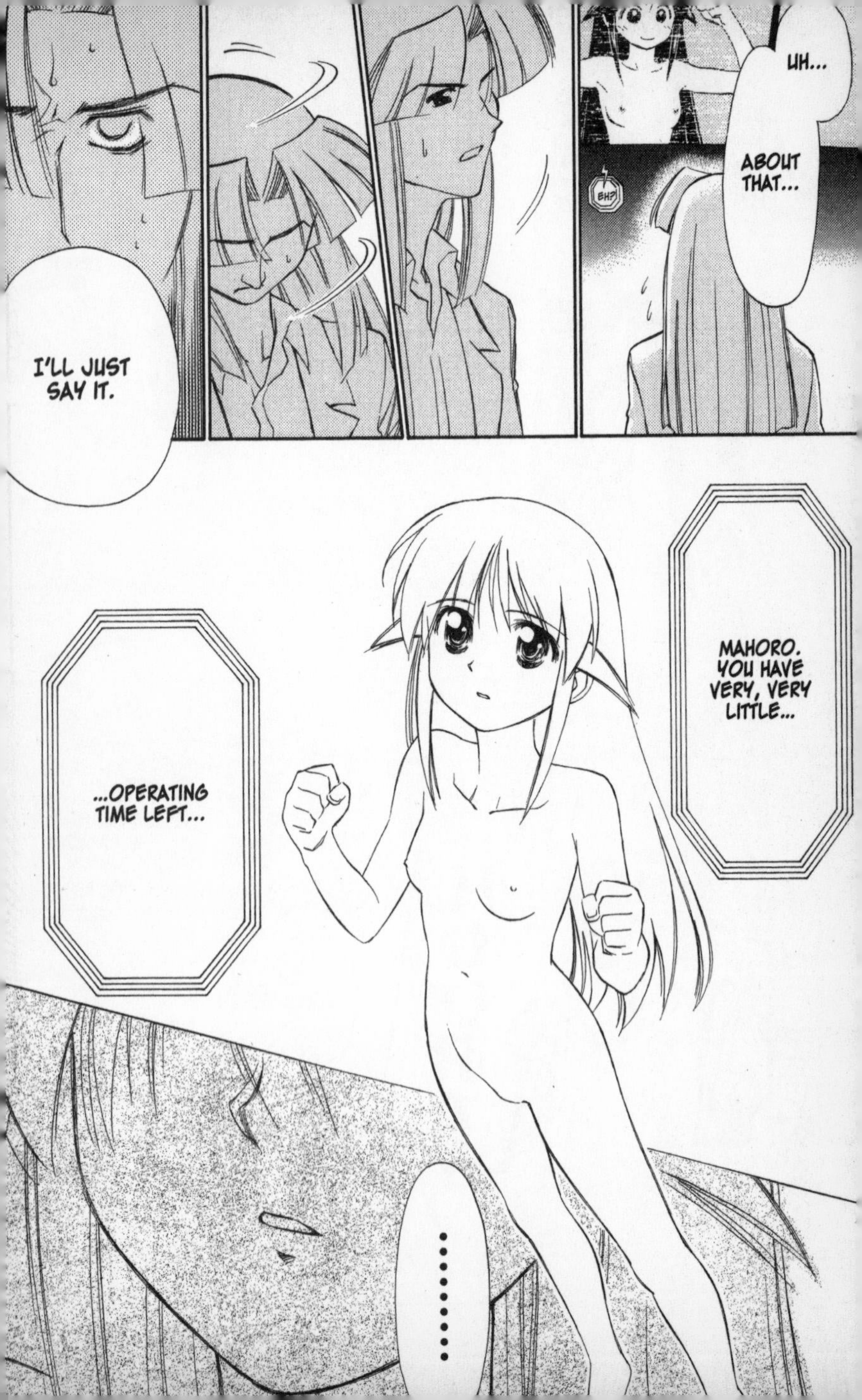
UH...
ABOUT THAT...
EH?!
I'LL JUST SAY IT.
MAHORO. YOU HAVE VERY, VERY LITTLE...
...OPERATING TIME LEFT...
......

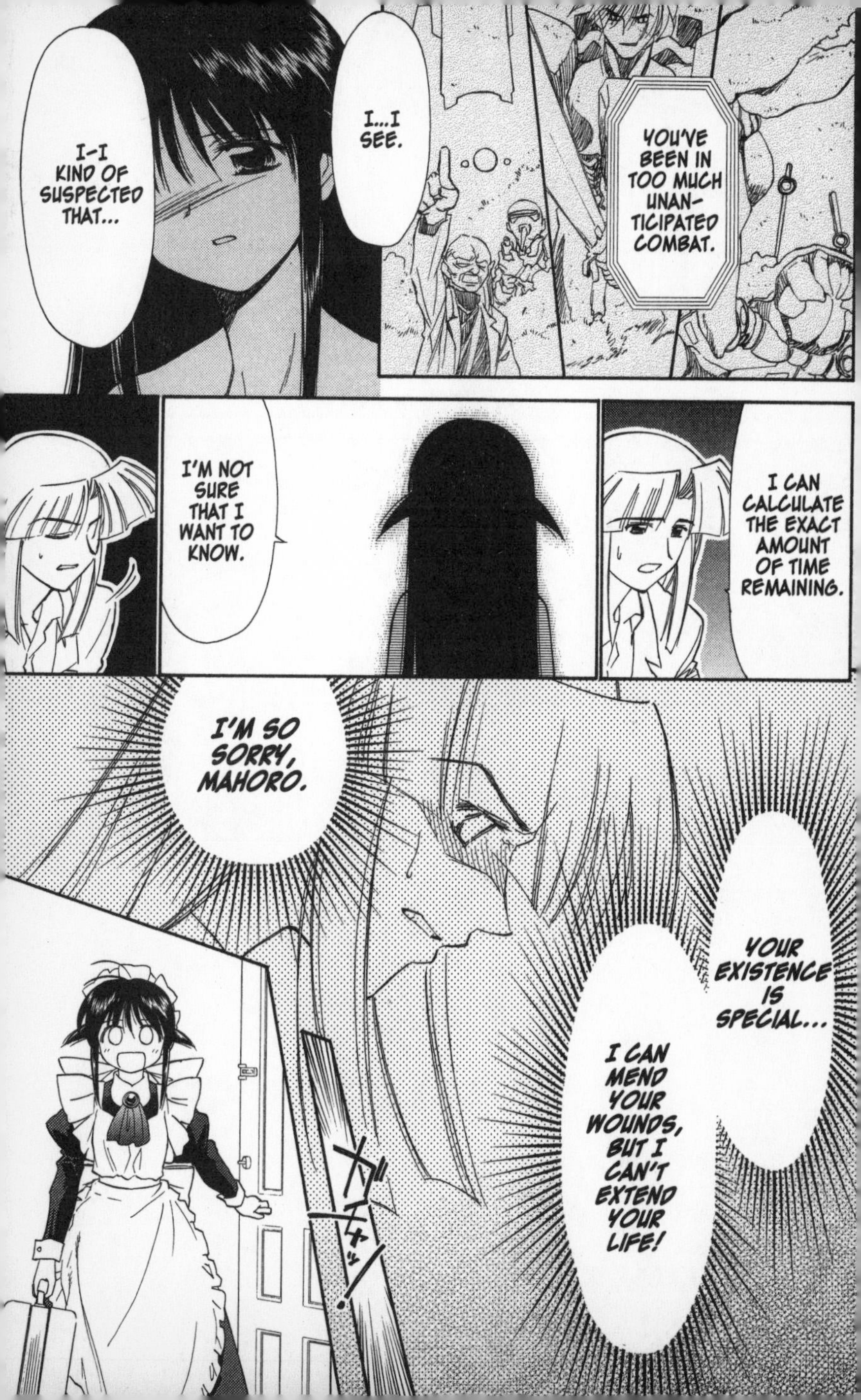
YOU'VE BEEN IN TOO MUCH UNAN-TICIPATED COMBAT.
I...I SEE.
I-I KIND OF SUSPECTED THAT...
I CAN CALCULATE THE EXACT AMOUNT OF TIME REMAINING.
I'M NOT SURE THAT I WANT TO KNOW.
YOUR EXISTENCE IS SPECIAL...
I CAN MEND YOUR WOUNDS, BUT I CAN'T EXTEND YOUR LIFE!
I'M SO SORRY, MAHORO.

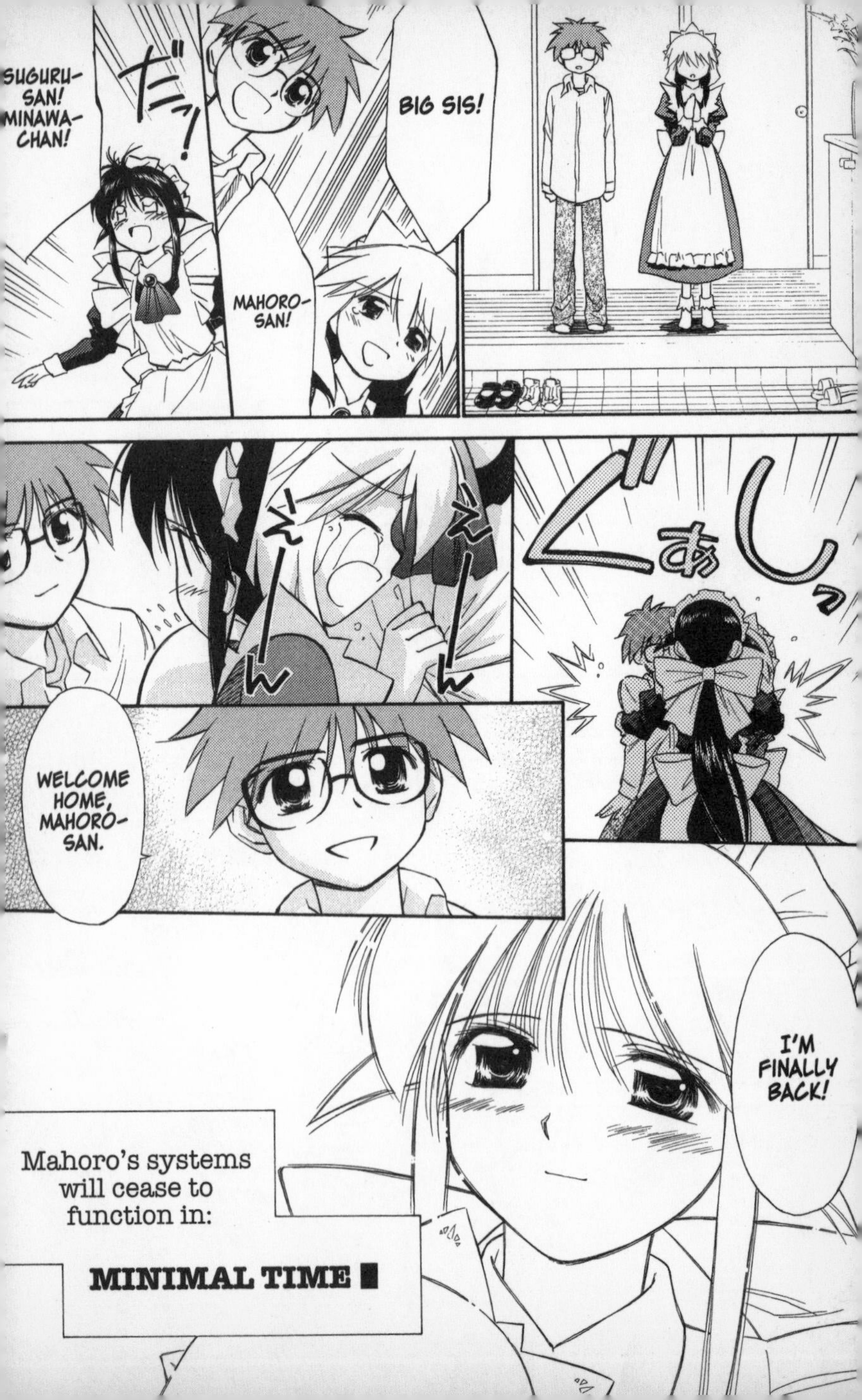
BIG SIS!
MAHORO-SAN!
ダーッ!
SUGURU-SAN! MINAWA-CHAN!
ぐぁしっ
えーん
えーん
WELCOME HOME, MAHORO-SAN.
I'M FINALLY BACK!
Mahoro's systems will cease to function in:
MINIMAL TIME

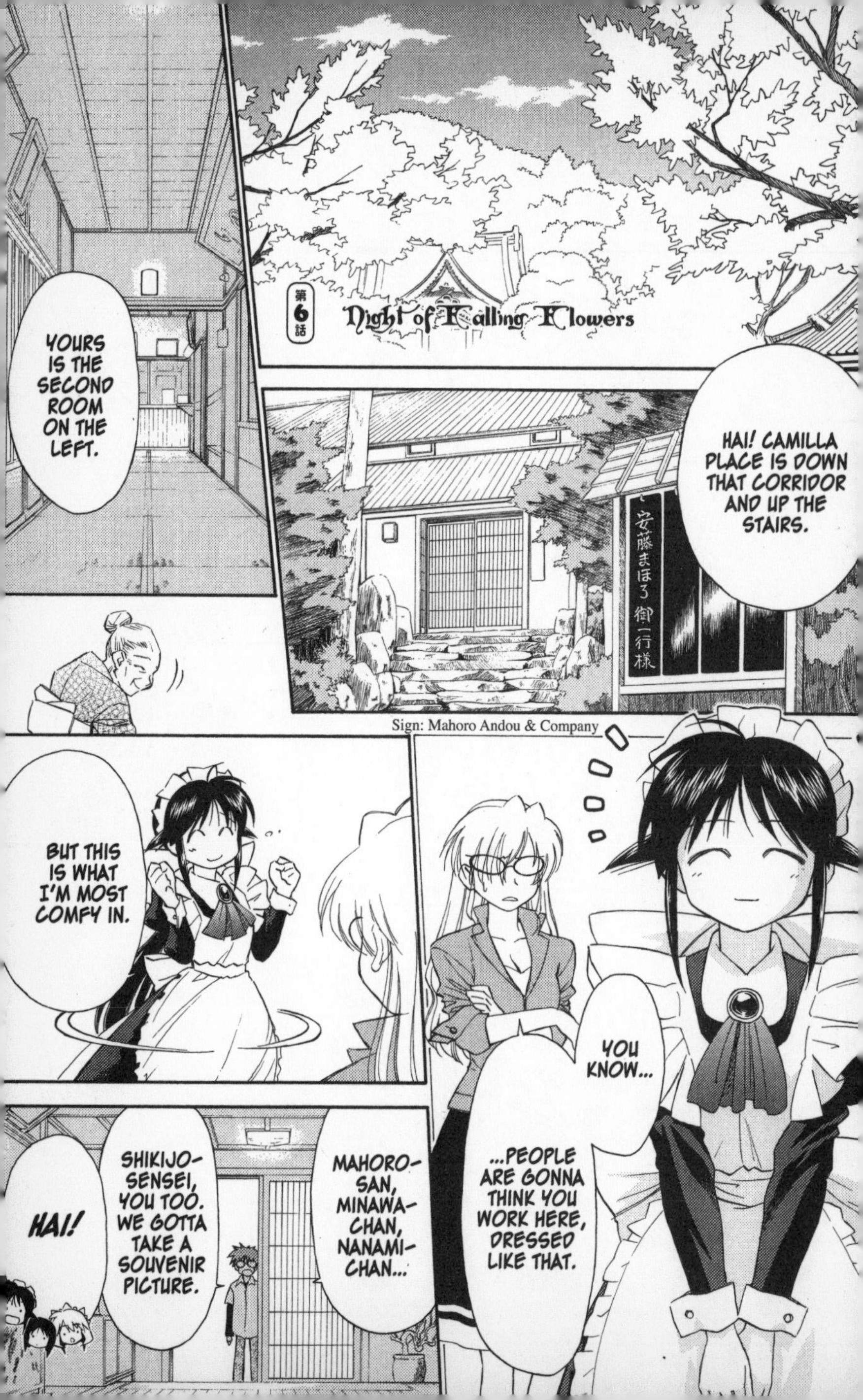
第6話
Night of Falling Flowers
HAI! CAMILLA PLACE IS DOWN THAT CORRIDOR AND UP THE STAIRS.
安藤まほろ 御一行様
Sign: Mahoro Andou & Company
YOURS IS THE SECOND ROOM ON THE LEFT.
YOU KNOW...
...PEOPLE ARE GONNA THINK YOU WORK HERE, DRESSED LIKE THAT.
BUT THIS IS WHAT I'M MOST COMFY IN.
MAHORO-SAN, MINAWA-CHAN, NANAMI-CHAN...
SHIKIJO-SENSEI, YOU TOO. WE GOTTA TAKE A SOUVENIR PICTURE.
HAI!

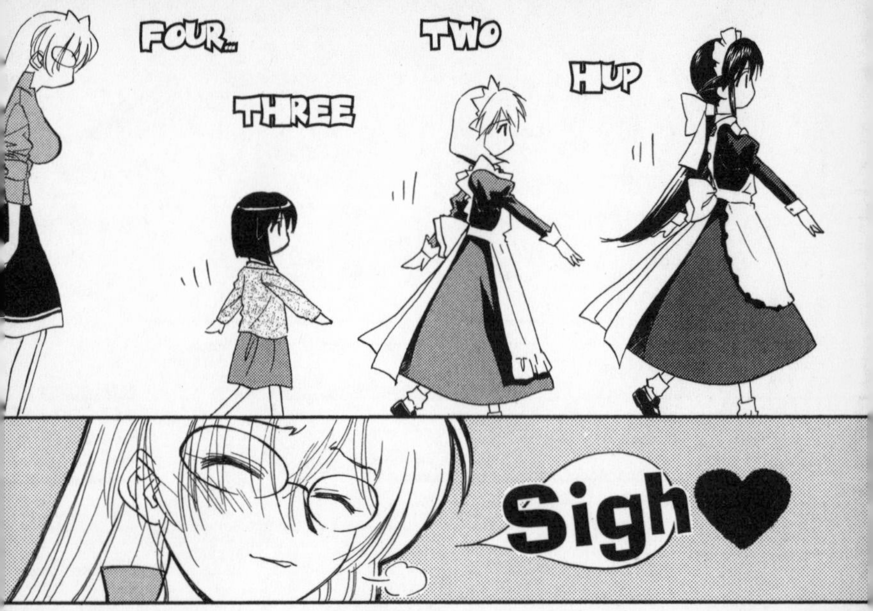
HUP
TWO
THREE
FOUR...
Sigh♥

第6話 Night of Falling Flowers

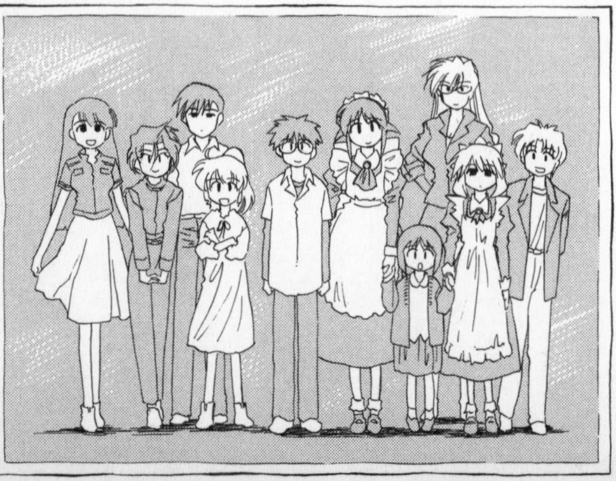

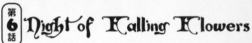

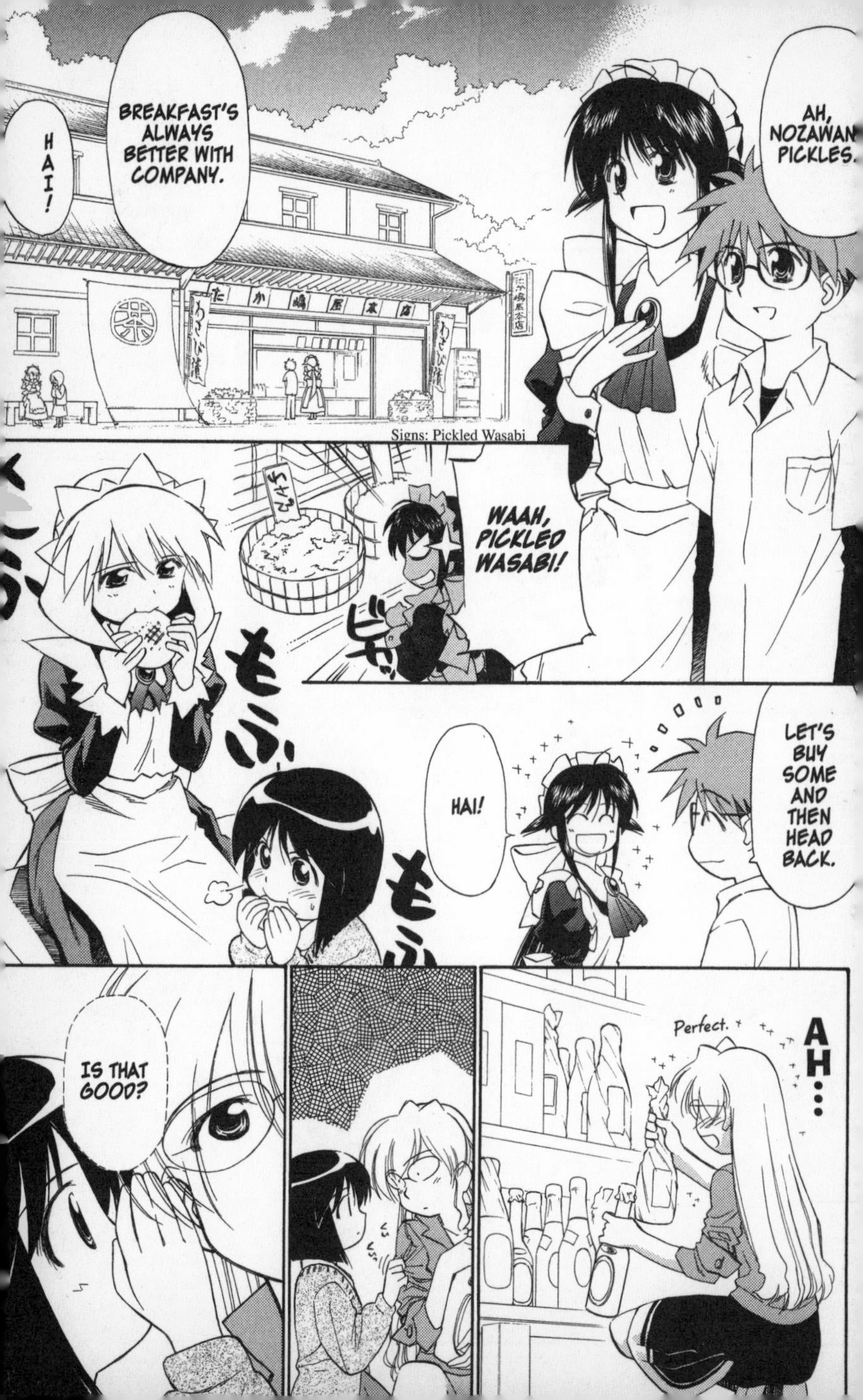
AH, NOZAWAN PICKLES.
BREAKFAST'S ALWAYS BETTER WITH COMPANY.
HAI!
Signs: Pickled Wasabi
WAAH, PICKLED WASABI!
LET'S BUY SOME AND THEN HEAD BACK.
HAI!
もふ
もふ
AH...
Perfect.
IS THAT GOOD?

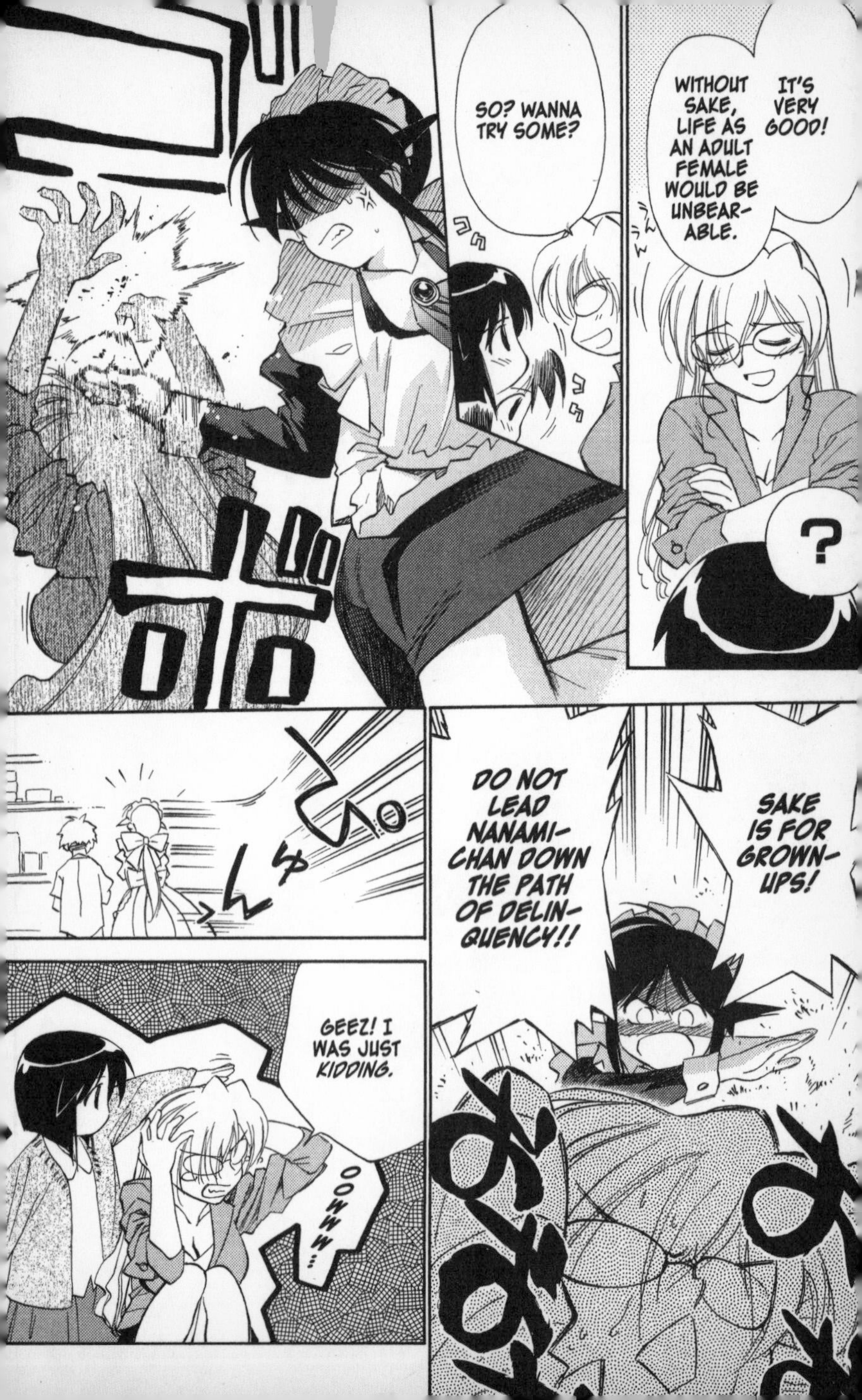
IT'S VERY GOOD!
WITHOUT SAKE, LIFE AS AN ADULT FEMALE WOULD BE UNBEARABLE.
?
SO? WANNA TRY SOME?
SAKE IS FOR GROWN-UPS!
DO NOT LEAD NANAMI-CHAN DOWN THE PATH OF DELIN-QUENCY!!
GEEZ! I WAS JUST KIDDING.
OOWWW...

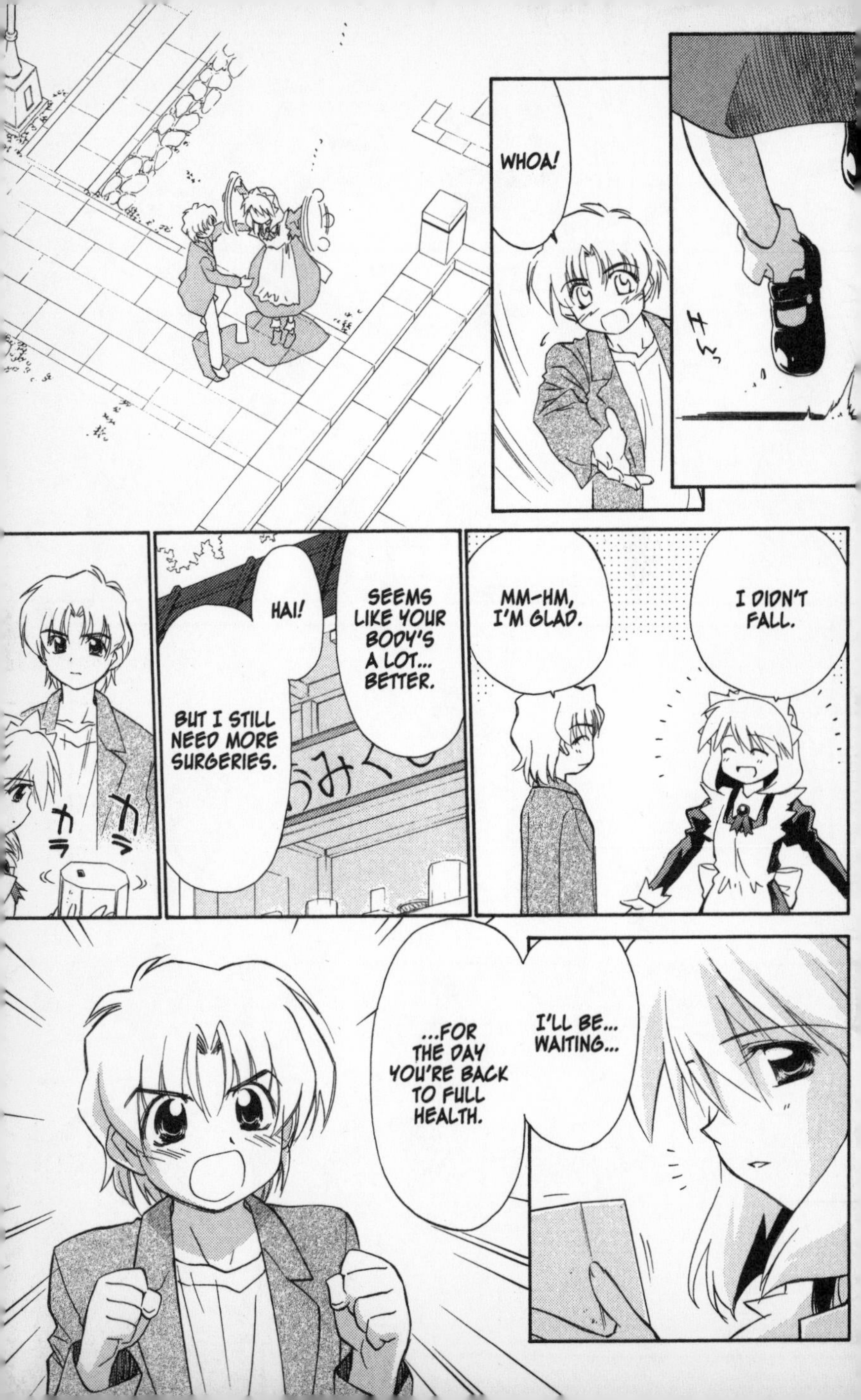
WHOA!
I DIDN'T FALL.
MM-HM, I'M GLAD.
SEEMS LIKE YOUR BODY'S A LOT... BETTER.
HAI!
BUT I STILL NEED MORE SURGERIES.
カラ カラ
I'LL BE... WAITING...
...FOR THE DAY YOU'RE BACK TO FULL HEALTH.

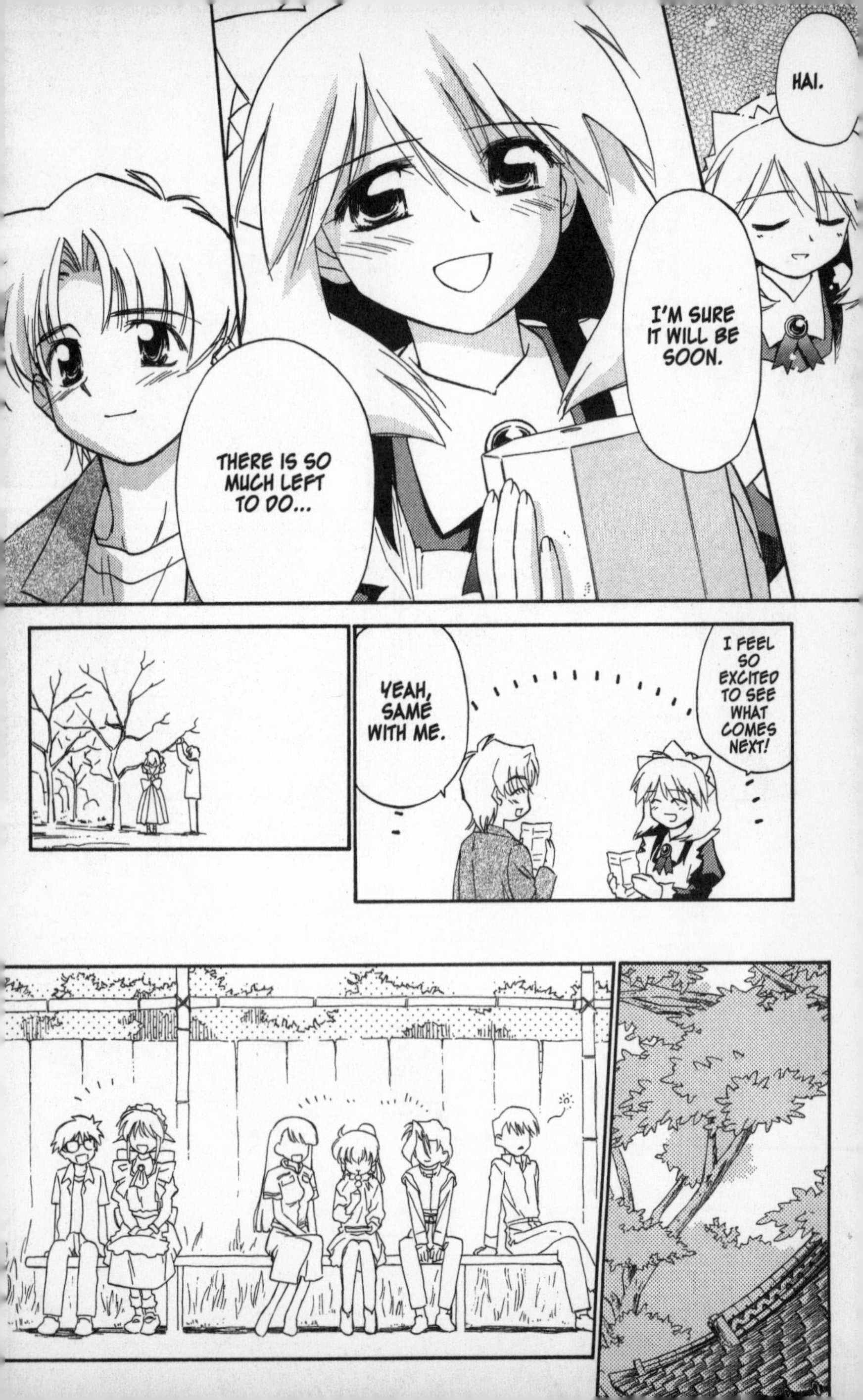
HAI.
I'M SURE IT WILL BE SOON.
THERE IS SO MUCH LEFT TO DO...
I FEEL SO EXCITED TO SEE WHAT COMES NEXT!
YEAH, SAME WITH ME.

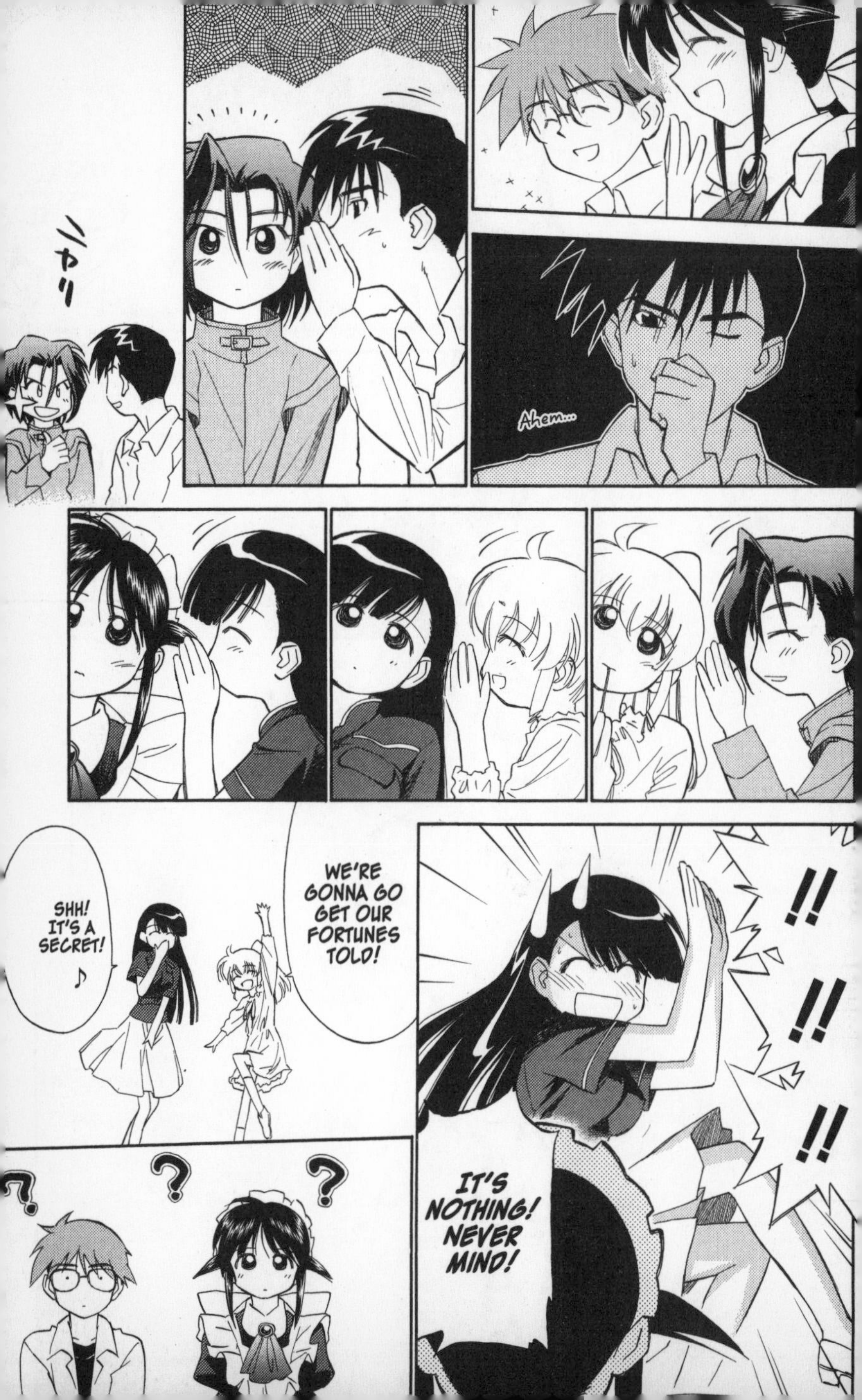
Ahem...
ニヤリ
!!
!!
!!
IT'S NOTHING! NEVER MIND!
WE'RE GONNA GO GET OUR FORTUNES TOLD!
SHH! IT'S A SECRET! ♪
?
?
?

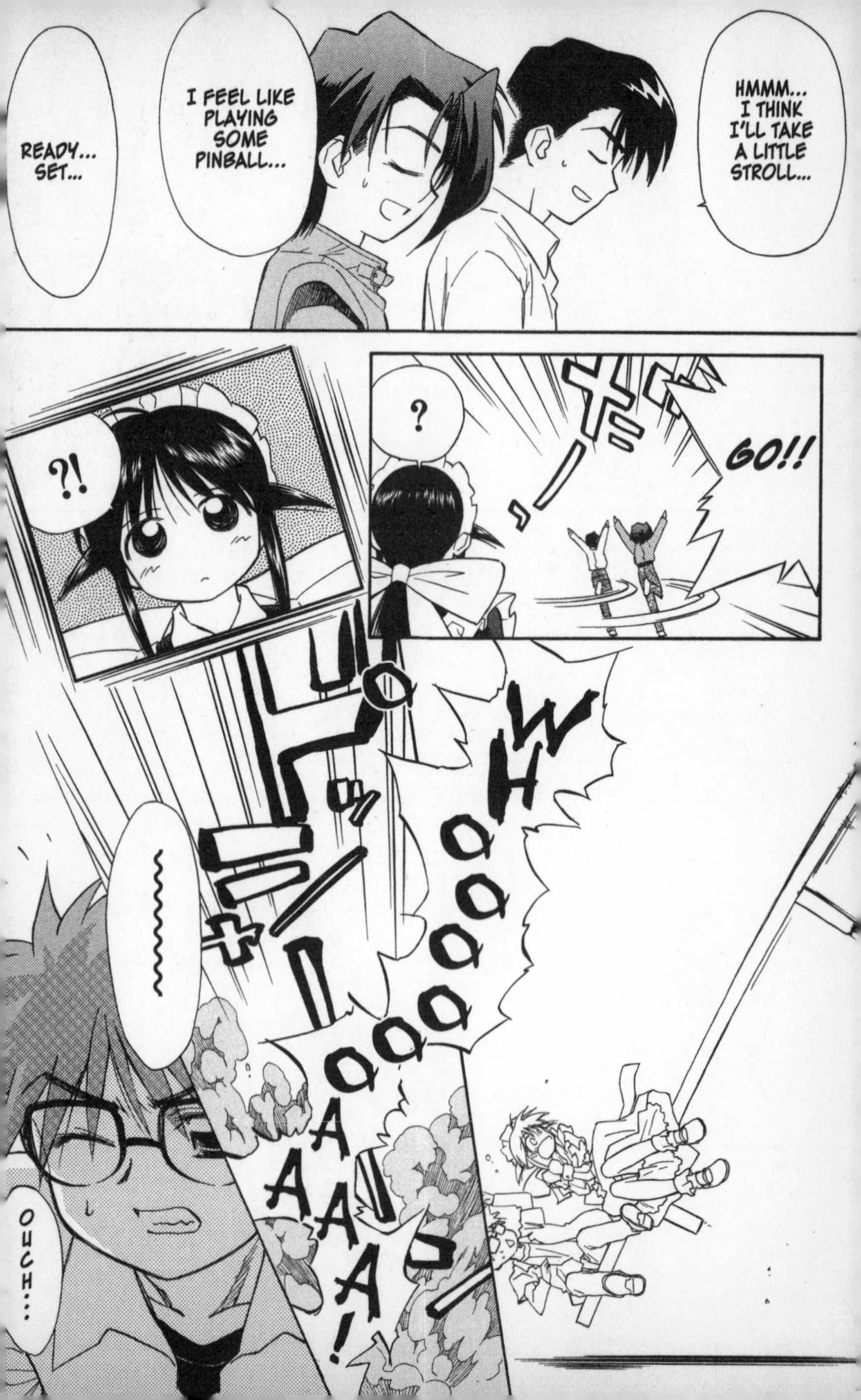
HMMM... I THINK I'LL TAKE A LITTLE STROLL...
I FEEL LIKE PLAYING SOME PINBALL...
READY... SET...
?
GO!!
?!
WHOOOOOOAAAA!
OUCH...

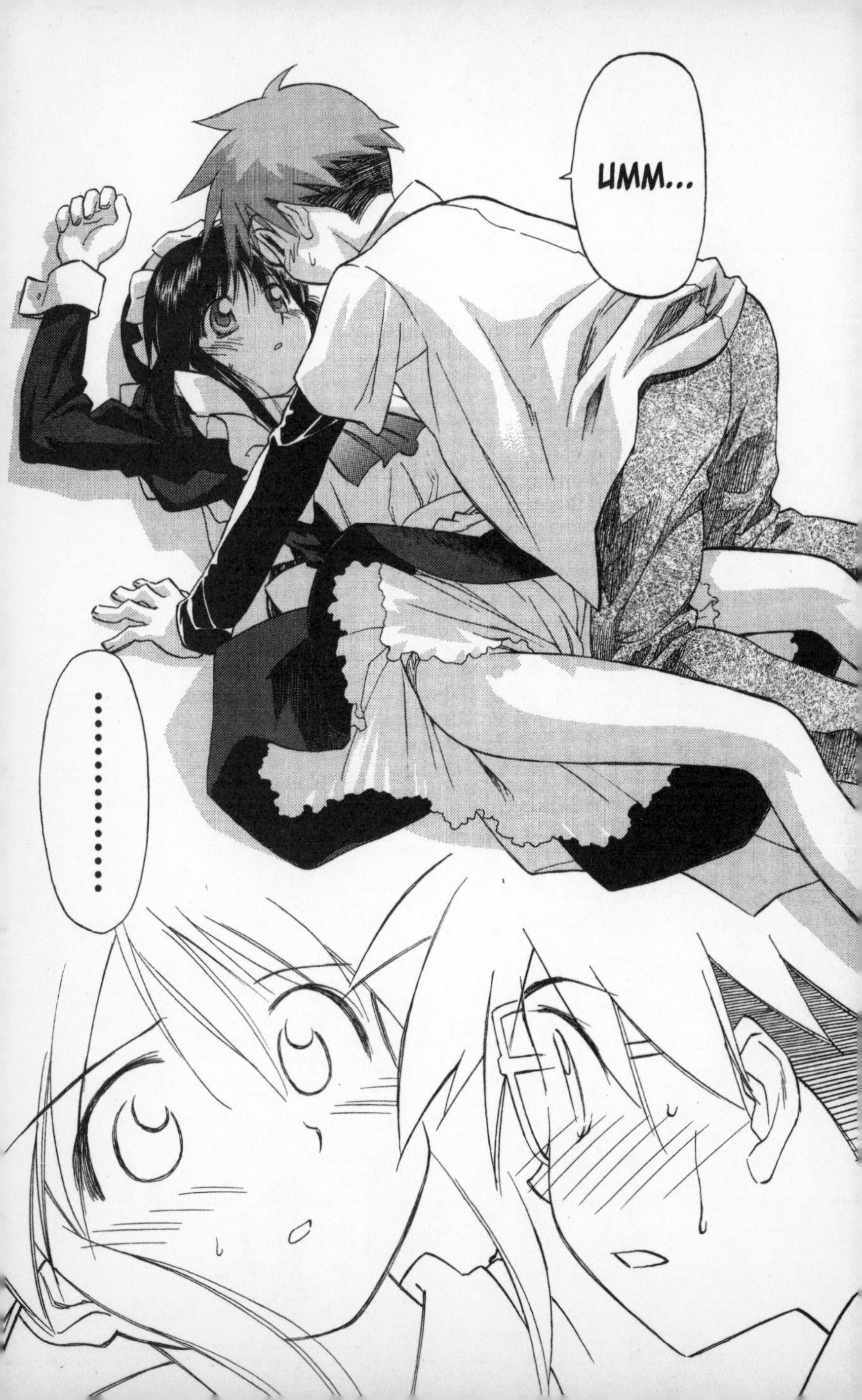
UMM...
....

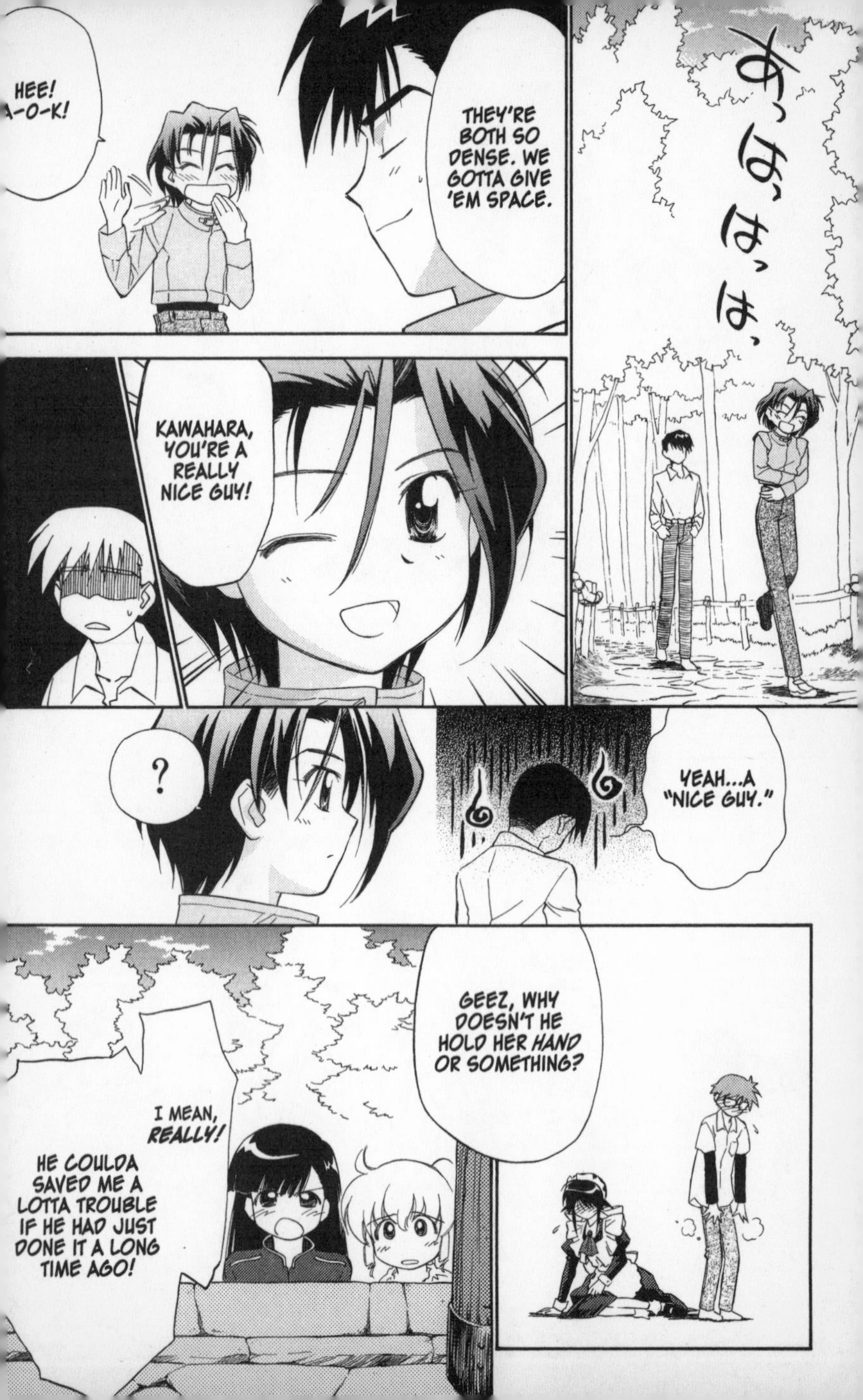
あっはっは、
THEY'RE BOTH SO DENSE. WE GOTTA GIVE 'EM SPACE.
HEE! A-O-K!
KAWAHARA, YOU'RE A REALLY NICE GUY!
YEAH...A "NICE GUY."
?
GEEZ, WHY DOESN'T HE HOLD HER *HAND* OR SOMETHING?
I MEAN, *REALLY!*
HE COULDA SAVED ME A LOTTA TROUBLE IF HE HAD JUST DONE IT A LONG TIME AGO!

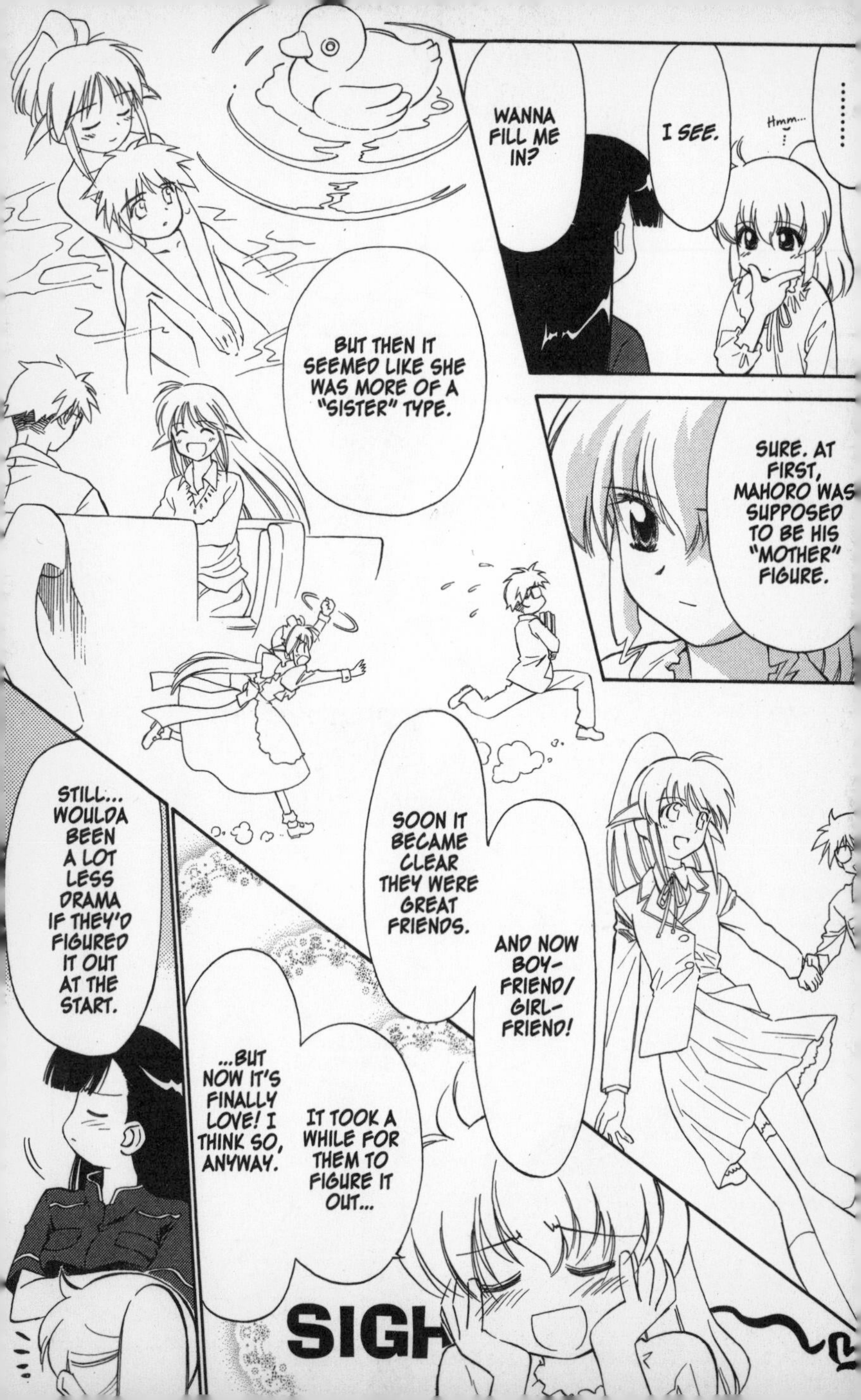

......
Hmm...
I SEE.
WANNA FILL ME IN?
SURE. AT FIRST, MAHORO WAS SUPPOSED TO BE HIS "MOTHER" FIGURE.
BUT THEN IT SEEMED LIKE SHE WAS MORE OF A "SISTER" TYPE.
SOON IT BECAME CLEAR THEY WERE GREAT FRIENDS.
AND NOW BOY-FRIEND/GIRL-FRIEND!
IT TOOK A WHILE FOR THEM TO FIGURE IT OUT...
...BUT NOW IT'S FINALLY LOVE! I THINK SO, ANYWAY.
SIGH
STILL... WOULDA BEEN A LOT LESS DRAMA IF THEY'D FIGURED IT OUT AT THE START.

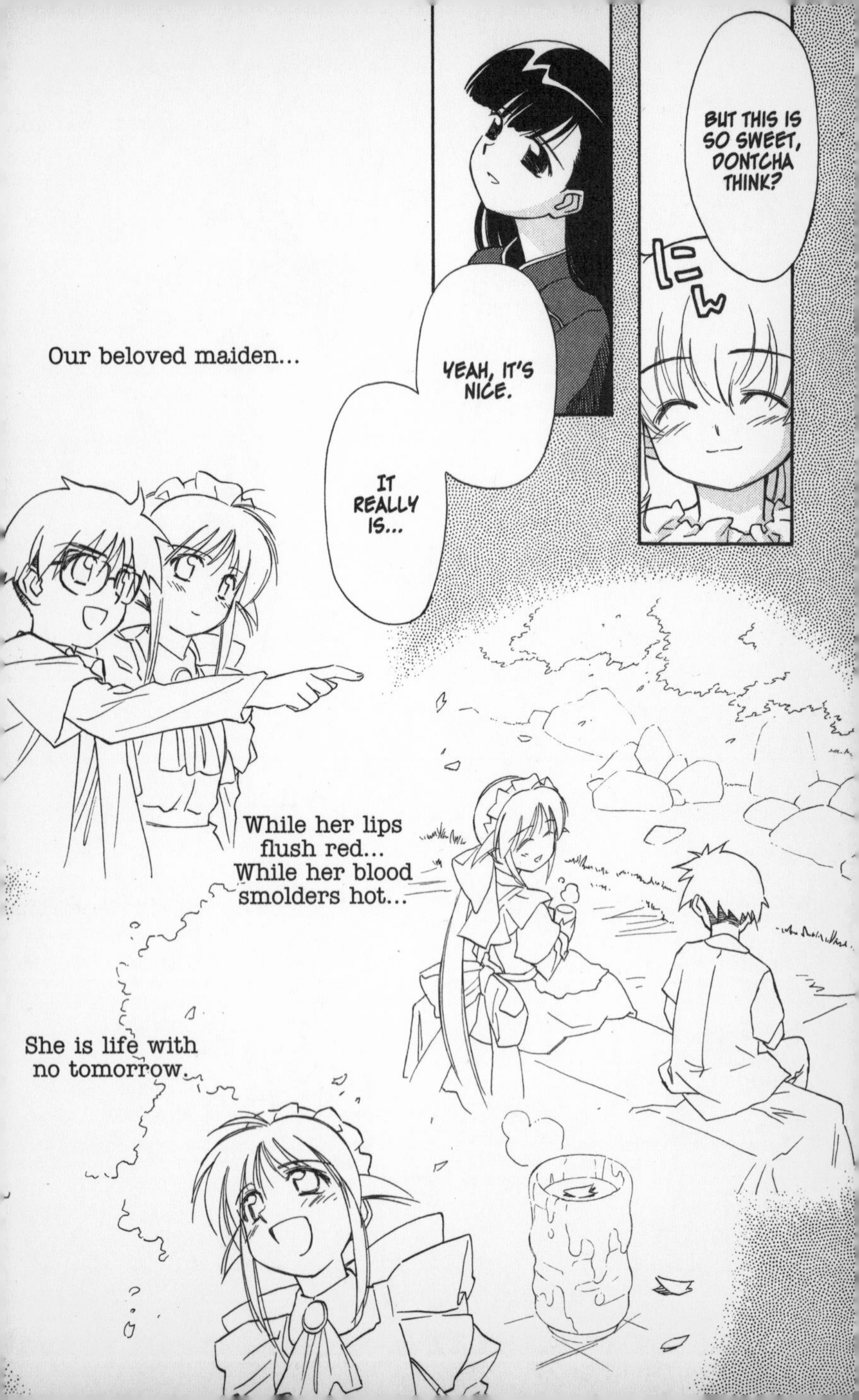
BUT THIS IS SO SWEET, DONTCHA THINK?
YEAH, IT'S NICE.
IT REALLY IS...
Our beloved maiden...
While her lips flush red... While her blood smolders hot...
She is life with no tomorrow.

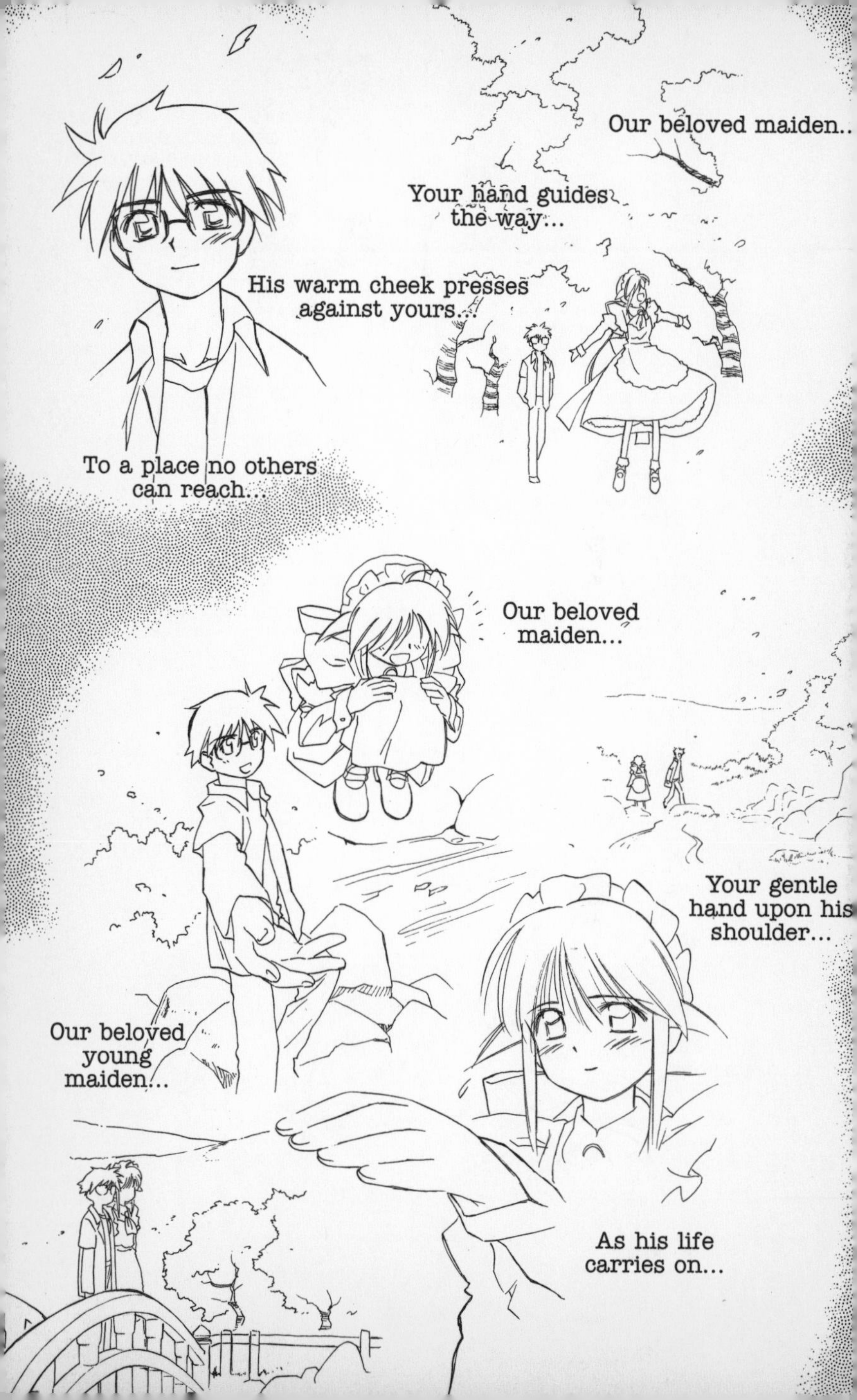
Our beloved maiden..
Your hand guides the way...
His warm cheek presses against yours...
To a place no others can reach...
Our beloved maiden...
Your gentle hand upon his shoulder...
Our beloved young maiden...
As his life carries on...

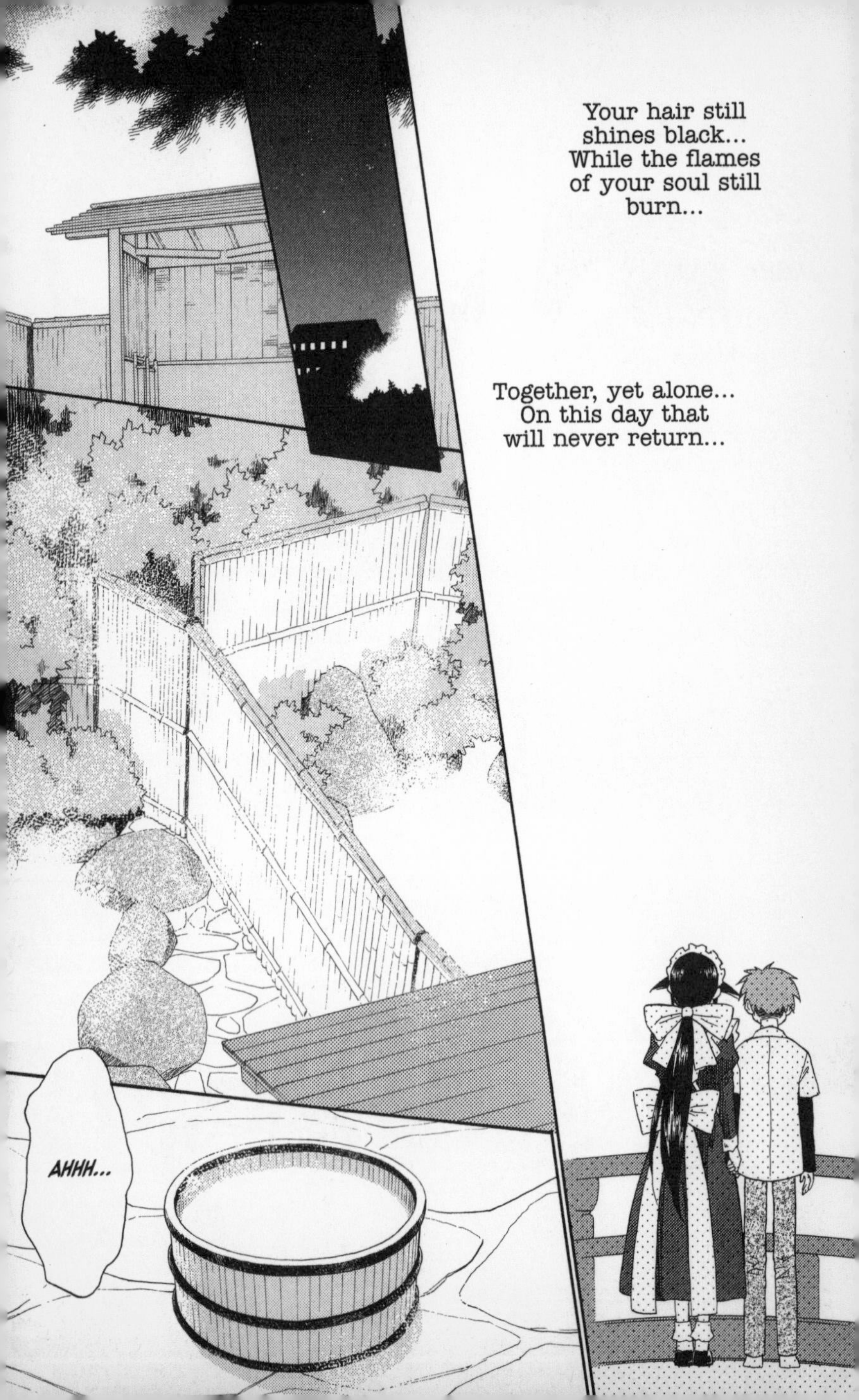
Your hair still shines black... While the flames of your soul still burn...
Together, yet alone... On this day that will never return...
AHHH...

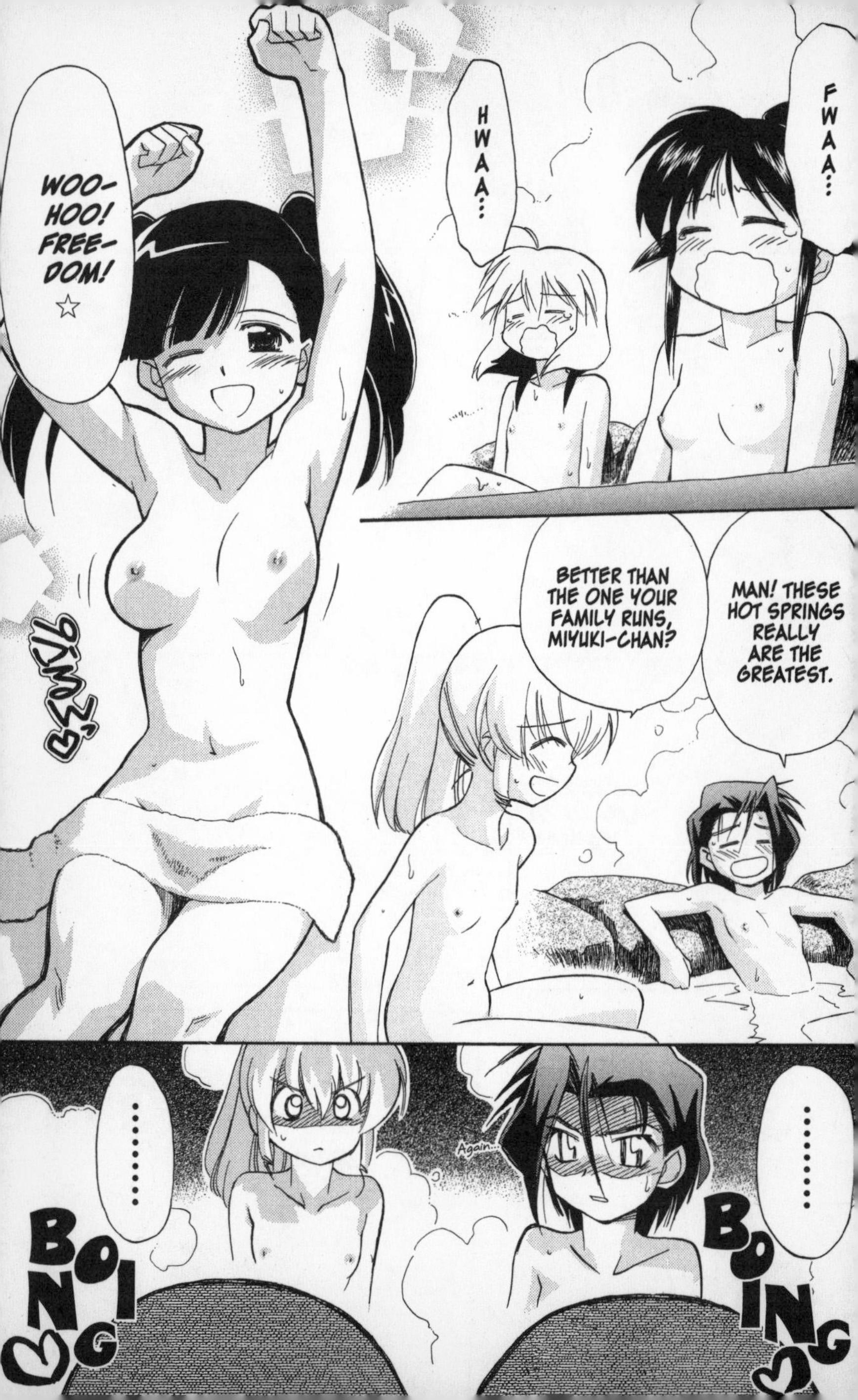
FWAA...
HWAA...
MAN! THESE HOT SPRINGS REALLY ARE THE GREATEST.
BETTER THAN THE ONE YOUR FAMILY RUNS, MIYUKI-CHAN?
WOO-HOO! FREE-DOM! ☆
......
BOING
Again...
......
BOING

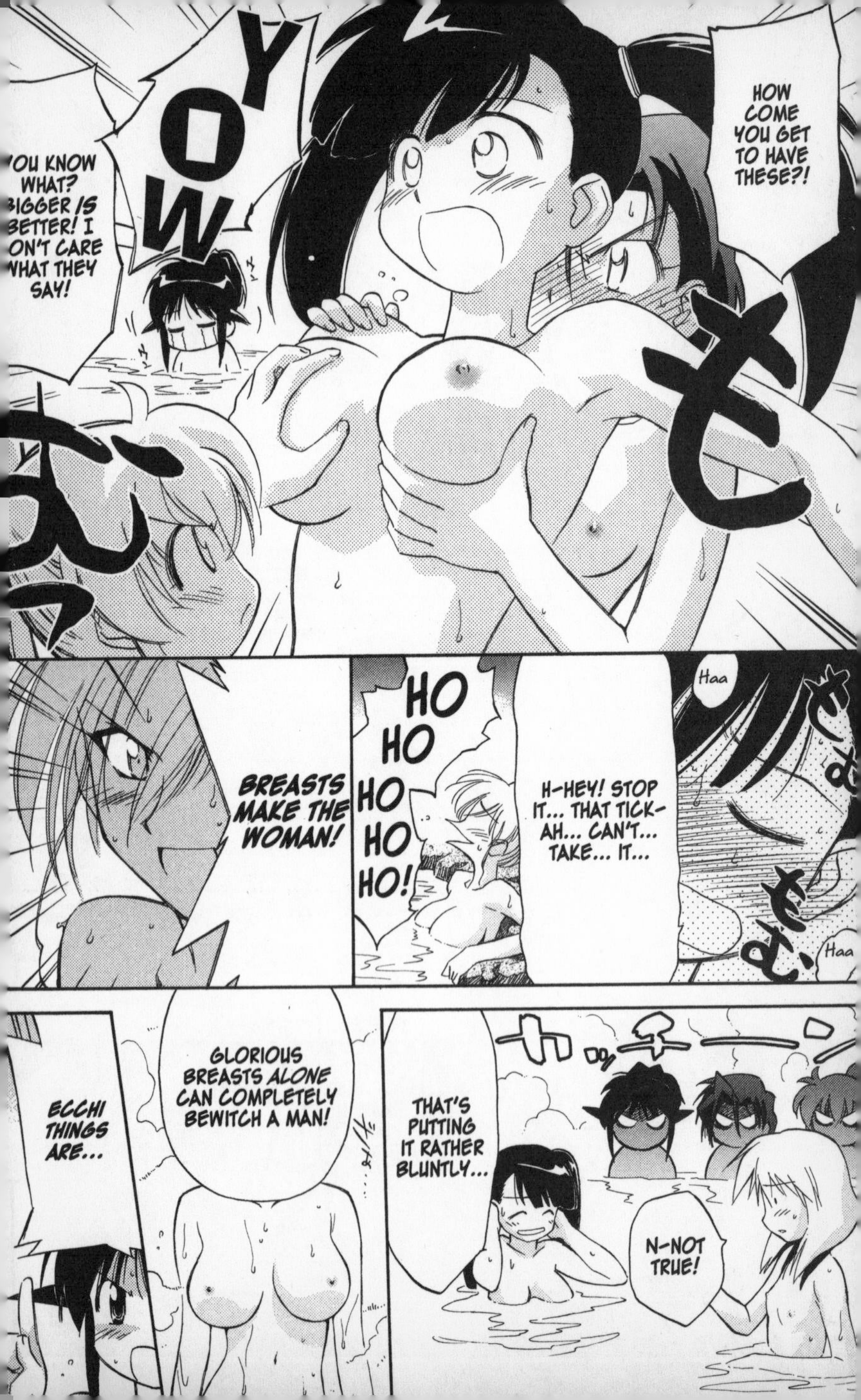
HOW COME YOU GET TO HAVE THESE?!
YOW
YOU KNOW WHAT? BIGGER IS BETTER! I DON'T CARE WHAT THEY SAY!
Haa
H-HEY! STOP IT... THAT TICK- AH... CAN'T... TAKE... IT...
Haa
HO HO HO HO HO!
BREASTS MAKE THE WOMAN!
THAT'S PUTTING IT RATHER BLUNTLY...
N-NOT TRUE!
GLORIOUS BREASTS ALONE CAN COMPLETELY BEWITCH A MAN!
ECCHI THINGS ARE...

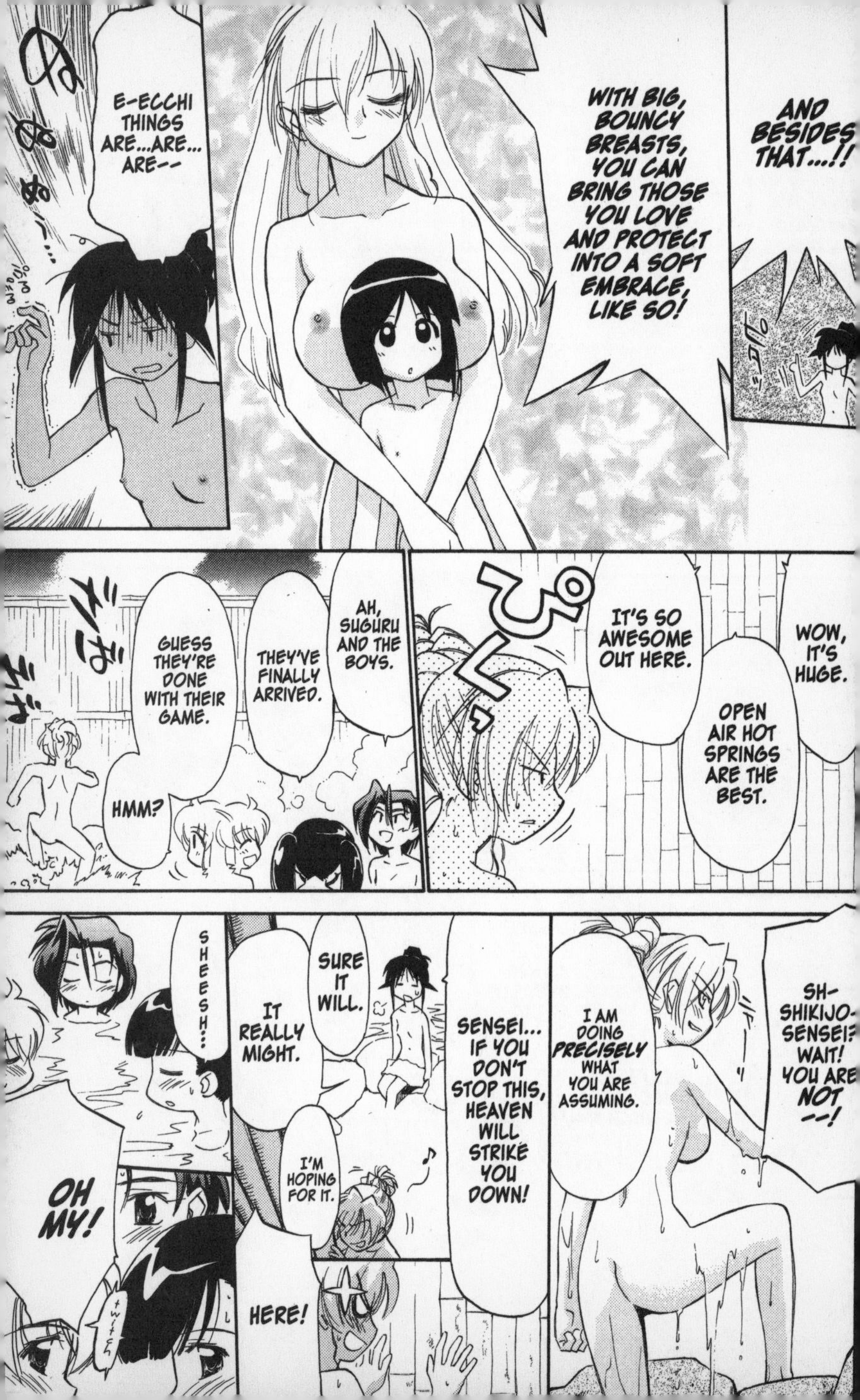
AND BESIDES THAT...!!
WITH BIG, BOUNCY BREASTS, YOU CAN BRING THOSE YOU LOVE AND PROTECT INTO A SOFT EMBRACE, LIKE SO!
E-ECCHI THINGS ARE...ARE... ARE--
WOW, IT'S HUGE.
IT'S SO AWESOME OUT HERE.
OPEN AIR HOT SPRINGS ARE THE BEST.
AH, SUGURU AND THE BOYS.
THEY'VE FINALLY ARRIVED.
GUESS THEY'RE DONE WITH THEIR GAME.
HMM?
SH-SHIKIJO-SENSEI!? WAIT! YOU ARE NOT --!
I AM DOING PRECISELY WHAT YOU ARE ASSUMING.
SENSEI... IF YOU DON'T STOP THIS, HEAVEN WILL STRIKE YOU DOWN!
SURE IT WILL.
IT REALLY MIGHT.
SHEESH...
I'M HOPING FOR IT.
HERE!
OH MY!
twitch

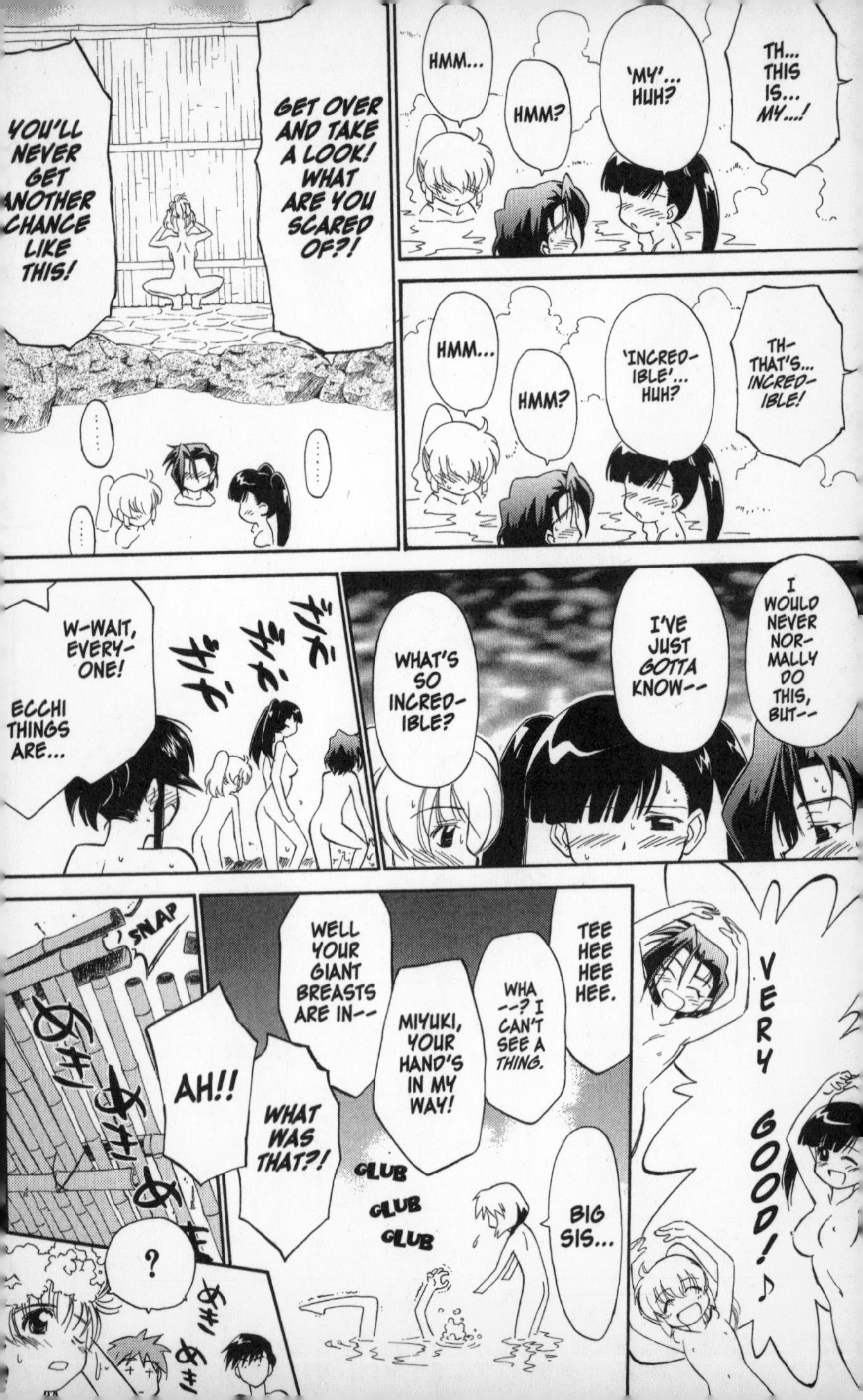
TH... THIS IS... MY...!
'MY'... HUH?
HMM?
HMM...
TH-THAT'S... INCREDIBLE!
'INCRED-IBLE'... HUH?
HMM?
HMM...
GET OVER AND TAKE A LOOK! WHAT ARE YOU SCARED OF?!
YOU'LL NEVER GET ANOTHER CHANCE LIKE THIS!
......
......
......
I WOULD NEVER NORMALLY DO THIS, BUT--
I'VE JUST GOTTA KNOW--
WHAT'S SO INCREDIBLE?
W-WAIT, EVERY-ONE!
ECCHI THINGS ARE...
VERY GOOD!♪
TEE HEE HEE HEE.
WELL YOUR GIANT BREASTS ARE IN--
WHA--? I CAN'T SEE A THING.
MIYUKI, YOUR HAND'S IN MY WAY!
BIG SIS...
GLUB
GLUB
GLUB
WHAT WAS THAT?!
AH!!
SNAP
?
めき めき

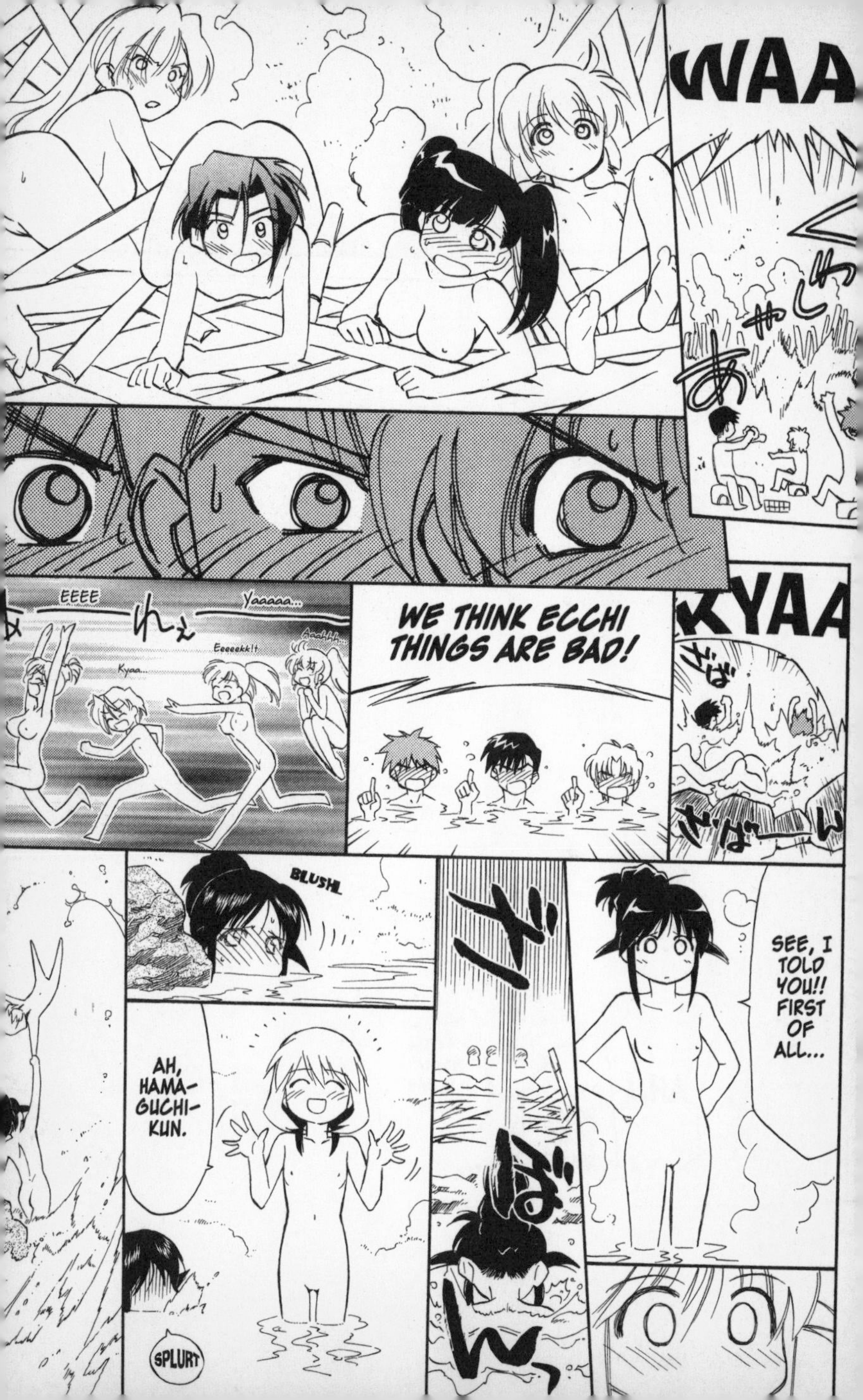
WAA
KYAA
WE THINK ECCHI THINGS ARE BAD!
EEEE
Yaaaaa...
Aaahhh...
Eeeeekk!!
Kyaa...
SEE, I TOLD YOU!! FIRST OF ALL...
BLUSH
AH, HAMAGUCHI-KUN.
SPLURT

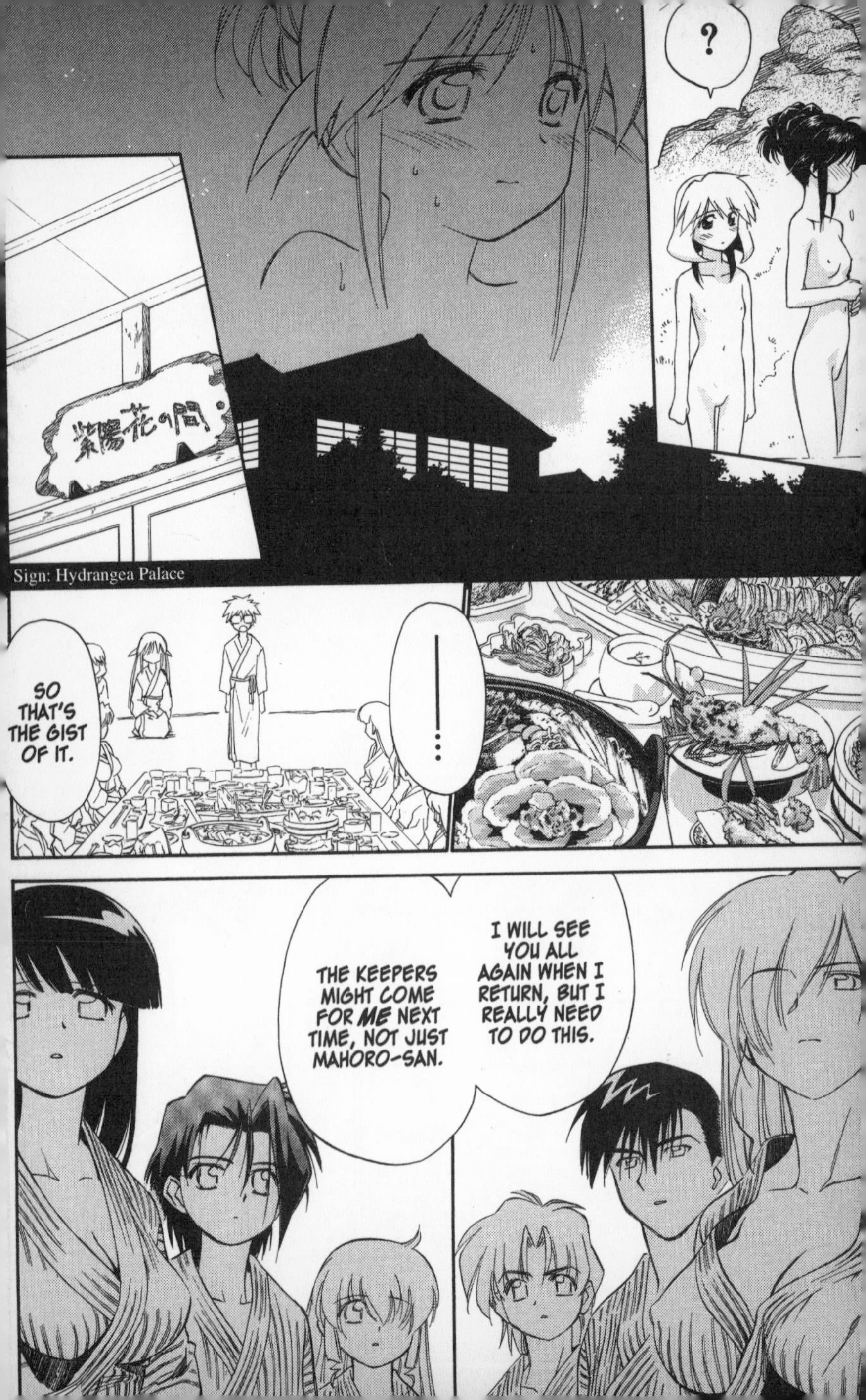
?
紫陽花の間
Sign: Hydrangea Palace
—...
SO THAT'S THE GIST OF IT.
I WILL SEE YOU ALL AGAIN WHEN I RETURN, BUT I REALLY NEED TO DO THIS.
THE KEEPERS MIGHT COME FOR *ME* NEXT TIME, NOT JUST MAHORO-SAN.

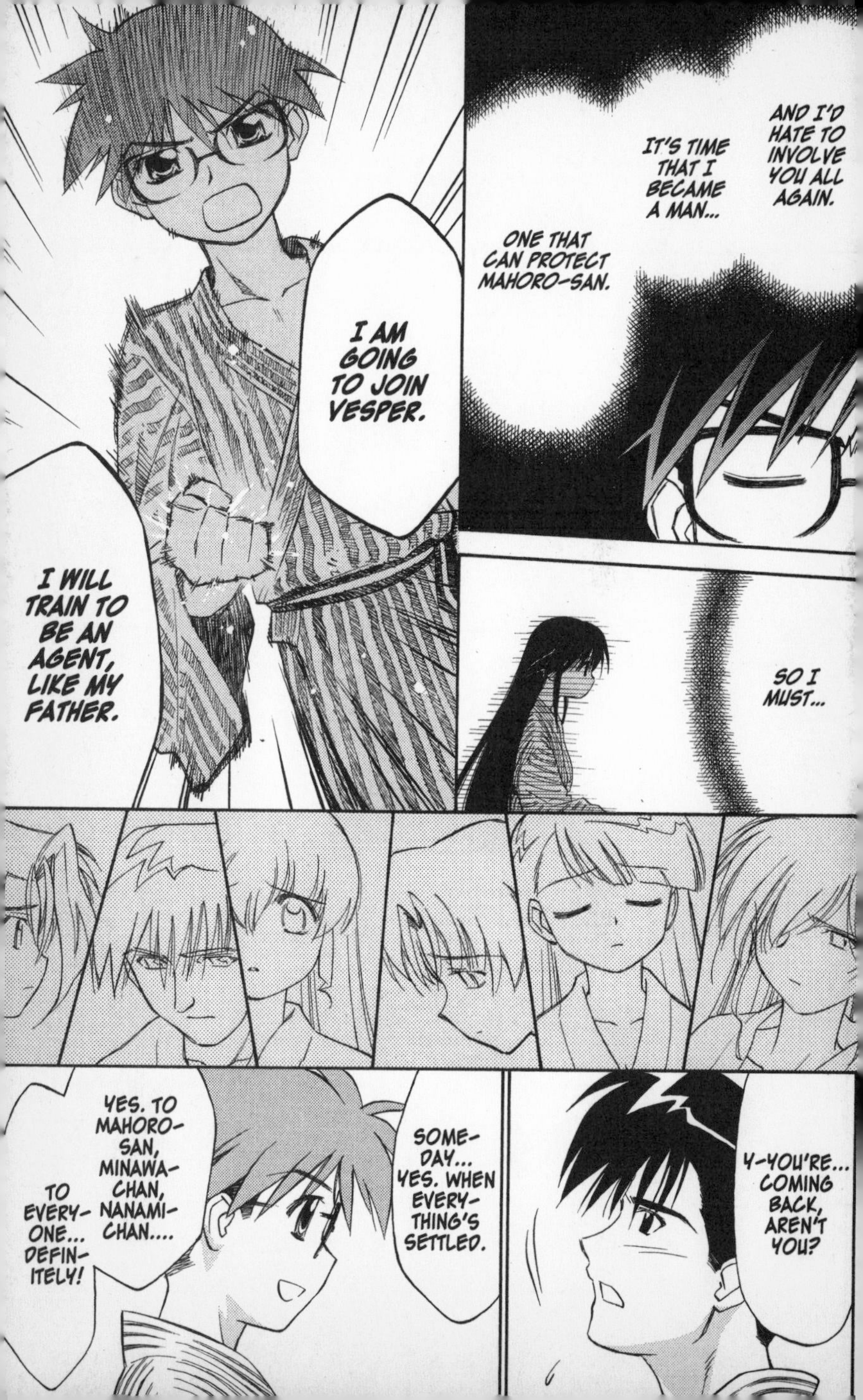
AND I'D HATE TO INVOLVE YOU ALL AGAIN.
IT'S TIME THAT I BECAME A MAN...
ONE THAT CAN PROTECT MAHORO-SAN.
SO I MUST...
I AM GOING TO JOIN VESPER.
I WILL TRAIN TO BE AN AGENT, LIKE MY FATHER.
Y-YOU'RE... COMING BACK, AREN'T YOU?
SOME-DAY... YES. WHEN EVERY-THING'S SETTLED.
YES. TO MAHORO-SAN, MINAWA-CHAN, NANAMI-CHAN....
TO EVERY-ONE... DEFINI-TELY!

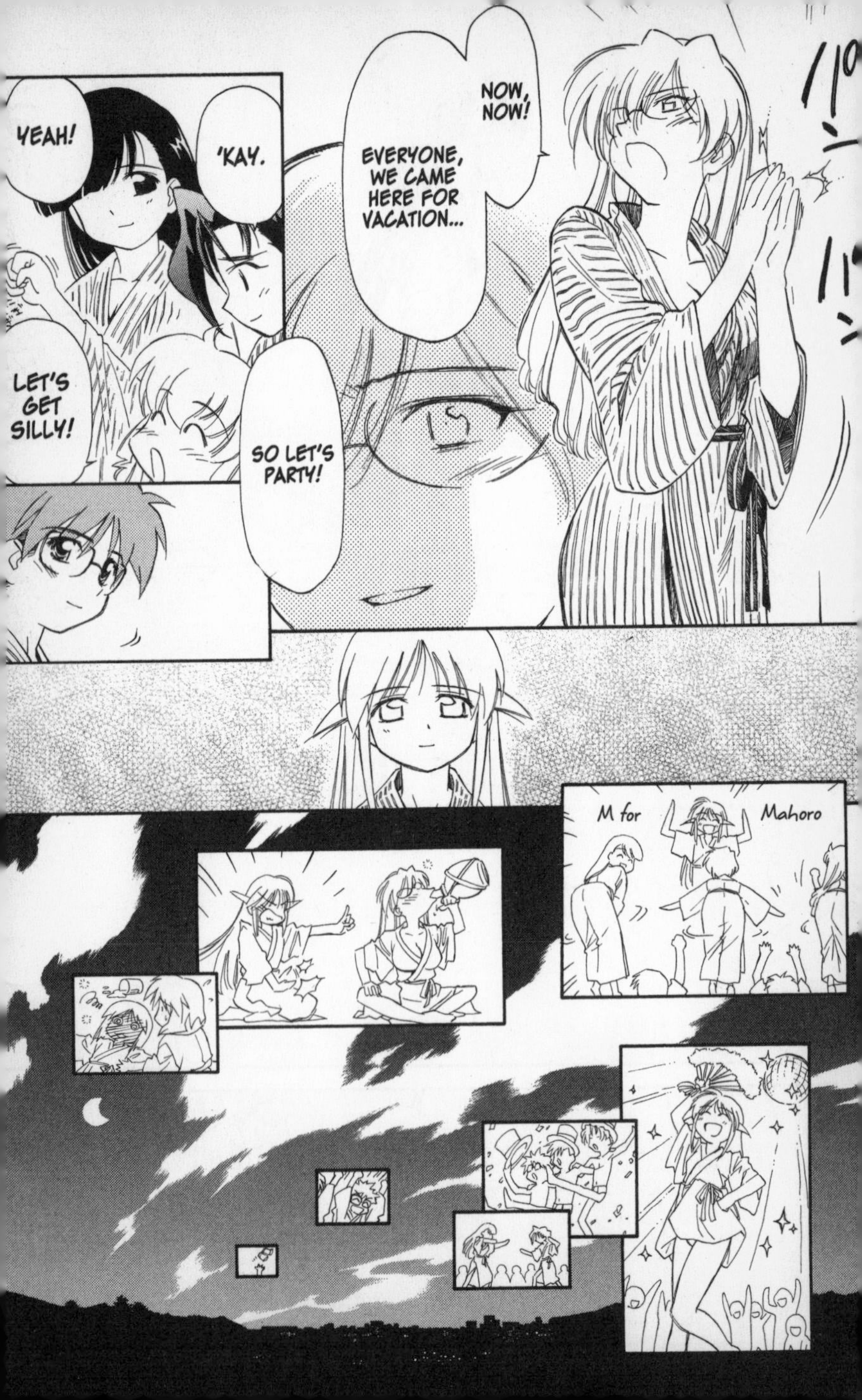
パン
パン
NOW, NOW!
EVERYONE, WE CAME HERE FOR VACATION...
SO LET'S PARTY!
'KAY.
YEAH!
LET'S GET SILLY!
M for Mahoro

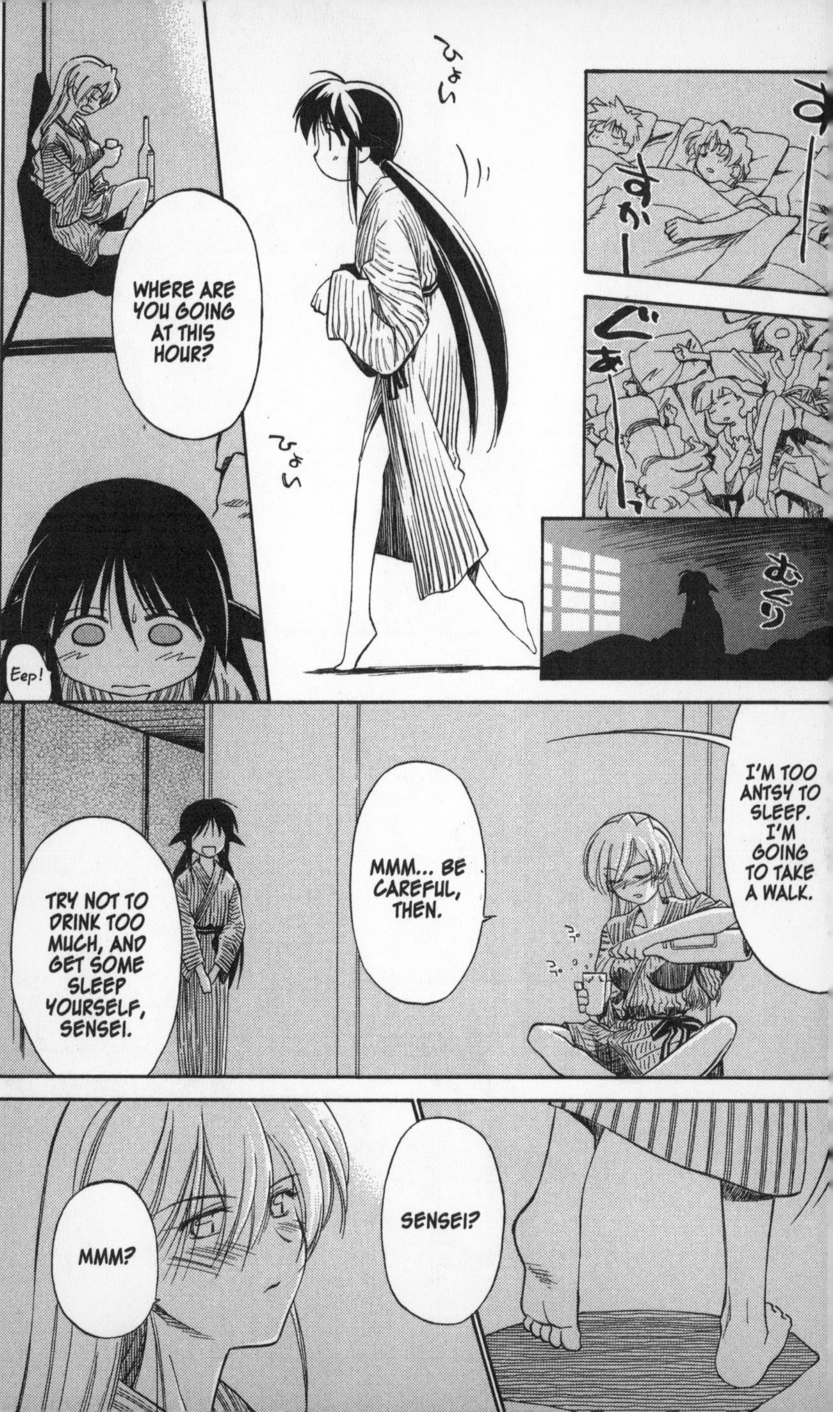
すー
すかー
ぐあーっ
むくり
ひょい
ひょい
WHERE ARE YOU GOING AT THIS HOUR?
Eep!
I'M TOO ANTSY TO SLEEP. I'M GOING TO TAKE A WALK.
MMM... BE CAREFUL, THEN.
TRY NOT TO DRINK TOO MUCH, AND GET SOME SLEEP YOURSELF, SENSEI.
SENSEI?
MMM?

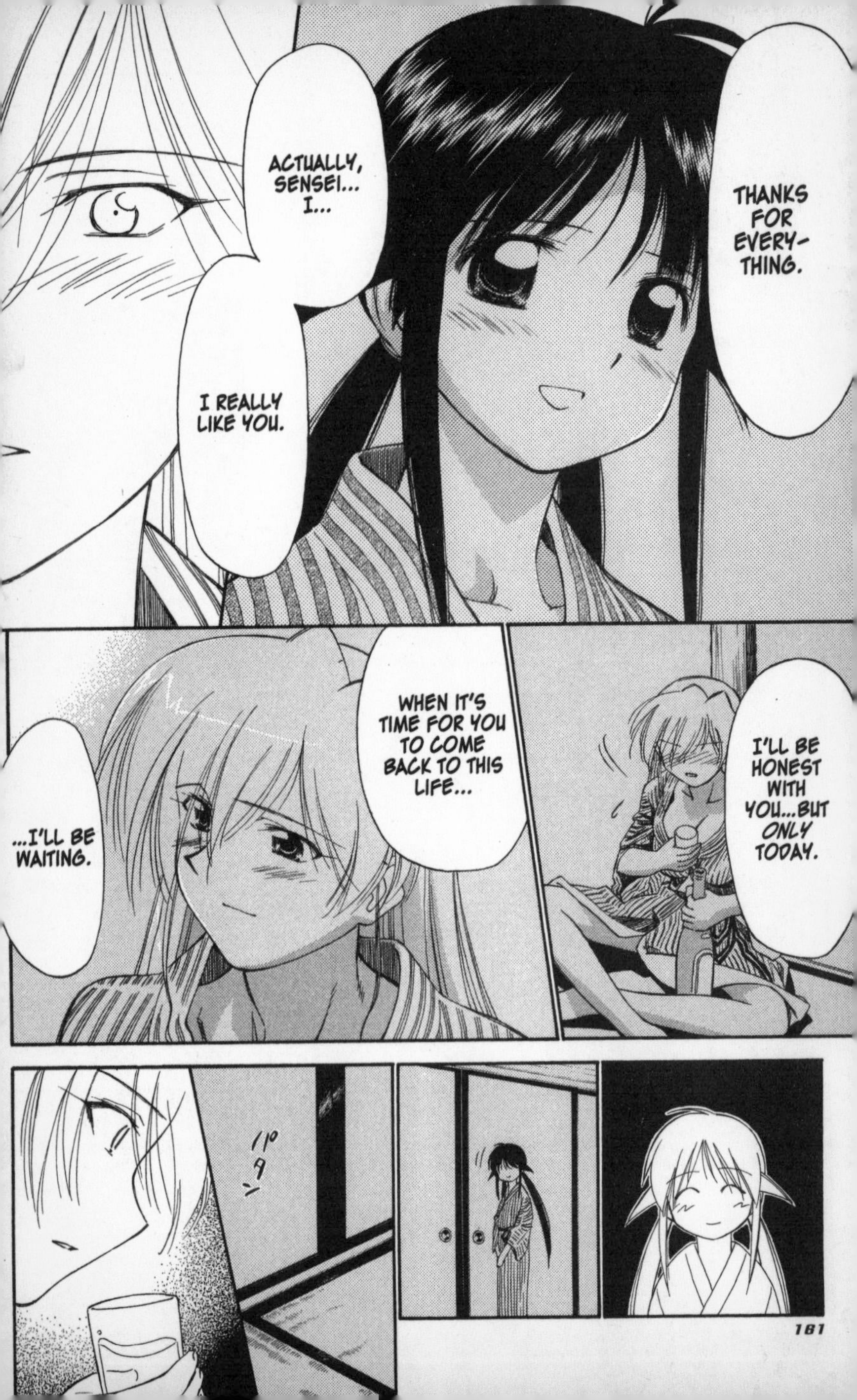
THANKS FOR EVERY-THING.
ACTUALLY, SENSEI... I...
I REALLY LIKE YOU.
I'LL BE HONEST WITH YOU...BUT ONLY TODAY.
WHEN IT'S TIME FOR YOU TO COME BACK TO THIS LIFE...
...I'LL BE WAITING.
パタン

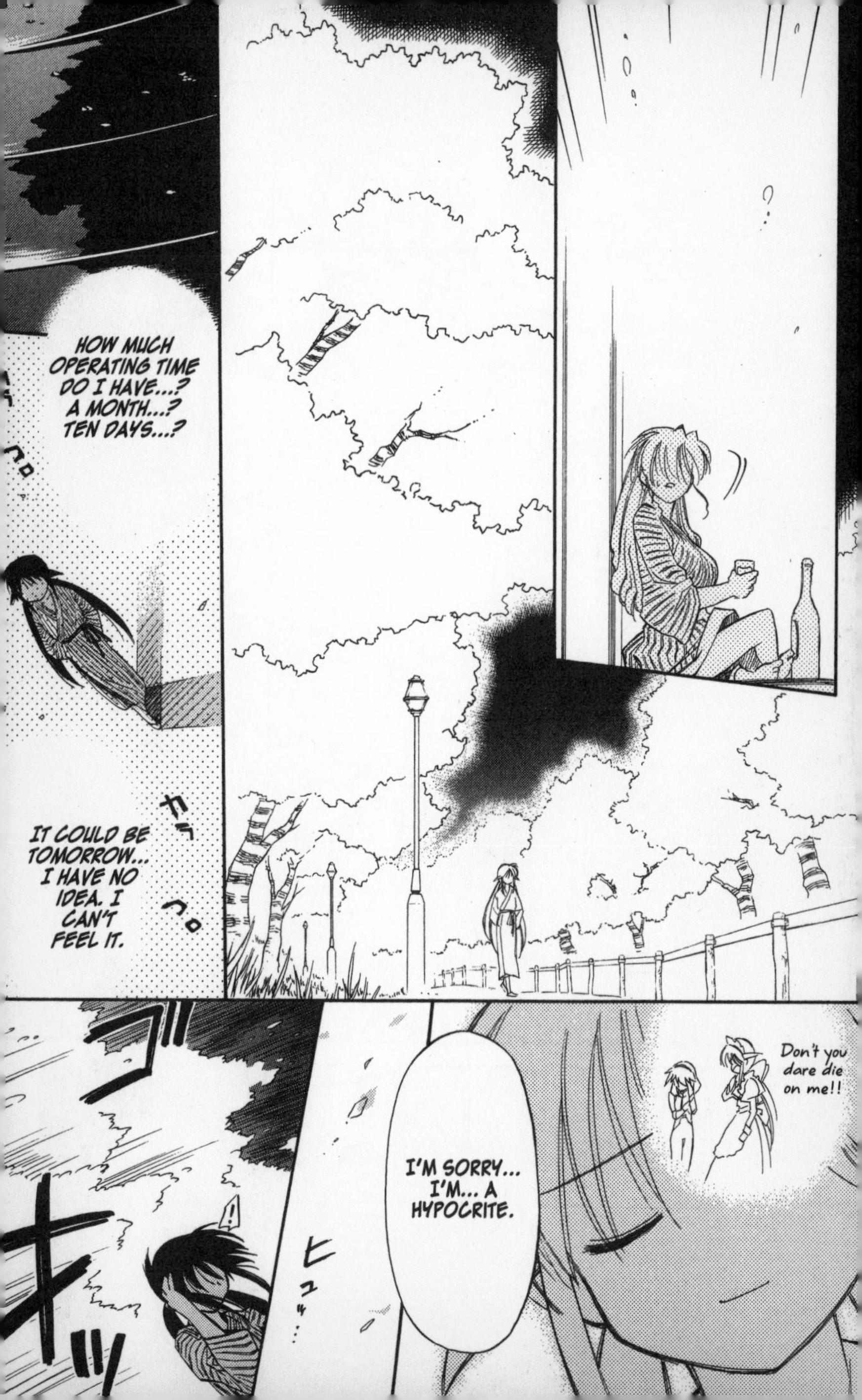
HOW MUCH OPERATING TIME DO I HAVE...? A MONTH...? TEN DAYS...?
IT COULD BE TOMORROW... I HAVE NO IDEA. I CAN'T FEEL IT.
Don't you dare die on me!!
I'M SORRY... I'M... A HYPOCRITE.
!

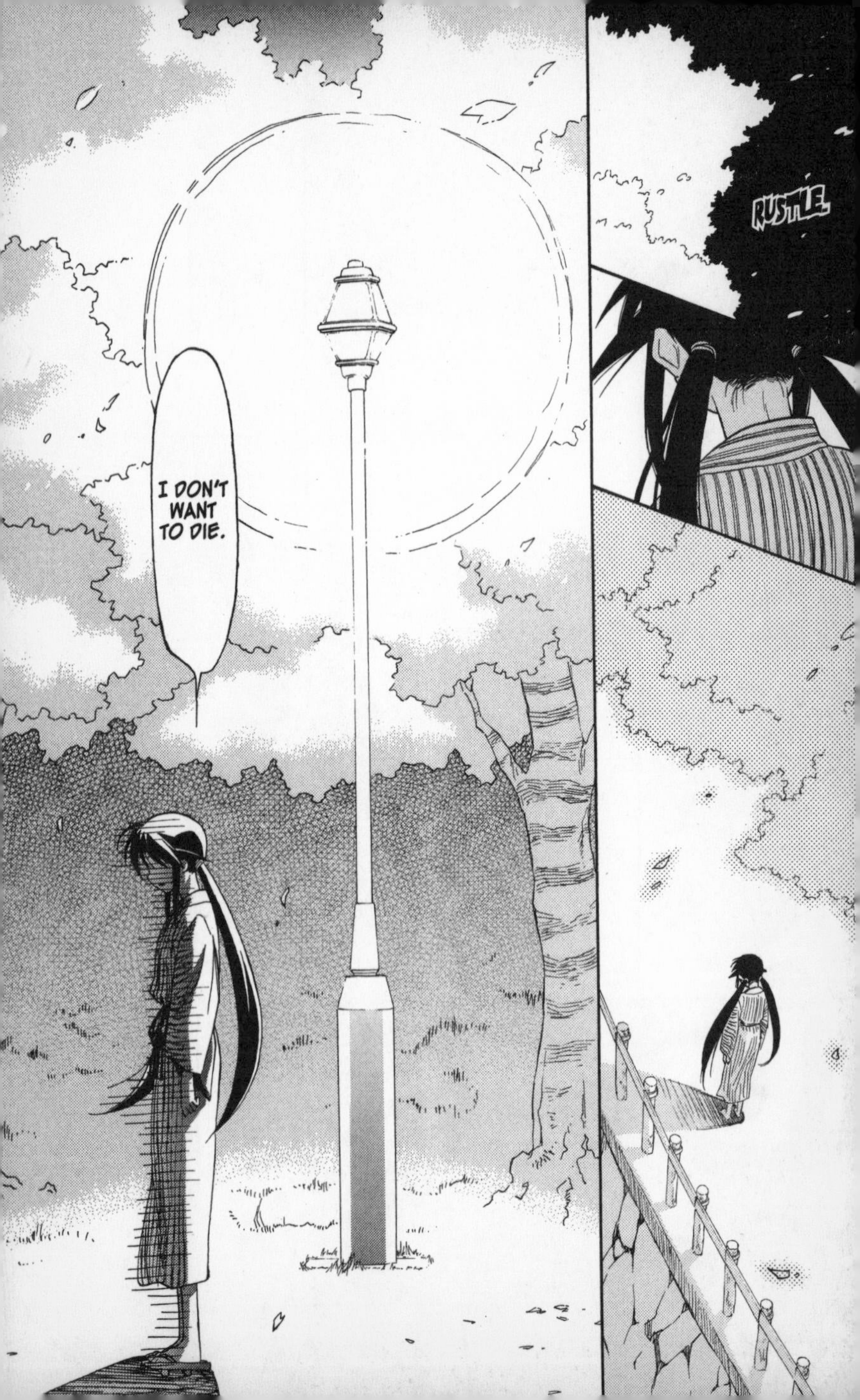
RUSTLE.
I DON'T WANT TO DIE.

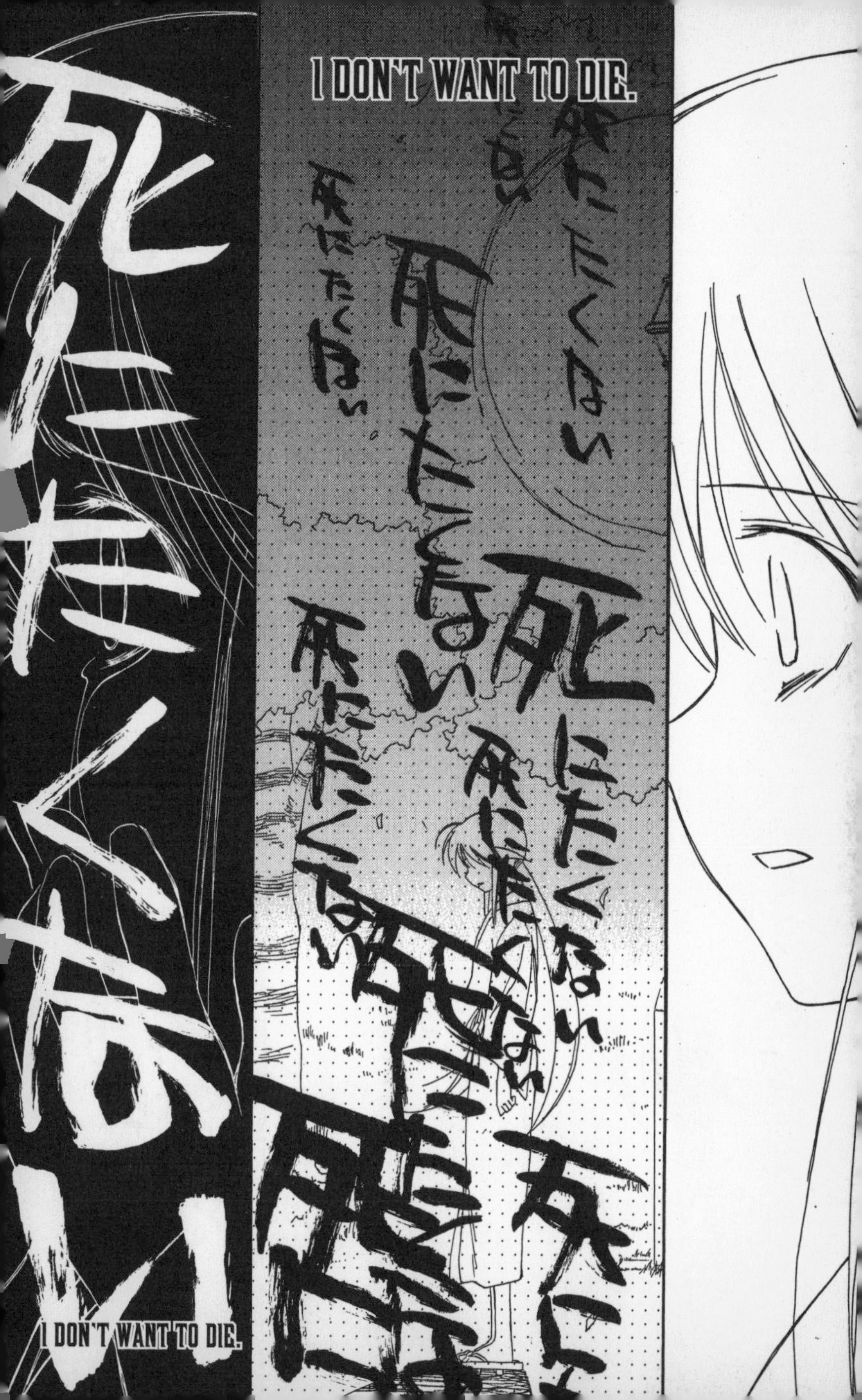
I DON'T WANT TO DIE.
死にたくない
死にたくない
死にたくない
死にたくない
死にたくない
死にたくない
死にたくない
死にたくない
I DON'T WANT TO DIE.

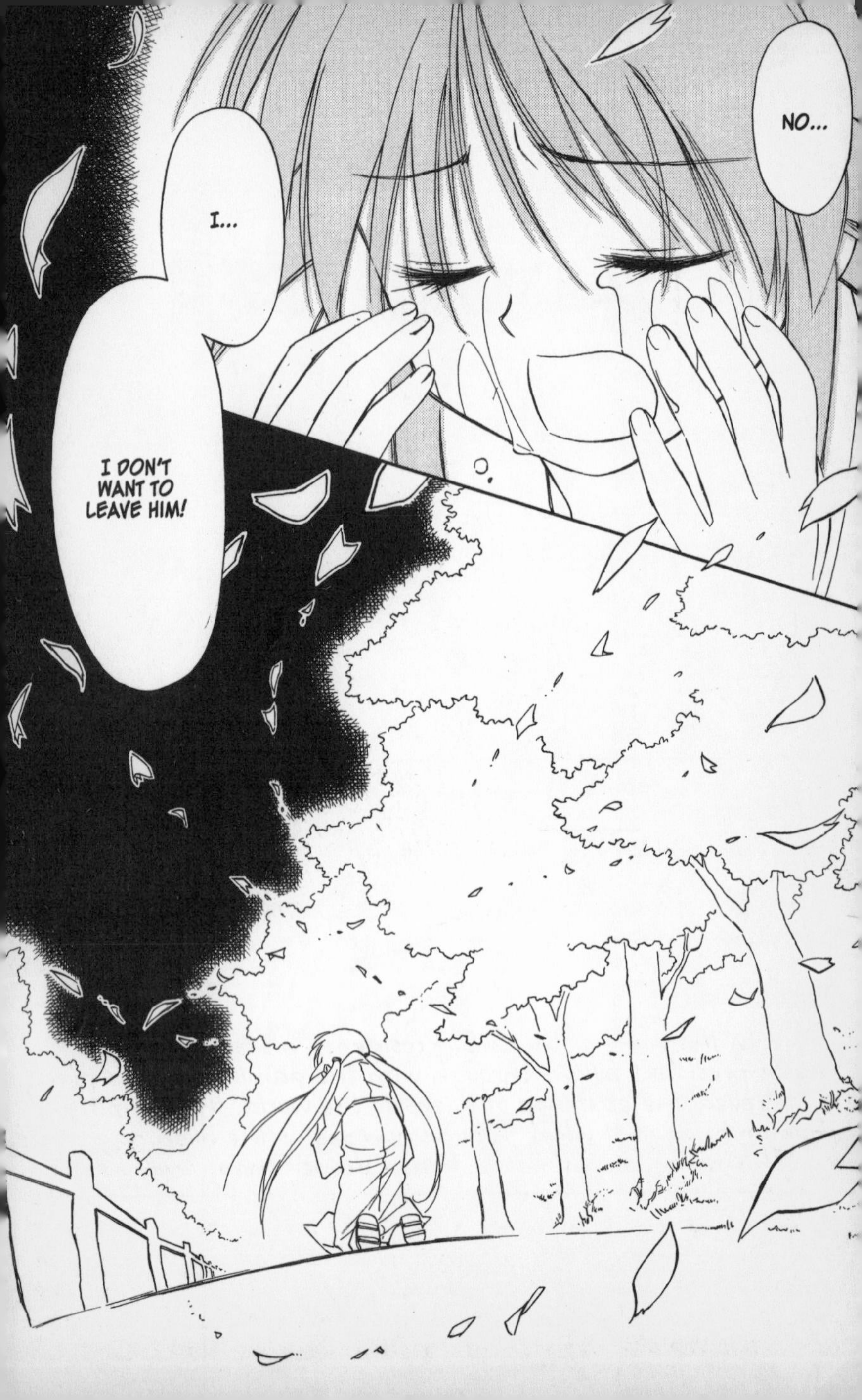
NO...
I...
I DON'T WANT TO LEAVE HIM!

Coming Soon

In the wake of the U.S. President's assassination, the vice-president follows through with the administration's plans to reveal the existence of aliens to the world, thereby pitting humanity against what they all now see as the alien aggressors. This new anti-alien fever brings Vesper under pressure, as the organization is labeled a traitor to the Earth in the public consciousness. And when a deflected energy beam causes a chain reaction that threatens the planet, all sides stampede toward all out interstellar war. But Mahoro and Suguru's love continues to blossom even as her imminent shutdown and the world's imminent destruction loom on the horizon.

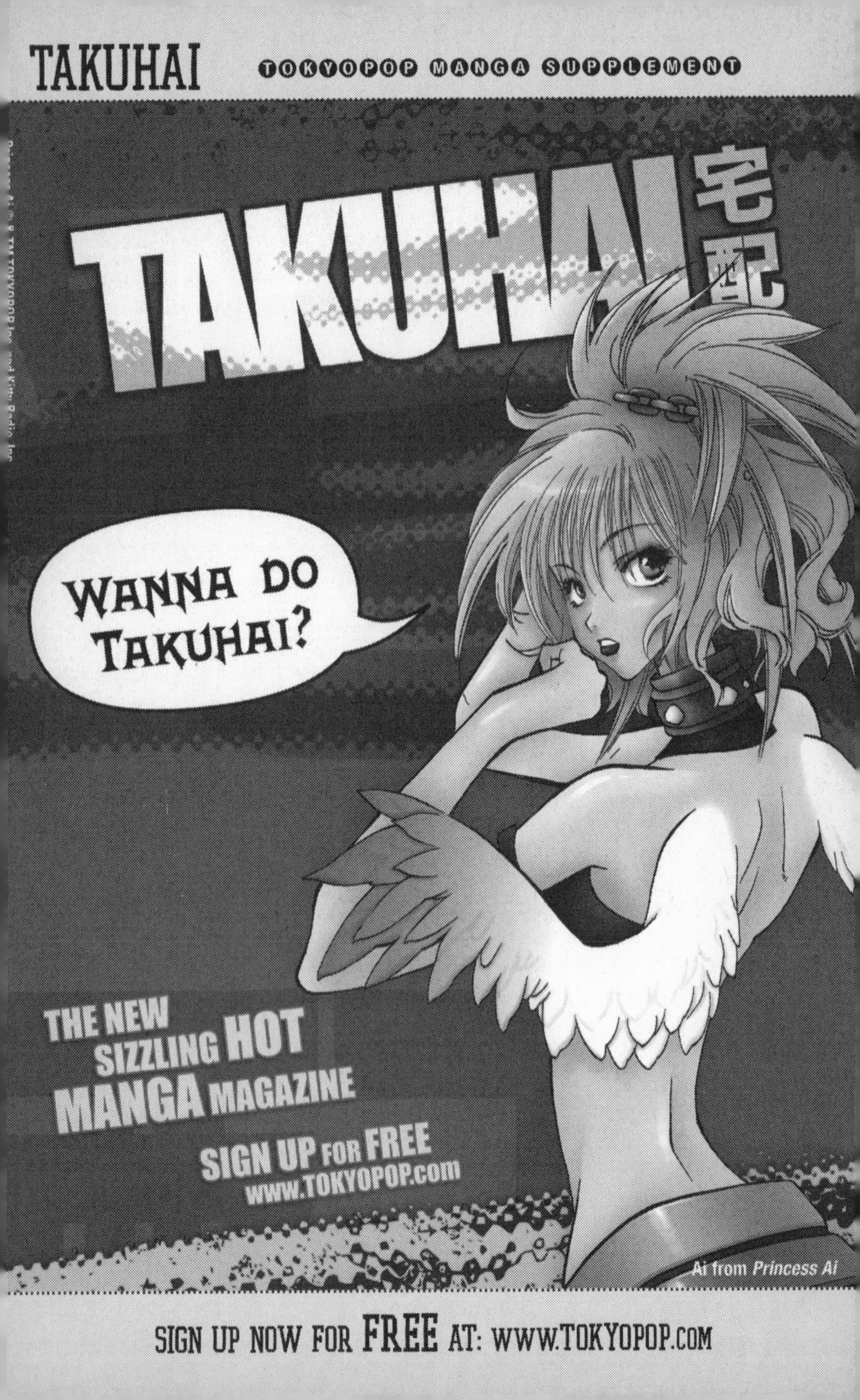
TAKUHAI 宅配
WANNA DO TAKUHAI?
THE NEW SIZZLING HOT MANGA MAGAZINE
SIGN UP FOR FREE
WWW.TOKYOPOP.com
Ai from *Princess Ai*
Princess Ai © & TM TOKYOPOP Inc. and Kitty Radio, Inc.

TOKYOPOP SHOP

WWW.TOKYOPOP.COM/SHOP

HOT NEWS!
Check out the
TOKYOPOP SHOP!
The world's best
collection of manga in
English is now available
online in one place!

I Luv Halloween
and other hot titles are
available at the store
that never closes!

KAMICHAMA KARIN

KANPAI!

I LUV HALLOWEEN

- LOOK FOR SPECIAL OFFERS
- PRE-ORDER UPCOMING RELEASES
- COMPLETE YOUR COLLECTIONS

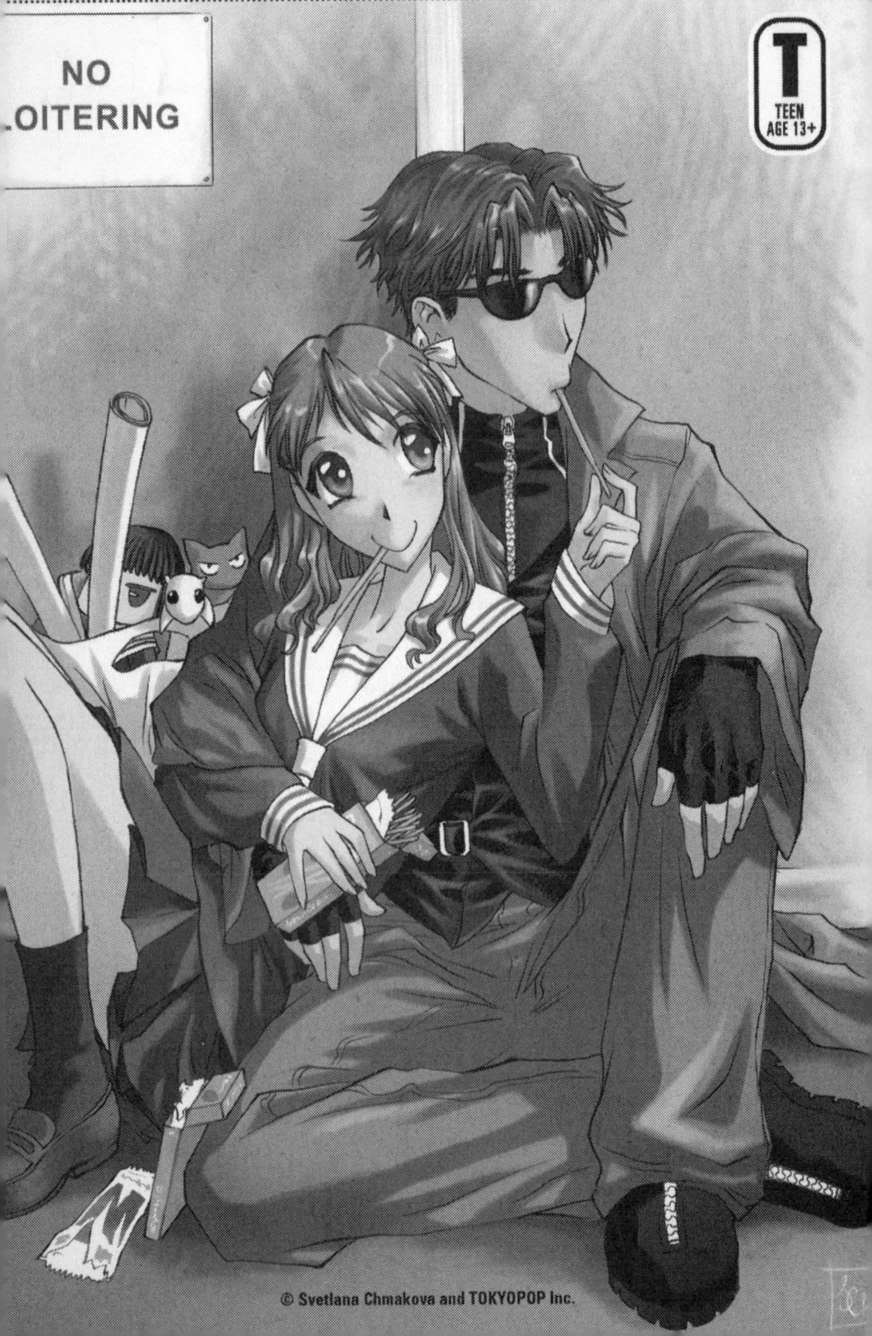
NO
OITERING
T
TEEN
AGE 13+

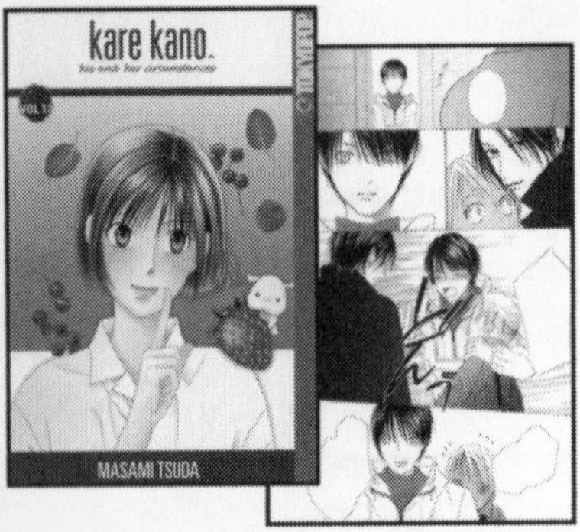
kare kano
MASAMI TSUDA

BY MASAMI TSUDA

KARE KANO

Kare Kano has a fan following for a reason: believable, well-developed characters. Of course, the art is phenomenal, ranging from sugary sweet to lightning-bolt powerful. But above all, Masami Tsuda's refreshing concept—a high school king and queen decide once and for all to be honest with each other (and more importantly, themselves)—succeeds because Tsuda-sensei allows us to know her characters as well as she does. Far from being your typical high school shojo, *Kare Kano* delves deep into the psychology of what would normally just be protagonists, antagonists and supporting cast to create a satisfying journey that is far more than the sum of its parts.

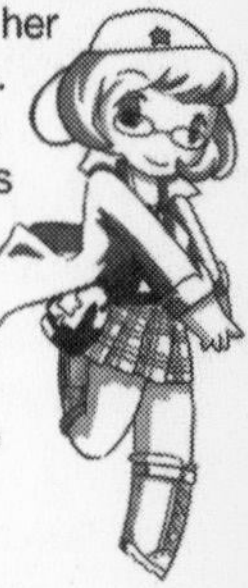

~Carol Fox, Editor

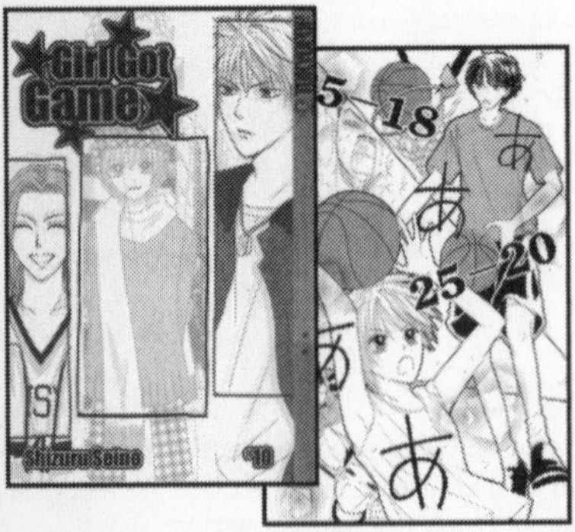
Girl Got Game
Shizuru Seino
10

BY SHIZURU SEINO

GIRL GOT GAME

There's a fair amount of cross-dressing shojo sports manga out there (no, really), but *Girl Got Game* really sets itself apart by having an unusually charming and very funny story. The art style is light and fun, and Kyo spazzing out always cracks me up. The author throws in a lot of great plot twists, and the great side characters help to make the story just that much more special. Sadly, we're coming up on the final volume, but I give this series credit for not letting the romance drag out unnecessarily or endlessly revisiting the same dilemmas. I'm really looking forward to seeing how the series wraps up!

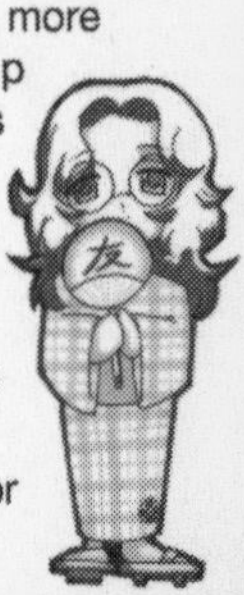

~Lillian M. Diaz-Przybyl, Jr. Editor

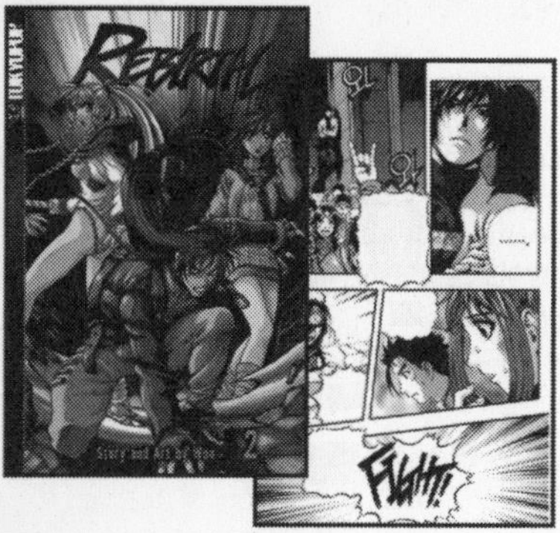
REBIRTH
TOKYOPOP
2
FIGHT!!

BY WOO

REBIRTH

Every manga fan has their "first love." For me, that book is *Rebirth.* I've worked on this series in one fashion or another since its debut, and this epic, action-packed vampire tale has never yet let me down. *Rebirth* is a book that defies expectations as well as first impressions. Yes, it's got the dark, brooding vampire antihero. And, sure, there's lots of bloodshed and tight-bodied maidens in peril. But creator Woo has interwoven an enthralling tale of revenge and redemption that, at its heart, is a truly heartbreaking tragedy. Were you a fan of TV's *Angel*? Do you read Anne Rice? Well, my friend, *Rebirth* is for you!

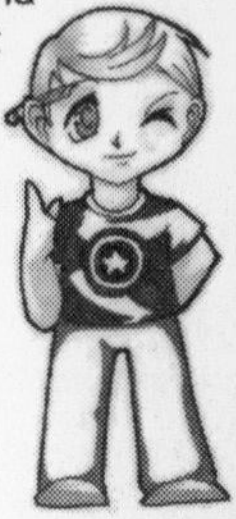

~Bryce P. Coleman, Editor

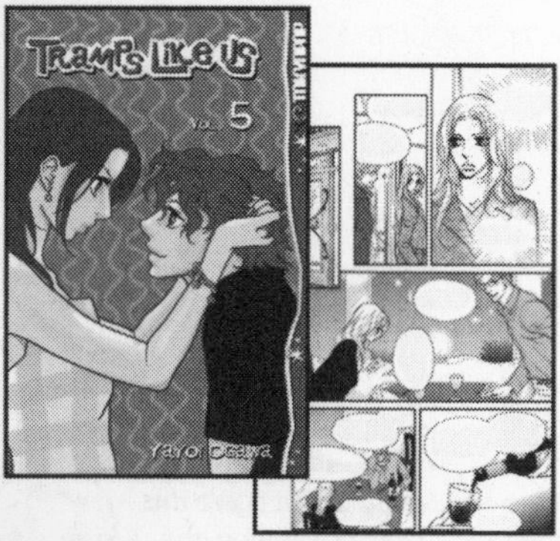
Tramps Like Us
Vol. 5
TOKYOPOP
Yayoi Ogawa

BY YAYOI OGAWA

TRAMPS LIKE US

Thrillingly erotic but relentlessly realistic, *Tramps Like Us* turns gender stereotypes on their head. Sumire Iwaya, a beautiful and busy news exec, is disappointed by the men in her life. So she takes in a gorgeous young boy and makes him her pet. As a man, am I offended? Not really. Actually, I find it really sweet. Sumire is no wide-eyed, skirted, young manga vixen. She's tall, womanly, with a wide mouth and serious, appraising eyes. Momo is cute as a puppy one minute, graceful and petite the next. But the book only indulges the fantasy aspect partway. The abnormal situation gets awkward and even burden-some. I love it. And the tone Carol Fox sets in the English adaptation is one of the best around.

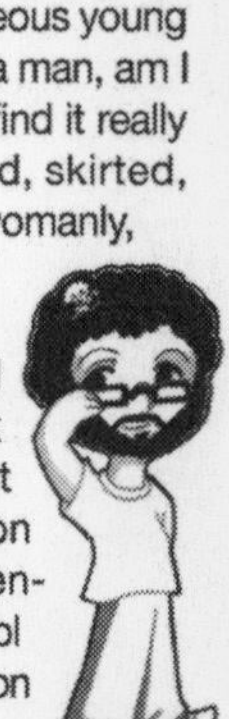

~Luis Reyes, Editor

© Myung-Jin Lee, Daiwon C.I. Inc.

LIGHTS OUT
BY MYUNG-JIN LEE

Gun has always been a problem kid, but after a tearful plea from his mom, he decides to turn over a new leaf. Vowing to abandon troublemaking, Gun transfers to a new high school and rents a room at the local coed dorm. There he falls for Seung-Ah the dorm owner's granddaughter. However, love is not to be for this couple, as sexy Ji-Ae's untimely advances always thwart Gun's attempts to woo the innocent Seung-Ah.

T TEEN AGE 13+

From the creator of _Ragnarok_, one of the top-selling Korean manga of all time!

KINGDOM HEARTS
BY SHIRO AMANO

Sora's whole world is shattered when a violent storm hits his island-paradise home and he is separated from his two closest friends, Riku and Kairi. The three friends are scattered to different and unknown worlds. At the same time, there's turmoil in Disney Castle...King Mickey is missing! Donald and Goofy meet Sora, and they join forces to search for Sora's friends and the King!

A ALL AGES

Based on the mind-alteringly popular Square/Disney videogame!

© Shiro Amano / Enterbrain, Inc. © Disney
Characters from FINAL FANTASY video game series
©1990,1997, 1999, 2001, 2002 Square Enix Co., Ltd.

OFF*BEAT
BY JEN LEE QUICK

Meet 15-year-old Tory Blake, a self-proclaimed genius who is more than a bit cynical about the world. Life is just tedious for Tory...until he befriends a mysterious boy his own age who moves in across the street. But this pursuit of friendship—and possibly something more—leads Tory to the one thing he wasn't expecting to discover.

T TEEN AGE 13+

© Jennifer Quick and TOKYOPOP Inc.

SOKORA REFUGEES™

Kana thought life couldn't get any worse—behind on her schoolwork and out of luck with boys, she is also the only one of her friends who hasn't "blossomed." When she falls through a magical portal in the girls' shower, she's transported to the enchanted world of Sokora—wearing nothing but a small robe! Now, on top of landing in this mysterious setting, she finds that her body is beginning to go through some tremendous changes.

SOKORA REFUGEES

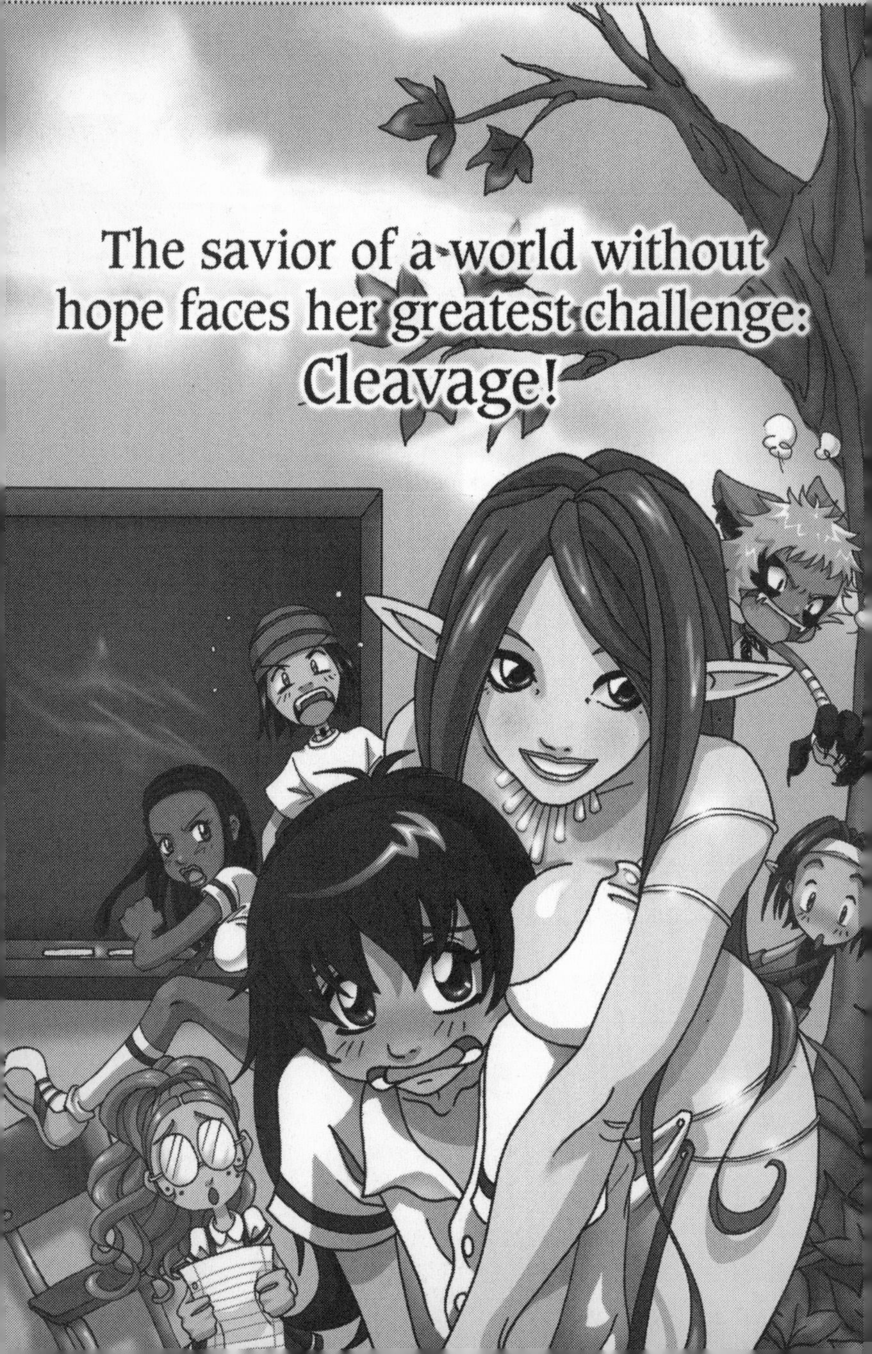
The savior of a world without
hope faces her greatest challenge:
Cleavage!

STOP!

This is the back of the book.
You wouldn't want to spoil a great ending!

This book is printed "manga-style," in the authentic Japanese right-to-left format. Since none of the artwork has been flipped or altered, readers get to experience the story just as the creator intended. You've been asking for it, so TOKYOPOP® delivered: authentic, hot-off-the-press, and far more fun!

DIRECTIONS

If this is your first time reading manga-style, here's a quick guide to help you understand how it works.

It's easy... just start in the top right panel and follow the numbers. Have fun, and look for more 100% authentic manga from TOKYOPOP®!

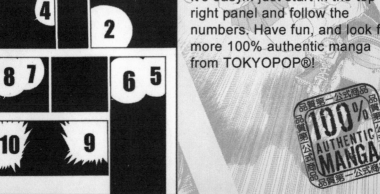